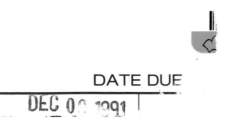

EU-805

CHELSEA HOUSE PUBLISHERS

Modern Critical Views

HENRY ADAMS
EDWARD ALBEE
A. R. AMMONS
MATTHEW ARNOLD
JOHN ASHBERY
W. H. AUDEN
JANE AUSTEN
JAMES BALDWIN
CHARLES BAUDELAIRE
SAMUEL BECKETT
SAUL BELLOW
THE BIBLE
ELIZABETH BISHOP
WILLIAM BLAKE
JORGE LUIS BORGES
ELIZABETH BOWEN
BERTOLT BRECHT
THE BRONTËS
ROBERT BROWNING
ANTHONY BURGESS
GEORGE GORDON, LORD BYRON
THOMAS CARLYLE
LEWIS CARROLL
WILLA CATHER
CERVANTES
GEOFFREY CHAUCER
KATE CHOPIN
SAMUEL TAYLOR COLERIDGE
JOSEPH CONRAD
CONTEMPORARY POETS
HART CRANE
STEPHEN CRANE
DANTE
CHARLES DICKENS
EMILY DICKINSON
JOHN DONNE & THE
    17th-CENTURY POETS
ELIZABETHAN DRAMATISTS
THEODORE DREISER
JOHN DRYDEN
GEORGE ELIOT
T. S. ELIOT
RALPH ELLISON
RALPH WALDO EMERSON
WILLIAM FAULKNER
HENRY FIELDING
F. SCOTT FITZGERALD
GUSTAVE FLAUBERT
E. M. FORSTER
SIGMUND FREUD
ROBERT FROST

ROBERT GRAVES
GRAHAM GREENE
THOMAS HARDY
NATHANIEL HAWTHORNE
WILLIAM HAZLITT
SEAMUS HEANEY
ERNEST HEMINGWAY
GEOFFREY HILL
FRIEDRICH HÖLDERLIN
HOMER
GERARD MANLEY HOPKINS
WILLIAM DEAN HOWELLS
ZORA NEALE HURSTON
HENRY JAMES
SAMUEL JOHNSON
BEN JONSON
JAMES JOYCE
FRANZ KAFKA
JOHN KEATS
RUDYARD KIPLING
D. H. LAWRENCE
JOHN LE CARRÉ
URSULA K. LE GUIN
DORIS LESSING
SINCLAIR LEWIS
ROBERT LOWELL
NORMAN MAILER
BERNARD MALAMUD
THOMAS MANN
CHRISTOPHER MARLOWE
CARSON MCCULLERS
HERMAN MELVILLE
JAMES MERRILL
ARTHUR MILLER
JOHN MILTON
EUGENIO MONTALE
MARIANNE MOORE
IRIS MURDOCH
VLADIMIR NABOKOV
JOYCE CAROL OATES
SEAN O'CASEY
FLANNERY O'CONNOR
EUGENE O'NEILL
GEORGE ORWELL
CYNTHIA OZICK
WALTER PATER
WALKER PERCY
HAROLD PINTER
PLATO
EDGAR ALLAN POE

POETS OF SENSIBILITY &
    THE SUBLIME
ALEXANDER POPE
KATHERINE ANNE PORTER
EZRA POUND
PRE-RAPHAELITE POETS
MARCEL PROUST
THOMAS PYNCHON
ARTHUR RIMBAUD
THEODORE ROETHKE
PHILIP ROTH
JOHN RUSKIN
J. D. SALINGER
GERSHOM SCHOLEM
WILLIAM SHAKESPEARE (3 vols.)
    HISTORIES & POEMS
    COMEDIES
    TRAGEDIES
GEORGE BERNARD SHAW
MARY WOLLSTONECRAFT SHELLEY
PERCY BYSSHE SHELLEY
EDMUND SPENSER
GERTRUDE STEIN
JOHN STEINBECK
LAURENCE STERNE
WALLACE STEVENS
TOM STOPPARD
JONATHAN SWIFT
ALFRED LORD TENNYSON
WILLIAM MAKEPEACE THACKERAY
HENRY DAVID THOREAU
LEO TOLSTOI
ANTHONY TROLLOPE
MARK TWAIN
JOHN UPDIKE
GORE VIDAL
VIRGIL
ROBERT PENN WARREN
EVELYN WAUGH
EUDORA WELTY
NATHANAEL WEST
EDITH WHARTON
WALT WHITMAN
OSCAR WILDE
TENNESSEE WILLIAMS
WILLIAM CARLOS WILLIAMS
THOMAS WOLFE
VIRGINIA WOOLF
WILLIAM WORDSWORTH
RICHARD WRIGHT
WILLIAM BUTLER YEATS

Further titles in preparation.

Modern Critical Views

WILLIAM FAULKNER

Modern Critical Views

WILLIAM FAULKNER

Edited with an introduction by

Harold Bloom

Sterling Professor of the Humanities
Yale University

1986
CHELSEA HOUSE PUBLISHERS
New York
New Haven   Philadelphia

THE COVER:

The cover illustration represents Faulkner's superb short novel, *The Bear*, where the beast, at once mythological and realistic, serves something of the function of the noble synecdoche of Melville's great White Whale, Moby Dick.—H.B.

Cover illustration by Cathy Saksa. Graphics courtesy of Bettmann Graphics.

10 9 8 7 6 5 4 3

Library of Congress Cataloging in Publication Data

William Faulkner.
    (Modern critical views)
    Bibliography: p.
    Includes index.
    1. Faulkner, William, 1897–1962—Criticism and
interpretation—Addresses, essays, lectures.
I. Bloom, Harold.   II. Series.
PS3511.A86Z985685   1986   813'.54   85–9610
ISBN 0–87754–652–5

Contents

Editor's Note

This volume gathers together, in the chronological order of its publication, a representative selection of the best criticism devoted to William Faulkner during the last quarter-century. A number of scholars regard this as the second phase of significant Faulkner criticism, following upon the first phase which dates from Malcolm Cowley's *The Portable Faulkner* (1946) and which can be said to culminate in *William Faulkner: The Yoknapatawpha Country* by Cleanth Brooks (1963).

After the editor's "Introduction," which centers upon Faulkner's agon with his own sense of belatedness, this volume begins with Cleanth Brooks at his strongest, analyzing Faulkner's "discovery of evil" in that grand shocker, *Sanctuary*, and its belated coda in *Requiem for a Nun*. Three other Faulkner critics of the sixties follow. Michael Millgate usefully charts Faulkner's Balzacian design in *The Hamlet* and the entire Snopes saga. Richard Poirier and James Guetti provide an interesting juxtaposition in two very different readings of *The Bear*, Poirier's centering upon American literary tradition and Guetti's upon the limits of trope, a reading carried over in Guetti's remarks upon *The Sound and the Fury*.

Criticism of the sixties is exemplified here by Joseph W. Reed Jr.'s rather formalist account of *Light in August* and then by Irving Howe's more socially aware defense of *The Wild Palms*. Hugh Kenner, the critical high priest of Anglo-American literary modernism, follows with his ironic celebration of Faulkner as "the last novelist," before the coming-on of the Post-Modernist fictions of Barth, Nabokov, and Pynchon. John T. Irwin's study of *The Sound and the Fury* and *Absalom, Absalom!* is the pioneering work that inaugurates the characteristic Faulkner criticism of the eighties, with its Freudian, Nietzschean, deconstructive and feminist components. The candid description of Faulkner's prevalent misogyny by Albert J. Guerard is another prelude to what have become the critical concerns of our moment.

Nearly half this volume is given over to those concerns, starting with David Minter's superb critical biography, represented here by the chapter on the genesis of *The Sound and the Fury* and *Sanctuary*. Richard H. King's *A Southern Renaissance*, which shares Minter's theme of Faulkner's obsessions with belatedness, contributes a sensitive reading of *Go Down Moses*. I have followed these essays with Alan Holder's analysis of *The Unvanquished* and Jan Bakker's reconsideration of *As I Lay Dying*, both of them good examples of revisionist meditations upon Faulkner and the traditions of Faulkner criticism.

A balanced feminist consideration of Faulkner's misogyny is provided by Judith Bryant Wittenberg. Freud's mappings of the psyche, influential in Faulkner criticism for some time, inform the very advanced analysis of *Absalom, Absalom!* by Peter Brooks. The final essay, by Judith L. Sensibar, returns to the origins of Faulkner's rhetorical art by centering upon the moment of transition from his poetry to his far stronger fictional prose.

Introduction

I

No critic need invent William Faulkner's obsessions with what Nietzsche might have called the genealogy of the imagination. Recent critics of Faulkner, including David Minter, John T. Irwin, David M. Wyatt and Richard H. King, have emphasized the novelist's profound need to believe himself to have been his own father, in order to escape not only the Freudian family romance and literary anxieties of influence, but also the cultural dilemmas of what King terms "the Southern family romance." From *The Sound and the Fury* through the debacle of *A Fable*, Faulkner centers upon the sorrows of fathers and sons, to the disadvantage of mothers and daughters. No feminist critic ever will be happy with Faulkner. His brooding conviction that female sexuality is closely allied with death seems essential to all of his strongest fictions. It may even be that Faulkner's rhetorical economy, his wounded need to get his cosmos into a single sentence, is related to his fear that origin and end might prove to be one. Nietzsche prophetically had warned that origin and end were separate entities, and for the sake of life had to be kept apart, but Faulkner (strangely like Freud) seems to have known that the only Western trope participating neither in origin nor end is the image of the father.

By universal consent of critics and common readers, Faulkner now is recognized as the strongest American novelist of this century, clearly surpassing Hemingway and Fitzgerald, and standing as an equal in the sequence that includes Hawthorne, Melville, Mark Twain and Henry James. Some critics might add Dreiser to this group; Faulkner himself curiously would have insisted upon Thomas Wolfe, a generous though dubious judgment. The American precursor for Faulkner was Sherwood Anderson, but perhaps only as an impetus; the true American forerunner is the poetry of T. S. Eliot, as Judith L. Sensibar demonstrates. But the truer precursor for Faulkner's fiction is Conrad, inescapable for the American novelists of Faulkner's generation, including Hemingway and Fitzgerald. Comparison to Conrad is dangerous for any novelist, and clearly Faulkner did not achieve a *Nostromo*. But his work of the decade 1929–39 does include four permanent books: *The Sound and the Fury, As I Lay Dying, Light* in August and *Absalom, Absalom!* If one adds *Sanctuary* and *The Wild Palms*, and *The Hamlet* and *Go Down, Moses* in the early forties, then the combined effect is extraordinary.

From Malcolm Cowley on, critics have explained this effect as the consequence of the force of mythmaking, at once personal and local. Cleanth Brooks, the rugged final champion of the New Criticism, essentially reads Faulkner as he does Eliot's *The Waste Land*, finding the hidden God of the normative Christian tradition to be the basis for Faulkner's attitude towards nature. Since Brooks calls Faulkner's stance Wordsworthian, and finds Wordsworthian nature a Christian vision also, the judgment involved necessarily has its problematical elements. Walter Pater, a critic in a very different tradition, portrayed a very different Wordsworth in terms that seem to me not inapplicable to Faulkner:

> Religious sentiment, consecrating the affections and natural regrets of the human heart, above all, that pitiful awe and care for the perishing human clay, of which relic-worship is but the corruption, has always had much to do with localities, with the thoughts which attach themselves to actual scenes and places. Now what is true of it everywhere, is truest of it in those secluded valleys where one generation after another maintains the same abiding place; and it was on this side, that Wordsworth apprehended religion most strongly. Consisting, as it did so much, in the recognition of local sanctities, in the habit of connecting the stones and trees of a particular spot of earth with the great events of life, till the low walls, the green mounds, the half-obliterated epitaphs seemed full of voices, and a sort of natural oracles, the very religion of those people of the dales, appeared but as another link between them and the earth, and was literally a religion of nature.

A kind of stoic natural religion pervades this description, something close to the implicit faith of old Isaac McCaslin in *Go Down, Moses*. It seems unhelpful to speak of "residual Christianity" in Faulkner, as Cleanth Brooks does. Hemingway and Fitzgerald, in their nostalgias, perhaps were closer to a Christian ethos than Faulkner was in his great phase. Against current critical judgment, I prefer *As I Lay Dying* and *Light in August* to *The Sound and the Fury* and *Absalom, Absalom!*, partly because the first two are more primordial in their vision, closer to the stoic intensities of their author's kind of natural piety. There is an *otherness* in Lena Grove and the Bundrens that would have moved Wordsworth, that is, the Wordsworth of *The Tale of Margaret*, *Michael* and *The Old Cumberland Beggar*. A curious movement that is also a stasis becomes Faulkner's pervasive trope for Lena. Though he invokes the imagery of Keats' urn, Faulkner seems to have had the harvest-girl of Keats' *To Autumn* more in mind, or even the stately figures of the *Ode to Indolence*.

We remember Lena Grove as stately, calm, a person yet a process, a serene and patient consciousness, full of wonder, too much a unitary being to need even her author's variety of stoic courage.

The uncanniness of this representation is exceeded by the Bundrens, whose plangency testifies to Faulkner's finest rhetorical achievement. *As I Lay Dying* may be the most original novel ever written by an American. Obviously it is not free of the deepest influence Faulkner knew as a novelist. The language is never Conradian, and yet the sense of the reality principle is. But there is nothing in Conrad like Darl Bundren, not even in *The Secret Agent*. *As I Lay Dying* is Faulkner's strongest protest against the facticity of literary convention, against the force of the familial past, which tropes itself in fiction as the repetitive form of narrative imitating prior narrative. The book is a sustained nightmare, insofar as it is Darl's book, which is to say, Faulkner's book, or the book of his daemon.

II

Canonization is a process of enshrining creative misinterpretations, and no one need lament this. Still, one element that ensues from this process all too frequently is the not very creative misinterpretation in which the idiosyncratic is distorted into the normative. Churchwardenly critics who assimilate the Faulkner of the Thirties to spiritual, social and moral orthodoxy can and do assert Faulkner himself as their preceptor. But this is the Faulkner of the Fifties, Nobel laureate, State Department envoy and author of *A Fable*, a book of a badness simply astonishing for Faulkner. The best of the normative critics, Cleanth Brooks, reads even *As I Lay Dying* as a quest for community, an exaltation of the family, an affirmation of Christian values. The Bundrens manifestly constitute one of the most terrifying visions of the family romance in the history of literature. But their extremism is not eccentric in the 1929–39 world of Faulkner's fiction. That world is founded upon a horror of families, a limbo of outcasts, an evasion of all values other than stoic endurance. It is a world in which what is silent in the other Bundrens speaks in Darl, what is veiled in the Compsons is uncovered in Quentin. So tangled are these returns of the repressed with what continues to be estranged that phrases like "the violation of the natural" and "the denial of the human" become quite meaningless when applied to Faulkner's greater fictions. In that world, the natural is itself a violation and the human already a denial. Is the weird quest of the Bundrens a violation of the natural, or is it what Blake would have called a terrible triumph for the selfish virtues of the natural heart? Darl judges it to be the latter, but Darl luminously denies the sufficiency of the human, at the cost of what seems schizophrenia.

Marxist criticism of imaginative literature, if it had not regressed abominably in our country, so that now it is a travesty of the dialectical suppleness of Adorno and Benjamin, would find a proper subject in the difficult relationship between the 1929 business panic and As I Lay Dying. Perhaps the self-destruction of our delusive political economy helped free Faulkner from whatever inhibitions, communal and personal, had kept him earlier from a saga like that of the Bundrens. Only an authentic seer can give permanent form to a prophecy like As I Lay Dying, which puts severely into question every received notion we have of the natural and the human. Darl asserts he has no mother, while taunting his enemy brother, Jewel, with the insistence that Jewel's mother was a horse. Their little brother, Vardaman, says: "My mother is a fish." The mother, dead and undead, is uncannier even than these children, when she confesses the truth of her existence, her rejecting vision of her children:

> I could just remember how my father used to say that the reason for living was to get ready to stay dead a long time. And when I would have to look at them day after day, each with his and her single and selfish thought, and blood strange to each other blood and strange to mine, and think that this seemed to be the only way I could get ready to stay dead, I would hate my father for having ever planted me. I would look forward to the times when they faulted, so I could whip them. When the switch fell I could feel it upon my flesh; when it welted and ridged it was my blood that ran, and I would think with each blow of the switch: Now you are aware of me! Now I am something in your secret and selfish life, who have marked your blood with my own for ever and ever.

This veritable apocalypse of any sense of otherness is no mere "denial of community." Nor are the Bundrens any "mimesis of essential nature." They are a super-mimesis, an over-representation mocking nature while shadowing it. What matters in major Faulkner is that the people have gone back, not to nature but to some abyss before the Creation-Fall. Eliot insisted that Joyce's imagination was eminently orthodox. This can be doubted, but in Faulkner's case there is little sense in baptizing his imagination. One sees why he preferred reading the Old Testament to the New, remarking that the former was stories and the latter, ideas. The remark is inadequate except insofar as it opposes Hebraic to Hellenistic representation of character. There is little that is Homeric about the Bundrens, or Sophoclean about the Compsons. Faulkner's irony is neither classical nor romantic, neither Greek nor German. It does not say one thing while meaning another, nor trade in contrasts between expectation and fulfillment. Instead, it juxtaposes incommensurable realities: of self and other, of parent and child, of past and future. When Gide maintained that Faulkner's people lacked souls, he simply failed to observe that Faulkner's ironies were Biblical. To which an amendment must be added. In Faulkner, only the ironies are Biblical. What Faulkner's people lack is the blessing; they cannot contend for a time without boundaries. Yahweh will make no covenant with them. Their agon therefore is neither the Greek one for the foremost place nor the Hebrew one for the blessing, which honors the father and the mother. Their agon is the hopeless one of waiting for their doom to lift.

III

Faulkner writes tragic farce rather than tragedy, more in the mode of Webster, Ford and Tourneur than that of Shakespeare. In time, his genius or daemon may seem essentially comic, despite his dark houses and death drives. His grand family is Dickens run mad rather than Conrad run wild: the hideous saga of the Snopes, from the excessively capable Flem Snopes to the admirably named Wallstreet Panic Snopes. Flem, as David Minter observes, is refreshingly free of all influence-anxieties. He belongs in Washington D. C., and by now has reached there, and helps to staff the White House. Alas, he by now helps to staff the universities also, and soon will staff the entire nation, as his spiritual children, the Yuppies, reach middle age. Ivy League Snopes, Reagan Revolution Snopes, Jack Kemp Snopes: the possibilities are limitless. His ruined families, burdened by tradition, are Faulkner's tribute to his region. His Snopes clan is his gift to his nation.

CLEANTH BROOKS

Discovery of Evil

The theme of *Sanctuary* is the discovery of the nature of reality with the concomitant discovery of evil, and it recurs throughout Faulkner's work. In *The Unvanquished* Bayard Sartoris triumphantly passes the crucial test of courage in which his initiation culminates. But in *Sanctuary* the initiation of Horace Benbow has a much more somber ending. Instead of victory and moral vindication, Horace receives a stunning defeat. Horace is, of course, a different kind of man from Bayard and furthermore the times have changed. The traditional society has given place to a modern world in which amoral power is almost nakedly present.

Here, as in *Sartoris*, Horace is the man of academic mind, who finds out that the world is not a place of justice and moral tidiness. He discovers, with increasing horror, that evil is rooted in the very nature of things. Horace represents a type that appears often in Faulkner's work, not only in the early novels but again prominently in his last novels. He is an "intellectual." He has a great capacity for belief in ideas and a great confidence in the efficacy of reason. In *Sanctuary* Faulkner has made Benbow ineffectual in his contest with evil, but Faulkner has succeeded so well that many of his readers accord Horace something less than his due. Yet he must have his due, for if Benbow is a mere weakling, one loses the very point of the novel, which is a sense of the horrifying power of evil.

The truth of the matter is that a stronger man and a more aggressive lawyer than Horace Benbow might have failed under the circumstances. Horace demonstrates a good deal of pertinacity, shrewdness,

From *William Faulkner: The Yoknapatawpha Country*. Copyright © 1963 by Yale University. Yale University Press, 1963.

and vigor. Having interested himself in Lee Goodwin and his wife, he works steadily to try to get his clients to talk. Lee Goodwin's own fatalism and his specific fear of the gangster Popeye's gun make it very difficult for Horace to get any help from his client. Later on, however, Ruby does give him a hint, namely that there was a girl on the Old Frenchman's Place the day that Tommy was shot. Horace tries to track down this mysterious girl, who may become his key witness. His getting the tip from Clarence Snopes has, of course, to be put down to sheer luck, but he follows up the tip vigorously and even wins the sympathy of Miss Reba, the madam of the brothel. This in itself is no small accomplishment. With her help, he persuades Temple Drake to agree to testify in favor of Lee Goodwin.

Horace takes what measures he can to ensure that Temple will remain in Memphis, where he can keep in touch with her as he awaits Goodwin's trial. This last point, by the way, is worth some comment, for at least one critic has reproached Benbow for waiting "until the night before the trial before he can decide to expose her as a witness. By that time it is too late." But Horace calls up Miss Reba about a week after he had visited Temple, some nine or ten days before the trial, "just to know if she's still there. So I can reach her if I need to." Miss Reba replies that Temple is still there all right, "but this reaching. I dont like it. I dont want no cops around here unless they are on my business." But Horace does call once more, the day before the trial, and this time finds that Temple has suddenly disappeared.

Horace is not, however, paralyzed by Temple's failure to show up at the trial. He carries on without her and has good hopes of success. (Had his sister, Narcissa, not betrayed him to the district attorney, he probably would have won his case.) What Horace, understandably, was not prepared for was Temple's *volte-face*—her appearance on the second day of the trial with perjured testimony against which almost any attorney would have contended in vain. It is true that Horace does collapse after this body blow. The fight has been taken out of him, his rebellion against family pressures is over, and he goes back to the wife whom he should never have married and whom he has tried to leave. But as Faulkner has plotted this novel, a man much more practical, hard-headed, and belligerent than Horace Benbow would have been defeated.

One has also to remember that *Sanctuary* shows the stamp of its time and of its genre. It is a gangster novel of a sort: the brilliance of the writing cannot conceal that fact. In a gangster story it is almost impossible to get the witnesses, including the gangster's victims, to testify against him. The gangster leads a charmed life, for the lethargic community, the corrupt public official, and the ordinary citizen, paralyzed with fear, allow him to escape punishment. All this is as true of stories laid in Cook County, Illinois, as of Yoknapatawpha County, Mississippi. In this connection, it may be worth noting that the real fatalist is the man on trial, Lee Goodwin, the rough-hewn hill man, and not his attorney, Horace Benbow, the son of a distinguished judge, with a love for Venetian glass and world-weary poetry. Lee Goodwin is certain that he is "doomed" and that Popeye, whether by a bullet through the jail window or by some other means, will see to it that he does not go free. By contrast, it is Benbow who remains hopeful to the end.

Sanctuary is not only a gangster novel; it is, as André Malraux has suggested, also something of a detective novel, in that the meaning of certain events is not revealed until the end, and the author builds suspense, complicates his plot, and presents his reader with sudden and surprising developments. Indeed, there is something of a puzzle about just what does happen in the courtroom scene at the end of the novel; and some readers have been puzzled also by Popeye's conduct after he has been arrested for murder.

Part of the difficulty arises because the author is obviously concerned with something more important than a mere story of crime, with its plot suspense and exciting action. But some of the difficulty is to be referred to certain of Faulkner's methods of presentation. For one thing, he deliberately refrains from entering into the minds of his characters at the moments when they make their decisions. For another, he refuses—perhaps for fear of killing the psychological suspense—to fill in certain gaps in the action. The result is that the motive for an act is often merely implied, and sometimes the act itself is merely implied. The reader may therefore be confused, not only as to why something happened but as to what actually did happen.

Faulkner's chosen methods are very effective for presenting scenes of action with almost intolerable immediacy, for rendering psychological states, and for building up a sense of foreboding and horror. In his concern with this mode of presentation, however, he has slighted the analysis of motive, the articulation of action with thought, and the usual methods for working out the plot. We are not, for example, allowed inside Popeye's mind as he awaits his execution. The scene is vividly rendered: the curious little man methodically crushing out his cigarettes and carefully arranging the butts in a neat line to form a sort of calendar marking the days that have elapsed. But what is going on inside his head? Why is it that he will not summon a lawyer? Has he resolved upon a kind of suicide? Or is it that he simply cannot believe that he is to be hanged? The author does not show us—or if he does, it is only through hints and suggestions.

In fact, a great deal of the power of the novel comes from the naked objectivity of such scenes as this of Popeye in prison or that of Temple Drake in the courtroom. They are rendered in compelling detail, though without explicit reference to the inner thoughts of the characters.

Having in mind Faulkner's use of this kind of technique, one may be tempted to call *Sanctuary* a mood piece rather than a novel proper. The interpretation of the situation is often mediated to the reader poetically rather than through the more normal modes of fiction. Consider what the author accomplishes in the mere description of a room in Miss Reba's brothel:

> The light hung from the center of the ceiling, beneath a fluted shade of rose-colored paper browned where the bulb bulged it. The floor was covered by a figured maroon-tinted carpet tacked down in strips; the olive-tinted walls bore two framed lithographs. From the two windows curtains of machine lace hung, dust-colored, like strips of lightly congealed dust set on end. The whole room had an air of musty stoginess, decorum; in the wavy mirror of a cheap varnished dresser, as in a stagnant pool, there seemed to linger spent ghosts of voluptuous gestures and dead lusts. In the corner, upon a faded scarred strip of oilcloth tacked over the carpet, sat a washstand bearing a flowered bowl and pitcher and a row of towels; in the corner behind it sat a slop jar dressed also in fluted rose-colored paper.

The style is what Joyce would have called "scrupulously mean." But though the mode is apparently that of naturalism, the whole passage glows with meaning. The physical picture is convincing and even compelling in its detail, but there is much more than the physical picture, and much more than a vague aura. The author relentlessly exposes the pretentious sleasiness of the room and the faked respectability that emanates from the machine-made lace curtains, the crazed "wavy" mirror, and the slop jar, swathed in rose-colored paper.

Another obvious example of Faulkner's descriptive power occurs in his celebrated view of Popeye at the spring: "His suit was black, with a tight, high-waisted coat. His trousers were rolled once and caked with mud above mud-caked shoes. His face had a queer, bloodless color, as though seen by electric light; against the sunny silence, in his slanted straw hat and his slightly akimbo arms, he had that vicious depthless quality of stamped tin."

The prose never becomes shrill, the attitude remains thoroughly detached, but the damnation is absolute. Here two figures of speech do most of the work of interpretation. They rob Popeye of substance and make him a sinister black silhouette against the spring landscape. "As though seen by electric light" justifies the description of his queer, blood-less color, but it does more: juxtaposed as it is to the phrase "against the sunny silence," it introduces the sense of the contrived and artificial, as though Popeye were a kind of monstrous affront to the natural scene. At the least it sets up notions of a sort that will be confirmed at the end of the sentence with the phrasing "depthless quality of stamped tin." Popeye is here not merely described physically, but interpreted and judged.

Thus the author, through the very rendering of scene and action, supplies the interpretation of its meaning. But has Faulkner done so sufficiently in the trial scene? Why does Temple Drake break her promise to Horace Benbow and commit perjury by accusing Lee Goodwin of the rape and the murder of which he was innocent? What is her motive? We are never told directly, nor are we allowed to follow the play of her thoughts and emotions, either at the time at which she decided to perjure herself or during the scene in which she actually gives her false testimony. Instead, there is only a powerful reporting of the trial scene as a spectator might have observed it. Detail after detail is picked out in a hard light. Some of Temple's responses to the district attorney are given verbatim, but others are simply implied; furthermore, many of the questions put to her are merely implied or summarized.

There are, to be sure, scenes in the novel in which we are allowed to see what goes on in Temple's mind. When she tells Horace Benbow the long and horrifying story about what happened at the Old Frenchman's Place, we are put very definitely and emphatically inside her mind and so inside her cringing and outraged flesh. But in this crucial scene of the trial we merely observe her from the outside. The psychiatrist Dr. L. S. Kubie notes that Faulkner makes no effort to explain "why [Temple] sacrifices Goodwin . . . to the furies of the mob and saves Popeye, her impotent malefactor."

One theory which has won a considerable measure of acceptance holds that Temple's perjury is the result of pressure from her family. According to this interpretation of the novel, Clarence Snopes, the corrupt state senator, having discovered Temple's hiding place in a Mem-phis brothel, looks up Temple's father, Judge Drake, and sells him this information. Judge Drake then collaborates with the district attorney in concocting the lie that Temple is persuaded to tell on the witness stand. The father's motive for having his daughter tell the lie is to protect the family honor: it must not come out that Temple has been living in a brothel from the time of the murder until the time of the trial. If Popeye committed the rape and murder, then the truth about his having kept Temple in the brothel will have to come out "either through necessity or [through] Popeye's malice"; but if the rape and murder can be fastened on Lee Goodwin, the man on trial, then the fact of Temple's having lived in the brothel can be concealed.

But this reasoning does not convince. If Temple Drake's father was indeed stage-managing her testimony, why does he have Temple disclose the rape at all? Why not, since the story is being fabricated out of whole cloth anyway, make it simply a story of murder? Popeye would not care. His only concern is that the murder should be pinned on another man. If Judge Drake is arranging the testimony in this manner to protect the good name of his daughter, then he is not only a corrupt judge, he is also a very stupid man.

There are a number of other things wrong with this account. In the first place, there is considerable evidence to indicate that Judge Drake had not seen his daughter until the day of the trial. According to Lisca's theory, Clarence Snopes came back from Jackson, Mississippi, after having conferred with Judge Drake, two days before the trial—that is, on June 18. But Popeye and Temple had already left Memphis—had at least left Miss Reba's—when Horace Benbow telephoned on the day before the trial (June 19), and there is every reason to believe that they had left two days before that, on the evening of the 17th, the day on which Popeye had shot Red. When Horace Benbow called Miss Reba on the night of the 19th to speak to Temple, Miss Reba told him that "they" had gone, and since she says that they left owing a week's rent, theirs must have been a sudden departure. Miss Reba goes on to remark to Horace: "Dont you read no papers?" The only possible meaning of this question is that the newspapers had attributed the death of Red to Popeye, and that if Horace Benbow had read the Memphis papers, he would not now expect to find Popeye and Temple in her house.

If, as Lisca implies, Clarence Snopes returned from a visit to Judge Drake in Jackson just two days before the trial (June 18), Judge Drake could not have used information given as late as that for the purpose of establishing contact with his daughter. For it is perfectly plain that Clarence Snopes did not know in advance that Popeye was going to shoot Red on the 17th and therefore could not have predicted the flight of Popeye and Temple. Popeye, of course, had not supplied a forwarding address.

Be this as it may, according to the theory we are examining, "the district attorney established a socially acceptable account of Temple's actions between the rape and the trial." The district attorney asks Temple: " 'Where did he [her father] think you were?' 'He thought I was in school.' [a lie, as we have seen] 'You were in hiding, then, because something had happened to you and you dared not—' " Thus goes the passage in *Sanctuary*, with Mr. Lisca's interpolations in brackets. But we need to look at the paragraph that immediately precedes the passage he has quoted. The district attorney asks Temple: " 'Where have you been living since May twelfth of this year?' Her head moved faintly, as though she would see beyond him. He moved into her line of vision, holding her eyes. She stared at him again, giving her parrotlike answers. 'Did your father know you were there?' 'No.' "

As I read it, the clear implication is that Temple *did* tell the district attorney where she was living. When he puts the question, she tries to avoid his eyes; but he forces her to look at him, and then evidently she answers him. For the district attorney's next question, "Did your father know you were there?" surely implies that Temple has confessed that she was at Miss Reba's house in Memphis. Temple's answer is "No," and the attorney then goes on to inquire: "Where did he think you were?" Temple evidently had not been provided with a "socially acceptable account" of her actions between the murder and her appearance in court. In spite of his pretensions of sympathy, the district attorney fully exposes her shame.

There are two further matters that must be taken into account by anyone who means to describe what happens at the trial. The first of these has to do with the Memphis "Jew lawyer," who turns up in the courtroom on the second day of the trial, June 21. The second is the action of Horace's sister, Narcissa, in visiting the district attorney and telling him that Clarence Snopes possesses some important information bearing upon the case.

As for the Memphis lawyer, it is significant that Horace Benbow is not really surprised when he sees him in the courtroom. . . . [W]e are told that Horace stopped just within the door. "It's a lawyer," he said, a "Jew lawyer from Memphis," and he evidently expects that now he will see Temple in the courtroom. Indeed he says, "I know what I'll find before I find it . . . She will have on a black hat."

Evidently, when he heard from Miss Reba that Popeye and Temple had suddenly fled, Horace had rather expected that something like this might happen. It is significant that the Memphis lawyer apparently takes no part in the courtroom scene at all, and this can only mean that he has conferred already with Eustace Graham, the district attorney. For Eustace Graham knows exactly what to bring out and what to say.

Graham's information as to what happened at the Old Frenchman's Place is detailed. He knows that Temple has been raped. Where did he get his information? From whom unless from Temple herself or a representative of Popeye's? Obviously, he did not get it from Horace Benbow; nor did he get it from the man on trial, Lee Goodwin, or from his common-law wife Ruby. He could not have got it from Narcissa directly, for when Narcissa called upon him, she tells him: "Three nights ago that Snopes, the one in the legislature, telephoned out home, trying to find him. The next day he [Horace] went to Memphis. I dont know what for. You'll have to find that out yourself. I just want Horace out of this business as soon as possible."

Presumably, as soon as Eustace Graham had been given the tip-off by Narcissa, he did get in touch with Clarence Snopes, and by using bribes or simply the various pressures available to him, extracted from Snopes all that he knew about Temple, including her Memphis address. Narcissa spoke with Eustace on the 4th of June. One supposes that Eustace wasted very little time in getting in touch with Temple and perhaps with her protector, Popeye. At any rate, he had plenty of time to do this before the 17th of June, the day on which they fled. Did Eustace exact from Temple a promise to appear in the courtroom and testify against Goodwin? And then after the murder of Red, did Popeye insist that Temple go on and keep her date with the district attorney in the courthouse? One can only speculate, but it would be hard otherwise to see how Eustace Graham could know so well just what to say and do. This hypothesis also provides a role for the Memphis lawyer, who presumably was commissioned by Popeye to see to it that Temple duly appeared in the courtroom.

There remains, however, the problem of why Clarence Snopes, who had some days earlier talked about going to Jackson on business, should turn up in Jefferson on the morning of the 18th, showing the marks of having been recently beaten up. What happened to Clarence? Who gave him the beating? Again we can only conjecture. When Clarence read the Memphis papers and found out that Popeye was alleged to have killed Red and had left town, did he then rush to Judge Drake to try to milk him of a hundred dollars, receiving the money but also a beating, possibly from one of Temple's brothers? But if so, why then is he scream-ing his revulsion at the "Jew lawyer": "We need laws against them. . . . When a jew lawyer can hold up an American, a white man, and not give him but ten dollars for something that two Americans. . . ." (Obviously, Clarence is referring to Judge Drake and Horace Benbow, each of whom had evidently paid him a hundred dollars.) Judge Drake would scarcely have hired a lawyer from Memphis, nor, with his legal connections, would he have employed this obviously raffish mouthpiece of the underworld. Moreover, the ten dollars paid to Clarence by the Memphis lawyer was evidently not paid on behalf of Judge Drake, who had already paid ten times that amount. Actually, it is difficult to see why the Memphis lawyer should have paid Clarence Snopes anything at all. Did Popeye's henchmen beat up Clarence when he came asking for money, and is Clarence lying about having been paid the ten dollars? Or was he given the ten dollars contemptuously after the beating? There is simply not enough evidence presented in the novel to allow any clear answers to these questions.

Again, we can do no more than speculate about the circumstances that brought Judge Drake to the trial. Someone had evidently told him that his daughter would appear in the courtroom at Jefferson. The way in which Temple reacts to her father and cringes from her brothers suggests that this is her first meeting with any of them since her disappearance. Perhaps Eustace Graham had at the last minute let Judge Drake know that his daughter would appear at the trial. (Graham would lose nothing by informing him on the eve of Temple's appearance, and to have failed to inform him at all would certainly have created resentment—resentment that Graham would not want to provoke in a man with powerful political connections within the state.)

What, then, was Temple's motive for perjuring herself? Did she do so out of fear of Popeye? Or because she had been corrupted by Popeye? Faulkner leaves the answer for the reader to infer, but everything in the novel suggests that in her lassitude and docility she was willing to carry out Popeye's command. At the trial she appears to be drained of energy, listless, like a person drugged. Apparently she had cared something for Red, and now that he is dead, she is so emptied of volition that she has no concern for anything. She may be so listless as to acquiesce even in the wishes of Red's murderer, Popeye. Certainly, that is the general impression that we get of her as the novel closes: Temple on a gray day at the end of a gray year, sitting in the Luxembourg Gardens, yawning behind her hand, taking out her compact, looking at her face, "sullen and discontented and sad," listening to the dying brasses of the army band.

When Faulkner, some twenty years later in *Requiem for a Nun*, reconsidered the character of Temple Drake, he made it quite plain that it was Popeye's hold upon Temple that caused her to testify against Goodwin. The Governor tells Temple that he remembers her from newspaper accounts, as the young woman who disappeared and reappeared "six weeks later as a witness in a murder trial in Jefferson, produced by the lawyer of the man who, it was then learned, had abducted her and held her prisoner—" In *Requiem* Faulkner thus makes it clear that the facts about Temple's rape and her stay in the Memphis brothel did get into the newspapers, where the Governor read them. Temple does not disagree with the Governor. She apparently accepts his version of the affair, namely that she was "produced" in the courtroom by the lawyer of the man who had abducted her.

I have been careful, however, to base my argument as to what happens in *Sanctuary* upon evidence found in that novel itself, for *Requiem for a Nun* may well present Faulkner's revised conception of the story. But at the least, the interpretation of Temple's actions that Faulkner gives in *Requiem* does not make it any easier to maintain that Temple's perjury was forced upon her by her father.

Sanctuary is clearly Faulkner's bitterest novel. It is a novel in which the male's initiation into the nature of evil is experienced in its most shattering and disillusioning form. After Horace has left Temple in the Memphis brothel, he thinks "perhaps it is upon the instant that we realize, admit, that there is a logical pattern to evil, that we die," and he thinks of the expression he had once seen in the eyes of a dead child and in the eyes of the other dead: "the cooling indignation, the shocked despair fading, leaving two empty globes in which the motionless world lurked profoundly in miniature."

In nearly every one of Faulkner's novels, the male's discovery of evil and reality is bound up with his discovery of the true nature of woman. Men idealize and romanticize women, but the cream of the jest is that women have a secret rapport with evil which men do not have, that they are able to adjust to evil without being shattered by it, being by nature flexible and pliable. Women are the objects of idealism, but are not in the least idealistic.

In the novel *Sartoris* Horace's younger sister, Narcissa, is depicted as a rather sweet girl, shy, quiet, and dependent upon her brother. But nine years later, the Narcissa of *Sanctuary* reveals a depravity that the reader, and certainly Horace himself, finds shocking. She is much upset that her brother has concerned himself with such people as the Goodwins, and midway through the novel Horace is forced to realize that it is his sister who has stirred up the "church ladies" to see that Ruby is evicted from the cheap room in which he had found lodgings for her. Horace, who has returned to his sister's house after trying to find another place for Ruby Goodwin, exclaims: "Just because she happens not to be married to the man whose child she carries about these sanctified streets. But who told them? That's what I want to know. I know that nobody in Jefferson knew it except—." Miss Jenny Du Pre puts in, "You were the first I heard tell it." Obviously, since only she and Narcissa have heard it from Horace, it is Narcissa who has arranged the eviction.

On the very next day Narcissa asks Horace who the district attorney is, and as she urges Horace to be quit of the murder case, it becomes perfectly plain to Horace how shallow and cruel Narcissa actually is. With regard to the murder, she exclaims: "I dont see that it makes any difference who did it. The question is, are you going to stay mixed up with it?" At this point, however, Horace could hardly have suspected that she would betray his case to the district attorney. (We are not told in the novel whether Horace ever does learn of her betrayal.) Next to Popeye, Narcissa is the most frightening person in this novel, as she pitilessly moves on to her own ends with no regard for justice and no concern for the claims of truth.

One most important facet of Horace's discovery of the true nature of women involves his stepdaughter, Little Belle. In the powerful scene which closes chapter 23, Horace has been looking at Little Belle's picture. Her face "dreamed with that quality of sweet chiaroscuro." But suddenly the room is filled with the odor of invisible honeysuckle and "the small face seemed to swoon in a voluptuous languor." Then "he knew what that sensation in his stomach meant." He hastily puts down the photograph and hurries to the bathroom, but as his stomach begins to retch, he has a terrible vision of Little Belle. Or is it Temple? "She" could be either: ". . . bound naked on her back on a flat car moving at speed through a black tunnel, the blackness streaming in rigid threads overhead, a roar of iron wheels in her ears." In the vision the car shoots out from the tunnel "in a long upward slant . . . toward a crescendo like a held breath, an interval in which she would swing faintly and lazily in nothingness filled with pale, myriad points of light. Far beneath her she could hear the faint, furious uproar of the shucks." In the last sentence Little Belle has not only been fused with Temple; she has fused with Horace himself, who in an agony of empathy has felt himself into the raped girl's ordeal.

This passage has been interpreted by several critics as a revelation to Horace of the evil within himself—incestuous feelings which he suddenly realizes he has for his stepdaughter. In Horace's unconscious mind there may indeed lurk such feelings, but I believe it would have required a psychiatrist to reveal them to Horace. (Toward his sister Narcissa, however, he clearly does have them and may well be aware of them.) But what troubles Horace in this scene are other matters: the evil to which a sweet young girl is exposed and, more darkly, the disposition to evil which lurks within such a girl. Earlier, Horace had told Miss Jenny that he thanked God that Little Belle wasn't his own flesh and blood. "I can reconcile myself to her having to be exposed to a scoundrel now and then, but to think that at any moment she may become involved with a fool."

This is after he had learned the consequences of Gowan's folly. As for a girl's own propensity to evil, Benbow has already been aware of that. He "looked at the familiar image [of Little Belle] with a kind of quiet horror and despair, at a face suddenly older in sin than he would ever be, a face more blurred than sweet, at eyes more secret than soft." This is why, when Horace returns from his shocking interview with Temple at Miss Reba's house and looks once more at Little Belle's photograph, the nausea rises in his stomach.

Horace's tendency to idealize women also receives a rather shattering blow from another quarter. He admires Goodwin's common-law wife, Ruby, for her loyalty, her power of endurance, her willingness to suffer anything in order to aid the man she loves. She tells Horace that she had once prostituted herself to raise money for her man when he was in jail. She makes it plain to him that she is willing to do so again, and indeed that she assumes that Horace means to demand her body as a fee for his legal services. He cries out in exasperation: "O, hell! Can you stupid mammals never believe that any man, every man—You thought that was what I was coming for? You thought that if I had intended to, I'd have waited this long?" Finally Horace whispers to her: "Good God. What kind of men have you known?" The term that Horace uses in addressing Ruby is revealing: "you stupid mammals." Women are peculiarly mammals, creatures that give suck, and to Horace, the appalled and outraged idealist, these human beings, whose function is so invincibly animal, are nowhere more so than in their unwillingness to believe in ideals.

Horace's grudge against women, against nature, against the irrational brutality of reality, comes out rather plainly when, after the verdict, he starts home. Narcissa has invited him into the car and asks him whether he wants to go "to the house" (that is, to Horace's house) or "out home" (that is, where she and Miss Jenny Du Pre live). Horace answers, "I dont care. Just home." A little later in the car "he began to cry, sitting in the car beside his sister." There was still a little "snow of locust blooms" on the drive. " 'It does last,' Horace said, 'Spring does. You'd almost think there was some purpose to it.' "

Sanctuary here shows the mark of the period in which it was written. Horace Benbow is not so much a product of a decadent Southern culture as a bookish, middle-aged inhabitant of the modern waste land. "April is the cruelest month, breeding" lilacs and locust blossoms "out of the dead land." It is the cruelest month because it promises a rebirth that is fraudulent and meaningless. And this is Horace's complaint here, "You'd almost think there was some purpose to it."

The reader may well ask whether Temple does not have some part in these rites of initiation or whether Faulkner regards them as strictly the prerogative of the male. Temple's discovery of evil is horrifying enough, but it takes a very different form from Horace's. In spite of the terror and violent affront that the girl feels, the experience is not so much a disillusionment as a discovery of her own capacities, resources, and deepest drives and desires. To say this is not to rely entirely upon *Requiem for a Nun*, in which Temple, eight years later, is very hard on herself and confesses that she discovered that she liked evil. Even in *Sanctuary* there is plenty of evidence to support this conception of her. Horace, for example, notices as Temple tells him the story of the rape that there is a kind of detachment and even pride in her account.

Her story is overpowering in its vividness. In the telling Temple seems to become a pure medium through which the sense of horror is being transmitted directly and with a terrifying immediacy. For example, describing Popeye's touch upon her skin, the girl says: "and my skin started jumping away from [Popeye's hand] like those little flying fish in front of a boat. It was like my skin knew which way it was going to go before it started moving, and my skin would keep on jerking just ahead of it like there wouldn't be anything there when the hand got there." Yet this appalling story is told, as it seems to Horace, "in one of those bright, chatty monologues which women can carry on when they realize that they have the center of the stage." Suddenly Horace realizes that Temple "was recounting the experience with actual pride, a sort of naive and impersonal vanity, as though she were making it up, looking from him to Miss Reba with quick, darting glances like a dog driving two cattle along a lane." The masterful simile at the end beautifully describes what Temple is doing or at least what it seems to Horace that she is doing. The searing experience is already mixed up with posturing and histrionics.

Or consider the episode in which the girl is being taken to Memphis by Popeye. She has been brutally raped, and as they drive through the spring landscape Temple begins to scream. But when the traffic thickens she is willing to hush, and when Popeye stops at a filling station in a small town, Temple does not scream. "She watched him go up the street and enter a door. It was a dingy confectionery." When Popeye comes back to the car, Temple has gone, but she has not rushed down the street in order to escape. Instead, Popeye finds her in the filling-station yard, cowering between a barrel and the wall. She whispers in terror to Popeye: "He nearly saw me! He was almost looking right at me!" When Popeye asks who, Temple tells him, "A boy. At school. He was looking right toward—." The desire not to be seen in these circumstances by someone she knows apparently drives out of her head any notion of escape. It is this kind of inordinate respectability that corrupts Narcissa, Benbow's sister, as well as Temple Drake. Later, in *Requiem for a Nun*, Faulkner is to make Temple realize this trait for what it is. She tells the Governor "I had two legs . . . and I could have simply screamed up the main street of any of the little towns we passed."

The fatal adaptability, the "social sense," the ability to accommodate to circumstances—any circumstances—these are the things that paralyze any impulse on Temple's part to flee the scene or to resist the evil. Having made her accommodation to evil, she will find that she has a positive liking for it.

But the liking comes later. It is one thing to say that Temple's very terror and self-consciousness serve to arouse the men at the Old Frenchman's Place and that the one mode of ingratiation which she has learned by her eighteenth year turns out to be precisely the worst behavior that she could use. It is, however, a very different thing to say that the terrified girl is actually trying to lead the men on and to provoke the sexual assault that finally occurs. Poor Temple's "grimace of taut, toothed coquetry" is not intended as an invitation to Popeye but as a way of placating him. So also with her cringing yet grinning demeanor, which elicits from Popeye simply the comment, "Make your whore lay off of me, Jack."

Ruby Goodwin, in her fury with respectable women and in her very lively concern lest Temple arouse Lee's lust, is very sharp with Temple and proceeds to read into her actions motives of which Temple was surely not conscious. But later, in talking to Horace, Ruby testifies to Temple's utter terror and her compulsive efforts to escape. What Temple discovers is that the world of nightmare evil is real. She tells Ruby, "Things like that dont happen. Do they?. . . You're just like other people." Temple's mind is thoroughly conventional—that is, good and evil do not exist; only what is proper and improper exist. It is a world which can be arranged if one has the money and the proper position, and the real shock to Temple is that she has suddenly fallen into a place in which money and position no longer avail. This is why she can do nothing but practice her little foolish grimaces of coquetry and protest, "My father's a judge; my father's a judge."

Faulkner has presented what happened at the Old Frenchman's Place with a multiple focus. Beginning with chapter 5, and extending through chapter 14, we have the omniscient author's third-person account with a good deal of conversation and occasional presentation of the various characters' inmost thoughts and feelings. But later on, in chapter 19, Ruby gives Horace her own account of what happened that night, with special reference to Temple's actions. Horace is very much concerned to make sure that the girl has not been touched. (Ruby evidently knows nothing of the rape, or, if she does, chooses not to tell Horace anything about it.) Their interview concludes with Horace's statement: "You know she was all right."

But there is still another focus on these same events. In chapter 23, when Horace visits Miss Reba's establishment, Temple tells her own story, with special reference to her fears and apprehensions. Hers is naturally a highly subjective account. The curious thing to Horace is that Temple seems fixated upon the night that she spent in the ruined house, "from the time she entered the room and tried to wedge the door with the chair, until the woman came to the bed and led her out. That was the only part of the whole experience which appeared to have left any impression on her at all: the night which she had spent in comparative inviolation." As for Horace's attempts to get her to talk about the crime itself, "she would elude him and return to herself sitting on the bed, listening to the men on the porch, or lying in the dark while they entered the room." " 'Yes; that,' she would say. 'It just happened. I dont know. I had been scared so long that I guess I had just gotten used to being.' "

What it is to be scared as Temple was scared has been brilliantly dramatized by Faulkner. The psychology is convincing to the reader but frequently puzzling to the victim herself. Consider the passage in which Temple "thinks" herself into a boy's body, or in which she imagines herself in a spiked chastity belt. She says to Horace: " 'Oh, yes; this was something else funny I did.' " It is the strange way in which she reacted when she felt Popeye approaching her bed. As she lay in the dark and sensed him approaching, she was silently saying to him: "Come on. Touch me. Touch me! You're a coward if you dont. Coward! Coward!" And she goes on to tell Horace, by way of explanation: "I wanted to go to sleep, you see. And he just kept on standing there. I thought if he'd just go on and get it over with, I could go to sleep. So I'd say You're a coward if you dont! . . . and I could feel my mouth getting fixed to scream, and that little hot ball inside you that screams."

In discussing Faulkner's brilliant handling of the psychology of terror, one should not fail to mention the phantasy in which Temple sees herself in the coffin. She tells Horace: "I did a funny thing. I could see myself in the coffin. I looked sweet—you know: all in white. I had on a veil like a bride, and I was crying because . . . they had put shucks in the coffin. I was crying because they had put shucks in the coffin where I was dead." A depth psychologist could doubtless do a lot with this passage, but the sensitive layman is able to get much of the force of it without professional help: death and loss of virginity fuse in this phantasy, with its overtones of self-pity, but the death has been robbed of dignity by a cruel joke—the dry rustling corn husks in the coffin, and their associations with the girl's unnatural rape in the corn crib.

Temple's respectability, conventionality, and pliability all have their part in her final betrayal of Lee Goodwin at the trial. But not least important in this matter is the ambiguity of her attitude toward Popeye. If she hates Popeye—and perhaps just because she does hate him for his power and authority—she finds in him something of a father. In *Requiem for a Nun* Temple tells the Governor that Popeye "was worse than a father or uncle. It was worse than being the wealthy ward of the most indulgent trust or insurance company." But this theory of her relationship to Popeye is not necessarily an afterthought on Faulkner's part, for in *Sanctuary* itself there are hints of a "fatherly" role. While Temple lives at Miss Reba's, Popeye showers her with gifts of all sorts and frequently simply sits by her bed: "Often in the night she would wake to smell tobacco and to see the single ruby eye where Popeye's mouth would be." She resents the close guard that Popeye keeps over her, and when she is angry at him she taunts him for not being a man; but when she tries to wheedle something out of him she calls him "Daddy," and when she fears that he is preparing to shoot her lover Red, she tries to get the pistol away from him by saying to him "Give it to me . . . Daddy. Daddy." If "Daddy" as used here could be the slang of the twenties for one's lover, nevertheless it carries in this context some sense of the father image too.

The comic scenes in this novel have won deserved praise. The adventures of Fonzo and Virgil trying to find a cheap hotel and, in their country innocence, putting up at Miss Reba's establishment and for two weeks speculating as to what Miss Reba does for a living are all very funny. So also, though in a different mode, is the account in chapter 25 of the wake that is held for Red and the subsequent beer party at Miss Reba's, in which the two other madams, Miss Myrtle and Miss Lorraine, philosophize about life and love and the difficulties that confront "us girls."

The comic scenes are not, however, extraneous to the novel. They provide, among other things, depth and substance to the nightmare. The evil in which Temple is involved is no shadowy specter; it has blood and bone and belly. Daylight, common sense, and humor can exorcise the mere nightmare. But the evil that can live in the daylight world of common sense is substantial. Insofar as *Sanctuary* has to do with Horace's initiation, the comic scenes associated with Miss Reba's establishment supply more than comic relief from horror; they comment upon his idealism and thus play their part in the initiation.

The meaning of the title, *Sanctuary*, has excited various conjectures. A student of mine once suggested that Faulkner must have had in mind the following passage in Joseph Conrad's *Chance* (p. 311 of the Uniform edition):

> A young girl, you know, is something like a *temple*. You pass by and wonder what mysterious rites are going on in there, what prayers, what visions? The privileged man, the lover, the husband, who are given the key of the *sanctuary* do not always know how to use it. For myself, without claim, without merit, simply by chance I had been allowed to look through the half-opened door and I had seen the saddest possible desecration, the withered brightness of youth, a spirit neither made cringing nor yet dulled but as if bewildered in quivering hopelessness by gratuitous cruelty; self-confidence destroyed and, instead, a resigned recklessness, a mournful callousness.
>
> (italics mine)

This passage about the girl named Flora de Barral is spoken by Conrad's Marlow, but it might very well have been spoken by Horace Benbow with reference to Temple Drake. In the long interview with Temple in Miss Reba's brothel, Horace had looked through a half-opened door and had seen, as Conrad has put it, "the saddest possible desecration." In that experience there was "gratuitous cruelty" indeed. Temple's conduct at the end of the book answers brilliantly to Conrad's phrase "a resigned recklessness" if we think of her at the trial of Lee Goodwin, and to a "mournful callousness" if we think of our last sight of her in the Luxembourg Gardens. One grants, of course, that if Horace Benbow had spoken these words with reference to Temple Drake, he would have been speaking of a very different situation from that recounted by Conrad and would have been using the words not wonderingly but bitterly. Indeed, Horace's creator, William Faulkner, may have felt that Conrad had understated woman's general situation and probably had misunderstood it—that in some instances a look within the "sanctuary" would have proved too shocking for Conrad to have credited, and that his own novel to be entitled *Sanctuary* might provide instruction in what indeed such a Temple could contain.

Did Faulkner then derive the title of his novel and the name of his heroine from this passage? Faulkner's titles are highly subjective and often whimsical. I think it certainly possible that the title *Sanctuary* came from Conrad's *Chance*; but in any case, the view of woman held by Conrad and expressed so explicitly in this novel certainly reminds one of the view entertained by Faulkner. For example, Marlow describes what he calls "the pathos of being a woman." Though a man can struggle, a woman's part is passive: "they are not made for attack. Wait they must. I am speaking here of women who are really women. . . . Nothing can beat a true woman for a clear vision of reality; I would say a cynical vision if I were not afraid of wounding your chivalrous feelings—for which, by the bye, women are not so grateful as you may think, to fellows of your mind." A disillusioned Horace might be speaking here.

I observed earlier that the Faulknerian male's discovery of evil and reality is bound up with his discovery of the true nature of woman. Women, though idealized by men, are themselves hard-headed realists. As is said of Narcissa, "Fiddlesticks. You dont wonder. You just do things and then stop until the next time to do something comes around." This is a bitter but quite just comment upon Narcissa, but it is a comment made by another woman, by Miss Jenny Du Pre. Yet if Narcissa and Temple terrify Horace with their lack of any final morality, one must remember that there are also in the novel women like Ruby and Miss Jenny, women who, for all their great differences and dissimilar attitudes, are both feminine and yet both fundamentally decent. Even Miss Reba has a kind of decency. After Temple's confession, Miss Reba begs Horace to take her away and not let her come back: "I'd find her folks myself, if I knowed how to go about it. But you know how . . . She'll be dead, or in the asylum in a year, way him and her go on up there in that room."

Yet if *Sanctuary* is in some respects Faulkner's most pessimistic novel, it is certainly one of his most brilliant, and the psychology of Temple as she goes through her various experiences is hair-raising in its power of conviction. No one knows just what would go through a girl's head were she to undergo Temple's experience, and yet most readers will feel that the account in *Sanctuary* carries conviction. However incredible the events narrated, Temple's reaction to them is compellingly credible, and the reader will acknowledge the veracity of Faulkner's searching look into her mind and heart.

Whatever its final meaning, the story of Temple Drake evidently remained with Faulkner as a fascinating problem. In *Requiem for a Nun* he asked himself what might have happened to people like Gowan and Temple. What Faulkner supposes to have happened does thorough credit to his sense of reality. Their marriage could hardly have been a really happy one. Temple would have found it difficult not to resent what Gowan had got her into and his pusillanimous conduct at the Old Frenchman's Place. Moreover, Temple would have been too conscious of the fact that he had married her because he had felt that this was the only honorable thing to do and thus would have been too conscious of the fact that he had done the decent thing. There was too much to be forgiven and too much for which to be grateful.

Faulkner as a good realist knows that Temple had, in her sojourn in the Memphis brothel, gone on past the tepid decencies of suburbia. As she puts it herself: "Temple Drake liked evil." In fact, she liked it so much that she longs for a confidant, and so chooses for a maid, Nancy, the Negro prostitute dope-fiend. Nancy can talk her language, and Temple can confide in her. Because Temple Drake really likes evil, she finds herself unprepared to resist when Red's younger brother comes up out of the past to blackmail her with the love letters that she had written to Red several years before. As Temple tells the Governor: "You've got to be already prepared to resist [evil], say no to it, long before you even know what it is." This is a comment shrewd enough to have come from the lips of a Jesuit confessor.

Faulkner's basic conception of his sequel, then, is perfectly sound. He is too good a realist to believe that it would have been very easy for either Temple or her husband to gloss over the fact of Temple's past. Before there could be any enduring bond between them, they would have had to be able to forgive each other the past, and that would have meant accepting the fact of the past. For either one to be capable of doing that would require some bitter and difficult struggle. Nancy Mannigoe's violent attempt to save Temple's home is thus justified, for Temple's case is one requiring the most drastic remedies. But Faulkner's choice of drastic remedies sets some very special and difficult problems. Most readers will be hard put to maintain complete sympathy with Nancy as she murders one of Temple's children in order to save the home for the other child. The difficulty is compounded by the fact that Faulkner has chosen to render all the action through a strict use of the dramatic mode. Thus there is no direct means for our getting inside Nancy Mannigoe's head or for looking into her heart as she goes about the terrible deed dictated to her by love. Her own speeches do not help too much, for she is not allowed many speeches; besides, she is a simple person, relatively inarticulate, and a great deal must therefore be left to the reader's inference.

Under the circumstances, Faulkner has done very well indeed. The play as performed carries a certain amount of power and conviction, particularly the last scene, in the jail, in which Nancy appears and speaks her good-bye to Temple, the woman for whose sake she is going to her death. But a measure of power and conviction is not enough to bring off this most ambitious work. By limiting himself to dialogue, and rather clipped and terse dialogue at that, Faulkner has pretty well cut himself off from the poetic resources that are really necessary if *Requiem for a Nun* is to succeed. To be sure, he has put a great deal of poetry into the book; but the poetry has been introduced in a very special way: before each block of dramatic matter, Faulkner has given us a long section of bardic prose on the courthouse, the scene of Nancy Mannigoe's trial; the statehouse, in which the Governor meets Temple and Gavin Stevens to hear Temple's plea for Nancy; and the jail, where Temple goes to see Nancy for the last time. These three sections are brilliantly written, particularly that entitled "The Courthouse," which gives us the early history of Faulkner's Jefferson. But though they evoke a general background rich in history for the events that take place in the play, they do not solve Faulkner's specific dramatic problems. The use of this material in just this fashion constitutes the most daring but perhaps the least successful solution of the structural problems attempted by Faulkner in any of his novels.

There is much that could be said for the ethical and psychological insights given us in *Requiem for a Nun*, and a great deal has to be said for the fine last scene. Here Nancy, illiterate and humble yet quietly confident, addresses herself to the problem of evil and the problem of suffering, and tries to answer Temple's anguished question: "Why do you and my little baby both have to suffer just because I decided to go to a baseball game five years ago? Do you have to suffer everybody else's anguish just to believe in God? What kind of God is it that has to blackmail His customers with the whole world's grief and ruin?" Nancy's answer is that God "don't want you to suffer. He don't like suffering neither. . . . He don't tell you to suffer. But He gives you the chance. He gives you the best He can think of, that you are capable of doing. And He will save you."

Nancy has faith, the kind that moves mountains, and for some readers she will have established the fact that she killed Temple's baby indeed because she loved it. But for others the credibility of Nancy's motive is more difficult. Their difficulty will be not so much with Nancy's theology, which is probably sound enough, but with the dramatic presentation, which may not be quite full enough, articulate enough, convincing enough to bring the whole work to success.

MICHAEL MILLGATE

"The Hamlet"

Faulkner said at the University of Virginia that he wrote *The Hamlet* "in the late twenties," mostly in the form of short stories, and that in 1940 he "got it pulled together." Writing to Malcolm Cowley in 1945, he had given a fuller account of the book's history:

> THE HAMLET was incepted as a novel. When I began it, it produced Spotted Horses, went no further. About two years later suddenly I had THE HOUND, then JAMSHYD'S COURTYARD, mainly because SPOTTED HORSES had created a character I fell in love with: the itinerant sewing-machine agent named Suratt. Later a man of that name turned up at home, so I changed my man to Ratliff for the reason thag [sic] my whole town spent much of its time trying to decide just what living man I was writing about, the one literary criticism of the town being 'How in the hell did he remember all that and when did that happen anyway?' Meanwhile, my book had created Snopes and his clan, who produced stories in their saga which arc to fall in later volume: MULE IN THE YARD, BRASS, etc. This over about ten years, until one day I decided I had better start on the first volume or I'd never get any of it down. So I wrote an induction toward the spotted horse story, which included BARN BURNING, AND [sic] WASH, which I discovered had no place in that book at all. Spotted Horses became a longer story, picked up the HOUND (rewritten and much longer and with the character's name changed from Cotton to Snopes), and went on with JAMSHYD'S COURTYARD.

There is no doubt that Faulkner began writing a Snopes novel some time in late 1926 or early 1927. In a newspaper article written at about that time Phil Stone spoke of two novels on which Faulkner was working: one was the book we now know as *Sartoris*, the other "something of a saga of an extensive family connection of typical 'poor white trash.' " Meriwether, quoting this article, also quotes from a letter which Stone wrote to him in 1957: "Bill once wrote fifteen or twenty pages on the idea of the Snopes trilogy which he entitled 'Father Abraham'. . . ." These comments substantiate Faulkner's own statements about the composition of the book, and help to date the 25-page manuscript of "Father Abraham" now in the Arents Collection of the New York Public Library.

This manuscript opens with an extended description of Flem as a symbolic and legendary figure, a by-product of the democratic principle in action and successor to the Southern gentleman as the representative figure of his region and his time. There follows an account of the Old Frenchman place and its legend, and of the inhabitants of Frenchman's Bend, which bears a direct and sometimes a close relationship to the opening pages of *The Hamlet*. Once the setting has been established the "Father Abraham" manuscript goes on to describe a number of characters, notably Uncle Billy Varner and his daughter Eula, and continues with a telling of the "spotted horses" story, from the standpoint of the omniscient author, that is similar in essentials to the version which appears in Chapter I of "The Peasants", the fourth book of *The Hamlet*. A typescript of "Father Abraham," now in the Alderman Library, introduces a number of features that are absent from the manuscript and develops in particular Mrs. Littlejohn's function as a silent commentator on the follies of the male world of horse-trading. It is apparently later than the manuscript and is certainly still closer to the version used in *The Hamlet*, although it seems to have gone no further than a point shortly following the moment when the injured Henry Armstid has been carried into Mrs. Littlejohn's boarding house.

The "Father Abraham" manuscript gives a more or less complete account of the whole "spotted horses" episode, but its last page, written on different paper and in different ink from the preceding pages, suddenly breaks off, as though Faulkner had abruptly abandoned an attempt to extend the material further and to develop it into the Snopes novel that he apparently had in mind. The "Father Abraham" typescript may have been completed shortly afterwards; on the other hand, it may have been a product of that later stage in the history of *The Hamlet* to which Faulkner referred in his letter to Cowley: "About two years later suddenly I had THE HOUND, then JAMSHYD'S COURTYARD." "The Hound" was first published in *Harper's* in August 1931, "Lizards in Jamshyd's Courtyard" in the *Saturday Evening Post* for February 27, 1932, but it is clear from the sending schedule which Faulkner kept for his early stories that they existed in completed form by November 17, 1930, and May 27, 1930. The short story "Spotted Horses" was published in *Scribner's* in June 1931, but a version may have been finished by August 25, 1930. "Centaur in Brass," a Snopes story first published in the *American Mercury* (February 1932) and later incorporated in *The Town*, also existed by August 1931. All of these stories, of course, may have been written at a somewhat earlier date. Faulkner says that his first attempt to write a Snopes novel did not go any further than "Spotted Horses" (i.e. "Father Abraham"), but there is no doubt that he had already worked up a great variety of Snopes material and already had in mind the general pattern of Flem's career.

Many years later he spoke of the moment when "I thought of the whole story at once like a bolt of lightning lights up a landscape and you see everything . . ." The comprehensiveness of this conception is apparent from the various references to the Snopes family in *Sartoris*—brief references, to be sure, but sufficient to delineate the ground-plan of almost the whole Snopes saga:

> [Montgomery Ward] Snopes was a young man, member of a seemingly inexhaustible family which for the last ten years had been moving to town in driblets from a small settlement known as Frenchman's Bend. Flem, the first Snopes, had appeared unheralded one day behind the counter of a small restaurant on a side street, patronized by country folk. With this foothold and like Abraham of old, he brought his blood and legal kin household by household, individual by individual, into town, and established them where they could gain money. Flem himself was presently manager of the city light and water plant, and for the following few years he was a sort of handy man to the municipal government; and three years ago, to old Bayard's profane astonishment and unconcealed annoyance, he became vice-president of the Sartoris bank, where already a relation of his was a bookkeeper.
>
> (*Sartoris*)

It is presumably to *Sartoris* that Faulkner is referring when he speaks of "my book [which] had created Snopes and his clan." The novel had also created Suratt, the sewing-machine agent, whose name, as Faulkner explains, he later changed to Ratliff, and it is conceivable that Faulkner—having first abandoned "Father Abraham" in order to work on *Sartoris*—returned to the Snopes material in the latter part of 1927, after the completion of the *Sartoris* typescript at the end of September. The final typescript of *The Sound and the Fury* was completed by October 1928, however, and it seems probable that the writing of this immensely ambitious work must have engrossed most if not all of Faulkner's energies during the intervening year. By the early summer of 1930, at all events, Faulkner had taken a fresh look at the Snopes material and had begun quarrying it for short stories. From the evidence of Faulkner's letter to Cowley, and in the absence of earlier manuscripts or typescripts, it would seem that "Spotted Horses," "The Hound," "Lizards in Jamshyd's Court-yard," and "Centaur in Brass" were written at this stage. The last three may have been written virtually from scratch, although Faulkner no doubt conceived of their essential features in that original vision of the whole Snopes sequence, but there is ample evidence to show that the writing of "Spotted Horses" and the subsequent incorporation of the episode in *The Hamlet* was by no means a simple process.

When composing the version of the Texas ponies anecdote which subsequently appeared in *Scribner's* as the story "Spotted Horses", Faulkner had a body of earlier material, including "Father Abraham," on which to draw, and in adapting this material he changed it radically. There is some evidence that at one stage—probably an early one—Faulkner may have experimented with a version of the story in which the "spotted horses" incident was divorced from any detailed account of Frenchman's Bend and its inhabitants; in the *Scribner's* version actually published Faulkner did not omit this scene-setting, but he greatly reduced it in length. The most important change was in the narrative point of view, for the story is told, not in the third-person of "Father Abraham" and the novel, but in the first-person, from the point of view of a man who, although not specific-ally identified, is clearly the sewing-machine agent, Suratt/Ratliff. The narrator tells the story as though to a group of friends—"You-all mind the moon was nigh full that night," he says at one point—and in vigorously colloquial language: "They was colored like parrots and they was quiet as doves, and ere a one of them would kill you quick as a rattle-snake." It is, in fact, essentially what the editor of *Scribner's* described it as being, "a tall tale with implications of tragedy"; but the point immediately to be made is that it is a by-product of the original Snopes conception, a story carved out of the material at a time when Faulkner, for whatever reason, felt unable or unwilling to work it up into a novel, and that the line of development between the original conception and *The Hamlet* does not pass through "Spotted Horses" as published in *Scribner's* but goes directly from "Father Abraham" to the novel. At the time when he was writing the version of the "spotted horses" episode which appears in the final section of *The Hamlet*, and also at the time when he was writing the present opening pages of the novel, Faulkner must certainly have had in front of him some version of the "Father Abraham" material; if he also had a copy of the *Scribner's* story he referred to it much less frequently.

When adapting for incorporation into *The Hamlet* the tale of Pat Stamper's horse-trading activities which had previously been told in the *Scribner's* story, "Fool About a Horse," Faulkner again seems to have worked primarily from an earlier typescript rather than from the published story, though no doubt he also had a copy of the story readily to hand.

Earlier in the letter to Cowley from which we have already quoted, Faulkner says that the *Scribner's* version of "Spotted Horses" was in the nature of a condensation of several chapters of *The Hamlet*, and it is entirely possible that Faulkner had actually got some way towards completing a Snopes novel at the time when "Spotted Horses" was written. Some day, indeed, firm evidence of this in the form of further manuscript or typescript material may become available, and in the meantime it is worth noting that Aubrey Starke, in his important article on Faulkner published in 1934, makes reference to "the long promised, and eagerly awaited 'Snopes saga',—chief title on Mr. Faulkner's list of unpublished work." Starke's further remarks on the Snopeses make clear how much material dealing with them Faulkner had already published by this time, and show that, to an intelligent reader, the whole trend of his treatment of them was already plain:

> And even if *The Snopes Saga* were not already promised we could safely predict that Mr. Faulkner would continue for some time to come the story of the Snopeses, for the rise of the class to which the Snopeses belong and the decay and disintegration of the class to which Sartorises and Compsons belong is surely the central, symbolic theme of Mr. Faulkner's comedy, as it—more than the traditional color problem—is the central problem of that part of the world in which Mr. Faulkner lives.

In fact, it was not until several years later that Faulkner "pulled together" the various segments of Snopes material, although even at this stage he got no further than *The Hamlet*. It was to be another seventeen years before the publication of a further volume, *The Town*, despite the fact that the conclusion of *The Hamlet* clearly invites a sequel—the final page of the typescript setting copy actually bears the deleted words, "end Volume One."

The final composition of *The Hamlet* apparently began some time late in 1938, and a considerable amount of manuscript and typescript material has survived from this stage, including a manuscript which is practically complete up to a point corresponding to the end of the second section of Book Three, Chapter II, of the published book, a complete typescript setting copy, and many miscellaneous pages of both manuscript and typescript. In the process of working towards the final version of the novel Faulkner made a great many minor additions and improvements, and the typescript setting copy is especially of interest for the evidence it provides of the many rearrangements which Faulkner made in the material of the book before eventually deciding on its final form. To take one example of many, it is clear that at one time the opening of the first new paragraph on page 128 of the published book appeared not in the first chapter of the "Eula" section but as the beginning of a proposed third chapter.

The most interesting features of manuscript and typescript alike, however, are the vestiges of Faulkner's experimentation with different opening chapters. Faulkner mentions to Cowley that when he began pulling *The Hamlet* together he wrote an "induction toward the spotted horse story"; he adds that the induction included "Barn Burning" and "Wash"—"which I discovered had no place in that book at all." It seems remarkable that Faulkner should ever have thought that "Wash", much of which he had already incorporated into *Absalom, Absalom!*, might find a place in the "Snopes Saga," and one can only surmise that he may have thought of giving an historical dimension to his largely economic study of the rise of the "poor white" Flem Snopes: he later used "Wash" to add such a dimension to his treatment of white-Negro relationships in *Go Down, Moses.* At all events, there appears to be no clear evidence to show that "Wash" was incorporated into any of the later versions of *The Hamlet*: there is no such evidence, at least, in the manuscript and typescript versions at the University of Virginia.

The case of "Barn Burning" is different. The 17-page manuscript of the story in the Alderman Library bears the heading "BOOK ONE/ Chapter I" in addition to the deleted title "Barn Burning," while the 32-page typescript bears no title at all but simply the heading "Chapter One." Deleted pagination in the typescript setting copy of *The Hamlet* shows that 32 pages have at some stage been removed and very clearly suggests that "Barn Burning" was until a fairly late stage incorporated into the novel as its opening chapter, with a version of the present first chapter as Chapter II. Sometime during the winter of 1938–1939, however, Faulkner must have changed his mind about the way the novel should open: among a group of rejected typescript pages in the Alderman Library there is a version of page 1, close to the first page of the published book, which bears the pencilled editorial note "Rec'd 3/20/39," while "Barn Burning" itself was published as an independent entity, and with only minor alterations from the typescript version headed "Chapter One," in *Harper's Monthly* for June 1939. Faulkner seems to have experimented with a number of other possible openings to the novel, including one which began with the first encounter between Jody Varner and Ab Snopes which now appears on page 8 of the published book. It is hard to think that this would have made a satisfactory opening, but there is no doubt that the deeply moving story of "Barn Burning" would have been in many ways an extremely effective introduction. We do not know why Faulkner finally decided to take it out, but it may have been in some measure the result of a decision not to use Colonel Sartoris Snopes, the boy of "Barn Burning," as a character elsewhere in the novel, or of some feeling that the episode gave too favourable an impression of the Snopes family to serve satisfactorily as a prologue to the history of Flem. The boy is certainly absent, apart from Ratliff's reference to another little Snopes whom he remembers having once seen, from the summary of the narrative events of "Barn Burning" which appears in the present opening chapter.

The long history of *The Hamlet* reveals it clearly as a novel conceived as a single whole but written over a period of many years, with many interruptions, much revision and reworking, and a continually enriching accretion of observation, anecdote and imagery; the finished book, far from being a series of loosely connected incidents, demands consideration as a carefully organised and wholly organic structure. An example of the care and deliberate artistry which went into the composition of *The Hamlet* is provided by Faulkner's extremely skilful incorporation of the "Fool About a Horse" and "Spotted Horses" episodes. As short stories "Fool About a Horse" and "Spotted Horses" are fairly straightforward and very funny tall tales of men being successfully and outrageously tricked in horse-trades. The stories remain firmly within the tall tale convention, with no wider implications. When these episodes appear in the wider context of the novel, however, the characters who in the short stories are little more than conventional counters become fully known to us as individuals, as human beings capable of suffering. In these circumstances Faulkner deliberately adapts and manipulates the tall-tale convention so that while it does not control and delimit the action, as it does in the short stories, it remains as an ironic background against which the events of the novel are played out, its restricted outlines providing an implicit contrast to the more fully realised characters and actions of the novel and at the same time offering one possible way of viewing these events. In a sense it is another example of that multiple point of view which is fundamental to so much of Faulkner's work. The "Spotted Horses" episode as we have it in *The Hamlet* is a brilliant variation on the traditional horse-trade theme, but it also tells us a great deal about the economic and social relationships operating within the world of Frenchman's Bend and brings out with painful clarity the suffering implicit for the losers in a horse-trade and for their wives and families—something which lies wholly beyond the limits of the tall tale. The episode also places Flem Snopes among his fellows, the other traders of genius, but at the same time distinguishes him from them: he appears as absolutely predatory and unpitying in his treatment of Mrs. Armstid, he employs an agent, and we see that he never treads the same path twice, his victims being not merely fresh scalps as they would be for Pat Stamper, but further upward steps on the ladder leading to the banker's mansion in Jefferson.

The "Spotted Horses" and "Fool About a Horse" episodes thus fall into place in the total pattern of the novel as versions of the tall tale, itself an essential feature of the novel's mode, and as stages in the central narrative of the rise of Snopesism. They have an even more important function, however, as variations on the theme of greed, one of the two major themes running throughout the book. The other principal theme is that of love, and the parallel and often inter-reflecting investigations of love and greed, of men dominated by the desire for sexual or economic possession, are pursued in terms of various episodes of love and marriage, on the one hand, and of trading and barter on the other. The view that this thematic pattern provides the chief unifying factor in *The Hamlet* seems first to have been clearly propounded by Robert Penn Warren, and it is now so firmly established that there is some danger of the novel's unity being thought of as exclusively thematic. It is true that the linear progression of the novel is constantly interrupted and diversified by a series of stories and episodes which are chiefly significant in terms of their relationship to the central themes. But such apparent diversions all possess strong narrative links with the main action, and in view of the criticisms which have often been made of *The Hamlet*'s "episodic" structure it seems necessary to emphasise the strong element of straightforward narrative continuity which runs throughout.

The theme which is the more closely tied to the narrative continuity of the book is that of greed and self-interest, and it is perhaps worth noting that it was this theme which seems to have dominated, almost exclusively, the Snopes material which Faulkner wrote during the early stages of his extended work on *The Hamlet* and its successors; the counterpointed theme of love seems to have been added during that final "pulling together" of *The Hamlet* in the late 1930's. In Book One of the novel, "Flem," as we follow the rise of Flem Snopes to the point where he is able to supplant Will Varner in his favourite flour-barrel chair at the Old Frenchman place, it is the theme of greed which predominates, although Book One also creates most of the characters who are to play major roles later in the novel as well as many of the situations through which Faulkner later develops the theme of love. The shift of interest to this latter theme in Book Two is heralded by its title, "Eula," but after the stories of the implacable passivity of Eula and the passionate fury of Labove have been told, Faulkner skilfully involves them in the theme of self-interested greed and swings the whole section into line with the central narrative by means of Eula's marriage to Flem and Ratliff's vision of Flem taking over Hell.

Book Three, "The Long Summer," is taken up with the stories of Ike Snopes, Houston, and Mink Snopes, each story merging smoothly into its successor: Ike's beloved cow belongs at first to Houston, Houston himself is murdered by Mink. These episodes relate primarily to the theme of love, but the theme of greed irresistibly enters, generally with tragic or ironic effects. It would be ridiculous to speak of Ike's passion for the cow as being endorsed by Faulkner, but the heightened language, the mythological allusions, and the sensitive evocation of nature all work to persuade us at least of its absolute sincerity and generosity; what finally appear as more grotesque and perverted than Ike's own role are the attempts of his relatives to exploit his love and, Ratliff suspects, to turn it to profit. The episode closes, however, with a shift of mood entirely characteristic of this immensely diversified novel, and we are given the almost unqualified humour of I.O.'s successful trickery of Eck, who finds himself paying far more than his fair share of the cost of buying the cow for slaughter and so protecting the Snopes name:

> "But I still dont see why I got to pay fifteen dollars, when all you got to pay is—?"
>
> "Because you got four children. And you make five. And five times three is fifteen."
>
> "I aint got but three yet," Eck said.
>
> "Aint that just what I said? five times three? If that other one was already here, it would make four, and five times four is twenty dollars, and then I wouldn't have to pay anything."
>
> "Except that somebody would owe Eck three dollars and twenty cents change," Ratliff said.
>
> "What?" I.O. said. But he immediately turned back to his cousin or nephew. "And you got the meat and the hide," he said. "Cant you even try to keep from forgetting that?"

Flem, absent throughout "The Long Summer," returns to Frenchman's Bend at the beginning of Book Four, "The Peasants"; his wife, Eula, has returned at the end of the previous book, bringing with her, Persephone-like, the end of that bitter winter "from which the people as they became older were to establish time and date events." The economic motif now again becomes dominant, first in the sale of the spotted Texas horses and finally in the defeat of Ratliff himself partly betrayed by cupidity, in the affair of the salted treasure hoard, and as Flem moves off on the last page we see that in linear terms *The Hamlet* can be simply and accurately described as the story of Flem's upward progress from near-rags to near-riches, from a dirt-farm to the ownership of a substantial bank-balance, a superbly handsome wife, and a half-share in a Jefferson restaurant. It is in the later novels of the trilogy that Faulkner completes what he must have recognised as being, among many other things, an ironic version of the American "success" myth.

Of the various episodes of the novel, it can be argued that the story of Labove is somewhat tenuously connected with the other events and characters; the others, however, are strongly bound to the central narrative line. All the episodes, including Labove's, are related in a multiplicity of ways both to the major themes of the novel and to each other. The various tales of barter and trading all throw light upon one another, and upon the whole economic and social situation of Frenchman's Bend at this particular moment in time. Similarly interrelated are the various marriages and love stories, and we can see that although the action of the novel tends to focus on the male world epitomised by the horse-swap, Faulkner also offers through his presentation of such characters as Ab's wife, Mink's wife, and Mrs. Armstid a series of comments on the role of women in this society, and especially on their capacity for sheer endurance. If we compare the short story, "The Hound," with the Mink Snopes portion of "The Long Summer," in which the same narrative material appears, we can see that although the short story is extremely powerful in its own right, the novel version has many additional qualities which it can accommodate simply because it is not a separate entity but a constituent part of a larger and intricately interrelated whole. The short story, for example, has no counterpart to the following passage in the novel:

> [Mink] watched the night emerge from the bottom and mount through the bitten corn, taking corn, taking the house itself at last and, still rising, become as two up-opening palms releasing the westward-flying ultimate bird of evening. Below him, beyond the corn, the fireflies winked and drifted against the breast of darkness; beyond, within it, the steady booming of the frogs was the steady pulse and beat of the dark heart of night, so that at last when the unvarying moment came—that moment as unvarying from one dusk to the next as the afternoon's instant when he would awake—the beat of that heart seemed to fall still too, emptying silence for the first deep cry of strong and invincible grief. He reached his hand backward and took up the gun.

In the limited framework of the short story such a passage would be wholly out of proportion. In the context of the novel, however, this description of the swamp lands near Mink's farm serves, at the simplest level, to extend a little further the overall description of the countryside around Frenchman's Bend, and, as such, it falls naturally into place in a larger pattern. But nature imagery is also being used here, as throughout the novel, to evoke and define the particular quality of the experiential moment and at the same time, as with a kind of visual rhetoric, to elevate moments and events to a higher, more general level of significance, and this is something of a quite different and more ambitious order. Throughout the novel Faulkner insists on the closeness to nature of the world of Frenchman's Bend, and his presentation of that world makes it possible for him to invoke nature imagery without any sense of arbitrariness or strain. This is especially, and most remarkably, true of the account of Ike Snopes's love for the cow, in which the rapturous evocation of the beauty and fecundity of nature is still further heightened by extravagant effects of rhetorical language and mythological allusion.

Stylistically, indeed, *The Hamlet* is one of Faulkner's greatest triumphs. Throughout the novel he exercises the utmost flexibility of style and language, ranging from direct and simple narrative to the colloquial vigour of Ratliff's telling of the "Barn Burning" and "Fool About a Horse" materials, to the baroque elevation of many of the passages describing Eula and, especially, Ike's idyll with the cow. Each episode is treated in a manner which brings out its individual quality but which also establishes its place in the structural and thematic patterns of the novel as a whole, and, where necessary, its relationship to more universal frames of reference: thus the mythological allusions in passages about Ike and Eula serve to suggest the degree to which their stories resemble those epitomisations of human experience embodied in ancient myth. This stylistic virtuosity is early established as an essential aspect of the novel's technique, and by the time Book Three has been reached it has clearly become irrelevant to wonder whether Mink himself, in the passage quoted, would have regarded the approach of darkness in quite this way. No more than in *As I Lay Dying* is Faulkner restricted to the vocabulary and manner of the characters whose attitudes and feelings he is describing: from the beginning of the novel he has established a mode which permits him to match rhetoric not so much to individuals as to emotional states and moments of crisis—of joy, agony, discovery, awareness of beauty—or, rather, to the significance of those states and moments in relation to the overall meaning of the novel.

That Faulkner is clearly aware of writing in a language foreign to his characters is evident from those moments when he skilfully plays off the richness of his formal language against the juxtaposed simplicity of colloquial speech. As Ratliff and his companions walk back to Mrs. Littlejohn's with Will Varner, who is to attend the injured Henry Armstid, we are given a description of the moonlit night:

> The moon was now high overhead, a pearled and mazy yawn in the soft sky, the ultimate ends of which rolled onward, whorl on whorl, beyond the pale stars and by pale stars surrounded. They walked in a close clump, tramping their shadows into the road's mild dust, blotting the shadows of the burgeoning trees which soared, trunk branch and twig against the pale sky, delicate and finely thinned. They passed the dark store. Then the pear tree came in sight. It rose in mazed and silver immobility like exploding snow; the mockingbird still sang in it. "Look at that tree," Varner said. "It ought to make this year, sho."
> "Corn'll make this year too," one said.
> "A moon like this is good for every growing thing outen earth," Varner said.

Here the simple remark, "Corn'll make this year," stands in a mutually enriching relationship to the elevated description of the "burgeoning" life of the spring landscape seen by moonlight; the characters themselves are clearly incapable of speaking of nature in the terms which Faulkner employs, but by placing the countryman's ostensibly practical observation in the context of the description he suggests that the men, for all their simplicity, are not unaffected by the beauty of what they see.

In the larger context of the novel the passage just quoted is also closely related to Faulkner's presentation of Eula Varner, as her father continues his remarks on the fecundating properties of the moon with an account of how Mrs. Varner lay in the moonlight after Eula had been conceived in order to ensure that the child would be a girl. Throughout the novel Eula is associated with fertility and the forces of nature and evoked in terms of repeated allusions to the pagan deities, to Helen and Venus and Persephone, and her marriage with Flem Snopes, that forced and grotesque union of fecundity and sterility, provides *The Hamlet* with its most disturbing, most affronting, symbol. Labove, the schoolmaster, whose own love for Eula takes on almost the nature of demonic possession, foresees the marriage of this Venus, this supreme embodiment of fertility and the sexual principle, to some "crippled Vulcan . . . who would not possess her but merely own her by the single strength which power gave, the dead power of money, wealth, gewgaws, baubles, as he might own, not a picture, statue: a field, say." Flem is the eventual Vulcan to Eula's Venus, marrying her not from love or even desire but in exchange for a cheque and the deed to the Old Frenchman place. This coincidence of Labove's vision with subsequent narrative events serves to illustrate once again how constantly and how intricately the thematic materials of the novel interact and coalesce in terms of the narrative line: for what is significant in both the vision and its realisation is the way in which possession of Eula is linked with the ownership and exploitation of land, effecting a conjunction of the themes of love and greed and setting both against the background of the land, which with its history, and its permanence transcending history and all human concerns, constitutes one of Faulkner's major preoccupations throughout his work.

At one stage in the writing of *The Hamlet* Faulkner apparently intended to apply to the whole book the title, "The Peasants," which he eventually used for the fourth and final section. One of Balzac's novels is called *Les Paysans*, and *The Hamlet* itself opens in almost Balzacian fashion with a precise and detailed description of the historical, geographical, social, and economic setting of the novel's subsequent events. Later in the book this basic framework is extended outwards by additional descriptions of places nearby, as, for example, when Faulkner supplies vivid and often precisely detailed impressions of Mink Snopes's farm and the land round about, and of the countryside through which Ike walks with the cow. An extract will suggest the degree of Faulkner's concern, in this novel, with the historical forces, both natural and man-made, which have shaped the landscape, and especially with the sad results of man's exploitation:

> A mile back he had left the rich, broad, flat river-bottom country and entered the hills—a region which topographically was the final blue and dying echo of the Appalachian mountains. Chickasaw Indians had owned it, but after the Indians it had been cleared where possible for cultivation, and after the Civil War, forgotten save by small peripatetic sawmills which had vanished too now, their sites marked only by the mounds of rotting sawdust which were not only their gravestones but the monuments of a people's heedless greed. Now it was a region of scrubby second-growth pine and oak among which dogwood bloomed until it too was cut to make cotton spindles, and old fields where not even a trace of furrow showed any more, gutted and gullied by forty years of rain and frost and heat into plateaus choked with rank sedge and briers loved of rabbits and quail coveys, and crumbling ravines striated red and white with alternate sand and clay.

But such passages do not stand isolated in the novel as mere historical footnotes loosely incorporated into the text. Faulkner is concerned to establish an image of a particular society in a particular place at a particular time; but the image is evoked primarily in terms of characters and their interaction, and the descriptive passages function also in terms of the human situation. The description of Mink's house, for instance, is important for its own sake, as an additional facet of the analytical portrait of the area, but it is also crucial to our understanding of Mink himself and of the reasons why he murders Houston. Thus there is obvious dramatic point in the utter poverty of the place being evoked through the eyes of Mink himself as he returns from the murder:

> It was dusk. He emerged from the bottom and looked up the slope of his meagre and sorry corn and saw it—the paintless two-room cabin with an open hallway between and a lean-to kitchen, which was not his, on which he paid rent but not taxes, paying almost as much in rent in one year as the house had cost to build; not old, yet the roof of which already leaked and the weather-stripping had already begun to rot away from the wall planks and which was just like the one he had been born in which had not belonged to his father either, . . .

Later, when Mink goes to the Negro's cabin to find his axe, his poverty is re-emphasised in the concrete terms of a comparison with the economic position of a Negro whose cabin is "shabbier than his" but whose surrounding corn is "better than his." Later still, as Mink is being taken to the jail in Jefferson, his own background is implicitly evoked in terms of his awareness of "the long broad rich flatlands lush with the fine harvest" around Whiteleaf store and of the trim and prosperous world of Jefferson itself:

> the surrey moving now beneath an ordered overarch of sunshot trees, between the clipped and tended lawns where children shrieked and played in bright small garments in the sunset and the ladies sat rocking in the fresh dresses of afternoon and the men coming home from work turned into the neat painted gates, toward plates of food and cups of coffee in the long beginning of twilight.

This is a world completely alien to Mink, as to the other inhabitants of Frenchman's Bend and its environs. The description at once extends, by contrast, the definition of these people's lives, and projects forward an image of the richer economic pastures to which Flem Snopes moves at the end of the novel. Nothing is wasted here. Instead of "clipped and tended lawns" the properties on which the poor whites like Mink, Ab Snopes, and Henry Armstid live have yards that are "weed-choked and grass-grown" and give an overall appearance of "cluttered desolation"; they have no "neat painted gates," for both Ab's and Mink's gates are broken and even their cabins paintless; their womenfolk wear "gray shapeless" garments, not "the fresh dresses of afternoon"; while their children, who are never presented as playing, have no "bright small garments" and are lucky, indeed, if they have a single pair of shoes between them.

In its sheer sociological richness *The Hamlet* recalls *Sartoris* rather than any other of Faulkner's earlier books, and it was *Sartoris* which first created in print many of the characters whose potentialities Faulkner here for the first time develops to the full. *The Hamlet* also demonstrates that sense of the slow inevitable procession of the seasons which provides an especially powerful undercurrent in *Sartoris*, but which figures to some degree in almost all of Faulkner's books from *The Marble Faun* and *Soldiers' Pay* onwards. The advance which *The Hamlet* marks over earlier novels, however, is in its wholly organic incorporation of themes and materials which had often appeared either sporadically, in set pieces, or in direct and usually ironic juxtaposition or counterpoint to the main action. One of the features of the novel which stays longest in the mind is the grouping, usually the pairing, of characters which emerges from Faulkner's thematic method. The opposition of Eula and Flem is one obvious example, but Flem's coldness and impotence is implicitly commented upon by Ike's yearning love for his cow, while the anti- or non-Snopesism of Ike is itself contrasted with the quintessential Snopesism of the other family idiot, St. Elmo. It is easy, too, to see intricate cross-references, particularly in view of Faulkner's early insistence on Eula's somewhat bovine placidity, between the Labove-Eula and Ike-cow situations. In a more direct confrontation, that between Houston and Mink Snopes, his murderer, we come to see that in large measure the very things they have in common—their fierce pride, their bitter isolation, their absolute capitulation to the women they marry—are those which most inflame their antagonism, although it should be added that Mink's principal motive for the murder seems to have been his fundamental anger at his ill-luck, especially in comparison with that of a relative like Flem or a neighbour like Houston. Even the greater attractiveness of Will Varner as compared with his son Jody—it is significant, in terms of the novel's particular scale of values, that Will Varner's sexual lustiness is not matched by his son—is also to some extent paralleled by the far greater condemnation which is reserved for Flem Snopes in comparison with his father. It has already been suggested that Faulkner may have abandoned "Barn Burning" as an opening chapter because of the extent to which it might generate undue sympathy for the Snopes family; even so, considerable sympathy for Ab's desperate economic plight is aroused in the present first chapter both by the version of the barn burning episode which Ratliff relates to Jody and by Jody's own mean calculations of how the maximum profit may be extorted from Ab's situation, while Ratliff's further recital of the Pat

Stamper episode, in a version of the material first used in published form in the story, "Fool About a Horse," also evokes an Ab Snopes who is by no means a wholly unattractive figure, although Ratliff repeatedly stresses that these events date from a period before Ab "soured."

The most important paired opposition in the novel, and the one upon which the action as well as the morality of the book largely turns, is that between Flem and Ratliff. The whole pattern of Flem's action is set by the early episode in which Jody, as the result of his own greed and over-confidence, has put himself in the position of having to bribe Flem with a job in the store in return for a protection against Ab's barn-burning tendencies which Flem does not even promise to provide:

> Once more Varner expelled his breath through his nose. This time it was a sigh. "All right," he said. "Next week then. You'll give me that long, wont you? But you got to guarantee it." The other spat.
> "Guarantee what?" he said.

It is characteristic of Flem that he puts nothing into words, that the blackmail is never stated, only implied, and that he exchanges nothing of value in return for the position which is to give him his first foothold in Frenchman's Bend. Throughout the novel Flem's silence is scarcely broken: his longest speech consists of 25 words, and he speaks only 244 words in all, with a further 33 in the Hell scene created in Ratliff's imagination. For long portions of the novel he is out of sight. He is never long out of mind, however, and usually another Snopes is present to remind us of his influence. In the second chapter of "The Long Summer," for instance, Flem is represented by one of his chief henchmen, Lump Snopes, his successor as the clerk in Varner's store. In his attempts to get his hands on the money which Houston carried, and in his complete disregard for all considerations of loyalty, humanity, or simple decency, Lump offers a concrete exemplification of greed in action which is simply a crude outward manifestation of qualities embodied more subtly but not less firmly by Flem himself. Here, as elsewhere in the novel, Faulkner uses Lump to demonstrate quite clearly the evil which Snopesism represents without needing to compromise his consistent presentation of Flem himself as a silent tactician and master strategist. The account of the sale of the spotted Texas horses which occupied most of the first chapter of "The Peasants" again shows Flem operating through substitutes, himself a silent witness or—during most of the auction and the whole of the subsequent court hearings—actually absent. Lump acts as his representative on this occasion, but not even Lump, it seems, is present to lend comfort to Mink Snopes at his trial in the Country Courthouse in Jefferson.

It is Ratliff, in a passage of bitter understatement, who links Mink's situation with that of Mrs. Armstid, the chief victim in the affair of the spotted horses. After describing the dreary round of Mrs. Armstid's life as she waits for her husband's leg to heal and for Flem Snopes to return the money paid for the horse, Ratliff continues:

> And after that, not nothing to do until morning except to stay close enough where Henry can call her until it's light enough to chop the wood to cook breakfast and then help Mrs. Littlejohn wash the dishes and make the beds and sweep while watching the road. Because likely any time now Flem Snopes will get back from wherever he has been since the auction, which of course is to town naturally to see about his cousin that's got into a little legal trouble, and so get that five dollars.

This linking of the two people who are vainly waiting for Flem to rescue them reveals in miniature the pattern of the whole novel, its establishment of a composite picture of Flem, his activities, their effect, and their significance. The heavily ironic diminutive, "a little legal trouble," as a description of the brutal murder for which Mink is to be tried, precisely catches the note of Ratliff's strenuous efforts to maintain that detachment which at this point still distinguishes him from the other actual and potential victims of Flem's machinations.

The final accolade of Flem's success in *The Hamlet* is a comment spoken by an unidentified local inhabitant, representative in his anonymity of the whole world of Frenchman's Bend:

> Couldn't no other man have done it. Anybody might have fooled Henry Armstid. But couldn't nobody but Flem Snopes have fooled Ratliff.

It is characteristic of the ironies implicit in Faulkner's working out of the book's thematic patterns that it should be Ratliff, the chief and most redoubtable opponent of Snopesism, who sells Flem the share in the restaurant which gives him his first foothold in Jefferson, just as it should have been Jody, who had most to lose from his coming, who had supplied Flem with his original opening in Frenchman's Bend. Ratliff had clearly recognised Jody's folly in the opening chapter of the novel, and throughout the book he remains almost entirely uninvolved in the activities of Flem and his relations: there is no danger of his buying one of the spotted horses, and in his one direct exchange with Flem, over the contract for the goats and the signed notes he accepts from Mink, he emerges with a clear, though not unqualified, victory. He is thus presented as a worthy opponent of Flem, and it is this which makes his final downfall so triumphant a conclusion to Flem's career in Frenchman's Bend. At the same time, the fact that one of Ratliff's motives is greed, and the cause of his defeat his over-confidence in his own reading of the situation and in his own understanding of Flem's character, fits precisely into the overall pattern of greed and self-delusion established by Jody Varner at the beginning of the novel.

Ratliff was clearly a character whom Faulkner regarded as being especially important, both for what he did and for what he represented. In the early short stories in which the sewing-machine agent appears—in "Lizards in Jamshyd's Courtyard," for example, in which he is still called Suratt—he remains essentially the same loquacious, dialect-speaking character with the "shrewd plausible face" whom Faulkner first presented in *Sartoris*. In *The Hamlet* the dialect element in Ratliff's speech has been greatly reduced, and he himself is no longer simply an engaging teller of tall tales. In an interview in 1955 Faulkner named Dilsey and Ratliff as his favourite characters in his own work: "Ratliff is wonderful," he said. "He's done more things than any man I know." In one of the discussions at Charlottesville in 1957 Faulkner developed his belief that man will prevail in terms of the human instinct to fight against Snopesism: "When the battle comes it always produces a Roland. It doesn't mean that they will get rid of Snopes or the impulse which produces Snopes, but always there's something in man that don't like Snopes and objects to Snopes and if necessary will step in to keep Snopes from doing some irreparable harm."

That Faulkner saw Ratliff as occupying a central and representative position in the battle against Snopesism, itself a microcosm of mankind's determined struggle to prevail, is clear from *The Hamlet* itself. Both as a character and as a representative figure, however, Ratliff is more complex than has generally been realised. He is, in the first place, very similar to Flem in many ways. He is a trader, making his living by buying and selling, and he has done well: starting from exactly the same background as Flem himself—"My pap and Ab were both renting from Old Man Anse Holland then," says Ratliff of the "Fool About a Horse" episode—he has, while still a comparatively young man, gained a steady economic position, a house in Jefferson, and a half-share in a restaurant there. In so far as Ratliff and Flem are both traders, there is a natural economic rivalry between them; on the moral plane it is Ratliff's practised skill at Flem's economic game which gives him at once the confidence and the capacity to challenge Flem on his own ground. Although he seems voluble where Flem is silent, we are specifically told that Ratliff always did "a good deal more listening than anybody believed until afterward." He is also like Flem in being something of an outsider to the world of Frenchman's Bend, different from its inhabitants in a way of which they themselves are a little antagonistically aware: "I thought something was wrong all day," says one of them when Ratliff appears after the finish of the horse auction. "Ratliff wasn't there to give nobody advice."

Ratliff, as he appears in *The Hamlet*, is *in* the world of Frenchman's Bend but by no means entirely *of* it. His detachment is insisted on throughout, and like Flem, though for different reasons, he tends to be absent from the scene at crucial moments, and especially when the local farmers are being cheated of what little money they have. The reasons for Ratliff's apparent withdrawal are worth examining in some detail. His detachment from Frenchman's Bend must be related to his powers of inner detachment, his gift for viewing himself and his own actions with the disenchanted eye of reason. Nowhere does this gift appear more clearly than in the exchange with Mrs. Littlejohn in which Ratliff plainly acknowledges the puritanical streak in himself which is urging him to stop the exploitation of Ike's love for the cow, and then as firmly declares his determination to act nonetheless, not ignoring what self-knowledge has told him, but embracing that awareness as part of the personal price to be paid:

> "I aint never disputed I'm a pharisee," he said. "You dont need to tell me he aint got nothing else. I know that. Or that I can sholy leave him have at least this much. I know that too. Or that besides, it aint any of my business. I know that too, just as I know that the reason I aint going to leave him have what he does have is simply because I am strong enough to keep him from it. I am stronger than him. Not righter. Not any better, maybe. But just stronger."
> "How are you going to stop it?"
> "I dont know. Maybe I even cant. Maybe I dont even want to. Maybe all I want is just to have been righteouser, so I can tell myself I done the right thing and my conscience is clear now and at least I can go to sleep tonight."

This intellectual quality of Ratliff's, which marks him off from the inhabitants of Frenchman's Bend, is both his strength and his weakness. As a trader, making his living by barter, Ratliff must operate within the established trading conventions as they are understood in the world of Frenchman's Bend. But his intelligence and his humanity will not allow him to remain blind to the implications of privation and suffering which the processes of trade, especially in their quintessential form of the horse-swap, may often carry for the defeated, and especially for their womenfolk. Ratliff is well aware of the traditional limits of the code, and especially of its principles of respect for the most skilful, of unconcern for the defeated, and, at all times, of non-interference in other men's trading:

"He done all he could to warn me," thinks Ratliff of Bookwright early in the novel. "He went as far and even further than a man can let his self go in another man's trade." The crucial question for Ratliff is whether he shall go outside the limits of the convention in order to try and combat Snopesism.

The clearest statement of Ratliff's position comes in answer to Bookwright's query as to whether he gave Henry Armstid the five dollars he lost to Flem in trading for one of the spotted horses:

> "I could have," he said. "But I didn't. I might have if I could just been sho he would buy something this time that would sho enough kill him, like Mrs Littlejohn said. Besides, I wasn't protecting a Snopes from Snopeses; I wasn't even protecting a people from a Snopes. I was protecting something that wasn't even a people, that wasn't nothing but something that dont want nothing but to walk and feel the sun and wouldn't know how to hurt no man even if it would and wouldn't want to even if it could, just like I wouldn't stand by and see you steal a meat-bone from a dog. I never made them Snopeses and I never made the folks that cant wait to bare their backsides to them. I could do more, but I wont. I wont, I tell you!"

The final cry recalls the agony of Quentin Compson at the end of *Absalom, Absalom!* when Shreve asks him why he hates the South: *"I dont. I dont! I dont hate it! I dont hate it!"* Ratliff longs for a continuation of the detachment he has practised, with only minor deviations, up to this point: he has, it is true, pitted his wits against Flem's over the matter of the goats, but this was a direct test of skill in the game of barter, with nothing seriously at issue. He knows that to intervene in "another man's trade," and especially to enquire what that trading means for the man's dependents, for women like Mrs. Armstid, inevitably brings pain to a man of his intelligence and humanity. He knows, in short, that involvement hurts, and that in detachment lies not merely discretion but self-protection. Yet he knows, too, that he must take action, become involved, and his "I wont. I wont, I tell you!" evokes the agony of his dilemma. Ratliff's hesitation, his reluctance to act, is presented as the inevitable concomitant of his personal intelligence and self-awareness, and, hence, as essential to Faulkner's conception of him. Equally essential, of course, is the courage, the moral commitment, which Ratliff displays when he decides nevertheless—again, not ignoring but accepting without self-deception what self-knowledge tells him—to abandon detachment and actively challenge Flem in a bid to stop his progress by the infliction of a resounding economic defeat.

In the event, of course, it is Ratliff who is defeated—partly because of the impetuousness which overcomes him in his eagerness to act, partly because of his disabling unfamiliarity with the nature and magnitude of the operation on which he embarks, and partly, it seems, because he too has been self-betrayed by some measure of that greed and over-confidence which had earlier brought defeat to Jody Varner and to so many others who thought themselves smarter than Flem. Once Ratliff acts, abandoning his customary devices of self-protection and stepping outside the accustomed bounds of his trader's experience to do so, it becomes inevitable not only that he should be defeated by Flem, but that he should be defeated on a scale exceeding any of Flem's previous conquests. It is essential to realise, however, that Ratliff's economic defeat is not accompanied by any defeat in human terms. The strength of Ratliff appears in the very moment of his realisation of Flem's victory, as he lingers luxuriously over his breakfast before resuming the digging which he already knows to be fruitless—"We even got a new place to dig," he thinks, with a humour which is not destroyed by its own wryness—and, a little later, as he bets Bookwright that he himself will have in his sack the oldest of the coins by which they have both been deluded. Once again, it is this capacity for combining decency and moral solicitude with clear-eyed intellectual detachment which gives Ratliff the ability to survive defeat and to continue, not merely the struggle against Snopesism, but the perpetual affirmation of life. Ratliff's opposition to Flem Snopes is obviously of great importance, but still more important is what he represents in himself, irrespective of the particular demands of the anti-Snopes campaign. It is extremely significant that Ratliff should be able to challenge Flem at his own game, but it is even more significant that Ratliff should continually demonstrate his aptitude for another and finer game than Flem's and thus affirm the persistence, whatever triumphs Snopesism may achieve, of those qualities by which, Faulkner believed, man will ultimately prevail. As Faulkner wrote to Warren Beck in 1941:

> I have been writing all the time about honor, truth, pity, consideration, the capacity to endure well grief and misfortune and injustice and then endure again, in terms of individuals who observed and adhered to them not for reward but for virtue's own sake, not even merely because they are admirable in themselves, but in order to live with oneself and die peacefully with oneself when the time comes. I don't mean that the devil will snatch every liar and rogue and hypocrite shrieking from his death-bed. I think liars and hypocrites and rogues die peacefully every day in the odor of what he calls sanctity. I'm not talking about him. I'm not writing for him. But I believe there are some, not necessarily many, who do and will continue to read Faulkner and say, "Yes. It's all right. I'd rather be Ratliff than Flem Snopes. And I'd still rather be Ratliff without any Snopes to measure by even."

RICHARD POIRIER

"The Bear"

One can admire other American writers more stylistically anxious than Emerson or Cooper without therefore preferring them. Other writers, like Thoreau, Melville, Mark Twain, James, and Faulkner, acknowledge how difficult it is to give authority to ideas, specifically those of the "poet" as the hero of relinquishment and possession, which are otherwise defenseless against the claims of conventional reality. Of course, any such comparative evaluations are tentative: one kind of accomplishment in literature is not all accomplishments, and in this instance Emerson and Cooper probably could have done fewer of the things they do so superbly had they been more stylistically defensive. Nonetheless, these other writers show greater willingness to make the investment by which a protective environment can be created for some of the images and themes they share with Emerson. In the complications of their language and in their structural ingenuities, they force the reader actually to participate in "the struggle for verbal consciousness" that is to liberate us from customary suppositions about the meaning of words like "possession" or "nature," "the poet" or "reality." Their best performances are known for their intricacy, their opaqueness, even to the point where they are discussed not as books but as "problems for interpretation."

The reason for this degree of complexity, the reason, too, why so many of these works are read so badly, is that they require not that we bring to them the same kind of awareness, even in a heightened form, that we bring to, say, most English novels of the nineteenth century, but that we submit to a discipline, imposed by the difficulties in the writing,

From *A World Elsewhere: The Place of Style in American Literature*. Copyright © 1966 by Oxford University Press.

that will develop in us a consciousness rarely called forth by English fiction before the works of Hardy, E. M. Forster, and Lawrence, English writers with an American penchant for moments of heightened awareness in which characters step beyond the boundaries of their daily environments. Ideally, the result of such writing—all of *Moby-Dick* and *The Bear* are conspicuous American illustrations—is the displacement of many of the reader's assumptions about reality, and a change in our expectations about the probable duration and sequence of events.

In *The Bear*, this effort to reshape the constituents of reality is called "relinquishment," a word which also describes Isaac's rejection of his inheritance and his visionary possession of the wilderness. But before that it refers, first, to a gutted log that is paradoxically said to be "healing with unbelievable speed, a passionate and almost visible relinquishment back into the earth"; later it describes how the boy surrenders to the wilderness and the bear by setting aside the instruments of industrial power—gun, compass, and watch—so that he "then relinquished completely to it"; and finally the word describes Isaac's relationship to his inheritance "not in pursuit and lust but in relinquishment." The genius displayed is in Faulkner's effort of style; his style makes "relinquishment" and "possession" a requirement as much for the readers as for his hero. Consider, for instance, the extraordinary use of negatives, almost from the beginning of the story:

> There was always a bottle present, so that it would seem to him that those fine fierce instants of heart and brain and courage and wiliness and speed were concentrated and distilled into that brown liquor which not women, not boys and children, but only hunters drank, drinking not of the blood they spilled but some condensation of the wild immortal spirit, drinking it moderately, humbly even, not with the pagan's base and baseless hope of acquiring thereby the virtues of cunning and strength and speed but in salute to them. Thus it seemed to him on this December morning not only natural but actually fitting that this should have begun with whisky.

It is noticeable that the description of things being dismissed by the negatives is never either foreshortened or contemptuous. The tone and balance of attention are deferential to those very aspects of reality that are being at the same time discarded. One can feel here a strength that is the essence of genius, a strength in having reached a conviction about reality that may indeed deny customary assumptions about its constituents but that is never merely hateful or contemptuous of them. And in any case the negatives do not apply merely to the practical view of a hunt; they apply just as energetically to literary myths about hunting (as in the references to drinking the "blood they spilled," or to the "pagan's base and baseless hope") which the reader is apt to conjure up once he is assured that this hunt is not an ordinary one.

Faulkner's style makes the reader's experience analogous to the hero's. The style requires that the reader divest himself of most of the conventional assumptions about hunting, people, and things that he brings to the story. At least Faulkner writes as if we do bring such assumptions to his work; that is precisely what makes him much more than a "Southern" novelist. He writes as if he could depend on very little public acceptance of the views he cherishes. Since Faulkner does acknowledge in the very grammar of refutation all that we might conventionally expect about the events he is narrating, his alternative version of them necessarily excites our attention and our consent. We experience thereby an unexpected extension of our consciousness of what such events might be. This sense of alternative possibilities is, in turn, located for us in the descriptive abstractions that pile up long before any object is attached to them. As we move through Faulkner's sentences we learn, having been denied expected supports, to grasp for those which *are* proffered, and these turn out to be the essentially visionary qualities of objects and accouterments associated with the hunt:

> He realised later that it had begun long before that. It had already begun on that day when he first wrote his age in two ciphers and his cousin McCaslin brought him for the first time to the camp, the big woods, to earn for himself from the wilderness the name and state of hunter provided he in his turn were humble and enduring enough. He had already inherited then, without ever having seen it, the big old bear with one trap-ruined foot that in an area almost a hundred miles square had earned for himself a name, a definite designation like a living man:—the long legend of corn-cribs broken down and rifled, of shoats and grown pigs and even calves carried bodily into the woods and devoured and traps and deadfalls overthrown and dogs mangled and slain and shotgun and even rifle shots delivered at point-blank range yet with no more effect than so many peas blown through a tube by a child—a corridor of wreckage and destruction beginning back before the boy was born, through which sped, not fast but rather with the ruthless and irresistible deliberation of a locomotive, the shaggy tremendous shape. It ran in his knowledge before he ever saw it. It loomed and towered in his dreams before he even saw the unaxed woods where it left its crooked print, shaggy, tremendous, red-eyed, not malevolent but just big, too big for the dogs which tried to bay it, for the horses which tried to ride it down, for the men and the bullets they fired into it; too big for the very country which was its constricting scope. It was as if the boy had already divined what his senses and intellect had not encompassed yet: that doomed

wilderness whose edges were being constantly and punily gnawed at by men with plows and axes who feared it because it was wilderness, men myriad and nameless even to one another in the land where the old bear had earned a name, and through which ran not even a mortal beast but an anachronism indomitable and invincible out of an old dead time, a phantom, epitome and apotheosis of the old wild life which the little puny humans swarmed and hacked at in a fury of abhorrence and fear like pygmies about the ankles of a drowsing elephant;—the old bear, solitary, indomitable, and alone; widowered childless and absolved of mortality—old Priam reft of his old wife and outlived all his sons.

Not merely the allusions at the end of this passage, but the style itself suspends us in time. It saturates us in a medium where objects are confused with the qualities of objects or with the values attached to those objects, so that "it" can refer to a cluster of impressions *about* the bear, while the bear itself can be named mostly by various abstractions, legends, and allusions. By such writing we are stripped, as Emerson wanted us to be, of dependable, conventional expectations, and our relation to reality is as open, mysterious, and expectant as that of someone newborn. Precisely the same process is being undergone by Isaac in these opening paragraphs. Faulkner's explicitness in this matter occurs, however, only after we, like Isaac, have been made to feel it, to sense it as inherent in the boy's experience and in the style which renders it. This is a fact of considerable importance: the story both in its style and in its fable insists that conceptions about experience derive from instincts and confrontations, not the other way around:

He entered his novitiate to the true wilderness with Sam beside him as he had begun his apprenticeship in miniature to manhood after the rabbits and such with Sam beside him, the two of them wrapped in the damp, warm negro-rank quilt while the wilderness closed behind his entrance as it had opened momentarily to accept him, opening before his advancement as it closed behind his progress, no fixed path the wagon followed but a channel nonexistent ten yards ahead of it and ceasing to exist ten yards after it had passed, the wagon progressing not by its own volition but by attrition of their intact yet fluid circumambience, drowsing, earless, almost lightless.

The language here is an inducement to feel the progress into the woods as a progress out of the womb—the actual entrance into consciousness (from "fluid" to something "almost lightless") evoking the passage of the foetus into its first tentative groping toward the external world. But the woods are a second, not a first entrance into history for Isaac, and of course they are not the initial entrance into history for us. They afford what William James meant by "second birth," and Isaac's progress in the woods thereafter prepares us for his later relinquishment of inheritance and redefinition of his place in history.

Faulkner, James, and Thoreau, in handling the theme of possession, reveal their characteristic faith in writing as an act of power, an act by which reality is seized and dominated. In the works of each of them style . . . is the final authority to which the reader may appeal for verifications of reality. Of course each of them honors something outside of style: in James it is often what he means by "experience" ("Experience is never limited and it is never complete"); in Faulkner what he calls "the things that touch the heart," a sort of atavism typically associated with notions of the organic community; and in Thoreau it is Nature in which he finds the creative agent. But if these powers are not wholly dependent for their existence upon the creative energy of the writer they are even more emphatically not dependent on any other kind of artifacts, other works of art or society, systems of any kind. The abstractions to which each of these writers feels subservient—"experience," "things that touch the heart," "nature"—are larger than any to which interpretive criticism can appeal. They refer us not to anything with a settled existence but rather to something of which the style itself is the synecdoche. The intense involvement in style required of the reader is notably strenuous in each of these writers, and there is always the temptation to escape from this involvement and to read the books as if they depended on more conventional social or psychological standards. These standards are often not so much irrelevant as below the mark in accounting for the extraordinary dislocations of our fixed ideas of reality that occur while we read James or Faulkner or Thoreau, the suspension and then the redirection of our way of seeing things and of feeling them through language.

JAMES GUETTI

"The Sound and the Fury" and "The Bear"

PART ONE

I shall confine my discussion, in this chapter, of Faulkner's work to an analysis of *The Sound and the Fury*, and my reasons for doing so are these. Although structural disorder in Faulkner is not always concomitant with an explicit preoccupation with the failure of imagination, such disorder is always indicative in Faulkner of certain assumptions about language and meaning that I shall discuss in my concluding remarks. Because this general disorder always implies, as I see it, a single view of language, it is unnecessary here to proceed through various novels and stories, remarking, for example, that structural disorder seems explicitly parallel with the inadequacy of language in *As I Lay Dying* whereas in *Light in August* such disorder seems to be presented with little clarifying emphasis upon the separateness of words and experience. That such structural disorder is, in fact, the dominant quality of Faulkner's writing, furthermore, has been shown—and, I think, thoroughly and conclusively—by Walter J. Slatoff. Slatoff traces the phenomena of unresolved ambiguities, incomplete patterns and approximate significances through the major fiction, and he leaves no doubt of the consistency and single-mindedness of Faulkner's deliberate preoccupation with structural confusion. His conclusion is to see this preoccupation as a "quest for failure," a quest which may have the effect of suggesting the greatness of

From *The Limits of Metaphor*. Copyright © 1967 by Cornell University. Cornell University Press, 1967.

what has been attempted but too often simply emphasizes the inconclusiveness and self-obfuscation of the attempt itself. My own concern, of course, is to examine this dual effect of Faulkner's persistent structurelessness in terms of its linguistic characteristics and consequences. It may be simply noted at this point that since the emphasis on general disorder in Faulkner has been recognized, there remains the matter of establishing more detailed relations between the particular use of language I have described and the various works that I have not considered.

"Each in its ordered place." With this last phrase of *The Sound and the Fury* we realize that the idiot Benjy's "order"—the difference between his placid and empty satisfaction and his total, bellowing despair—depends upon the permanence of a simple spatial movement from "left to right" as he rides to and from the cemetery. Faulkner suggests consistently in this novel, however, that all the attempts at imaginative control that the story contains are equivalent to the order created in the mind of an idiot. To Benjy's mind the world takes the form of a small number of catchwords, the principal of which is "Caddy" or, as the men in his pasture-turned-golf-course say, "caddie." The presence of Caddy, his sister, gives Benjy his greatest stability and security; the awareness of her absence—constantly re-emphasized for Benjy by her "symbolic" presence in the word "caddie"—triggers the inarticulate moaning that seems the essence of profound chaos.

The same tendency to build a world around exclusive "symbols" may be seen in Jason Compson IV, whom Faulkner has called "the first sane Compson since before Culloden." Jason exhibits his "sanity," we may suppose, in his pragmatic vision, in his avowed reluctance to meddle—which may seem a recognition of the invincible and confused separateness of persons and of experiences—and in his particular lack of moral scruples and his general unwillingness to take any human rule or totem seriously. And yet the meaning that Jason sees in his existence—that which justifies his losses to the "New York Jews," the tedium of his life at the store, and his continual and frantic financial juggling—depends upon a symbolic view that is as specious as Benjy's own: "Of his niece he did not think at all, nor the arbitrary value of the money. Neither of them had had entity or individuality for him in ten years; together they merely symbolized the job in the bank of which he had been deprived before he ever got it." Jason's concern with his niece and the money, as well as with Quentin his brother and Caddy, is concentrated in his feeling of deprivation and his fanatical belief that this deprivation is in fact the metaphor by which his identity is established: he is the eternal loser, sufferer, and underdog.

It is not only the emptiness of Benjy's or Jason's imaginative order, however, that is apparent in this novel. The vision of resurrected religious truth that moves Dilsey so deeply, as an example of the sort of "truth" with which Faulkner presents us, is the standard product of a theatrical specialist in such visions, the monkeylike preacher with the great voice, Shegog, the power of whose speech is directly proportional to its incoherency. The entire Easter framework of the story, moreover, is conspicuously hollow and ironical—in which Jason crucifies himself by transforming his particular losses into the eternal metaphor of the righteous, sacrificial loser and Benjy is suggested by the Easter chronology to be harrowing hell.

The most penetrating account in the novel of the struggle for order, however, lies outside the Easter mythology, in Quentin's account of the day of his suicide, and it exhibits his attempt to detach himself from all such struggle. Quentin's "confession" to his father of incest with Caddy is received by Mr. Compson as a futile attempt to render experience meaningful; Quentin recalls the conversation as follows:

> . . . and i i wasnt lying i wasnt lying and he you wanted to sublimate a piece of natural human folly into a horror and then exorcise it with truth and i it was to isolate her out of the loud world . . . and he and now this other you are not lying now either but you are still blind to what is in yourself to that part of general truth the sequence of natural events and their causes which shadows every mans brow even benjys you are not thinking of finitude you are contemplating an apotheosis in which a temporary state of mind will become symmetrical above the flesh and aware both of itself and of the flesh it will not quite discard you will not even be dead and i temporary. . . .

Quentin's father celebrates the "finitude" of existence, of course, the mortal "sequence of natural events," by drinking himself to death, but his pronouncements have crucial effect. Quentin comes to understand that his desire for incestuous consummation is merely an attempt to deny the nature of the confusions of experience as "temporary" states of mind; it is an attempt to establish order by means of transforming momentary "folly" into eternal "sin."

It is not because of incestuous desire, in other words, that Quentin commits suicide, nor is it because of Caddy's aborted marriage—to pay for which, along with Quentin's year at Harvard, Benjy's pasture was sold—but because he has been deprived of any way in which he might see the desire and the marriage, as well as the suffering of his brother, his sister, and himself, in a meaningful perspective. He has become aware through his father that his attempt to transform the temporal complexity of his experience into an "apotheosis"—as I infer, into an eternal and significant order—is as empty as experience itself, is itself an example of mortal futility and confusion. The result of this awareness—of a recognition and acceptance of the meaninglessness of human experience—is his suicide: "It's not when you realise that nothing can help you—religion, pride, anything—it's when you realise that you dont need any aid."

This novel does not simply provide us with an excellent example of Faulkner's concern with imaginative failure, but defines that failure in terms that are different from any that we have previously encountered. Quentin's striving for coherent meaning is consistently equated with his concern with time, and not only in the fact that his attempt to make his experience meaningful is inseparable from destroying its temporariness. His search for order is an attempt at the eternal, certainly, but it is interesting to note that the search itself—in its endless, mechanical, and inescapable persistence—is associated with time and clocks. Quentin's father describes this association as "that constant speculation regarding the position of mechanical hands on an arbitrary dial which is a symptom of mind-functioning." But for Quentin such "speculation" has become not simply the "symptom" but the symbol of consciousness—the consciousness that he will relinquish. His destruction of his father's watch and his flight away from the bells and whistles that mark time are simply metaphorical pre-enactments of his suicide. The arbitrary measurement of time has become representative, we may suppose, of the arbitrary but ceaseless function of the mind itself, of the emptiness of the order that the mind continually must strive to create. Because Quentin is aware of this arbitrariness, he can conquer time—like consciousness—not by an act of ultimate and immutable vision but only by an act of relinquishment.

PART TWO

Why should a reader respond to verbal contradiction and complexity with a feeling that the inexpressible has been communicated? Why does the expectation of meaning, which seems necessary to this sort of response, often continue to exist in spite of the fact that such complexity is sustained? And why, finally, should a writer present language that seems antithetical to the traditional moral and imaginative certainties of fiction? Once again I would like to postpone more direct consideration of the matter for a moment, as the answers to these questions may be suggested by examining a work in which the use of language is parallel to the novels I have described, but in which the emphasis upon moral failure and complete confusion is not so great as it is in "Heart of Darkness" or *Absalom, Absalom!*: Faulkner's "The Bear."

In the general outlines of the major portion of its narrative, "The Bear" seems a neat parallel to *Moby-Dick* and "Heart of Darkness." The hunt in general is suggested to be an attempt to give order to something that may be finally beyond order, the wilderness and the quintessence of the wilderness, the bear. In order even to see the bear, however, Ike McCaslin finds it necessary to put aside his gun, his compass, and his watch, to relinquish, in fact, the very idea of a hunt or of any search with implications of ultimate resolution. Gun, compass, and watch, it may be noted, all seem representative of ways of rendering experience intelligible, and it would thus appear that in order to know the bear Ike must give up all the means of such intelligibility at his command.

This idea is reinforced by the fact that upon every occasion when Old Ben is encountered or brought to bay, the basic terms of the encounter always reflect the absence of the simplest sort of order. The first example, of course, is the necessity of Ike's losing himself in the woods before he can confront the bear. Later, when Ike and Sam Fathers bay Old Ben, they do so with a "fyce," a seemingly insignificant mongrel whose shrill courage is indistinguishable from folly. Lion himself, the dog who is essential to the killing of the bear, is as inscrutable in his power as Old Ben; he is a part of the wilderness, lending himself—on a kind of sufferance—to men. Boon Hogganbeck, finally, is incoherency personified. He has never been known to hit anything with his gun, he has the body of a brute and the mind of a child, and he accomplishes the death of the bear by entering into a chaotic, knife-to-claw struggle with it that is another sort of nullification of the rules of the hunt, of its dignity and restraint.

The character in whom the possibilities of response to the idea of "wilderness" are most articulated, again, is Ike himself. Ike looks, but he does not shoot; he refuses to resolve the hunt, which may be seen as a tension between order and disorder, and his refusal, as we learn later, has something to do with "truth." On the one hand, Ike's refusal is just that, a deliberate gesture and thus a kind of controlled uncontrol; on the other hand, it is somehow not deliberate but simply an inability to act or to consummate. The refusal and the inability, furthermore, appear inseparable. It may be that one must refuse to kill Old Ben just because once killed he is only a dead bear, because he loses all the vague significance of the wilderness, just as the wilderness itself is slowly being plotted and destroyed. It may be also that what is involved is the kind of fantastic paradox that we find in "The Old People," in which Walter Ewell, who never misses with his rifle, shoots at the great deer, the "grandfather," and hits a spike-horned yearling. In "The Old People" the ineffable spirit of the wilderness exists—the deer leaves tracks, for example—but it continues to be real only if one does not attempt to apprehend it in a final way: the capturing or the killing can have the effect only of anticlimax and unsatisfaction. There is this flavor of anticlimax about the death of Old Ben in "The Bear," but there is also another suggested consequence of the attempt to apprehend the "reality" of the wilderness.

When Ike returns to the wilderness for the last time he finds Boon—and this passage seems one of the most powerful in all American literature—sitting at the base of the huge Gum Tree:

> . . . the whole tree had become one green malestrom of mad leaves, while from time to time, singly or in twos and threes, squirrels would dart down the trunk then whirl without stopping and rush back up again as though sucked violently back by the vacuum of their fellows' frenzied vortex. Then he saw Boon, sitting, his back against the trunk, his head bent, hammering furiously at something on his lap. What he hammered with was the barrel of his dismembered gun, what he hammered at was the breech of it. The rest of his gun lay scattered about him in a half-dozen pieces while he bent over the piece on his lap his scarlet and streaming walnut face, hammering the disjointed barrel against the gun-breech with the frantic abandon of a madman. He didn't even look up to see who it was. Still hammering, he merely shouted back at the boy in a hoarse strangled voice:
>
> "Get out of here! Dont touch them! Dont touch a one of them! They're mine!"

Faulkner has glossed this passage for us; he tells us that Boon is trying to *repair* his gun, in which a shell has jammed, and that he doesn't want anyone to shoot the squirrels until he can. But there appears here, in distinct contrast to this idea of repairing, a decided emphasis upon fanatical destruction of the gun, and it cannot be doubted that, whether repairing or destroying his gun and consequently the idea of the hunt, Boon is at the moment completely insane. As the killer of Old Ben, it may be that he now possesses the mystery, that he has apprehended the reality of the wilderness, and his passion of ownership can now take the form only of an intense and futile confusion.

It thus appears in "The Bear" that the only possible approach to the wilderness, the reality or the "truth" of it, is Ike's method; this is the only alternative to anticlimax or to madness. The fundamental idea of this approach that is not an approach is, again, the maintaining of imaginative distance, the refusal to bring to issue or to resolve, and an insistence upon

one's lack of imaginative control. As an imaginative attitude, it is charac-
terized by McCaslin Edmonds' reference to Keats' "Ode on a Grecian
Urn": " 'She cannot fade, though thou hast not thy bliss,' McCaslin said:
'Forever wilt thou love, and she be fair.' "

And it is here that one of the primary ambiguities of "The Bear"
and most of Faulkner's writing becomes apparent: this ambiguity lies in
the motivation of the "suspension" that I have described. Insofar as Ike's
motives for relinquishing his patrimony are similar to those for his adopt-
ing a suspended attitude wherever "truth" becomes an issue, a reader has
the feeling that there is no mystery here at all. The land has a curse on it,
we are told, a curse of slavery and miscegenation and incest, and the
pursuit of "truth" cannot be successful or even attempted until the curse
has ended. The failure to order, in other words, springs from a conviction
that a certain kind of order exists, and it is not a failure at all, but a
condition of the "hell" in which we live and which some day may become
"heaven," or at least Eden, again. There is no way of doing away with this
problem in Faulkner, I think, but it is possible to suggest that his moral
conviction of a curse may be frequently subsumed under a more general
conviction of a basic quality of language and imagination, and whether
this quality is seen by him to be the result of a curse or the fall of man or
anything else is secondary to the pervasive effects and less fabulous
assumptions of the quality itself.

For a reader cannot fail to notice the parallels between the manner
in which Ike McCaslin approaches the "truth" of the wilderness and the
usual form of Faulkner's own rhetorical methods. The insistence upon
incoherency, upon the abrogation of rules, and upon permanent unresolution
as positive values that have been seen to be characteristic of Faulkner's
imagination are all expressed metaphorically in Ike's attitudes. The very
suspension of pursuit upon which Ike relies, in fact, as well as his reliance
upon losing his way, is the dramatic equivalent to Faulkner's use of verbal
suspensions, the long and seemingly directionless sentences that never
come to issue. If we follow this parallel to its logical conclusion, we may
establish the proposition that "truth" depends somehow upon this sort of
suspension; it depends upon what we might normally assume to be the
antithesis of truth—upon the refusal and inability to structure experience
or, in the language of my discussion, to create a metaphor. Why this
should be so, however, is a more complicated question.

JOSEPH W. REED, JR.

"Light in August"

Well, a man's future is inherent in that man. . . . That is, . . . there is no such thing as was. That time is, and if there's no such thing as was, then there is no such thing as will be. That time is not a fixed condition, time is in a way the sum of the combined intelligences of all men who breathe at that moment.

—Faulkner in the University

Memory believes before knowing remembers. Believes longer than recollects, longer than knowing even wonders.

—Light in August

Light in August is character-dominated as is no other of Faulkner's books—not even *The Sound and the Fury* or *As I Lay Dying*. One result of this is that each character carries his own structure with him and to a certain extent imposes it on the book. The structure of the whole cannot completely rule any of these individual narrative patterns, yet the whole is clearly greater than the sum of its parts: an explication of these individual patterns is not a decent explication of the book, and some strong general narrative forces have no root in the individual patterns. The enigma of *Light in August* is the relationship between these individual worlds and the book's cosmic forces. Individual worlds, islands of privacy, exist side by side for a time, then impinge on each other or interpenetrate. Some are kept private longer than others, only to be smashed into each other finally. The book has thus been taken to be compound rather than complex; in Malcolm Cowley's terms, it "combine[s] two or more themes having little relation to each other."

I think that the tracing of narrative strategy can make more sense of this than any thematic system. This multiple progress of all the private, segregated parts and their violent conjunction brought about by the force of the whole makes, for instance, an elaborate proliferation of time schemes: the small time scheme for each character must govern that private world until the grand time scheme of the whole book seizes it. In *The Sound and the Fury* the past was the inherited burden of group and of individual. In *As I Lay Dying* the function of the past was reduced to little more than individual memory: each narrator's past operated according to his own rules, sometimes breaking out to affect his or someone else's present, but in every instance each was far less significant and far more securely individual than any of the individual parts in *Light in August*. Here the past is central: individual freedom or compulsion is primarily determined by a character's success or failure in dealing with his past—in coming to terms with the unspoken or, frequently, the inarticulate residue of what he has known, believed or done. And this past more or less determines his present. Characters who can successfully integrate what they have been into what they are now manage to escape. Of those who cannot, some smash themselves up when their present meets another's present or when their *was* begins to constitute for them a *must be*: Hightower finds a happy entrapment by submitting himself to a chosen past, selected to replace and supplant permanently his present.

All the issues of the book—of past and present, of individual and group, of cosmic and human cause—emerge from those multiple functions of time, or in one way or another from the two quotations set as epigraph to this chapter, from man's "inherent" future or from memory believing. But no overview comprising a single unifying theme or narrative strategy will "solve" the whole or unify its disjunctions. Even the "solution" of a part is illusive because that part's identity is in continual flux, subject to change as the book progresses because of its dynamic relationship to other parts and the dynamic tension of the whole. Either the whole or another part can at any time rather arbitrarily change it or determine its fate.

One third of the book narrates events of the deep or intermediate past, and all of this is manifested in the pasts of individuals: Joe, Joanna and her family, Lena, Hightower, the Hineses. Each of these is rendered in a different way and comes upon us rather unexpectedly. We move to Joe's past earlier than we expected (if we expected it at all). Lena's past is continually present because she is pregnant—everyone infers a simple past for her and that is not far from the truth. Joanna tells Joe about her past in the middle of the book's arbitrarily timed but strictly chronological tracing of *his* past. The narrative deals with four levels of time: present, imperfect, the deep past, and an intermediate level between the historical chronicle of the deep and the almost-immediate of the imperfect. The passage tracing the Burden family history which begins in objective narra- tion and passes into Joanna's narrative to Joe is cast in the deep past in a style resembling the disconnected objectivity of the *Dictionary of American Biography*. Hightower's childhood (in chapter 20) is also of the deep past, but it is cast rather as a reverie of memory. Joe's deep past (say, everything up to Bobbie) is more objectively narrated than Hightower's, but it never approaches the coldness of the Burden section. The intermediate past (Lena's family, Hightower and his church, Joe's "phases" with Joanna) is also subject to considerable variation in tone and style.

The point is that we are led to believe that all this has relevance to the present moment, but we are given no warning when the next time shift may come. The narrative presence seems to accept as his donnée that his sense of timing is unquestionable and he need not consult our comfort or our wishes in the matter.

No past in this book is safely sealed off from the present. Hightow- er's past continually rises to the surface to haunt him in the present and to allow Faulkner to connect him with Joe and Joanna on the level of plot. Doubts about Joe's race haunt the book, partly imposed by his own internal doubts and habitual action in the present and partly trailing him out of the past in what people have heard. Because the barrier between the present and the past is so thin, the plot cannot be charted in proper Dickensian patterns of early incident and late significance: for individuals the past is never really gone—there is no such thing as *was*—but for the whole, the reader never knows whether what is past will stay safely sealed away or will erupt into the present. Hines behaves like a proper Dickens character, popping up when least expected with an identifying phrase out of the past ready on his lips. But McEachern, abandoned on the school- house floor, doubtfully dead, a much more likely subject for coincidental resuscitation, never returns. Character dominance and arbitrary accidence combine to create a strong sense of doubt in the reader. Accidental triggers rouse the past, chance encounters rule the present. They never establish *Sanctuary*'s cosmos of accidence but, enforced by narrative mo- mentum, they become by the end a web of inevitability.

This pattern of individual parts, the arbitrary eruption of pasts into presents, is set within an even more puzzling chronological scheme in the whole. Take *Sanctuary* as a point of reference. There Horace gives us exposition as he wanders into the Frenchman's Bend enclave and gives us more exposition when he gets back to Jefferson. We return to the enclave for the Perils of Temple and the narrative proceeds to shift back and forth between the outlaw camps of Frenchman's Bend/Memphis and the law and order of Jefferson, in the conventional manner of a gangster movie or western of the thirties. *Light in August* defies such an order. It opens with a narrative neither puzzling in its content nor expositional in its intent: the essentially static action of a character who later seems rather tangential. We move by what seems to be an accidental train of narrative association through Byron Bunch and Gail Hightower to Joe Christmas. There is frantic and unexplained action. Then we backtrack into the past of Joe Christmas, a character who has not concerned us for the first quarter of the book. We finally find connections between these disparate elements when we are more than halfway through, and then they are not conventional connections but only happenstance encounters. The Lena thread is tied up, the Christmas thread is brought to a dramatic end, we pause for more character exposition with Hightower, and then Lena and Byron move us out of the book. Disjunction here goes far beyond just a confused chronology or overturned conventional expectations. The reader has to become content to move where and when the author chooses, give himself up to a flow of characters, events, information, and encounters, and to draw his meanings and arrive at his responses where he can. Action, drama, or the conventional involvement of plot will not carry him comfortably along.

This narrative unconcern, the Teller's apparent lack of concern for the Hearer, is also present in the book's most puzzling time device, the arbitrary switches of tense from present to imperfect and back again. We might well expect such alternation to resemble the relationship between deep past and immediate narrative (as might a chronological narrative reordered to satisfy requirements of suspense and calculated revelation: this is what happened and this is how that motive originated). If the alternation of tense were arranged systematically around the arbitrary locus of the column of smoke from the Burden house, for instance, the story might be narrated in the present as it advanced from that point and in the imperfect for events leading up to that point. Instead we find that shifts between present and imperfect (in chapters, 1, 2, 14, and 18) are from the very outset almost completely arbitrary. Since this switching accomplishes no locating purpose it must be for effect, to enhance immediacy and dramatic closeness. The use of the present tense (especially in returns to the present from dominant imperfect) slams the reader up against the action. Switches back and forth also lead to a peculiar uprooted quality, and this enforces the narrative power of moments of crisis such as the pursuit of Joe and Byron's pursuit of Brown.

But beyond this there is a more important function more closely related to the book's other time disjunctions. Once we as readers discover that we can function in the uncertain fluctuation between present tense and imperfect, we begin to get the idea that there is little difference between them: that pasts tend to persist in the present; that a past which has risen to the surface of the present several times becomes a stronger past and tends to convert a future *might be* into *must be*; that recurrence is a pattern in which it doesn't much matter where you stand because it's the same all the way forward and all the way back. Switches back and forth not only level distinctions between past and present (the past is present and the present is never really past), but suggest to us that for an individual, time might work in both directions. We can thus seek an explanation for the confusing, apparently arbitrary present in the incoherent, chaotic, inarticulate past. At the same time the narrative strategy invites us to look forward to the unforeseen results of tiny impulses started in the past.

Finally there is the contrast between our sense of time and distance at the beginning and at the end of the book. The novel opens in Lena's journey, timeless and distanceless because of her nature and her present condition. Ponderous moving and apparent non-moving here are contrasted to inexorable, inevitable movement at the end. From the pursuit of Brown through the death of Joe the book is compulsively driven to its conclusions, emanating from The Player's movements and culminating in Grimm's killing of Joe. The early concentration on present tense has already been accounted for in the way Lena's *is* presents her *was* to all who see her. But there is a further explanation: both Lena's helplessness as isolated stranger, subject of the town's sometimes cruel and automatic care, and her character of patient and timeless endurance are essential at the outset, both to define her place in the book—as a possible Ishmael—and to make believable her attraction to Byron. The downhill narrative propulsion at the end can also be accounted for, because Joe's *was* becoming an *is* necessitates a *must be*, and as it does the narrative gives over its arbitrary switches from tense to tense and takes up the inexorable drive to its fated end. The Player steps in.

But The Player has always been there. In our sense of the whole the omnipresence of the past and the narrative presence's omniscience about it, the Teller's apparent disregard of our sense of order and expectations, and the book's rather chilling objectivity have all been preparations for him, or perhaps even extensions of him back into the novel. He is the logical conclusion, the personified agent of all the habits to which the book's strategy has been accustoming us. And in the "Emily" sense, he is *us:* we, because of what the book's patterns of objectivity, justice, and accidence have instilled in us, have become The Player as surely as it is we who break down the door to Emily's room.

Seen in terms of the triple issue I have posed—time, individual, cause, and effect—the book's rather intimidating time disjunctions make sense. Each narrative device responds to the immediate need, whether of part or of whole, and the disjunctions between part and part or part and whole are illusory. Eventually everything in the book responds to the story's necessities. The novel as a whole moves forward chronologically (rather slowly because so little of it narrates the immediate action at hand), and each of its discrete parts tends backward, from accomplishment to source. Lena enters the book pregnant; we learn how she got pregnant and begin a search for the father. We then see Hightower in deep isolation and examine the events which led to that isolation. We see Hines without knowing who he is, then see him nearly mad and move back to a point which precedes our first encounter with him to look for the sources of his madness. The burning house appears in the narrative before the crime does, Byron's weekend concerns appear without an explanation for them (Faulkner never really gets back to this), and Christmas's wanderings just prior to the killing of Joanna are traced before we see any of the causes for his fitful "thinking" or his psychosis. Later we know Lena has given birth before the birth is narrated, and know Christmas is dead before we have met his killer or traced his pursuit. And just before the end, we are given a yet more remote past for Hightower—the backward look itself looking backward. We might well expect to find such omissions and reversals at the beginning of the novel since Faulkner's opening move is so frequently suspense by omission; but the reversals begin early and persist throughout. None of Faulkner's other books—not even *Absalom, Absalom!*—reveals so consistent a set of reversed parts.

We are able to move through all this with comparative ease, in part because of the narrative landmark of the burning Burden house. It stands as a pillar in the center of the book, and the remotest reaches into the deep, the intermediate, or the immediate past are never far away from that mark. As with the house, all paths, figurative, narrative, and causal, lead there.

I have charted the relationship between parts and whole first in time schemes because our deep involvement in the book while we are reading it so peculiarly distracts us. The introduction of Lena sets up a red herring which, if we happily pursue it, can bring us to disappointment in the end. Even concentration on the central part, the narrative thread of Joe Christmas, is a disservice to the whole because it denies the significance of his dynamic relationship to the book's world; concentration on him can distract us from the greater effect of the chilling cosmos the whole novel embodies. Relating the parts to each other without undervaluing any of them is difficult but I think essential. Part of this depends on the double sense of time—cause can be traced forward or backward.

Each character sets off concentric waves, some of them out of his past, some from his present, and these waves meet the waves set off by others, resulting themselves in more complex waves. Small and harmless actions, moving through different individuals and their differing systems of values, become larger and larger, out of proportion and unrecognizable from their origins in force and result. The hermit, the eccentric, the outlaw—each moves and is moved in a private dance called by elaborate combination with the private dances of others.

A similar law works in the opposite direction: an unremembered action, an answer, a word deep in the past can prove to be the root cause of a complex response or violent action erupting in the present. Every individual is a puzzle, a set of nested Chinese boxes of cause and motive. *Light in August* gives us appearance first, the outside box, then a group-think analysis by the town or another group, and then by stages seems to move us toward the heart of the final box. The explanation of this final root cause is not given; frequently it is resolved in action rather than in cause or motivation, but this, too, in its own way, builds the novel's power.

A colleague once said to me that he liked *Light in August* because it was the greatest study he knew of the origins of evil. I agreed at the time and still agree, but more and more wonder which origins of what evil. Both Joe's self-pursuit and the town's pursuit of Joe produce evil but are not themselves its cause. Each individual pattern, its particular residue of memory, knowledge, belief, abstract system, can be benign in private but in combination with just the right pattern in another provide a formula for malignancy. Some benign residual patterns can even operate for good in combination with others. Lena's particular state and pattern call forth Byron's protection and (in spite of his own defensive patterns) his love. His love in turn conditions his response to others and his appeal to Hightower to leave his isolation.

But those individual patterns which contain adaptations of rigid abstract systems tend to become malign when they combine with others. Hines's compulsive poison and his and McEachern's private and individually manufactured hells of Calvinism contribute to Joe's eventual poisonous combination with Joanna. Hines returns and triggers malignancy in others. But to say that Joe's crime is the product of his reaction to their Calvinism is simplistic. Personal adaptations of almost any institutional or abstract form can be equally poisonous: the Calvinist work-ethic, prostitution, motherhood (or foster-motherhood), community pride, racism, benevolent uplift, moralistic self-degradation. Each is more or less benign in itself, but when cultivated by rigorous personal adaptation and met with just the right combination in another individual, any of these can lead to evil.

Joanna's carpetbagger and reformer instincts, far from evil in themselves, become evil when they rather than her human feelings determine her relationship to Joe. They interpose external forms (even as McEachern and Hines interpose their individual adaptations of Calvinism) as a substitute for human flexibility. The form of automatism promoted by abstract ideals, the hardening of responses and feelings into habits or reactions, is one of the chief subjects of the biographical digressions. Joe throughout his affair with Bobbie takes on more and more automatic patterns of behavior: to avoid being looked upon as an outsider he takes on protective coloration which will make him less conspicuous in the diner; he develops affectations in smoking and wearing his hat which bring him closer to Mame and Max. But these are secondary adaptations and he the experimental subject for the primary adaptations and automatic reactions in others. Thus adaptations or cruelty in others conditions in Joe a stock response to every contact until he finally finds all the shapes of his past—of kindness, of feeding, of love, of evangelical attempts at redemption, of racial attitudes—in the body of one woman and can kill them all once and for all by taking off her head.

Reciprocal interaction is the key to the fictional realization of all this and to the particularly flexible third-person method which Faulkner adopts as its essential narrative medium. The processes of cruelty are almost always dependent upon reciprocal fear—in the dietitian, McEachern, Bobbie, Joanna, in Lena and Burch. The tension in these confrontations is not just between subject and object, but between what the character knows and cannot know, between what he remembers and does not remember, what he knows and what he believes, what he thinks and what lies too deep for thought. The rhythm and frequency of third-person variation is capable of a much more delicate and sensitive response to momentary vacillation, the tiny vibration between appearance and consciousness, than is that of the first person.

The dietitian sequence seen only through Joe's eyes could never have revealed the dietitian's essential fear. Joe fears punishment for eating the toothpaste. The dietitian hasn't even noticed. She fears exposure and dismissal if Joe reveals something he cannot reveal because he hasn't noticed and is too young to understand. Joe rendered in the first person would have sacrificed the reciprocity of fear, the intense way in which the object of fear is played against the fearing sentient being.

A great deal of *Light in August* is devoted to the momentary examination of just what *As I Lay Dying* had to omit: the immediate response of consciousness to consciousness, the slippage between assumption or formulation of one consciousness about another, and what is actually going on inside another.

In casting this book in the third person rather than the first Faulkner did not want to sacrifice all the immediacy just to gain total objectivity. He salvages some of the first person's immediacy by switching into present tense but, more important, by a peculiar device designed to render thoughts and point of view. The framework for this is set forth early in Lena's journey:

> From the corner of his eye he watches her profile, thinking *I dont know what Martha's going to say* thinking, 'I reckon I do know what Martha's going to say. I reckon womenfolks are likely to be good without being very kind. Men, now, might. But it's only a bad woman herself that is likely to be very kind to another woman that needs the kindness' thinking *Yes I do. I know exactly what Martha is going to say.*

The first quotation in italics of Armstid's "thinking" is at a level just below speech, more or less formulated for speech. The second (in single quotation marks) lies at a lower level, more articulate as it appears here than the thought it represents (as in "Barn Burning"). The third, again in italics, returns to the level just below speech but incorporates a conclusion formed at the lower level. This is a very simple example of the 322 similar patterns in the book, but it represents well the typical movement of even the most complex pattern. Complexity increases as the book proceeds. Joe has more instances of "thinking" than anyone else; Hightower is next with a more continuous development between one "thinking" and the next; Byron's are more infrequent but seem to move deeper in these isolated instances.

The venture into Lena's consciousness which opens the book is an example of the way in which Faulkner brings a comparatively simple device to complexity by its conjunction with other narrative devices. The first pattern is an inner soliloquy very much in her style and speech, but speech repressed. This is followed by a second version coming from somewhere a bit deeper in the consciousness. Lena has come a long way and is farther from home than she has ever been. This could have been handled more efficiently by Faulkner in a bit of mind-reading by the narrative presence, but he chooses this more complex way because Lena's process of thought carries a meaning beyond its substance. *Is* and *was* are mixed for Lena Grove. The present dominates in her own mind but those who help her see her in terms of her past. Lena's pregnancy represents a past of which she has been made innocent by the man's abandonment and her simpleminded search for him. People treat her kindly because they believe in her condition (*was* surviving in *is*) as surely as they reject Joe Christmas because of what they believe about him; that is, that he is black. The whole opening section represents Lena's attempt to impose a *was* on what for her is a continual present of squeaking wagons. By showing her inability to do so, Faulkner demonstrates in short compass something essential about her.

The next three instances reflect her innocence but, more important, her fatalism, which, rather strangely, is one thing that makes the present so dominant for her. All three of these "thinkings" are out of the past, and her thinking carries us back there so she can tell us about it as if she were still in that time. But her consciousness as she tells us is only of the present ("If it had been this hard to do before"). She amplifies this with "my hearing before my seeing." Since the noise forms her consciousness of the wagon, it seems that she was in it half an hour before she got in, and after she gets out, will in that sense continue in it for another half-hour. The present encloses her in the repetition of faces, kindness, wagon squeaks. The present encompasses both the past and the future, which she develops by a fantasy of happiness, the vicarious adaptation of what Lucas Burch, she feels, will be thinking: "I will be riding within the hearing . . . before his seeing. He will hear the wagon, but he wont know, so there will be one within his hearing before his seeing. And then he will see me and he will be excited. And so there will be two within his seeing before his remembering." The fantasy is generous and more than a little innocent, but this is Lena's characteristic mode. Faulkner soon contrasts this unseen generosity to the unseen stock cruelties which lie behind Armstid's and Varner's kind words. But generally her effect on others produces good. Everything in Lena that is of the present causes the characters she meets to re-examine their pasts and try to change them: Byron gives up Saturday nights for her; Lena as catalyst brings Hightower to re-examine his place in the town and his isolation and to be tempted to change some of his *was* rules: to consider again having a woman in the house, to sally forth again as midwife, tempting all that old trouble, finally to realize fully his past.

All of this could be seen as a rather clumsy way to introduce a consciousness, pushing Lena's essential innocence so hard. But Faulkner has also involved us in Lena's sense of time and change: even as she adopts Burch's consciousness she further explicates her own. In the "hearing-seeing" relationship there is the suggestion of a Darl-like formulation, never developed fully, but perhaps completed in another individual, when hearing jolts Byron out of his dream of love for Lena the virgin and he sees Lena in labor. For Byron Lena represents so certain an *is* and so hopeless a *was* that he is able to suspend her from both *was* and *will be*, a suspension not broken until the baby is born and Byron is faced with a reassessment of what she has been and what he must become.

Faulkner's desire for unity and coherence in the pattern is not as strong as is his desire for truth to individual response. When Byron comes to that moment of reassessment, his mind works in its own way, one not so much marked by a literary mode common with Lena's, the similarity of his "thinking" patterns to hers, as it is by individual and immediate response to his situation. His pursuit of Brown in chapters 17 and 18 demonstrates some of the same volitionless movement as Joe does at points of decision, something of that same mental numbness which follows points of realization: "And then, just outside the cabin door where he had stopped, he heard the child cry once and something terrible happened to him." This is the echo of Joe's fears as he "waited for what came next," and the echo is repeated again for Byron in chapter 18 ("his insides were afraid that . . . something terrible would happen"). For Byron the present is his involvement with Lena (signaled in the text by the repetition of "Byron Bunch knows this"). For Hightower and for us, Byron's past is that enigmatic cause of his weekend hegira. The town sees Byron's present as his job, and they don't know or care if he ever had a past. We never find out much about the past, and he abandons it completely when he meets Lena and is thus able to break free of whatever obligation it had imposed upon his present.

The surface similarity between Byron's and Joe's premonitions, far from enforcing the dominance of a common fate or even a common consciousness, suggests instead that even fate is individual. Byron's premonition does not prove true. "What came next" offers him a path for escape because his realization is not tragic but almost comic. It involves the adjustment of a dream to conform with present reality: "It was like for a week now his eyes had accepted her belly without his mind believing. 'Yet I did know, believe,' he thought. 'I must have knowed, to have done what

I have done: the running and the lying and the worrying at folks.' . . . Yet still he did not believe." Byron has planned, assessed, calculated—all hermetic "thinking" directed to the end of serving and saving Lena. The narrative presence steps in with a metaphor for this:

> He was working fast, yet thinking went slow enough. He knew why now. He knew now that thinking went slow and smooth with calculation, as oil is spread slowly upon a surface above a brewing storm. "If I had known then," he thought. "If I had known then. If it had got through then." He thought this quietly. . . . "Yes. I would have turned my back and rode the other way. Beyond the knowing and memory of man forever and ever I reckon I would have rode." But he did not.

Joe's "thinking" is hermetic, but by contrast it is internally, not vicariously, compulsive. Byron has moved to complete his relationship with Lena, but it fails to satisfy his premises or resolve his identity. Thus for him the process cannot end with simple realization: he must carry the realization back to his former assumptions and change them.

> *It was not until . . . I heard her and saw her face and knew that Byron Bunch was nothing in this world to her right then, that I found out that she is not a virgin* And he thought that that was terrible, but that was not all. There was something else. . . . *I'll have to tell him now. I'll have to tell Lucas Burch. . . . Why I didn't even believe until now that he was so. It was like me, and her, and all the other folks that I had to get mixed up in it, were just a lot of words that never even stood for anything, were not even us, while all the time what was us was going on and going on without even missing the lack of words. Yes. It aint until now that I ever believed that he is Lucas Burch. That there ever was a Lucas Burch.*

"Thinking" about himself has been prevented by the surface calculation he has devoted to helping Lena, and by believing. Now both are called into question by the believing he has failed to do. The surface has been enough to lead his memory, his knowing, and his believing into falsehood, to protect him from the danger to his self-esteem which lurks in "thinking" about himself. His volitionless movement responds to external necessity—helping Lena. He has been kept from Joe's kind of "thinking," from Joe's self-compulsion by a false believing, which has made it possible to lie, meddle, and care in a way which Joe's self-thought would have cut short. In other words, he has been in love.

Realization has come to him by way of the external, unavoidable, and incontrovertible fact of a noise and a sight, and it has brought with it a question about the basis of his action, meddling, compulsion, and love. When the adjustment comes it is not *anagnorisis* but inverted *anagnorisis*—

essentially comic because it permits him to restore his order and to pass out of time and distance (in chapter 18) and back in. Then (free of this false pattern of believing) he can escape the book into some kind of future with Lena.

> The world rushes down on him like a flood, a tidal wave. It is too huge and fast for distance and time; hence no path to be retraced. . . . It is as though he has already and long since outstripped himself, already waiting at the cabin until he can catch up and enter. *And then I will stand there and I will.* . . . But he can get no further than that. . . . He does not give up, however, *Even if I cant seem to get further than that.* . . . *And then I will. Look at her. Look at her. Look at her.*

He gets no farther because what lies beyond is a leap of faith and a breaking of his accustomed pattern. He must move forward from realization to action—to make another try at what has been based in a false belief, and to have the courage to replace it with real belief.

Hightower's pattern at a similar point of realization results in entrapment. He begins (chapter 20) in a comfortable retrospective mood, shifting into his deep past: "Thinking goes quietly, tranquilly, flowing on, falling into shapes quiet, not assertive, not reproachful, not particularly regretful." But the quiet and comfortable (somewhat self-condemning) process hits a snag, and the narrative presence steps in with a metaphor: "Thinking begins to slow now. It slows like a wheel beginning to run in sand, the axle, the vehicle, the power which propels it not yet aware. . . . The wheel of thinking slows; the axle knows it now but the vehicle itself is still unaware." For Hightower the past is present in the rushing hooves every evening. He fled the present and the community that surrounded him to seek his present isolation in the cultivation of that past. The town thinks Hightower's past is what they said of him then that made him what he is now. And to Hightower the town is his *was*, as he is theirs. It is safer for both that way.

But now when he throws himself the old sops they don't work. He wants to continue to conceal from himself that his martyr's exile from the church was simply self-indulgence.

> "But I was young then," he thinks. "I too had to do, not what I could, but what I knew." Thinking is running too heavily now; he should know it, sense it. Still the vehicle is unaware of what it is approaching. . . . "It is any man's privilege to destroy himself, so long as he does not injure anyone else, so long as he lives to and of himself—" He stops suddenly. . . . He is aware of the sand now; with the realization of it he feels within himself a gathering as though for some tremendous effort. Progress now is still progress, yet it is now indistinguishable from the

recent past like the already traversed inches of sand which cling to the turning wheel, raining back with a dry hiss that before this should have warned him. . . .

His agony comes in the slow process of realizing what he is thinking, of seeing the false thinking within it. Again the narrative renders this by a collaboration between the narrative presence's mind-reading and direct quotation of "thinking." Byron's realization came on the instant and made all of the difference at once, to be consolidated only by the slow process of reassessment after realization. Hightower's is strongly contrasted to this.

> Out of the instant the sand-clutched wheel of thinking turns on with the slow implacability of a mediaeval torture instrument, beneath the wrenched and broken sockets of his spirit, his life: "Then, if this is so, if I am the instrument of her despair and death, then I am in turn instrument of someone outside myself. And I know that for fifty years I have not even been clay: I have been a single instant of darkness in which a horse galloped and a gun crashed. And if I am my dead grandfather on the instant of his death, then my wife, his grandson's wife . . . the de-baucher and murderer of my grandson's wife, since I could neither let my grandson live or die . . ." The wheel, released, seems to rush on with a long sighing sound. . . . It is going fast and smooth now, because it is freed now of burden, of vehicle, axle, all.

The wheel freed can move on to Byron and Lena, to Grimm and Christmas, the last two faces confused in his mind. He utters a final lament ("I wanted so little. I asked so little. It would seem . . . ") and the wheel turns on, on its own, because Hightower is back with the "whipping ribbons . . . and eager lances." His realization is tragic because he cannot use it to move beyond himself but instead falls back into his earlier fantasy. The last glimpse of him, objectified in his window, a bandaged head upon the twin blobs of his hands, as distant from life (although perhaps not from self-knowledge) as Emily, "like an idol in a niche," is as poignant as anything in Faulkner.

In Hightower protection of the self has taken precedence over all. He has broken some of his resolutions of self-protection and ventured out, but where Byron's realization ends in escape, Hightower's must end in entrapment. Hightower has been trapped in a dream of harmless insignificance, Byron has believed in a dream of altered reality. Hightower's fall from the dream must be to a horrifying realization of self-deception, while Byron can escape by reassessment. Hightower comes to realize that he is what he was and what all before him have been, Byron that he can be what he is willing to be. We leave Hightower as an object, in a present dominated by a past. We leave Byron as a man in a *will be* formed of his past and his present. The "thinking" device finds its poetic statement and its major force in Joe Christmas. All other patterns of "thinking" are less absolute—controls for the compulsive and absolute integrity of his pattern: "Memory believes before knowing remembers. Believes longer than recollects, longer than knowing even wonders. Knows remembers believes a corridor." This is not just an overt statement of this most effective narrative device but its organizing principle. Memory is inarticulate and can believe without formulating. Belief contains the sense of both a leap of faith and a false self-deception. The inarticulate operates before the articulate takes over, and can persist even when the articulate has taken over some of its functions. *Before* gives memory not just chronological priority but primacy of incidence: it not only precedes the remembering of knowing in the child, but can also be dominant later, can cause knowing to be ineffectual ("longer than recollects, longer than knowing even wonders"). Memory can reach farther back in time than knowing, and can last longer—can outlast even knowing's failure to recollect, wondering why it does not.

This formula can be made to approximate roughly Wordsworthian categories: an infancy of direct sensations whose residue forms memory, a childhood of knowing and conning another part of facts and external truth, the youth's believing and the adult's remembering. But to make Faulkner's formula fit into such a rigid schematic pattern is neither necessary nor particularly useful (and commits the critical sin of preferring systematic arrangement to sense.) Faulkner needs only a limited system, to define the rough limits of these words (memory, believe, know, remember) and some others (think, see, say), so that he can then count on them to operate by controlled diction.

The main aim of the verbal limitation is to get at the central fact of the character of Joe Christmas: he is ruled by inarticulate memory. He knows, remembers, forgets, builds up self-knowledge and self-definition in a system of recurrence and repetition. Darl in *As I Lay Dying* sought freedom by trying to get away from time and distance formulation in an attempt to get at what *is* as contrasted to the appearances of what *is-not*. Joe is caught by the recurrence of what *was* and what *is*, and this forms his knowing, believing, remembering, being, doing, and necessity. Recurrence supports and feeds his remembering (which in some cases involves forgetting), his knowing (which is sometimes only formulation to replace a lack of knowing), and his believing (which, as with most believing, often involves a condition contrary to fact). The repetition and recurrence of what *was* in what *is* produces a necessary belief in (and indeed a strong likelihood of) what *must be* ("He was waiting for the rest of it to begin; the part that would not be pleasant, whatever it would be,"; *"Something is going to happen to me. I am going to do something."*

For Joe the past is what he was then—not big enough, not sure enough, not adapted enough. The present is thinking, believing, remembering—everything that has accrued to him from encounters in his past. *Was* for him is an ever-present recurrence demonstrated in physical fact by the return of Hines to his life, proved to Joe's own satisfaction by the uniformly stereotyped behavior of his women. *Was* is constant. Women (in a sense, always the same woman) are always a part of his *is.* He defines himself in terms of what she *is,* but first makes her become what other women have been to him. He has lost the power to escape from this form of dependence. For the town, Joe's past is a stereotyped offense of race and his present a stereotype of the mad-dog fugitive killer. It manufactures this by combining its stock reaction to his blackness with its stock reaction to Joanna's reforming zeal. For the town, the perfect victim has met the dream aggressor.

In Joe's patterns of "thinking" we see most clearly that the technical device is a continual response to narrative need, the same need to which the time disjunctions responded: there is no such thing as *was;* every moment of the present and every moment of action involves a deep residue of reference, connection, and even determination from the past. With Joe, Faulkner concentrates on the notion of the experience or fact he has forgotten (in the sense that he cannot call it up consciously) that still operates on his consciousness. Faulkner is trying to get at something that lies deeper than telling. We know but Joe does not what is determining many of his momentary movements and responses. Almost everything of significance that happens in the novel is the product of subverbal (or at least unspoken) weighing, calculation, or arrangement.

Joe's "thinking" falls into so many different patterns that any discussion which did not replicate the length and thickness of the novel would do a disservice to its subtlety and nuance, but a most representative sample can be found in his relationship with Joanna. The end of chapter 10 brings Joe to this final, decisive liaison. But already in chapter 5 (paralleling the general outlines of effect-to-cause movement in the book) we have observed Joe's wanderings just before he gets back to the matter of Joanna. Then in chapters 6 through 8 we accumulate data with him, watch the formation of a consciousness and objectively retain all—some of which he subjectively forgets, slurs over, and obliterates. In chapter 8 (the encounters with Bobbie) recurrence begins, and represents not just an input of experience but also the inductive process in which experience and recurrence operate in rapid mutual acceleration. The residual product of earlier input begins to determine new input. For instance, in his scene with Mrs. McEachern after striking down her husband Joe performs and uses the words he might in a condemnation of Bobbie which could follow her refusal of him (if he ever got the chance to play out that condemnation). The combination of experience-input and repetition-echo results in a reaction which is already almost predetermined by the previous input. Lena is immersed in the process of travel, which obliterates time, distance, *was* and self. Joe is immersed in the process of recurrence which makes all of these one and determines his response. Perpetual warfare with his current woman involves continual warfare with himself as he watches, helpless, voluntarily moving again into a cycle, knowing his adversary must in the end win out but defying her nonetheless. He quite literally sees himself as object, even as he hears his mouth saying, sees his hand hurling the dishes against the wall, as he sees himself moving back to try the kitchen door again when all he really wants to do is get away. He is rendered will-less by the process, because inasmuch as he is rootless and a fugitive he exercises free will. As experience accumulates, so must his fatalism. Joe in a sense makes the web himself by his initial judgment of his women and the performance determined by that judgment. Casting the various women always in the archetypal role imprisons them and him in a web of preordained action. In Joanna he finds the perfect adversary, one who matches each of his archetypal expectations with a stock response of her own, so that although she continually fulfills the role he casts her in, she does it in a perfect way which he has not met before. She draws him on by the fascination of her variety (she is a combination of all of her predecessors) and perfectly satisfies his expectation of the archetype.

At the end of chapter 10 he is already trapped.

> He did not know that he had even wondered or tasted until his jaw stopped suddenly in midchewing and thinking fled for twenty-five years back down the street, past all the imperceptible corners of bitter defeats and more bitter victories, and five miles even beyond a corner where he used to wait in the terrible early time of love, for someone whose name he had forgot; five miles even beyond that it went *I'll know it in a minute. I have eaten it before, somewhere. In a minute I will* memory clicking knowing *I see I see I more than see hear I hear I see my head bent I hear the monotonous dogmatic voice which I believe will never cease going on and on forever and peeping I see the indomitable bullet head the clean blunt beard they too bent and I thinking How can he be so nothungry and I smelling my mouth and tongue weeping the hot salt of waiting my eyes tasting the hot steam from the dish* "It's peas," he said, aloud. "For sweet Jesus. Field peas cooked with molasses."

When Joe connects field peas and molasses with Mrs. McEachern, he infers the next step in the recurrence, saying that he won't be trapped, that he is under no necessity to love—but what he thinks he's saying is "won't eat." With Joanna he says he won't eat, won't love, won't go to school, won't pray—establishes a series of final lines of defense and then successively finds a rationalization for retreat from each one, largely because Joanna's patterns of attack demonstrate such variety and so surprise his suspicions and satisfy his imaginations of disaster. Possibly he might even have found a retreat from her praying, had she not pulled a gun on him. Joanna's patterns of memory, believing, knowing, remembering are operating in just the way which foreordains a conclusive end for Joe's patterns of recurrence. So the gun—perhaps a gun from the Sartoris duel—must be pulled, and Joe, to complete his own internal patterns, must kill her.

After the rather overt tracing of the process of recurrence and recapitulation in chapter 10, the narrative changes its method. The recurrence and the complexity of responses to experience are assumed, and Joe's experience with Joanna is developed with all the narrative richness of mixed chronology, variant focus and individual confusion.

Chapter 11 opens with a passage which firmly establishes the relativity of time in this part of the narrative.

> By the light of the candle she did not look much more than thirty, in the soft light downfalling upon the softungirdled presence of a woman prepared for sleep. When he saw her by daylight he knew that she was better than thirtyfive. Later she told him that she was forty. "Which means either fortyone or fortynine, from the way she said it," he thought. But it was not that first night, nor for many succeeding ones, that she told him that much even.

The first sentence takes up where the preceding left off. Then we move in a series of time shifts which dissolves our attention to chronology, so clearly built up since the beginning of chapter 6. "It was a year after he had remarked without curiosity the volume of mail which she received and sent." The text is studded with references to particular times or periods of time and the relationships between one and the other, but order is gone. "And when he entered the house at night it was as he had entered it that first night; he felt like a thief, a robber, even while he mounted to the bedroom where she waited." That moment most beloved of trash fiction, the moment of first physical contact, is slurred over here, so that we are never quite sure when it happened. Joe's childish defiance of her "manlike surrender" clearly follows this first experience; his almost volitionless decision to "blow" and his subsequent return to the kitchen with the food-throwing follows on that, so that the general chaos is interrupted by passages of chronological order. Chronology is conceived of in a filmic way: it is here out of focus and there in focus, depending on the function of the particular moment—whether the event is to be dealt with in terms of the preceding narrative or in the more general terms which apply to the progress of the new connection, the new adversary, the new cycle. The distance serves narrative necessity by getting out a lot more exposition than Faulkner has the leisure to cover (point by point). In the midst of the general, rather distant narrative of the "three phases" Faulkner can insert the chronicle of the Burdens, then casually give us the impression that Joanna has recited all this, or something like it, to Joe.

The product of this development of the "thinking" patterns is a rich narrative of consciousness—consciousness which seems at times to be nothing much more than a surface level of twitches and knee-jerk survival, at others to go to the depths of now-forgotten patterns which form Joe's later actions. The process begins at a distance. Joe is an object of town curiosity, seen at a distance shoveling sawdust across the way. We move closer and see him in a series of enigmatic, almost autistic reactions, then become intimate as only a thoroughgoing chronological biography can make us intimate, watch him moment by moment and through a summary of a long period of development given in short compass. Then we see him pursued, get even deeper objective origins (in chapters 15 and 16). His end is at the greatest distance. We hear about it at the end of chapter 18, follow his pursuit in 19—when he is nothing more than a glint of handcuffs in the distance, again the fugitive outlander over there across the way, as he began—and finally we see the bleeding corpse. Except for that last-minute closeup, he has returned to his original state of the stranger.

Only we, like Hightower, cannot forget. We know too much. Faulkner has taken an impossible case for sympathetic attachment and empathetic participation and has not only made him accessible but has made the outside world of the town (which we accept at the outset) foreign to us because of our association with the outlander. This characterization is tour de force in the highest sense of his use of that term—tour de force which involves not just knowing what you want to do and then doing it, but stacking the deck at the outset against doing it, and involving all of the techniques of fiction to overcome the stacked deck.

The time disjunction subjects us to both the compelling immediate effect of narrative details and the thematic results produced by narrative strategy. We begin in ponderous moving/not-moving and end in inexorable propulsion. The variety of our developing responses to Lena, Byron, Hightower, and especially to Joe—from objectivity through intimacy and back to objectivity again—moves us deeply into the individual power of parts without dissipating the overpowering effect of the whole.

One familiar narrative structure of this whole is yet to be discussed: our relationship to the town. It brings forth its consciousness in a complex imitation of the patterns of "thinking" familiar in individual consciousnesses. The residual patterns of the members of the community are generalized at the fire as a macrocosmic personality. Individual patterns of automatic reaction become as one. When community personality meets with the force of an abstract ideal in Percy Grimm everyone can embrace it because of their automatism—Grimm justifies their fears and at the same time can seem to represent a call to higher action, while still permitting them to retain their cherished modes of individual respectability and behavior. The macrocosm can become a whole by gaining in Grimm the will and force which they as individuals would never have known: with Grimm, the archetypal blind conscience, they can become as one for the pursuit of Christmas, the archetypal foe.

The subtle development of this needs to be traced in detail. Chapter 1 establishes basically the same pattern we saw in *As I Lay Dying*. Lena, wrapped in her subjective oblivion of time and distance, totally preoccupied with her search, is regarded by Armstid and Varner in much the same way Armstid and McGowan regard the Bundrens. They feel superior to the outsider in their experience and the innocence they assume for her along with several false attitudes which are functions of the archetypal role they have cast her in. Varner even reads Lena's mind, and the narrative presence immediately provides us with a correction to this reading, indicating that Lena is even more innocent than Varner had assumed, and that the process of community concern rests on a rather shaky foundation of assumptions and unsuccessful sympathetic identification. The community is in trouble from the beginning, then; it can neither appeal to our sympathies nor demand our adoption of its attitudes. It is unworthy of them because it is essentially mistaken.

In chapter 3 Hightower's career is followed in a narrative pattern strongly reminiscent of the pattern in "Emily." The subgroups are present but they have a less significant function here, only to illustrate the unanimity of the community's attitude. There is no central sensible, tough-minded observer as in "Emily" to which they can react by contrast.

The community displays uniform smugness and misunderstanding at every level, acts upon attitudes rather than feelings, and consequently our opinions are neither engaged nor directed. They may be trying to enlist us, but because we see them objectively we will not share their attitudes or finally their guilt. The "elders" here put us off almost as much as the "party of masked men," partly because of familiar associations from experience and from other literature, but the novel seems not to be manipulating even this distaste.

Chapter 4, operating within the small subgroup of the men at the sawmill, contains perhaps our strongest invitation to join the town. Byron's point of view and statement, assessment, observation, are alternated with those of individuals and groups at the mill. All are clearly directed against Christmas and Brown as outsiders, and in this unanimity of opinion and the strong temptation to join in the camaraderie (compare similar feelings of kinship in the groups of "Hair," and "A Bear Hunt") we are for the first time persuaded toward alliance.

The effect of this persuasion, however, is gone by chapter 13, after we have been through Joe's biography and autobiographical commentary. After we have seen this complexity, beside which the simplicity of the town's attitude to an "outsider" is an absurdity, the possibility of an alliance with them is gone. In chapter 13 the town has become an attitude-machine for the production of damaging oversimplifications. At just this point the narrative presence announces quite clearly where all this ambiguity has been leading us. "Within five minutes after the countrymen found the fire, the people began to gather." They come together in a passage heavy with atmosphere, filled with the detailed treatment of small-town passage and flux which marks similar passages in *Sanctuary* and *Intruder in the Dust*. They are not gathering to serve as an obedient chorus or as atmospheric background but rather to provide the omniscient narrative presence with the materials for a thematic statement.

> She had lived such a quiet life . . . that she bequeathed to the town in which she had been born and lived . . . a kind of heritage of astonishment and outrage, for which, even though she had supplied them at last with an emotional barbecue, . . . they would never forgive her and let her be dead in peace and quiet. Not that. Peace is not that often. So they moiled and clotted, believing that the flames, the blood, the body that had died three years ago and had just now begun to live again, cried out for vengeance, not believing that the rapt infury of the flames and the immobility of the body were both affirmations of an attained bourne beyond the hurt and harm of man. Not that. Because the other made nice believing. Better than the shelves and the counters filled with long-

familiar objects bought not because the owner desired them or admired them, could take any pleasure in the owning of them, but in order to cajole or trick other men into buying them at a profit; and who must now and then contemplate both the objects which had not yet sold and the men who could buy them but had not yet done so, with anger and maybe outrage and maybe despair too. Better than the musty offices where the lawyers waited lurking among ghosts of old lusts and lies, or where the doctors waited with sharp knives and sharp drugs, telling man, believing that he should believe, without resorting to printed admonishments, that they labored for that end whose ultimate attainment would leave them with nothing whatever to do. And the women came too, the idle ones in bright and sometimes hurried garments, with secret and passionate and glittering looks and with secret frustrated breasts (who have ever loved death better than peace) to print with a myriad small hard heels to the constant murmur *Who did it? Who did it?* periods such as perhaps *Is he still free? Ah. Is he? Is he?*

This is a remarkable passage of condemnation, almost vituperation. It has two foundations, one in our understanding of Joanna built up in preceding chapters and another in an ironic statement of the distance between the town's false beliefs about Joanna and its contented hypocrisy about itself. The narrative presence is able to convey both the town's developing point of view of belief and his own ironic denial of the validity of this belief. The machinelike professional or vocational functions of individuals in the town (their adaptations of system) have so far supplanted humanity that their reaction is not feeling but rather outrage on Joanna's behalf (secretly, because she has attained peace, the narrative presence tells us). The fire is an excuse for a momentary escape from the unsatisfying mechanism their passionless and soulless pursuits have forced them into. The passage is a denunciation, self-contained on one page, of the emptiness of man's usual workaday pursuits and the hypocritical excuse this emptiness provides for his madness in crowds. It is as bitter a reading of human motivation as is to be found in Faulkner, and it rules all of this book's prior references to community.

The narrative presence has been unequivocal throughout. When Varner attempts to read Lena's mind, the narrative presence steps in to tell us, "She is not thinking about this at all." He reminds us again, about Byron, "Man knows so little about his fellows. In his eyes all men or women act upon what he believes would motivate him if he were mad enough to do what that other man or woman is doing." He then goes on to assert that no one (certainly not his landlady) knows of Byron's life beyond his work. Mechanics and automatism have supplanted human relationships. Each man moves in his own track until he happens to draw the attention of the mob. Then it moves toward him, not to care or help but to destroy. Behavioral mechanism is suggested in another of Byron's observations on Hightower's progress: "As though, Byron thought, the entire affair had been a lot of people performing a play and that now and at last they had all played out the parts which had been allotted them and now they could live quietly with one another." Byron also suggests that only he knows why Hightower sits in the window, that the town does not know that he sits there or know that Byron knows. As it turns out, even Byron does not know what Hightower sees from the window.

But failed knowledge is less important than failed caring. Byron observes of Brown: "The thing was, there was no reason why he should have had or have needed any name at all. Nobody cared, just as Byron believed that no one (wearing pants, anyway) cared where he came from nor where he went nor how long he stayed. Because wherever he came from and wherever he had been, a man knew that he was just living on the country, like a locust." There is a kind of resigned inevitability in the town's insistence on the uncaring automatism of its behavior: "Then the town was sorry with being glad, as people sometimes are sorry for those whom they have at last forced to do as they wanted them to." Individuals are caught each in his own, largely self-made, pattern, and the community is caught in a pattern of automatic recurrence of boredom and automatic relief in righteous outrage. The stage is set for a terrible collision.

> Later, as the town quieted for the night, . . . Grimm's platoon began to drop off too. He did not protest, watching them coldly; they became a little sheepish, defensive. Again without knowing it he had played a trump card. Because of the fact that they felt sheepish, feeling that somehow they had fallen short of his own cold ardor, they would return tomorrow if just to show him. . . .
> Somehow the very sound of the two words [Grand Jury] with their evocation secret and irrevocable and something of a hidden and unsleeping and omnipotent eye watching the doings of men, began to reassure Grimm's men in their own makebelieve. So quickly is man unwittingly and unpredictably moved that without knowing that they were thinking it, the town had suddenly accepted Grimm with respect and perhaps a little awe and a deal of actual faith and confidence, as though somehow his vision and patriotism and pride in the town, the occasion, had been quicker and truer than theirs. His men anyway assumed and accepted this; after the sleepless night, the tenseness, the holiday, the suttee of volition's surrender, they were almost at the pitch where they might die for him, if occasion arose. They now moved in a grave and slightly aweinspiring reflected light which was almost as palpable as the khaki would have been which Grimm wished them to wear, wished that they wore, as though each time they returned to the orderly room they dressed themselves anew in suave and austerely splendid scraps of his dream.

A system is accepting converts and they will be able to move in a dance called not by themselves but by something higher. Community has finally taken its final shape. After starting as something we could almost share, passing through a stage which invited our conventional disapproval of its conventional smugness, it has passed from the dissatisfying mechanism of individual tasks into the terrifying form of the collective individual, happily donning the uniform of an adopted system, an adopted ideal, an adopted force, more attractive than individual feeling because it is potent, committed, idealistic—more dangerous for the same reasons. We have known that the town was capable of this since chapter 4, but only now does the full impact of that capability emerge. Then it was only a crucible for the production of frustration. Now it is a power unto itself.

Percy Grimm's individual destiny has just the characteristics which make it perfect for combination with the community's. His past never was—or rather he manufactures a past out of what he wasn't, repairing the lack of the war out of due time, now, in the present. His present, then, is a recompense for what his past failed to supply. He is madder than McLendon of "Dry September" in that he is trying to recapture what he never had in the first place. He is somewhat similar to Hightower: both are what the community has made them; in both a lack of *was* has led to a failure of *is*. But Grimm is striving to change the town's memory of him, and Hightower is striving to remain safely within the memory the town had made of him. Grimm, unlike Hightower, is the collective individual in small, seeking gratification in recapturing a power he never had. Thus the pattern of his part of the narrative corresponds so closely to the pattern of the whole that he operates the way we expect characters in novels to act, as functions of the advance of the whole (unlike Joe and Lena and Hightower).

The narrative, then, does not attempt to form an alliance between us and community. Yet in the confusion of conflicts between individual parts and collective whole our first instinct is to find a safe alliance or identification—someone to act as our locus if not as our guide. In *As I Lay Dying* we could elect to adopt Darl as guide to both general complexity and difficult individual relationship. He failed in the end and was carted off, but he served the purpose for most of the book. Here no one gets quite far enough away from involvement in events (as Darl does there through formulations and his dedication to abstraction) to act as our constant guide, or even to provide some indication of a direction to follow. Byron comes closest because he has greater objectivity about himself than the others. In chapters 17 and 18 this objectivity is called into question and he finally proves it to have been self-deception, but his questioning process even here is more objective than anyone else's. Lena, of course, is the most consistent force in the book, but we cannot accept her as guide because we cannot share enough of her approach to things—we don't know what it is.

But we need a guide for *Light in August* because, with the mixture of subjective intimacy and objective coldness, we have been given no consistent pattern of *us* and *them*. We at least tentatively empathize with Lena and Byron: Byron as perfect expositor delivers exposition to Hightower, the perfect straight man for exposition, and the burden of exposition is one of the constant characteristics of narrative locus of the *us*-surrogate. The man with the facts not only attracts our identification with him as he is delivering them but makes us tend to look to him in the future for more explanation. And this is a book in which eagerness for explanation, or expectation that explanation is possible, is one of the reader's most strongly felt responses. That Lena and Byron escape from the town and, to a certain extent, from its guilt and the local web of inevitability, gives them the added attraction of Ishmaels. And as with Ishmael, personal peculiarities or moments of doubt are less significant for us in the final accounting than is the fact of escape.

The Lena–Byron portions then make one locus. Hightower serves as mediator of action between this group of actions and some actions even more remote than his own, with Byron acting as information-giver and Hightower as Hearer. We can assert from this a rather clumsy order for our identification with the book's actions—a division of individuals into us-figures, mediator, and others: one part to share with us and provide for our escape, connected through another part to the more remote events of Joe Christmas.

But the trouble (and here the complexities of our several relationships to individual characters and their individual narrative patterns are most apparent) is that we spend so much of our time caring about and empathizing with Joe. He can't be our guide, but he is our center: we cannot escape with him but we find ourselves caring most about his fate. We can measure some of this strange empathy by the distance we feel from Byron when he shows marked indifference to Joe in trying to protect Lena. Even the characters in the book who are able to care cannot care for Joe or affect what must be for him. They can listen and sometimes comprehend, but they can never understand or enter into his situation.

We can—more than Byron or Hightower, and more important, more than Joe can. We can see the structures, archetypes, and individuals which must attract him, reject him, spell his doom, because we hold (by virtue of what his part of the narrative has given us) more knowing than he can call up by remembering. Compare what we share with Joe with the way we came to share the collective memory in "Emily." There we move backward in the narrative in three steps and forward in ten, so that by the time we return to the present we have not only been given the memory but have been taken up in some of the processes of remembering. Here we build up experience as Joe does, but do so in very short compass, so tangibly and with such compression that it is possible for us to remember everything—even some that he forgets.

We know in abstraction and retain all. Joe knows in totality and retains only shapes and repetitions. Byron knows of Joe what he hears. The town knows next to nothing and supplies its lack with ready-made archetypal beliefs about what it thinks he is—a nigger and a mad-dog killer. Again the central pattern seems to return to knowing and not knowing (as in the community's knowledge), the distance between what is and what is thought to be, the town's objective formulations from appearance and Joe's subjective compulsion from his past.

This split between *us*-surrogate and the book's strongest empathy does not help to resolve its unity. The independence of the progress of individual parts from the progress of other parts and from the progress of the whole will never, of course, yield a perfectly gratifying unity. This lack of schematic unity is surely part of its conscious design: part of the book's impact rests on the failure of its cosmos to provide unity for anything but disaster.

The solution of the problems of the rather enigmatic ending helps a bit. If we can connect even the surface of the Byron-Lena-Hightower events to the Christmas events we will have something. But there is a problem in even this minimal unity of surface: If Christmas exists only to bring Hightower to self-realization, then he died in vain, since we never find out if that realization is significant or just a momentary interlude before another surrender to the mad galloping hooves. The failure of this surface connection provides a clue: if the book is seen as a double structure on the surface, one part leading up to the death of Joe and the other to the birth of Lena's baby, some rude unity emerges. Byron and Hightower are the mediators—Byron because he must get involved with Joe's problems in order to help Lena, Hightower because the town's pursuit of Joe is parallel to his exile by the congregation and because he involuntarily becomes involved with Joe's end. The birth of Lena's baby is, of course, connected by Mrs. Hines with the birth of Joe, but this is just frosting on the cake in the manner of Faulkner's other rather offhand Christ-parallels. The birth releases Brown and frees the Hineses to return to Mottstown. It also confronts Byron with reality and prepares him for his decision, which eventually delivers him from entrapment in *was* and provides for a change in Lena's station from a prisoner of the automatic kindness and secret cruelty of strangers to an open situation in which she can move by her own volition to her own ends. In terms of freedom and the freeing of individuals, the birth is as significant as Joe's death is in terms of final entrapment.

To insist upon a double surface structure resolves most of the apparent confusions of the ending. Our most intimate glimpse of High-tower and his most realistic view of himself must come at chapter 20 because it must be triggered by Joe's death. But more important, it has to come there because it must come after it is too late to do any good for anything or anyone at all except perhaps Hightower himself (and, of course, the book). It moves Hightower into a tragic measure (depending on how one reads the permanence of his realization and the prevalance of his tendency to madness) and provides the book with a time lapse in which what has happened has time to sink in—that we have been less moved by the whole event than by each of the individual narratives of its parts, that what we have seen has told more than it revealed at the time, that meaning here is a matter of making a number of leaps of faith. Then Byron and Lena must get together in the last chapter, at even greater distance from us, and escape.

The ending is more than Jane Austen's tidying up in the last chapter and sending all the Bennet sisters down the road into the future. It is an escape which we must hear about from a distance because for us as for Hightower, the past and what has happened have become more important, and form more of the core of the meaning of our experience of the book, than they have for anyone who has escaped. We retain every-thing they have lost in the process. The ending does not even bring us to an apt tidying up, but indeed to a point beyond any surface ending.

This sort of unity is no answer to Cowley's reading, of course. But it is to my colleague who puzzled over the book's aura of evil. And for this the narrative devices which indicate the particular origins of a particular past are less significant than the structures of the whole which act to frustrate any such fictional certainty. *Light in August* is, after all, less a definition of the origins of good and evil than it is a profound moral and philosophical ambiguity. What falls into place in the book, the climaxes of decision and motivation, seem to be attempts at solving the *why* which events have raised rather than just bringing to conclusion the *whats:* hence the backward movement of each of the discrete parts in the slow chronological movement forward. As Faulkner traces back through a sequence toward a cause or back through a biography toward a root event, we discover that he is giving us only so much and no more. Faulkner continally indicates—in narrative structure, in time disjunction, in the overt statements of the narrative presence—that we should seek explanation and answer in the cause rather than in its effects, in the source which (he indicates) the reader has perhaps slighted in his rush to conclusions. Then he traces out a pattern of multiple roots and continual conditioning which finally suspends moral and philosophical certainty between the opposed mirrors of multiple cause and magnified effect. The time structure and its searchings for cause in individual pasts are continually building up our information, accumulating more and more materials for subjective understanding. Our alliance with particular individuals grows as the book proceeds. At the same time a rudimentary alliance with the community of the town, established early in Armstid and Varner and in the sawmill group's examination of Joe and Lucas, gradually decays. In other words, the time structure and the progress of individuals reveal a growth of the subjective and internal, the whole and the groupings reveal a structure of the objective and distant. Our search for general principles is frustrated by our knowledge of particular exceptions.

Sanctuary dealt with an amoral cosmos: the stock good of innocence in Temple and the stock evil of corruption in Popeye are unaffected either by the immanent force of Nature's traditional order or the justifying redressal of the society's established forms. The effects were ironically detached from their causes in a mythical universe of mistaken execution and accidental blooming, arbitrary reward and punishment. Gratuitous circumstance led to arbitrary fate. *Light in August* is neither so ironic nor so detached. There is a sense here that a cause exists for every effect, but its source may be rather accidental and cause wildly disproportionate effect. Everyone in the book pursues his own ends in a world filled with combinations and patterns in other humans which may at any moment turn against him. Each plows a mined field without a map: apparently no conventional guide to virtue will see him safely through. The community proves that it is not enough to mind one's own business, but in taking up with Percy Grimm, it questions the advantage of an abstract ideal. Bunch finds that even caring can be carried too far—into a form of blindness, and Hightower concludes that there is no haven in the present or safety in the future. Our sense of relief in following Byron and Lena out of the book at the end is not just a product of our identification with them, but the strong feeling that having escaped from the community they (and we with them) have escaped from the world of the book.

Light in August gives us at once a growing faith in our knowledge of details and a profound chaos in structure. We can always approach the truth about the characters and the events and the meanings in the book, continually coming closer and closer; but the surrounding meetings, confrontations, and combinations between individuals retain their essential and evocative mystery, the ambiguity of life. What the book makes for us while we are reading it differs from what it makes after we have read it and are away from it. It combines *As I Lay Dying*'s satisfaction of pattern with *Sanctuary*'s mythic and brooding world.

Tour de force I suppose it is not (in spite of the characters of Joe and Hightower) because, as with any product of literary genius, it is impossible to maintain the assumption that it was written by one man who intended all the meanings and structures which emerge from it. But if it is possible to maintain a binocular vision—to see with one eye Old Bill snapping his galluses and talking about storytelling and with the other to see objectively the effect upon us of the death of Christmas—then literary genius must exist.

IRVING HOWE

"The Wild Palms"

M ost of Faulkner's influential critics have agreed that *The Wild Palms* is a failure and that its two intersecting stories—"Wild Palms" and "Old Man" need not be printed together as they were in the original edition. In his *Portable Faulkner* Malcolm Cowley reprints "Old Man" by itself; other editors and publishers have followed his lead. I propose to question this view, both as regards the structure and value of the novel. By looking somewhat closely at their plots, it should be possible to see whether the two parts of the book are genuinely bound together through theme and atmosphere.

A study in middle-class romanticism, "Wild Palms" is probably the most depressing and painful narrative Faulkner has ever written, if only because the self-destruction of its characters proceeds from a desire in itself admirable. The story opens at the point where the disintegration of its leading figures is almost complete. Charlotte Rittenmeyer, a young woman of powerful ego and compulsive sexuality, and Harry Wilbourne, a rather pliant hospital interne, leave New Orleans after a brief, intense love affair. Charlotte abandons a conventional marriage, Harry the promise of a conventional career. Together they seek a life beyond the city, uncertain whether their rebellion is against bourgeois norms or the very fact of society itself. This confusion of purpose is to be a major source of their troubles, for only if controlled by a precise awareness of both goal and limits could their flight possibly succeed. Soon their behavior seems a painful demonstration of how perilous the romantic view of life can be, how violently it can exhaust and then consume those who are most loyal

From *William Faulkner: A Critical Study.* Copyright © 1951, 1952 and 1975 by Irving Howe. The University of Chicago Press.

to it—romantic in this instance signifying a refusal to live by any terms except those which cannot be enforced. As Charlotte tells Harry:

> Listen; it's got to be all honeymoon, always. Forever and ever, until one of us dies. It can't be anything else. Either heaven, or hell; no comfortable safe peaceful purgatory between for you and me to wait in until good behavior or forbearance or shame or repentance overtakes us.

Charlotte is not a fool; if she were, "Wild Palms" could not build up to the tension it does. She can be so fanatically self-destructive as to demand "all honeymoon, always," but she can also express her outlook in terms that are more impressive: " 'They say love dies, between two people. That's wrong. It doesn't die. It just leaves you, goes away, if you are not good enough, worthy enough. It doesn't die; you're the one that dies.' "

The two young people believe they are turning to a blazing sensuous life, an utter purity of instinct and touch. Their relationship is eagerly, programmatically physical; only the clash of bodies, they feel, is an act free of social deceit. Charlotte wants no disabling or melting tenderness. She makes love to Harry by "striking her body against him hard, not in caress but exactly as she would grasp him by the hair to wake him from sleep." The comparison is acute. Vital enough to strain for a release of suppressed energies, courageous and admirable in her readiness to take chances, Charlotte deceives herself only in supposing that an unencumbered act of natural living, an embrace of the sun, can be a sufficient means toward personal fulfillment.

Charlotte and Harry wander off to Chicago; they have difficulty in finding work but that is not their most vexing problem. What really troubles them is that in rejecting the impersonality of the city and the deadness of middle-class existence they cannot find a way of life that might transcend the violence of their rejection. They trap themselves in a frozen gesture of protest, beyond which they cannot move. As soon as they begin eating regularly they wonder if they are not in danger of sliding into bourgeois complacence. To avoid this danger they abandon the city, moving to a desolate mining camp in Utah. Faulkner is crucially involved in this flight, for he has nothing in common with the middle-aged wisdom—perhaps merely middle-aged resignation—which would sneer at it. He is always ready to extend his sympathy to anyone who lives to the limit of power or desire. Yet he is also perceptive enough to see that the flight of Charlotte and Harry is fundamentally incoherent; and in a biting passage he shows the civilization from which the lovers had fled seeping into the remote mining camp—Harry is cheated of his wage, he has to perform an illegal abortion on the supervisor's wife: again, the moral ugliness of the city.

Destitute, the lovers drift south, back to the Mississippi basin, where Charlotte reveals herself to be pregnant and Harry performs his second abortion, this time a failure. Now, in the opening scene of the novel, the couple is living in penniless inertia, Charlotte resentful and broken, Harry a cartoon of the independent man he had hoped to become. When Charlotte dies after the botched abortion, Harry is taken off to prison, there to nurture memories of love, in safety and emptiness—yet not total emptiness, for in some desperate way he remains faithful to the vision he could not live by. In jail he experiences a moment of overwhelming, perhaps fulfilling, reflection:

> . . . and in the night he could face it, thinking *Not could. Will. I want to. So it is the old meat after all, no matter how old. Because if memory exists outside the flesh it won't be memory because it won't know what it remembers so when she became not then half of memory became not and if I become not then all of remembering will cease to be.—Yes*, he thought, *between grief and nothing I will take grief.*

Thrusting its characters into a fierce, somewhat muddled yet ultimately impressive struggle against reality, "Wild Palms" elevates that struggle to a principle of life: "Love and suffering are the same thing . . . the value of love is the sum of what you have to pay for it . . ." But the story also complicates and partly abandons this romantic view. The destination of flight proves as unacceptable as its starting point, perhaps because finally there is not so much difference between the two. Neither society nor isolation can satisfy Charlotte, and Harry's satisfaction is but a dependency of hers. Living too rigidly by a preconceived code, which transforms her passion for freedom into a mode of self-tyranny, she destroys both herself and her lover. The destruction, as I say, is impressive, far more so than the usual run of adjustments; still, it is destruction. So streaked is the life of Charlotte and Harry with the neurotic colors of the world they refuse, so fanatical is their fear of a settled existence, that they render themselves unfit for the natural haven to which they would retire. In the most extreme rural isolation they continue to live by the standards of the city, and at the end it is Harry's ineptness at abortion, a technique of civilization, which causes their catastrophe. Between the city from which they would escape and the natural world they dream of finding, there is no intermediate area of shade and rest. The act of rejection having consumed their energies, nothing remains for the act of living.

A simpler story, "Old Man" concerns an unnamed Mississippi convict. "About twenty-five, flat-stomached, with a sunburned face and Indian-black hair and pale, china-colored, outraged eyes," this tall convict, as he is called, is one of Faulkner's natural men. Limited in mental power, he is superbly in control of his immediate environment and endowed with a fine, even overacute sense of moral obligation. He has, however, grown so accustomed to the harsh security of the prison-farm that he does not take his freedom when he can.

Brought with other convicts to the Mississippi River to help control a flood, the tall convict is instructed to rescue a woman perched on a cypress snag and a man stranded on a cotton-house roof. Rowing furiously, he finds the woman, who is far gone in pregnancy, and through his instinctive skill in adapting himself to the river they manage to drift crazily down the flood waters. Neither intimacy nor affection sweetens the life of convict and woman; two people thrown together, they must cooperate if they are to survive, but more they will not do. It is a kind of honesty, free of the language of romanticism.

The woman, helped by the convict, has her baby. At the first mouth of the river they end their journey, settling in Cajun country where the convict becomes the partner of an alligator hunter and again, with his marvellous affinity to natural life, proves highly successful. For the first time freedom tempts him: "Yes. I reckon I had done forgot how good making money was. Being let to make it . . . I had forgot how it is to work." But a malicious twist of circumstances forces him to leave the alligator country and return to the prison area. "Yonder's the boat," he tells the prison guard, "and here's the woman. But I never did find that bastard on the cotton house." A final cut of injustice, the climax of "Old Man" is the sentencing of the convict to ten more years for "attempted escape." What impresses him more than this injustice, however, is his memory of how difficult it was to rid himself of the pregnant woman during his time of freedom. As in most Faulkner novels, freedom proves to be elusive, and when found, limited.

Simply sketched, these are the plots of "Wild Palms" and "Old Man." Faulkner has divided each story into five parts, alternating a part from one with a part from the other. To follow the pattern of the novel, envisage an interweaving of the following sections:

"WILD PALMS"	"OLD MAN"
1. Failure of abortion, Charlotte close to death.	2. Convict leaves for flood.
3. Flashback: Charlotte and Harry leave New Orleans.	4. "Lost" in flood.

5. Flashback: drifting from country to Chicago.

6. Drifting with pregnant woman on flood waters.

7. Flashback: haven in a mining camp.

8. Haven with Cajun.

9. Charlotte's death, Harry's imprisonment.

10. Return to prison.

Is this crossing of stories mechanical and arbitrary? That Faulkner may have composed them separately and then spliced them together is not very important; the problem is, why did he connect these two stories in so unusual a way? He has said that "I did send both stories to the publisher separately and they were rejected because they were too short. So I alternated the chapters of them." But he has also referred to *The Wild Palms* as one story of "two types of love," and has recently declared that he wrote "Old Man" to bring the other story "back to pitch" by contrast with its "antithesis." The remark is very shrewd, for "Wild Palms" by itself is almost intolerably painful and needs very much to be brought "back to pitch."

Even a glance at the above pattern of the novel should show some rough parallels between the two stories. There is the possibility that if taken together they will yield a dissonant irony or "counterpoint" which neither could yield alone. The possibility that any two stories by the same writer could be made to yield interesting contrasts and continuities cannot be denied; but at stake here is a relation much more detailed and intimate. Each story charts an escape from confinement to a temporary and qualified freedom and then to an ultimate, still more confining imprisonment. Two opposite intentions—one derived from extreme romanticism, the other a grudging response to circumstances—lead to the exhaustion of both intern and convict, and in that exhaustion there is a kind of common fate. Coincidence this may be, but the correspondences and joined oppositions between the two stories are so numerous and suggestive that we are obliged to take them seriously, as elements of a literary design.

Both the intern and the convict are socially homeless men who discover how intractable the world can be and how little one's hopes and ideas can move it. They are radically different men, but in the end the differences do not count for much. The convict is more resourceful and creative than the intern, perhaps because he is able to float upon the wave of circumstance rather than to dash himself against it. Where the convict helps bring new life into the world, though admittedly life for which he has no more than an abstract responsibility, the intern can only abort— and that unsuccessfully. In "Old Man" the life principle does rise to a rueful sort of triumph, yet it brings neither resolution nor satisfaction: it is a triumph that simply keeps the circle of existence turning. In "Wild Palms" a diseased hunger, not merely for life but also for clamping a rigid scheme upon life, becomes the catastrophe.

Still, in noting such contrasts we should not succumb to any pat assumption that Faulkner favors the convict over the intern, primitivism over civilization, nature over the city. The survival of the convict, ambiguous triumph though it may be, has been purchased at the price of a self-denial of personality, a rather awesome suppression of natural desires, and a loss of the vision of freedom—none of which either the characters of "Wild Palms" or Faulkner himself could tolerate. If in some sense the convict proves to be more durable than the intern, there is no reason (except an indulgence in literary primitivism) to ignore the cost of that durability. At the end both men are trapped, and the familiar distinction between will and fate, character and circumstance tends to be dissolved into an ironic perception of their gradual merger.

Faulkner, I think, lends conditional assent to the rebellion of Charlotte and Harry, but with the tacit warning that rebellion becomes suicidal if pressed to a fanatic grasping for total freedom. "Old Man," with a good many sardonic qualifications, proposes a counter-term of acceptance, but this too is carried to an extreme by the convict. Rebellion and acceptance, by the end of the book, shrink in importance beside the overwhelming fact of exhaustion.

In both stories the imprisonment of the leading character is at least partly due to excesses of conscience and ideal, and Faulkner's implicit conclusion—one may decide—is that our emotional economies thrive best on restraint. But when reading the novel itself, this is hardly the impression one is left with. The idea of restraint as a possible resolution seems, for this book, too distant and contained, inadequately rooted in the actual happenings, not a genuine option. At some points it may dimly visit us, but the true and overpowering energy of the book is directed toward another idea: that a suffering man encounters his fate through a total fulfillment of his chosen task. Both intern and convict are caught up in floods, the one a flood of passion, the other a flood of nature, the one a flood wilfully sought after, the other a flood that cannot be escaped. It hardly matters, the novel seems to say, which kind of flood a man lives through; in the end it will break him, and his humanity will be marked by the fullness, the courage of his struggle against it.

The Wild Palms points to the gap between aspiration and realization, the way in which the incommensurable becomes man's fate; and it suggests that this fate cannot be avoided through rebellion or acceptance, aggression or passivity. In the world of this novel, as perhaps in the world of all Faulkner's novels, emotion exceeds possibility, response fails situation, and for the welling of human passion there is never a properly receptive object. It is perceptions such as these which lie behind the strain and fury of Faulkner's prose, and which it is the function of the double plot in *The Wild Palms* both to release and qualify.

By starting "Wild Palms" near its climax, Faulkner magnifies its painfulness, for once he turns to trace the history of Charlotte and Harry it is impossible to feel any hope for them. "Old Man," beginning at its chronological outset and sweeping forward with a humorous and rhythmic equanimity, serves as emotional ballast. The two stories, it should be noted, are of unequal merit and interest, "Old Man" being much superior simply as a piece of writing and "Wild Palms" touching upon problems that are likely to seem more urgent to a modern reader. "Old Man" releases Faulkner's gifts for the fabulous, a mode of narrative in which a human action can be subsumed under, and gain magnitude from, an imposing event in nature. "Wild Palms," because so much of the behavior of its two lovers is caused by a wilfulness bordering on stupidity, cannot reach the tragic limit toward which it strains. Uncertain in its treatment of Northern locale, the story suffers even more seriously from a grating hysteria, an eagerness to hoard and multiply pain, and Faulkner's desperate— yet in some ways admirable—involvement with the two lovers. But whatever one's judgment of the stories, they do sustain each other through a counterpoint of response and should be printed, as they were offered, together.

Probably of little use to anyone but himself, Faulkner's device of alternating sections of the two stories may be judged a *tour de force* that partly succeeds. The novel can hardly be considered one of Faulkner's major works: it will not bear comparison with *The Sound and the Fury* or *Light in August*. But neither is it the negligible effort or outright failure it is too often taken to be. A serious, occasionally distinguished book which contains some admirable parts and is arresting in its general scheme and intent, *The Wild Palms* merits our respect.

HUGH KENNER

The Last Novelist

The *Sound and the Fury* (1929); it is permissible to dislike it; there are things that are important beyond all this fedaddle. Reading it, however, with perfect contempt for it, one discovers:

> I ran down the hill in that vacuum of crickets like a breath travelling across a mirror. . . .

and

> The shell was a speck now, the oars catching the sun in spaced glints, as if the hull were winking itself along. . . .

and

> . . . the last light supine and tranquil upon tideflats like pieces of broken mirror. . . .

These are all from Part II, the monologue of Quentin Compson, where the quotabilities swarm. The high finish on the language of Quentin Compson (obit June 2, 1910, in Cambridge, Mass., by suicide [drowning]) suggests that he has, like Stephen Dedalus, "aesthetic" affiliations; sure enough, he is partly traceable to a drowned Pierrot in a one-act play, *Marionettes*, written by the undergraduate William Faulkner circa 1920.

In those years William Faulkner affected a cane and was nicknamed "The Count." He was writing imitations of Verlaine and Mallarmé and Austin Dobson, and drawing competent black-and-white designs that descend from Beardsley via Art Nouveau. The young folk in the drawings—

From *A Homemade World: The American Modernist Writers*. Copyright © 1975 by Hugh Kenner. Alfred A. Knopf, Inc., 1975.

rhythmically posed, toes pointed, faces afloat in consummate boredom—are the very dandies and flappers whose apotheosization by John Held, Jr., would later itself apotheosize the twenties. Seeing Faulkner's renderings next to Faulkner's poems of the same period, in the little posthumous book called *Early Prose and Poetry*, we cannot miss seeing how that particular line of American iconography stemmed from a British decadence by then twenty-five years gone: from *The Yellow Book*, say, and from rumors of *Under the Hill*. The naughty young folk of the twenties, the flaming youth by whom buyers of Horace Liveright books were so deliciously scandalized, played solemnly at an historical charade which they innocently ascribed to modern facilities, notably bathtub gin and Stutz roadsters, and Scott Fitzgerald's corresponding rhetoric—the moth, the pink dawn, the tuning fork struck on a star—uncannily recreates from blurred exemplars the vocabulary of Pierrot-and-Columbine poems he may not even have read.

Having a more orthodox literary sensibility than had Fitzgerald, Faulkner began writing with a clearer idea of the sources from which the American twenties were derived. In the year in which Fitzgerald was basing the rhetoric of *The Beautiful and Damned* on Compton Mackenzie and Michael Arlen (not to mention Mencken and Nathan), Faulkner was making verse pastiches of the nineties which Mackenzie and Arlen echo.

> Columbine leans above the taper flame:
> Columbine flings a rose.
> She flings a severed hand at Pierrot's feet.
>
> Behind, a perpendicular wall of stars,
> Below, a gleam of snows.
> Pierrot spins and whirls, Pierrot is fleet;
> He whirls his hands like birds upon the moon. . . .
>
> Swift the wisps of motion blown across the moon;
> Columbine flings a paper rose,—
> Pierrot flits like a white moth on blue dark. . . .

White moth, blue dark: Wallace Stevens fiddled with pretty patterns like that, when he was finding ways to make his language as arbitrary as he sensed it had to be. But Stevens had no taste for the color of spilled blood this aestheticism used to attract. Faulkner had. "She flings a severed hand at Pierrot's feet": the Salome motif is detectable, and the severed head of St. John as Mallarmé and Flaubert celebrated it, with for visual counterpart the bejeweled savagery Gustave Moreau gave it in the painting that Mallarmé prized. Faulkner's miscalled Mississippi Gothic is more nearly a Mississippi aestheticism. The savageries his blood-saturated rustics ritualize are of frozen Art Nouveau sumptuousness. The diction of his mature novels too keeps remembering these Art Nouveau beginnings.

> When laggard March, a faun whose stampings ring
> And ripple the leaves with hiding: vain pursuit
> Of May's anticipated dryad, mute
> And yet unwombed of the moist flanks of spring . . .
> (1925)

is comparable with

> There is the one fierce evening star, though almost at once the marching constellations mesh and gear and wheel strongly on. Blond too in that gathering last of light, she owns no dimension against the lambent and undimensional grass. . . .
> (1940)

in its trick of playing verbal affinities across syntactic ones, so that we barely trouble to follow the syntax (in the poem it is not there to be followed) and receive the words in chewy gobbets: "unwombed of the moist flanks of spring"; "no dimension against the lambent and undimensional grass." This *impasto* of diction has affinities with *Symbolisme*, with for instance

> Mon doute, amas de nuit ancienne, s'achève
> En maint rameau subtil, qui, demeuré les vrais
> Bois mêmes, prouve, hélas! que bien seul je m'offrais
> Pour triomphe la faute idéale de roses.

—"L'Après-Midi d'un Faune," Mallarmé, 1876; and Faulkner's first published writing was a poem in the *New Republic* (August 6, 1919) called "L'Après-Midi d'un Faune."

Mallarmé's effort, he let readers of his prose understand, was toward simultaneity, the successive words dissociations of a chord. Some words in every language seem triumphantly expressive: *crimson* (to invent an English example), a sumptuous word for a sumptuous color. Others seem perfunctory: *red* shirks the simulation of blood and fire. And some words we may want are simply lacking: we must synthesize. Making up for these deficiencies, thought Mallarmé, the line of verse offers its rituals in place of poor semantic designations. Were the words right, as in Adam's legendary speech, we should have no need to compose, no need for the poet to appease that disquiet

> Dont le frisson final, dans sa voix seule, éveille
> Pour la Rose et le Lys le mystère d'un nom.

Faulkner took a similar view of the writer's obligations. When in 1962 an undergraduate asked him directly about his run-on sentences and chaotic pronoun references, he adduced the desire of any painter, writer, musician, to reduce all that he has experienced to "one single tone or color or word, which is impossible."

> And the obscurity, the prolixity which you find in writers is simply that desire to put all that experience into one word. Then he has got to add another word, another word becomes a sentence, but he's still trying to get it into one unstopping whole—a paragraph or a page—before he finds a place to put a full stop.

"My ambition," he told Malcolm Cowley, "is to put everything into one sentence—not only the present but the whole past on which it depends and which keeps overtaking the present, second by second"—Mr. Faulkner, as he said in another connection, "trotting along behind" with paper and pencil.

A writer with ambitions of this order cannot but grow obsessed with ceaseless Time: the time that takes away syllables as they are uttered, eroding all possibility of that one polyvalent word; that consumes antecedent actions, compelling him to retrieve them by raids on the past; that consigns the vivid actual to myth; that segments and scatters and blurs and consumes all those lives, volitions, passions whose pressure on the momentary *now* lends it the meaning he sets out to capture—at what cost, in what serial stratagems. For the show of analysis, the show of syntax, are stratagems forced on the Symbolist by Time. Faulkner was neither an analytic nor a syntactic thinker, but a teaser into words, into sentences, paragraphs, chapters—all necessary, all unwelcome—of what was, to start with, a simple unverbalizable pulsating impulse.

On more than one occasion Eliot, another post-Symbolist, gave a not dissimilar account of how his poems were written. They began, he said, with a germinating *need*; the poet "does not know what he has to say until he has said it; and in the effort to say it he is not concerned with making other people understand anything. . . . He is going to all that trouble, not in order to communicate with anyone, but to gain relief from acute discomfort. . . ." This is a post-Symbolist embryology for post-Symbolist poems. Ben Jonson, who wrote out his sense in prose before finding verse, would have given a different account.

So Faulkner could recall after thirty-five years an aesthetic discomfort that commenced to alleviate itself as he visualized the muddy seat of a little girl's drawers: a "doomed little girl" climbing a pear tree to see a funeral: to see, more exactly, through the parlor window, "what in the world the grown people were doing that the children couldn't see." The ignorance of the muddy-seated little girl in the pear tree might effectively be redoubled, he supposed, by showing her "through the eyes of the idiot child who didn't even know, couldn't understand what was going on": death at a double remove of impercipience: an epiphanic moment suitable (he thought) for concentration onto a radiant pinhead, but apt to require in this imperfect world a few pages to get it all in. "I thought it was going to be a ten-page short story." Here is the germinal incident:

> "Push me up, Versh." Caddy said.
> "All right." Versh said. "You the one going to get whipped. I aint." He went and pushed Caddy up into the tree to the first limb. We watched the muddy bottom of her drawers. Then we couldn't see her. We could hear the tree thrashing.
> "Mr. Jason said if you break that tree he whip you." Versh said.
> "I'm going to tell on her too." Jason said.
> The tree quit thrashing. We looked up into the still branches.
> "What you seeing." Frony whispered.

This presents a scene but of course expresses nothing, since we do not know that it is death the house conceals. We need to know, and yet, by the Symbolist economy, we must not be told ("To name is to destroy," said Mallarmé.) We must gather it, then, from knowledges the children have. Thus they know that tonight authority is disrupted (" 'We've got company.' Caddy said. 'Father said for us to mind me tonight.' "). The Negro children, moreover, Frony and Versh, can know more than the white elders are allowing the white children to know, and can let things slip. Frony asks,

> "Is they started the funeral yet."
> "What's a funeral." Jason said.
> "Didn't mammy tell you not to tell them." Versh said.
> "Where they moans." Frony said. "They moaned two days on Sis Beulah Clay." . . .
> "Oh." Caddy said, "That's niggers. White folks dont have funerals."
> "Mammy said us not to tell them, Frony." Versh said.
> "Tell them what." Caddy said. . . .
> "I like to know why not." Frony said. "White folks dies too. Your grandmammy dead as any nigger can get, I reckon."

We are to imagine that an idiot is recalling this, in an idiot's eternal present. A work conceived as Faulkner conceived his art could hardly not have generated an idiot. The idiot's usefulness is that he can be supposed not to ask questions. His mind is a timeless mosaic of pieces, not even remembered as normal minds remember, but all on one plane of time, edge matching edge, associatively fitted. Questions entail time, sequence, consequence, but epiphanic visions disregard time. So it is in an idiot mind that the pieces whose interlocking may make this epiphanic vision intelligible can be supposed to exist uninterrogated. The mind of Benjy Compson is not a process, but a kind of *place* for the elements of the story to exist in. We need not be surprised to learn that he isn't, in medical terms, a plausible idiot, though a doctor writing in the *American Journal of Mental Deficiency* took the trouble to find him "fabricated," "stuffed," in fact "literary." Of course he is literary; no more than anything in literature is he a person. He is the name of a principle on which some 20,000 words are organized: about 100 pages, having finished which, said Faulkner, "I still hadn't told that story." The trouble with the idiot consciousness, otherwise so attractive, is that the reader can hardly make head or tail of its lucubrations.

Continuing the account of his struggles with *The Sound and the Fury*, Faulkner dropped into the readiest convention of his later years, the tall tale: "So I chose another one of the children, let him try. That went for a hundred pages, and I still hadn't told that story. So I picked out the other one, the one that was nearest to what we call sane to see if maybe he could unravel the thing. He talked for a hundred pages, he hadn't told it, then I let Faulkner try it for a hundred pages. And when I got done, it still wasn't finished" (though anyway it was published, 400 pages of it) "and so twenty years later I wrote an appendix to it, tried to tell that story."

He was a born storyteller, and this is itself a funny story: the future Nobel laureate struggling against hope, against language, against the grain of fiction, against the very nature of things, to show us nothing more than a child with muddy drawers peeping at a funeral, and not succeeding, not after two decades. It is myth; we are not to believe it; and yet it contains exegetical truth, displaying what forced him to make *The Sound and the Fury* so complicated. "That's all I was doing on the first page," he stated, "trying to tell what seemed to me a beautiful and tragic story of that doomed little girl climbing the pear tree to see the funeral." Yet it's an incident most readers will barely remember, the weight of the narrative having shifted so massively toward exegesis of that exact word "doomed." It is only because Caddy is "doomed" that her rearward aspect in the pear tree is "beautiful and tragic," and spinning the threads that will render her doom intelligible came to occupy most of the novel's space.

Her doom, as it proved, was not to be wholly specified until the 1945 Appendix, where we learn how Caddy's fortunes leaped not only out of the 1929 book but clear out of any conceivable circle of consciousness the 1929 book could have contained. Her trajectory brought her ("ageless and beautiful, cold serene and damned") to the shining car, and implicitly the bed, of a German staff general in occupied France: this, for a Mississippi Compson, a bitter, defiant, compounded harlotry: willed doom. In the 1929 novel she has simply been gone since 1911, when, cast off by her Indiana husband, she left her child (not his) at her family home and departed. True to the Symbolist principle of indirection, the novel concentrates on the doom of the child, from which we infer the scale of Caddy's doom. The novel, in fact, occupies itself with the child—no, it doesn't; she barely appears until it's more than half over. Start again. The novel, in fact, comes to theoretical focus around the child's decisive act of rebellion; for on April 8th of 1928 the child, named Quentin after her drowned uncle, "swung herself by a rainpipe from the window of the room in which her [other] uncle had locked her at noon" to the window of the uncle's bedroom, where she stole nearly $7,000 and "climbed down the same rainpipe in the dusk and ran away with the pitchman who was already under sentence for bigamy. And so vanished. . . ."

But wait, that's wrong too, though the wording is Faulkner's from the 1945 Appendix. The writer of the 1929 novel had specified several times that Miss Quentin climbed down the pear tree, the same in which her mother had sat with muddy drawers, and moreover had used it in the manner of the "Merchant's Tale": a mechanical allegory, this, which he himself forgot before Malcolm Cowley's enthusiasm for the coherence of the Yoknapatawpha Saga had spurred him to this piece of incoherence.

Let that pass. The novel (we were saying) comes to theoretical focus on this act of Miss Quentin's, because the idiot Benjy's monologue (Part I) is dated the day of the evening Miss Quentin went down the pear tree (or rainpipe), and incorporates ancillary glimpses we can't at that stage decipher—Miss Quentin in the swing with a vulgar fellow (*"They sat up in the swing quick. Quentin had her hands on her hair. He had a red tie."*), Miss Quentin spatting with her uncle Jason (*"I hate this house. I'm going to run away."*); moreover because uncle Jason's monologue (Part III) is dated the day before that, and details his effort to take charge of her, and his new policy of locking her up; and lastly because the final narrative (Part IV) begins on the morning after, when her absence is discovered and all hell breaks loose. So insofar as our impulse as we read is to make out what is happening in the novel, what we make out is Miss Quentin's flight.

Yet the flight is unimportant, just as Quentin herself is unimportant: a slatternly rebelliousness, thinly characterized. Though she does do something explicit, she is a peripheral character, really; a means for making known to us the estrangement, long before, of her mother,

Caddy, whom Faulkner first thought of as a little girl with muddy drawers, aloft in a pear tree. Quentin's promiscuity re-enacts Caddy's (and the idiot's glimpse of Quentin necking in a swing is confused, in a way rereading will only partly disentangle, with a similar earlier glimpse of Caddy). Quentin's flight with a carnival pitchman re-enacts Caddy's flight, the one that took her to a movie magnate's bed and later to a Nazi officer's. The rough-cast saliences, these are the things a good Symbolist avoids dwelling on: rather their torques, their eddies, their reflections. The doom of the doomed little girl, which is what all this started with, the doomed little girl in the tree, we glimpse refracted through the cheaper doom of her daughter, and through the exacerbations of the brother who was closest to her, the brother for whom she named that daughter, the brother who drowned himself in 1910 after spending the day we spend with him in Part II, where much poetry of death does not really declare his termination, any more than his incest with Caddy is declared. And the suicide, we understand at last, did occur, but the incest did not; Quentin consummated only one of the two violences that haunted him. (Only the Appendix really settles—if it does—the question whether the incestuous liaison of Quentin with Caddy occurred or not.)

What Quentin did do, when his sister gave herself to a lover, was offer to kill her; he held a knife to her throat, but somehow dropped it. She had thrown herself supine in shallow water, "her head on the sand spit the water flowing about her hips . . . her skirt half saturated," and with the knife at her throat Quentin remembered her earlier violation by muddy water:

> . . . do you remember the day damuddy died when you sat down in the water in your drawers
>> yes
> I held the point of the knife at her throat . . .

—Those muddy drawers again: a *leitmotif*. The day damuddy (grandmother) died she had muddied them out of willfulness. There is willfulness, too, in the saturated skirt today, the day she was violated (and let herself be). A symbol, then, of the degraded woman of the house of Compson? Rather, a piece of pathos on the earlier occasion, a novelist's linking device on the later. You haven't got time, Faulkner told a questioner, to be thinking about images and symbols. You've got all you can manage without that. Writing a novel, he said, is like trying to nail together a henhouse in a hurricane.

Faulkner's "symbols" have been talked about as loosely as those of his first mentors, the Symbolists, who used symbols seldom. The fault is as much his as anyone's. Nailing his henhouse of the moment together, he let matching knotholes guide his choice of boards, or remembered details from distinguished architects. When Caddy (on page 234) is reminded that her paw told her to stay out of that tree, and rejoins that that was a long time ago, we cannot put aside the thought that Faulkner has remembered something similar from the book of Genesis, without taking time (since the tree became a rainpipe later) to decide how seriously he meant us to dwell on the parallel. A Symbolist poem, like an ideal Faulkner novel—one of the archetypes we shall maybe read in Heaven—elaborates verbal formulae, verbal interactions, creating a world dense with specificity but difficult to specify. (The tree Caddy's paw told her to stay out of is just at that moment insufficiently verbal; it looms up, an Edenic allegory.) The Symbolist work, avoiding symbols, prolongs what it cannot find a way to state with concision, prolongs it until, ringed and riddled with nuance, it is virtually camouflaged by patterns of circumstance. (You cannot skim a Faulkner story.) With good will, an identifiable world emerges, which, seeing the lavish trouble the writer has taken, we are apt to try to "interpret." This is usually a mistake. It is a mistake to exclaim portentously over Caddy's muddied drawers, or to see the Doom of the Old South in the decline of the Compsons (though Faulkner himself, in ill-considered moments, spurs us on). Readers who want to see the Doom of the Old South in everything Faulkner contrived are indulging, probably, extra-literary satisfactions. He shows no special sign of thinking the Old South more doomed than any other sector of humanity. It was simply the sector he knew. The reader's desire to find symbols derives from the desire to interpret, which in turn is apt to be linked to the desire to be horrified by epiphanic goings-on in a region where one congratulates oneself on not living. Shakespeare's groundlings thought of Italy thus. *Mais la lecture ne peut pas y consister.*

For Faulkner's root need was not to symbolize (a condensing device) but to expand, expand: to commence with the merest glimpse and by way of wringing out its significance arrange voices and viewpoints, interpolate past chronicles, account for just this passion in just this ancillary passion, and tie the persons together, for the sake of intimacy, intensity, plausibility, with ties of blood and community and heritage.

Those, not the "symbols," are Faulkner's real ties. One can guess, for instance, what made him spatch in that Edenic allusion. He meant it not for a real allegory, but as notation for the child's puzzled attempt to understand what Death is, something portentous. All is portentous; all, in his sense of things (which was not Cartesian), must reach vaguely beyond itself. The fiction writer's plots, by emphasizing linkage and fit, tend to conceal that reach, which helps explain Faulkner's efforts to submerge his plots, sometimes in their own intricacies. He needed linkages that were not causal, that did not resemble the internal linkages of machines. What the Old South gave him, what is inseparable from his preferred way of working, making possible in fiction what is essentially a method for poetry, was a society of which he could plausibly postulate that everything in it affects everyone. He needed inarticulate blood ties. When he relaxed his reliance on the Old South, and tried instead (see A *Fable*) to project Significance with the help of Allegory, the result is dreadful. A parallel between 1918 events and events traditionally dated 33 A.D. was something his method simply could not assimilate. (What method could is a question we needn't face; but the bewilderment A *Fable*'s failure occasioned tells us something about the critics' misunderstanding of his method.)

And as no Faulkner incident can yield its significance until it has entangled circumambient lives and circumstances even to the third and fourth generations, so no Faulkner novel really cuts off at its boundaries. Characters pass from one to another, a story illuminates the early history of a family we will later meet in a novel, people in a new book serve as analogues and reflectors for other people the author conceived years previously. Jason Compson (*The Sound and the Fury*, 1929) is nowhere more devastatingly "located" than by the sentence (Appendix, 1945) that tells us he "competed and held his own with the Snopeses." The Snopeses, who run through Faulkner country like a geological fault (they "took over the little town following the turn of the century as the Compsons and Sartorises and their ilk faded from it"), came late into his chronicles if only because a man must do one thing at a time; though Flem Snopes is mentioned in *Sartoris* (1929), their full and manic proliferation commences only with *The Hamlet* (1940), which in turn grew out of the story called "Spotted Horses" (1932). When Malcolm Cowley first pointed out in 1945 how the Faulkner books interlock, nine of them were still to appear; ideally we should have his entire work before us at once, including—also, alas, ideally—the books he would have written in a second lifetime; which is only to say that his work was impossible to finish, and even, in detail, impossible to accomplish. God himself has not yet stopped.

As years went by, the vast interdependent *oeuvre* came to seem like a feat of planning, though it was more like a marathon improvisation. And the convention toward which his fictions approximated, retreating from the highly "literary" convention of *The Sound and the Fury*, a book written by a man who had just read *Ulysses*, was that of the tall tale spun on a timeless afternoon.

In having all time at his garrulous disposal, the taleteller is the next best thing to an idiot, and considerably more amenable to fiction. He needs no sense of proportion; he need not foreshorten; he can dilate, he can expatiate, he can make us grasp by sheer explicitness all that was so wonderful about the bare anecdote, filling in meditations, preliminaries, relationships. He can assume, moreover, that he need not think about how to perform the most troublesome of all the novelist's tasks, which is "introducing" characters, for we and he, our feet together at a wooden railing, know the town, know the families, know without being told those things the conventional novelist must be at pains to plant and develop and imply: who is whose cousin, who is whose natural father; who is rumored to carry Negro blood, whose fortunes despite appearance were long ago lost, whose brother rattles the bars of what remote jail.

> . . . this was not something participated in or even seen by himself, but by his elder cousin, McCaslin Edmonds, grandson of Isaac's father's sister and so descended by the distaff, yet notwithstanding the inheritor, and in his time the bequestor, of that which some had thought then and some still thought should have been Isaac's, since his was the name in which the title to the land had first been granted from the Indian patent and which some of the descendants of his father's slaves still bore in the land. . . .

"That which some had thought then and some still thought" isn't taleteller's speech—the quotation is from the formal overture to *Go Down, Moses*—but it uses as its convention the taleteller's attitude: that everyone knows these genealogies and these lines of inheritance, that from inside the community of taleteller and listeners they are not at all labyrinthine. Manipulating this convention, Faulkner can give us past deeds in a hieratic idiom, like that one, or in a colloquial idiom, like this one:

> And after that, not nothing to do until morning except to stay close enough where Henry can call her until it's light enough to chop the wood to cook breakfast and then help Mrs. Littlejohn wash the dishes and make the beds and sweep while watching the road. Because likely any time now Flem Snopes will get back from wherever he has been since the auction, which of course is to town naturally to see about his cousin that's got into a little legal trouble and so get that five dollars. 'Only maybe he won't give it back to me,' she says, and maybe that's what Mr. Littlejohn thought too, because she never said nothing. . . .

By the standards of *Madame Bovary* or of *Dubliners* or, for that matter, of *Tender Is the Night*, this is a miserable narrative technique. The lines of action do not stand clear at all. By the standards of local gossip it is phonographic realism. And by the standards of the kind of fiction Faulkner worked out over many years, it is vivid and funny provided you have learned to pay, in many preceding pages, the kind of attention by which you get the hang of the community almost like a native, and intuit the proper vectors when a name like "Flem Snopes" is simply mentioned.

But notice what has happened now. Out of its sheer need to keep spinning out circumstances, the arty mode of narration we encountered in *The Sound and the Fury* has in a very few years discovered a convention that makes it look artless. It is like the way Cubist drawings people thought "any child could do" evolved from an accomplished mode of portraiture that happened to contain within it the ambition to analyze space. The route the artist travels, that is what counts; and Faulkner came to the folk tale in a new way, which was not, for example, the *faux naïf* way of Sherwood Anderson.

The consequence is important to understand. Faulkner discovered, whether by cerebration or by trial and error, that the Symbolist expansion of an incident, provided we imagine the incident in a real world and not in an art-world like that of Mallarmé's *Igitur*, expands it into a kind of unbounded interrelatedness, the kind taletellers count on everyone knowing. The Symbolist's ideal timelessness becomes the taleteller's ideal leisure. Faulkner could therefore use the taleteller's convention as a natural expansion of the Symbolist's convention; could use it, even, to go on with a vast tapestry in which "Symbolist" fiction like *The Sound and the Fury* also figured, so that *The Sound and the Fury* comes to seem not a false start within the oeuvre but an integral part of it. And to this method Flaubert's kind of fiction, and Joyce's and Conrad's, the kind of fiction that underlay *The Sound and the Fury*, comes to seem irrelevant, since their well-made fiction postulates a self-contained artifact, bounded, integral.

Integritas, Stephen Dedalus thought, is the first thing we perceive, the self-sufficiency of the work before us; *consonantia* next, the interrelation of its parts (like those of a "machine made out of words") and lastly *claritas*, the radiant affirmation. But Faulkner seems not to care for such Grecian-urn criteria. A story, in his usage, was a unit of attention within the large *oeuvre*. The stories in *Go Down, Moses* make up a chronological panorama, the fine "Delta Autumn" not really intelligible without its five predecessors, and "The Fire and the Hearth" completed in curious ways by a different book altogether, by no means one of his best yet irreplaceable, *Intruder in the Dust*.

From nearly total neglect in the early 1940's, Faulkner by the 1960's had risen in critical esteem to the rank of major novelist. This happened in part because he was "ahead of his time," which means that a change in the assumptions of fiction occurred earlier in his work than it occurred in the mind of the reading public. His development, in short, was paradigmatic: a development that left the "closed" novel behind. The self-sufficient information machine, coextensive with its physical package, the equilibrium of geodesic forces *Ulysses* apotheosized, had become by the 1960's an elaborate practical joke, a strange end for the dominant literary form of nearly a hundred years.

Conrad and Ford Madox Ford and Joyce, all their generation in modernism's heroic age, had struggled to replace what seemed to them scribbled fiction with something both more artful and more real. (There was a time when *Ulysses* seemed raw life.) Their craft remains unimpugnable, but their image of life is no longer as plausible as it was. As assumptions neither he nor his readers were aware he was making now cause the work of the Victorian novelist to look "Victorian," so other assumptions of which no one was aware now stamp the enclosed fiction as the product of a time for which we do not yet have a label. One of these may have been the synecdochic assumption, the assumption that the part is eloquent of the whole, the remark of the mind, the behavioral tic of the person, so that the artist is an artisan of signifying parts, and the aesthetic whole a pre-established nestling of significances. Hence its cross-references; hence its ideal suitability to exegesis; and Joycean scholarship has virtually become part of Joyce's text. It is not surprising that the scholar became an absurdity, and the sleuth-eyed reader the butt of fictional jokes. So that great bounded work, with nestled within it all that might be required to minister to its understanding, the artifact in typographic space on the margins of which penciled notes could accumulate: this pantechnicon, this well-packed Ark, this (in Karl Shapiro's phrase) cuckoo clock of literature, is today, along with the scholarship it entails, a vehicle for erudite humor. When Nabokov's *Pale Fire* was greeted as a masterpiece the criteria of the "closed" novel were becoming absurd. How well *Pale Fire* answered to those criteria!—a novel's thousands of pieces shuffled and arranged, without loss of cohesion, to yield a 999-line poem and an obsessed commentator's 200 pages of scholarship. "It is one of the very great works of art of this century," said one of the century's more emphatic critics. But *Pale Fire* is a mirthless hoax and so is its successor, *Ada, or Ardor*: ingenious ships-in-bottles riding plastic seas to the awe of teaching assistants. Less vindictively hollow, Thomas Pynchon's *V*, amid its intricate promise of significances it is careful never to deliver, proclaims that all the world's a comic book. The big books that make a game of soliciting our note cards are mocked in John Barth's *Giles Goat-Boy*, which itself makes a hollow game of having been machine-written from computer cards. Barth next puts in a personal appearance ("bald as a roc's egg") in

Chimera, to explain to his two newest characters that he's at an impasse. "My name's just a jumble of letters; so's the whole body of literature: strings of letters and empty spaces, like a code that I've lost the key to." Strings of letters and empty spaces: much as the "classic" detective novel, that puzzle box, has died utterly away, the big book full of Piranesi corridors now insists on its own illusoriness, and fades.

And with it goes the sense of life it fostered: the dialogue exactly heard, honed, polished; the absolute scientific typicality that stemmed from Flaubert's notebooks where he wrote down what people *always* said, and that got arranged according to Ford's conviction that since people never listen to other people, a conversation in a novel should be a fugue of purposeful cross-purposes. The writing schools have taught these wiles so well they now seem formulaic.

JOHN T. IRWIN

Doubling and Incest

To what extent, then, does the story that Quentin tells in *Absalom* resemble his own life story in *The Sound and the Fury?* We noted first of all that Quentin's failure to kill Candace's seducer and thus fulfill the role of protective brother has its reverse image in Henry's murder of Bon to safeguard the honor of their sister. Also, Quentin's incestuous love for Candace is mirrored by Bon's love for Judith. That Quentin identifies with both Henry, the brother as protector, and Bon, the brother as seducer, is not extraordinary, for in Quentin's narrative they are not so much two separate figures as two aspects of the same figure. Quentin projects onto the characters of Bon and Henry opposing elements in his own personality—Bon represents Quentin's unconsciously motivated desire for his sister Candace, while Henry represents the conscious repression or punishment of that desire. This separation of the unacceptable elements from the acceptable elements in the self, this splitting of Quentin's personality into a bad half and a good half, with the subsequent tormenting of the good half by the bad and the punishment of the bad half by the good, involves a kind of narrative bipolarity typical of both compulsion neurosis and schizophrenia. The split is the result of the self's inability to handle ambivalence, in this case, Quentin's failure to reconcile his simultaneous attraction to and repulsion by the incestuous desire for his sister. The solution is primitive and effective: one simply splits the good-bad self into two separate people. Indeed, at the very beginning of the novel when he first visits Miss Rosa, Quentin is presented as a divided self: ". . . he would listen to two separate Quentins now—the Quentin Compson preparing for Harvard in the South, the deep South dead since 1865 and peopled with garrulous outraged baffled ghosts, listening, having to listen, to one of the ghosts which had refused to lie still even longer than most had, telling him about old ghost-times; and the Quentin Compson who was still too young to deserve yet to be a ghost, but nevertheless having to be one for all that, since he was born and bred in the deep South the same as she was—two separate Quentins now talking to one another in the long silence of notpeople, in notlanguage. . . ." If at points during the narrative Quentin divides his personality between the characters of Bon and Henry, at other points Henry and Bon merge into one figure by exchanging roles. For example, though Henry ends up as the avenging brother, yet, as Mr. Compson says, "it must have been Henry who seduced Judith, not Bon: seduced her along with himself. . . ." And though Bon dies playing the role of the dark seducer, yet he offers to give up Judith and never trouble the Sutpens again if his father will only acknowledge his existence. When Sutpen ignores him, Bon's deliberate provoking of Henry amounts almost to a suicidal self-punishment.

Clearly, the relationship between Henry and Bon is a form of doubling: the hero-worshiping Henry imitates Bon's manners, speech, and dress, while Bon (as Shreve conjectures) looks at Henry and thinks "not *there but for the intervening leaven of that blood which we do not have in common is my skull, my brow, sockets, shape and angle of jaw and chin and some of my thinking behind it, and which he could see in my face in his turn if he but knew to look as I know but there, just behind a little, obscured a little by that alien blood whose admixing was necessary in order that he exist is the face of the man who shaped us both out of that blind chancy darkness which we call the future; there—there—at any moment, second, I shall penetrate by something of will and intensity and dreadful need, and strip that alien leavening from it and look not on my brother's face whom I did not know I possessed and hence never missed, but my father's, out of the shadow of whose absence my spirit's posthumeity has never escaped."* On another occasion Bon, debating this family resemblance with himself, divides into two voices that reflect Quentin's own splitting: "one part of him said *He has my brow my skull my jaw my hands* and the other said *Wait. Wait. You cant know yet. You cannot know yet whether what you see is what you are looking at or what you are believing."* That last remark is an apt description as well of Quentin's relationship to the story of Charles Bon, for it is impossible for us to tell whether many of the things that Quentin says about Bon are what he knows or what he simply believes.

In the doubling between Bon and Henry, Bon plays the role of the shadow—the dark self that is made to bear the consciously unacceptable desires repudiated by the bright half of the mind. Throughout the novel, Bon is identified with the image of the shadow. Mr. Compson speaks of Bon's "impenetrable and shadowy character. Yes, shadowy: a myth, a phantom: something which they engendered and created whole themselves; some effluvium of Sutpen blood and character, as though as a man he did not exist at all." Miss Rosa calls Bon "a shadow with a name." And she says that "he had left no more trace" in her sister's house than if "he had been but a shape, a shadow." At one point, Quentin and Shreve's reconstruction of Bon's character is described as "the creating of this shade whom they discussed (rather, existed in)." The contrast between Bon's role as the dark self and Henry's as the bright self is made particularly clear in Bon's imagined appraisal of his younger brother: *"this flesh and bone and spirit which stemmed from the same source that mine did, but which sprang in quiet peace and contentment and ran in steady even though monotonous sunlight, where that which he bequeathed me sprang in hatred and outrage and unforgiving and ran in shadow."* Realizing that Quentin projects his own unacceptable impulses onto Bon as the shadow self, we understand the deeper significance of the imagery that Quentin employs in imagining the final confrontation between the brothers. Bon and Henry ride up to the house, one falls behind or one draws ahead, they face each other and speak, *"Dont you pass the shadow of this post, this branch, Charles; and I am going to pass it, Henry."* And when Quentin unwillingly accompanies Rosa Coldfield out to the Sutpen place to discover the secret of the old dark house, he approaches the rotting gate posts and looks apprehensively about, "wondering what had cast the shadow which Bon was not to pass alive" and "wishing that Henry were there now to stop Miss Coldfield and turn them back."

Bon serves as the shadow self of Quentin by acting within Quentin's narrative as the shadow self of Henry. That Henry vicariously satisfies his own desire for his sister Judith by identifying himself with her lover is first suggested by Mr. Compson. He says that Henry pleaded his friend's suit better than Bon could himself, "as though it actually were the brother who had put the spell on the sister, seduced her to his own vicarious image which walked and breathed with Bon's body." And he comments, ". . . perhaps this is the pure and perfect incest: the brother realizing that the sister's virginity must be destroyed in order to have existed at all, taking that virginity in the person of the brother-in-law, the man whom he would be if he could become, metamorphose into, the lover, the husband; by whom he would be despoiled, choose for despoiler, if he could become, metamorphose into the sister, the mistress, the bride.

Perhaps that is what went on, not in Henry's mind but in his soul." Clearly, the relationship between Henry and Bon is ambivalent—that characteristic love/hate between the bright and the dark selves. Mr. Compson says that Henry loved Bon and that Bon "not only loved Judith after his fashion but he loved Henry too and . . . in a deeper sense than merely after his fashion. Perhaps in his fatalism he loved Henry the better of the two. . . ." Indeed, Mr. Compson suggests that Bon's marriage to Judith would have represented a vicarious consummation of the love between Bon and Henry. Yet between the two there is a veiled antagonism as well. Bon's dark Latin sensibility is galled by Henry's clodhopper Puritanism. When Bon and Henry are in New Orleans, Bon gradually reveals the existence of his octoroon mistress to prevent Henry, with his shocked provincial morality, from challenging him to a duel, for, as Bon sardonically remarks, he would have to give Henry the choice of weapons and he would prefer not to fight with axes. And later, in an imagined conversation, Henry tells Bon, "I used to think that I would hate the man that I would have to look at every day and whose every move and action and speech would say to me, I have seen and touched parts of your sister's body that you will never see and touch: and now I know that I shall hate him and that's why I want that man to be you. . . ."

As Otto Rank has pointed out in his classic study of doubling, the brother and the shadow are two of the most common forms that the figure of the double assumes. Rank locates the origin of doubling in narcissism, specifically in that guilt which the narcissistic ego feels at "the distance between the ego-ideal and the attained reality." In this case the ego's towering self-love and consequent overestimation of its own worth lead to the guilty rejection of all instincts and desires that don't fit its ideal image of itself. The rejected instincts and desires are cast out of the self, repressed internally only to return externally personified in the double, where they can be at once vicariously satisfied and punished. The double evokes the ego's love because it is a copy of the ego, but it evokes the ego's fear and hatred as well because it is a copy with a difference. It is this element of sameness with a difference that gives the figure of the double that quality of the uncanny which we will discuss later in relation to the repetitive structure of doubling. The difference that the ego senses in the double is the implicit presence of the unconscious and particularly that form of unconsciousness which the narcissistic ego finds most offensive to its self-esteem—death. In the myth, Narcissus sees his image reflected in the water; he recognizes the image as himself, yet sees that it is shadowed on a medium whose fluidity, whose lack of differentiation, whose anarchy continually threaten to dissolve the unity of that image at the very moment that the medium itself seems to supply the force to sustain that image. What Narcissus sees is that unified image of his conscious life buoyed up from moment to moment by a medium whose very constitution, in relation to the ego, seems, paradoxically, to be dissolution and death. Rank points out that in myth and literature the appearance of the double is often a harbinger of death and that just as often the ego attempts to protect itself by killing the double, only to find that this is "really a suicidal act." It is in the mechanism of narcissistic self-love that Rank finds the explanation for that "denouement of madness, almost regularly leading to suicide, which is so frequently linked with pursuit by the double. . . ." In this mechanism, the ego does not so much fear death as find unbearable "the *expectation* of the unavoidable destiny of death. . . ." Rank quotes Wilde's Dorian Gray: "I have no terror of Death. It is only the *coming* of Death that terrifies me." Or as Poe's Roderick Usher says, "In this unnerved—in this pitiable condition—I feel that the period will sooner or later arrive when I must abandon life and reason together, in some struggle with the grim phantasm, Fear." Roderick is driven mad by the image of his own fate which he sees in the progressive physical dissolution of his twin sister Madeline, and he is literally frightened to death when Madeline, whom he has prematurely buried in an unconscious attempt at self-defense, returns from the tomb as a figure of death-in-life. The narrator succinctly remarks that Roderick fell "a victim to the terrors he had anticipated." Rank notes that "the normally unconscious thought of the approaching destruction of the self—the most general example of the repression of an unendurable certainty—torments these unfortunates with the conscious idea of their eternal inability to return, an idea from which release is only possible in death. Thus we have the strange paradox of the suicide who voluntarily seeks death in order to free himself of the intolerable thanatophobia." There is as well about the suicidal murder of the double a suggestion of the *liebestod*, as if the only way that the ego could be joined with the beloved yet fearful other self is by a reflexive death in which the ego plunges itself into the otherness of the unconscious evoked by the double.

Both the narcissistic origin of doubling and the scenario of madness leading to the suicidal murder of the double help to illuminate the internal narrative of Quentin Compson's last day given in *The Sound and the Fury* and in turn to illuminate the story he tells in *Absalom*. In the fictive time of the novels, Quentin and Shreve's joint narration, which occupies the last half of *Absalom*, takes place in January 1910, and Quentin's suicide occurs six months later on June 2, 1910, but the account of that suicide is given in a novel that appeared seven years before

Absalom. Since we already know Quentin's end when we observe his attempt in *Absalom* to explain the reason for Bon's murder, we not only participate in that effort but also engage at the same time in an analogous effort of our own to explain Quentin's murder of himself. And it is only when we see in the murder of Bon by Henry what Quentin saw in it—that Quentin's own situation appears to be a repetition of the earlier story— that we begin to understand the reason for Quentin's suicide. And this whole repetitive structure is made even more problematic by the fact that the explanation which Quentin gives for Bon's murder (that Bon is black, i.e., the shadow self) may well be simply the return of the repressed— simply an unconscious projection of Quentin's own psychic history. Quentin's situation becomes endlessly repetitive insofar as he constantly creates the predecessors of that situation in his narration of past events. And to escape from that kind of repetition, one must escape from the self.

Like Narcissus, Quentin drowns himself, and the internal narrative of his last day, clearly the narrative of someone who has gone insane, is dominated by Quentin's obsessive attempts to escape from his shadow, to "trick his shadow," as he says. When Quentin leaves his dormitory on the morning of his death, the pursuit begins: "The shadow hadn't quite cleared the stoop. I stopped inside the door, watching the shadow move. It moved almost perceptibly, creeping back inside the door, driving the shadow back into the door. . . . The shadow on the stoop was gone. I stepped into the sunlight, finding my shadow again. I walked down the steps just ahead of it." Later, standing by the river, he looks down: "The shadow of the bridge, the tiers of railing, my shadow leaning flat upon the water, so easily had I tricked it that it would not quit me. At least fifty feet it was, and if I only had something to blot it into the water, holding it until it was drowned, the shadow of the package like two shoes wrapped up lying on the water. Niggers say a drowned man's shadow was watching him in the water all the time." Like Narcissus staring at his image in the pool, Quentin stares at his shadow in the river and, significantly, makes a reference to Negroes in relation to that shadow. I say "significantly" because at crucial points during Quentin's last day this connection between the shadow and the Negro recurs, most notably on the tram ride down to the river when Quentin sits next to a black man: "I used to think that a Southerner had to be always conscious of niggers. I thought that Northerners would expect him to. When I first came East I kept thinking *You've got to remember to think of them as coloured people not niggers,* and if it hadn't happened that I wasn't thrown with many of them, I'd have wasted a lot of time and trouble before I learned that the best way to take all people, black or white, is to take them for what they think they are, then leave them alone. That was when I realised that a nigger is not a person so much as a form of behavior; a sort of obverse reflection of the white people he lives among." If, in Quentin's mind, blacks are the "obverse reflection" of whites, if they are like shadows, then in Quentin's narrative projection of his own psychodrama in *Absalom*, Charles Bon's role as the dark seducer, as the shadow self, is inevitably linked with Bon's Negro blood. Further, since Quentin's own shadow has Negro resonances in his mind, it is not surprising that on the day of his suicide Quentin, who is being pursued by his shadow, is told by one of the three boys that he meets walking in the country that he (Quentin) talks like a colored man, nor is it surprising that another of the boys immediately asks the first one if he isn't afraid that Quentin will hit him.

If Quentin's determination to drown his shadow represents the substitutive punishment, upon his own person, of the brother seducer (the dark self, the ego shadowed by the unconscious) by the brother avenger (the bright self, the ego controlled by the superego), then it is only appropriate that the events from Quentin's past that obsessively recur during the internal narrative leading up to his drowning are events that emphasize Quentin's failure as both brother avenger and brother seducer in relation to his sister Candace—failures which his drowning of himself is meant to redeem. On the one hand, Quentin is haunted by his inability to kill Candace's lover Dalton Ames and by his further inability to prevent Candace from marrying Herbert Head, whom he knows to be a cheat. But on the other hand, he is equally tormented by his own failure to commit incest with his sister. In this connection it is significant that one of the obsessive motifs in the narrative of Quentin's last day is the continual juxtaposition of Quentin's own virginity to his sister's loss of virginity: "In the South you are ashamed of being a virgin. Boys. Men. They lie about it. Because it means less to women, Father said. He said it was men invented virginity not women. Father said it's like death: only a state in which the others are left and I said, But to believe it doesn't matter and he said, That's what's so sad about anything: not only virginity, and I said, Why couldn't it have been me and not her who is unvirgin and he said, That's why that's sad too; nothing is even worth the changing of it."

In Quentin's world young men lose their virginity as soon as possible, but their sisters keep their virginity until they are married. The reversal of this situation in the case of Quentin and Candace makes Quentin feel that his sister has assumed the masculine role and that he has assumed the feminine role. Quentin's obsessive concern with Candace's loss of virginity is a displaced concern with his own inability to lose his virginity, for, as both novels clearly imply, Quentin's virginity is psycho-logical impotence. Approaching manhood, Quentin finds himself unable to assume the role of a man. Consider his failure as the avenging brother when he encounters Dalton Ames on the bridge—Ames whom Quentin has earlier associated with the figure of the shadow. He tells Ames to leave town by sundown or he will kill him. Ames replies by drawing a pistol and demonstrating his marksmanship. He then offers the pistol to Quentin:

> youll need it from what you said Im giving you this one because youve seen what itll do
>> to hell with your gun
>> I hit him I was still trying to hit him long after he was holding my wrists but I still tried then it was like I was looking at him through a piece of coloured glass I could hear my blood and then I could see the sky again and branches against it and the sun slanting through them and he holding me on my feet
>>> did you hit me
>>> I couldn't hear
>>> what
>>> yes how do you feel
>>> all right let go
>>> he let me go I leaned against the rail

Later, sick and ashamed, Quentin thinks, "I knew he hadnt hit me that he had lied about that for her sake too and that I had just passed out like a girl. . . ." Quentin, by rejecting the use of the pistol with its phallic significance and thus avoiding the necessity of risking his life to back up his words, relinquishes the masculine role of avenging brother and finds suddenly that in relation to the seducer he has shifted to a feminine role. Struggling in Ames's grasp, Quentin faints "like a girl," and Ames, because he sees the sister in the brother, refuses to hurt Quentin and even lies to keep from humiliating him.

Quentin's failure of potency in the role of avenging brother is a repetition of an earlier failure in the role of brother seducer. On that occasion, Quentin had gone looking for Candace, suspecting that she had slipped away to meet Dalton Ames, and he found her lying on her back in the stream: ". . . I ran down the hill in that vacuum of crickets like a breath travelling across a mirror she was lying on her back in the water her head on the sand spit the water flowing about her hips there was a little more light in the water her skirt half saturated flopped along her flanks to the waters motion in heavy ripples going nowhere. . . ." Forcing Candace to get out of the water, Quentin begins to question her about

Ames, only to find that the questioning suddenly turns to the subject of his own virginity:

Caddy you hate him dont you
    she moved my hand up against her throat her heart was hammering there . . .
    Yes I hate him I would die for him I've already died for him I die for him over and over again everytime this goes . . .
    poor Quentin
    she leaned back on her arms her hands locked about her knees
    youve never done that have you
    what done what
    that what I have what I did
    yes yes lots of times with lots of girls
    then I was crying her hand touched me again and I was crying against her damp blouse then she lying on her back looking past my head into the sky I could see a rim of white under her irises I opened my knife
    do you remember the day damuddy died when you sat down in the water in your drawers
    yes
    I held the point of the knife at her throat
    it wont take but a second just a second then I can do mine I can do mine then
    all right can you do yours by yourself
    yes the blades long enough benjys in bed by now
    yes
    it wont take but a second Ill try not to hurt
    all right
    will you close your eyes
    no like this youll have to push it harder
    touch your hand to it . . .
    but she didnt move her eyes were wide open looking past my head at the sky
    Caddy do you remember how Dilsey fussed at you because your drawers were muddy
    dont cry
    Im not crying Caddy
    push it are you going to
    do you want me to
    yes push it
    touch your hand to it
    dont cry poor Quentin . . .
    what is it what are you doing
    her muscles gathered I sat up
    its my knife I dropped it
    she sat up

what time is it
I dont know
she rose to her feet I fumbled along the ground
Im going let it go
I could feel her standing there I could smell her damp clothes
feeling her there
it's right here somewhere
let it go you can find it tomorrow come on
wait a minute I'll find it
are you afraid to
here it is it was right here all the time
was it come on . . .
its funny how you can sit down and drop something and have to
hunt all around for it.

Candace says that she has died for her lover many times, but for the narcissistic Quentin the mention of sexual death evokes the threat of real death, the feared dissolution of the ego through sexual union with another, the swallowing up of the ego in the instinctual ocean of the unconscious. And Quentin, tormented by his virginity, by his impotence ("poor Quentin youve never done that have you"), can only reply to Candace's sexual death by offering a real *liebestod*. He puts his knife to his sister's throat and proposes that they be joined forever in a murder/suicide—a double killing that represents the equivalent, on the level of brother/sister incest, of the suicidal murder of the brother seducer by the brother avenger. For if the brother-seducer/brother-avenger relationship represents doubling and the brother/sister relationship incest, then the brother/brother relationship is also a kind of incest and the brother/sister relationship a kind of doubling. In at least one version of the Narcissus myth (Pausanias 9.31.6), Narcissus is rendered inconsolable by the death of his identical twin sister, and when he sees himself reflected in the water he transfers to his own image the love that he felt for his dead twin. In this light, consider once again the image that begins the scene: Quentin says, "I ran down the hill in that vacuum of crickets like a breath travelling across a mirror she was lying on her back in the water. . . ." The narcissistic implication is that his sister lying on her back in the stream is like a mirror image of himself, and indeed, one of the recurring motifs in Quentin's internal narrative is the image of his sister in her wedding dress running toward him out of a mirror. Further, Quentin says that Ames was always "looking at me through her like through a piece of coloured glass. . . ."

It would appear that for Quentin the double as a male figure is associated with the shadow and the double as a female figure is associated with the mirror image. If so, then his suicide represents the attempt to merge those two images. During his walk in the country on the afternoon of his death, Quentin senses the nearness of a river and suddenly the smell of water evokes a memory of his desire for his sister and his desire for death:

> The draft in the door smelled of water, a damp steady breath. Sometimes I could put myself to sleep saying that over and over until after the honeysuckle got all mixed up in it the whole thing came to symbolise night and unrest I seemed to be lying neither asleep nor awake looking down a long corridor of grey halflight where all stable things had become shadowy paradoxical all I had done shadows all I had felt suffered taking visible form antic and perverse mocking without relevance inherent themselves with the denial of the significance they should have affirmed thinking I was I was not who was not was not who.
>
> I could smell the curves of the river beyond the dusk and I saw the last light supine and tranquil upon tide-flats like pieces of broken mirror. . . . Benjamin the child of. How he used to sit before that mirror. Refuge unfailing in which conflict tempered silenced reconciled.

The image of Benjamin, Quentin's idiot younger brother, staring at himself in a mirror, locked forever in mental childhood, is a forceful evocation of the infantile, regressive character of narcissism, and it is in light of that infantile, regressive character that we can understand Quentin's drowning of himself in the river as an attempt to merge the shadow and the mirror image. Quentin's narcissism is, in Freudian terms, a fixation in secondary narcissism, a repetition during a later period in life (usually adolescence) of that primary narcissism that occurs between the sixth and the eighteenth months, wherein the child first learns to identify with its image and thus begins the work that will lead to the constitution of the ego as the image of the self and the object of love. The fixation in secondary narcissism in which the ego at a later period is recathected as the *sole* object of love condemns the individual to an endless repetition of an infantile state. This attempt to make the subject the sole object of its own love, to merge the subject and the object in an internal love union, reveals the ultimate goal of all infantile, regressive tendencies, narcissism included: it is the attempt to return to a state in which subject and object did not yet exist, to a time before that division occurred out of which the ego sprang—in short, to return to the womb, to reenter the waters of birth. But the desire to return to the womb is the desire for incest. Thus, Quentin's narcissism is necessarily linked with his incestuous desire for his sister, for as Otto Rank points out, brother-sister incest is a substitute for child-parent incest—what the brother seeks in his sister is his mother.

And we see that the triangle of sister/brother avenger/brother seducer is a substitute for the Oedipal triangle of mother/father/son. Quentin's drowning of his shadow, then, is not only the punishment, upon his own person, of the brother seducer by the brother avenger, it is as well the union of the brother seducer with the sister, the union of Quentin's shadow with his mirror image in the water, the mirror image of himself that evokes his sister lying on her back in the stream. The punishment of the brother seducer by the brother avenger is death, but the union of the brother seducer and the sister is also death, for the attempt to merge the shadow and the mirror image results in the total immersion of both in the water on which they are reflected, the immersion of the masculine ego consciousness in the waters of its birth, in the womb of the feminine unconscious from which it was originally differentiated. By drowning his shadow, Quentin is able simultaneously to satisfy his incestuous desire and to punish it, and as we noted earlier it is precisely this simultaneous satisfaction and punishment of a repressed desire that is at the core of doubling. For Quentin, the incestuous union and the punishment of that union upon his own person can be accomplished by a single act because both the union and its punishment are a *liebestod*, a dying of the ego into the other.

In the confrontation between Quentin and Candace at the stream, this linking of sexual desire and death centers for Quentin around the image of Candace's muddy drawers and the death of their grandmother, "Damuddy." The image recalls an incident in their childhood when, during their grandmother's funeral, they had been sent away from the house to play. Candace goes wading in the stream, and when Quentin and Versh tell her that she'll get a whipping for getting her dress wet, she says that she'll take it off to let it dry, and she asks the black boy Versh to unbutton the back:

> "Dont you do it, Versh." Quentin said.
> "Taint none of my dress." Versh said.
> "You unbutton it, Versh." Caddy said, "Or I'll tell Dilsey what you did yesterday." So Versh unbuttoned it.
> "You just take your dress off." Quentin said. Caddy took her dress off and threw it on the bank. Then she didn't have on anything but her bodice and drawers, and Quentin slapped her and she slipped and fell down in the water.

Candace splashes water on Quentin, an act that in retrospect is sexually symbolic, and Quentin's fear that now they will both get a whipping destroys his attempt to play the role of the protective brother. Shifting from an active to a passive role, Quentin sees Caddy take charge and lead the children back to the house while he lags behind, taunted by Caddy. When they reach the house, Caddy climbs the tree outside the parlor window to see the funeral, and at that point the image of her muddy drawers seen by the children below is fused with the image of Damuddy's death. It is significant that Quentin's obsessive linking of these two images (his sexual desire for his sister and death) involves the repetition, in each case, of the same word—the word "muddy" in Candace's "muddy drawers" and "Damuddy's" funeral, for the threat that sexual union poses to the bright, narcissistic ego is, in Quentin's mind, associated with the image of mud—soft, dark, corrupt, enveloping—the image of being swallowed up by the earth. In the scene where Candace interrupts an abortive sexual encounter in the barn between Quentin and a girl named Natalie ("a dirty girl like Natalie," as Candace says), Quentin retaliates by jumping into the hog wallow and then smearing his sister with mud:

> She had her back turned I went around in front of her. You know what I was doing? She turned her back I went around in front of her the rain creeping into the mud flatting her bodice through her dress it smelled horrible. I was hugging her that's what I was doing. . . .
>
> I dont give a damn what you were doing
>
> You dont you dont I'll make you I'll make you give a damn. She hit my hands away I smeared mud on her with the other hand I couldn't feel the wet smacking of her hand I wiped mud from my legs smeared it on her wet hard turning body hearing her fingers going into my face but I couldn't feel it even when the rain began to taste sweet on my lips. . . .
>
> We lay in the wet grass panting the rain like cold shot on my back. Do you care now do you do you
>
> My Lord we sure are in a mess get up. Where the rain touched my forehead it began to smart my hand came red away streaking of pink in the rain. Does it hurt
>
> Of course it does what do you reckon
>
> I tried to scratch your eyes out my Lord we sure do stink we better try to wash it off in the branch. . . .

Later, when Quentin identifies with his sister's lover Dalton Ames and imagines Ames and Candace making "the beast with two backs," the image of Quentin and Candace smeared with mud from the hog wallow metamorphoses into the image of the swine of Eubœleus—the swine that are swallowed up into the earth when Hades carries Persephone down to be the queen of the dead. And a variant of this image occurs in Quentin's last internal monologue before he drowns himself when he imagines the clump of cedars where Candace used to meet her lovers: "Just by imagining the clump it seemed to me that I could hear whispers secret surges smell the beating of hot blood under wild unsecret flesh watching against

red eyelids the swine untethered in pairs rushing coupled into the
sea . . ."

Since Quentin's incestuous desire for his sister is synonymous with
death, it is no surprise that in the scene by the branch, where Quentin
puts his knife to his sister's throat and offers to kill her and then himself,
their conversation parodies that of sexual intercourse:

> will you close your eyes
> no like this youll have to push it harder
> touch your hand to it . . .
> push it are you going to
> do you want me to
> yes push it
> touch your hand to it

It is a mark of the brilliance and centrality of this scene that its imagery
evokes as well the reason for that fear which continually unmans Quentin
whenever he tries to assume the masculine role. When Quentin puts his
knife to his sister's throat, he is placing his knife at the throat of someone
who is an image of himself, thereby evoking the threat of castration—the
traditional punishment for incest. The brother seducer with the phallic
knife at his sister's throat is as well the brother avenger with the castrating
knife at the brother seducer's throat—the father with the castrating knife
at the son's penis. The fear of castration fixes Quentin in secondary
narcissism, for by making sexual union with a woman synonymous with
death, the castration fear prevents the establishment of a love object
outside the ego. Quentin's fear of castration is projected onto the figure of
his sister, incest with whom would be punished by castration. Thus in her
encounters with Quentin, Candace becomes the castrator. When Candace
tells him to go ahead and use the knife, his fear unmans him; he drops the
phallic knife and loses it, and when he tells Candace that he will find it in
a moment, she asks, "Are you afraid to?" Recall as well that in the scene
at the hog wallow Candace says that she tried to scratch Quentin's eyes
out. Having failed in the masculine role of brother seducer in relation to
Candace, Quentin shifts to a passive, feminine role, and Candace assumes
the active, masculine role. It is a shift like the one that Quentin undergoes
when he fails in the masculine role of brother avenger in relation to the
seducer Dalton Ames; Quentin immediately assumes a feminine role,
fainting like a girl in Ames's grasp. Indeed, brooding on that fear of
risking his life that caused him to reject Ames's offer of the phallic pistol,
Quentin thinks, "And when he put Dalton Ames. Dalton Ames. Dalton
Ames. When he put the pistol in my hand I didn't. . . . Dalton Ames.

Dalton Ames. Dalton Ames. If I could have been his mother lying with open body lifted laughing, holding his father with my hand refraining, seeing, watching him die before he lived."

The explanation for this shifting from a masculine to a feminine role is to be found in the son's ambivalence toward his father in the castration complex. On the one hand, there is an aggressive reaction of the son toward the castrating father, a desire for the father's death, a desire to kill him. But on the other hand, there is a tender reaction, a desire to renounce the object that has caused the father's anger, to give up the penis and thus to retain the father's love by assuming a passive, feminine role in relation to him—in short, to become the mother in relation to the father. In this second situation (the tender, passive reaction) the fear of castration turns into a longing for castration, and since, as Freud points out, the fear of death is an analogue of the fear of castration, this transformation of the castration fear into a desire for castration within the incest scenario has as its analogue, within the scenario of narcissistic doubling, that fear of death that becomes a longing for death—the paradox, as Rank says, of a thanatophobia that leads to suicide. What the fear of castration is to incest the fear of death is to doubling, and as the fear of castration and the fear of death are analogues, so too are incest and doubling. We need only recall in this connection that the characteristic doubling scenario of madness leading to suicide often includes incidents of self-mutilation, for self-mutilation is simply a partial form of self-destruction. During the walk in the country that Quentin takes on the day of his suicide, he stops on a bridge and looks down at his shadow in the water and remembers,

> Versh told me about a man mutilated himself. He went into the woods and did it with a razor, sitting in a ditch. A broken razor, flinging them backward over his shoulder the same motion complete the jerked skein of blood backward not looping. But that's not it. It's not not having them. It's never to have had them then I could say O That That's Chinese I dont know Chinese. And Father said it's because you are a virgin: dont you see? Women are never virgins. Purity is a negative state and therefore contrary to nature. It's nature is hurting you not Caddy and I said That's just words and he said So is virginity and I said you dont know. You cant know and he said Yes. On the instant when we come to realise that tragedy is second-hand.
>
> Where the shadow of the bridge fell I could see down for a long way, but not as far as the bottom.

In a real or imagined conversation with his father, bits of which recur during his internal narrative, Quentin confesses that he and Candace have committed incest, and he seeks a punishment, he says, that will isolate himself and his sister from the loud world. When his father asks him if he tried to force Candace to commit incest, Quentin replies, "i was afraid to i was afraid she might." It is as if in seeking to be punished for incest, to be castrated, Quentin would have proof that his masculinity had ever been potent enough to constitute a threat to the father; castration would constitute the father's acknowledgment of the son's manhood. The similarity between Quentin's situation and Charles Bon's becomes clearer, for Bon's decision to go ahead and commit incest by marrying his half sister Judith is motivated less by his love for Judith than by his desire to force his father to acknowledge his existence, and when Bon learns that the reason that Sutpen refuses to acknowledge him is that he is black, then it becomes the desire to force Sutpen to acknowledge his manhood, even if that acknowledgment means forcing his father to kill him through his surrogate, Henry. It is as if Bon, realizing that he will never have his father's love in any normal sense, seeks to have that love in an inverse sense through a *liebestod* with that substitute for the father, the avenging brother. Henry's murder of his half brother, the dark double, is an incestuous love-death. And the paradox of Bon's solution is that in order to force his father to acknowledge his masculinity in this manner Bon must submit to being feminized. He must assume a passive role in relation to Sutpen and Henry: he announces his intention to marry Judith, knowing the danger involved, but he does not kill Sutpen or Henry; rather, he offers his own pistol to Henry in a scene that reminds us of Dalton Ames's offer of his pistol to Quentin:

> *Now it is Bon who watches Henry; he can see the whites of Henry's eyes again as he sits looking at Henry with that expression which might be called smiling. His hand vanishes beneath the blanket and reappears, holding his pistol by the barrel, the butt extended toward Henry.*
>   —Then do it now, he says. . . .
>   —You are my brother.
>   —No I'm not. I'm the nigger that's going to sleep with your sister. Unless you stop me, Henry.
>   *Suddenly Henry grasps the pistol, jerks it free of Bon's hand stands so, the pistol in his hand, panting and panting. . . .*
>   —Do it now, Henry, he says.
>   *Henry whirls, in the same motion he hurls the pistol from him and stoops again, gripping Bon by both shoulders, panting.*
>   —You shall not! he says. —You shall not! Do you hear me? . . .
>   —You will have to stop me, Henry.

But while Quentin rejects the pistol, never to use it, Henry rejects it only to use it later to kill Bon. Indeed, one has been prepared for Bon's ultimate feminization by references at various points in the novel to a certain feminine quality in him, as when Quentin and Shreve theorize that Henry must have learned from Bon "how to lounge about a bedroom in a gown and slippers such as women wore, in a faint though unmistakable effluvium of scent such as women used, smoking a cigar almost as a woman might smoke it, yet withal such an air of indolent and lethal assurance that only the most reckless man would have gratuitously drawn the comparison." The result of Henry's murder of his black half brother is the kind of regression that one would expect from the suicidal murder of the double: Henry ends his life hidden in the womb of the family home where, helpless as a child, he is nursed by his black half sister Clytie. In a way, Henry's end repeats the fate of his maternal grandfather who at the beginning of the Civil War nailed himself into the attic of his home and who, though cared for by his daughter Rosa, eventually starved himself to death.

Clearly, for Quentin the triangle of Candace, Dalton Ames, and himself appears as a repetition of the earlier triangle of Judith, Bon, and Henry, and in both triangles the danger of castration that lies at the core of narcissistic doubling is evoked by the woman's name. In the Apocrypha, Judith decapitates the Assyrian general Holofernes. In his essay "The Taboo of Virginity," Freud, commenting on Hebbel's drama *Judith und Holofernes*, says, "Judith is one of those women whose virginity is protected by a taboo. Her first husband was paralyzed on the bridal night by a mysterious anxiety and never again dared to touch her. 'My beauty is like belladonna,' she says. 'Enjoyment of it brings madness and death.' " And of Judith's murder of Holofernes, Freud remarks, "Beheading is well-known to us as a symbolic substitute for castrating." Candace's name recalls the incident in the Acts of the Apostles (8:26–40) when Philip meets the eunuch of Queen Candace of Ethiopia:

> . . . and, behold, a man of Ethiopia, an eunuch of great authority under Candace queen of the Ethiopians, who had the charge of all her treasure, and had come to Jerusalem for to worship, was returning, and sitting in his chariot read Esaias the prophet. Then the Spirit said unto Philip, Go near, and join thyself to this chariot. And Philip ran thither to him, and heard him read the prophet Esaias, and said, Understandest thou what thou readest? And he said, How can I, except some man should guide me? And he desired Philip that he would come up and sit with him. The place of the scripture which he read was this, He was led as a sheep to the slaughter; and like a lamb dumb before his shearer, so opened he not his mouth: In his humiliation his judgment was taken away: and who shall declare his generation? for his life is taken from the earth. And the eunuch answered Philip, and said, I pray thee, of whom speaketh the prophet this? of himself, or of some other man?

When Philip clarifies the text, the eunuch asks to be baptized, and Philip and the eunuch descend together into the water. Quentin's incestuous desire for his sister and the disabling fear of castration that she embodies for him have made Quentin in effect Candace's eunuch—impotent with his sister and yet obsessed with preventing her from making love to other men. As we suggested earlier, Quentin's brother Benjy is in certain respects a double of Quentin—in his arrested, infantile state, in his obsessive attachment to Candace, in his efforts to keep Candace from becoming involved with anyone outside the family, Benjy is a copy of Quentin, and when their brother Jason has Benjy gelded for attempting to molest a little girl, Benjy's physical condition doubles Quentin's psychological impotence, acting out the fate of the brother seducer at the hands of the brother avenger. Jason is, of course, named after his and Quentin's father.

In the Biblical account of Philip's baptism of the eunuch of Queen Candace, the detail of Philip and the eunuch's descent together into the water is worth noting, for when Quentin kills himself by descending into the river to join his shadow, there is in his internal narrative a religious significance attached to the act. Quentin wonders whether his bones will rise from the water at the general resurrection, a resurrection for which baptism makes one a member of the elect. Quentin thinks, "And I will look down and see my murmuring bones and the deep water like wind, like a roof of wind, and after a long time they cannot distinguish even bones upon the lonely and inviolate sand. Until on the Day when He says Rise only the flatiron would come floating up." And again later, "And maybe when He says Rise the eyes will come floating up too, out of the deep quiet and the sleep, to look on glory." The date of Quentin's section of *The Sound and the Fury* is June 2, 1910, while the dates of the other three sections of the novel are April 6, 7, and 8, 1928, that is, Good Friday, Holy Saturday, and Easter Sunday. As Quentin's suicide is associated in his mind with the image of the general resurrection, so the dating of the other sections in the novel associates Quentin's death with Christ's death and resurrection, establishing for Quentin's suicidal murder of the brother seducer by the father-surrogate a religious context in which the archetypal son sacrifices his life to appease the anger of the archetypal father. As the dates of three of the sections have a liturgical significance, so too does the date of the fourth section: June 2, the day of Quentin's drowning, is the feast day of St. Erasmus (also known as St. Elmo), who is the patron saint of sailors, particularly of sailors caught in a storm, and thus the saint whose special care it is to prevent drownings.

In *As I Lay Dying* (1930), the novel that Faulkner published immediately after *The Sound and the Fury*, the triangle of a mentally unbalanced brother, a promiscuous sister, and a seducer recurs. Darl Bundren discovers that his sister Dewey Dell has made love to her boyfriend Lafe, and Dewey Dell thinks, ". . . then I saw Darl and he knew. . . . and I said 'Are you going to tell pa are you going to kill him?' without the words I said it and he said 'Why?' without the words. And that's why I can talk to him with knowing with hating because he knows." Dewey Dell is pregnant, and when Doc Peabody comes out to be at her mother's deathbed, Dewey Dell tells herself that the doctor could help her out of her trouble if he only knew: "I would let him come in between me and Lafe, like Darl came in between me and Lafe. . . ." The implication at various points in the novel is that there exists, at least on Darl's part, an incestuous attachment between brother and sister, an attachment that represents for Darl a displacement of his love for his mother Addie. In a fantasy that is the reverse of the scene in which Quentin puts his knife to Candace's throat, Dewey Dell, riding into town with Darl, thinks, "The land runs out of Darl's eyes; they swim to pinpoints. They begin at my feet and rise along my body to my face, and then my dress is gone: I sit naked on the seat above the unhurrying mules, above the travail. *Suppose I tell him to turn. He will do what I say. Dont you know he will do what I say?* Once I was waked with a black void rushing under me. I could not see. I saw Vardaman rise and go to the window and strike the knife into the fish, the blood gushing, hissing like steam but I could not see. *He'll do as I say. He always does. I can persuade him to anything. You know I can. Suppose I say Turn here.* That was when I died that time. *Suppose I do. We'll go to New Hope. We wont have to go to town.* I rose and took the knife from the streaming fish still hissing and I killed Darl."

When at the end of the novel Darl is being taken to the state asylum, one of the two guards accompanying him must ride backwards in the railroad coach (so that the guards are facing each other), and Darl thinks, "One of them had to ride backward because the state's money has a face to each backside and a backside to each face, and they are riding on the state's money which is incest. A nickel has a woman on one side and a buffalo on the other; two faces and no back. I dont know what that is. Darl had a little spy-glass he got in France at the war. In it it had a woman and a pig with two backs and no face. I know what that is." The image of "a woman and a pig with two backs and no face" recalls Quentin's fantasy of Candace and Ames making love: ". . . *running the beast with two backs and she blurred in the winking oars running the swine of Euboeleus running coupled within how many Caddy.*" And the image of the coin with "two faces and no back" balanced against the image of the two guards facing each other evokes the psychic splitting, the doubling, that has taken place in Darl's personality. This doubling is clear from the very start of the section in which Darl describes his departure for the asylum, for Darl talks about himself in the third person, and then the first-person Darl carries on a dialogue with this other self:

> Darl has gone to Jackson. They put him on the train, laughing down the long car laughing, the heads turning like the heads of owls when he passed. "What are you laughing at?" I said.
> "Yes yes yes yes yes."
> . . . "Is it the pistols you're laughing at?" I said. "Why do you laugh?" I said. "Is it because you hate the sound of laughing?"
> . . . Darl is our brother, our brother Darl. Our brother Darl in a cage in Jackson where, his grimed hands lying light in the quiet interstices, looking out he foams.
> "Yes yes yes yes yes yes yes yes."

We should at this point make a clear distinction between the spatial aspect of doubling—the way in which one person can be a spatial repetition of another person who is his contemporary—and the temporal aspect of doubling—the way in which one person later in time recognizes another person earlier in time as a double of himself and thus sees his own condition as a fated repetition of that earlier life, or the way in which one pair of doubles later in time repeats another pair of doubles earlier in time. An indication of how interested Faulkner was in the temporal aspect of doubling at the period when he wrote *The Sound and the Fury* is to be found in the novel that he published in the same year, *Sartoris* (1929). *Sartoris* is the story of two pairs of brothers named John and Bayard Sartoris, three generations apart. The first pair goes off to fight in the Civil War; Bayard is killed and John returns. John has a son named Bayard Sartoris II, who in turn has a son named John Sartoris II, who in turn has twin sons named John Sartoris III and Bayard Sartoris III. The twins go off to fight in the First World War, and this time John is killed and Bayard returns. At home, Bayard marries a girl who, the novel implies, was in love with Bayard's dead twin brother and who unconsciously seeks, by marrying the surviving twin, to regain her lost love. Predictably enough, the girl's name is Narcissa. Bayard, however, is so haunted by the death of his twin brother that he launches into a series of self-destructive acts and finally manages to duplicate his brother's death by killing himself in a plane crash—killing himself on the very day that his son is born.

We learn from another book, *The Unvanquished* (1938), that besides the doubling of the two pairs of brothers in the Sartoris family there is as well a repetition of incest episodes. John Sartoris, the surviving brother of the first pair, returns home after the Civil War to live with, and eventually marry, his cousin Drusilla Hawk, and his son Bayard II, at the age of twenty-four, has an incestuous, though unconsummated, affair with Drusilla, who is both his stepmother and his cousin. During the period when Drusilla is living with John Sartoris prior to their marriage, Drusilla's mother writes letters begging her to stop disgracing Southern womanhood by her conduct. One of the letters is delivered to the Sartoris place by Mrs. Compson, presumably the great-grandmother of Quentin and Candace, and in this letter Drusilla's mother says that she hopes that Mrs. Compson has "been spared the sight of her own daughter if Mrs. Compson had one flouting and outraging all Southern principles of purity and womanhood that our husbands had died for," since, as the letter implies, Mrs. Compson, in delivering the message to Drusilla, was not spared the sight of Mrs. Hawk's daughter doing just that. It is a nice touch of irony when one considers Quentin's obsession in *The Sound and the Fury* with the "flouting and outraging" of "all Southern principles of purity and womanhood" by Mrs. Compson's great-granddaughter Candace.

In *The Unvanquished* when Sartoris's son, Bayard II, is twenty years old and just beginning to be attracted to his stepmother, he and Drusilla, while walking in the garden one evening, discuss his father's ruthless conduct in rebuilding Jefferson after the war, and Bayard compares his father to Thomas Sutpen who has been equally ruthless in his dream of rebuilding a lost world. Bayard remarks of Sutpen that "he lost everything in the War like everybody else, all hope of descendants too (his son killed his daughter's fiancé on the eve of the wedding and vanished." When Sartoris is himself killed by his former partner Redmond, and Bayard returns from college to avenge his father's death, Drusilla, in a scene filled with sexual overtones, gives Bayard his father's dueling pistols to accomplish the revenge, implying that her love will be the reward for his courageous action: "She faced me, she was quite near; again the scent of the verbena in her hair seemed to have increased a hundred times as she stood holding out to me, one in either hand, the two duelling pistols. 'Take them, Bayard,' she said, in the same tone in which she had said 'Kiss me' last summer, already pressing them into my hands, watching me with that passionate and voracious exaltation, speaking in a voice fainting and passionate with promise: 'Take them. I have kept them for you. I give them to you. . . . Do you feel them? the long true barrels true as justice, the triggers (you have fired them) quick as retribution, the two of them slender and invincible and fatal as the physical shape of love?'." But, as one would expect from other scenes in Faulkner where one person offers a pistol to another, Bayard rejects his father's dueling pistols, having decided that he will face his father's killer unarmed and either be killed or drive Redmond out of town by the sheer moral force of his presence. It seems likely, however, that on a deeper level Bayard's willingness to risk his own life to avenge his father's death is a displaced attempt to confront the vengeance due another wrong done to the father, an effort on Bayard's part to face the punishment for his own sin of desiring his father's wife and thus for the implicit sin of desiring his father's death. It is worth noting that the punishment for the active, masculine sin of desiring the step-mother and unconsciously desiring the death of the father involves the son's willingness to assume a passive, feminine role in relation to his father's killer, who in this scenario would act as a substitute for the father. Bayard, unarmed, allows Redmond to fire his pistol at him twice. If Redmond had killed Bayard, the avenging of the father would have been accomplished by the feminization of the son. But Bayard's courage unmans Redmond, and the characteristic shifting of roles occurs: Bayard assumes the active, masculine role and Redmond the passive, feminine role; Redmond drops his pistol and leaves town. By defeating Redmond, Bayard seems to have avenged his father's death, but another interpretation is even more likely: by defeating the man who killed his father, Bayard has proved himself a better man than his father; he has supplanted that overpowering, debilitating image of the father in the life of the son by psychically doing away with the threatening father-surrogate. In defeating his father's killer, Bayard is symbolically killing his father, and when Bayard confronts Redmond, the man who actually did what Bayard had unconsciously desired to do as an implicit part of his incestuous desire for his stepmother, i.e., kill his father, Bayard confronts a double of himself. It is a theme that Faulkner never tires of reiterating: by courageously facing the fear of death, the fear of castration, the fear of one's own worst instincts, one slays the fear; by taking the risk of being feminized, by accepting the feminine elements in the self, one establishes one's mascu-linity. And it is by allowing the fear of death, of castration, of one's own instincts, of being feminized, to dominate the ego that one is paralyzed, rendered impotent, unmanned, as in the case of Quentin. Considering *Sartoris* and *The Unvanquished* in relation to *Absalom* and *The Sound and the Fury*, one cannot help but be struck by how closely linked doubling and incest, narcissism and the castration complex are in Faulkner's imagi-nation, and by how these twin structures bind together the lives of the three principal families in the novels—the Compsons, Sartorises, and Sutpens—so that incidents in one family story will almost inevitably be doubled by incidents in one of the other family stories.

In examining the temporal aspect of doubling, we must keep in mind as well the temporal aspect of incest—the way in which incidents of incest or of incestuous attachment recur at intervals within the same family or within the three related families. For Faulkner, doubling and incest are both images of the self-enclosed—the inability of the ego to break out of the circle of the self and of the individual to break out of the ring of the family—and as such, both appear in his novels as symbols of the state of the South after the Civil War, symbols of a region turned in upon itself. Thus, the temporal aspects of doubling and incest evoke the way in which the circle of the self-enclosed repeats itself through time as a cycle, the way that the inability to break out of the ring of the self and the family becomes the inability of successive generations to break out of the cyclic repetition of self-enclosure. In one of his conferences at the University of Virginia, Faulkner was asked if "the miscegenation and incest of Roth Edmonds in 'Delta Autumn' complete a cycle of incest and miscegenation begun by old McCaslin," and Faulkner replied, "Yes, it came home. If that's what you mean by complete a cycle, yes, it did." The cycle began in 1833 when Carothers McCaslin had a son, Terrel, by his black daughter Thomasina. Eunice, Thomasina's mother, drowned herself because of this outrage. From then on, the white and black branches of the family are fatally enmeshed, and when Roth Edmonds has a baby by a black girl who he does not know is his cousin he unwittingly completes one cycle of incest and miscegenation only to begin another cycle in the same act. Uncle Ike's sense of the situation is less that something has ended than that something has started all over again. Indeed, by a renunciation of his inheritance, a renunciation that permanently alienated his wife and thus rendered him childless, Uncle Ike had tried to free himself and his family from just such a generative affront that would continue to bind white and black together in an endless cycle of guilt and retribution.

This sense of a cyclic repetition within whose grip individual free will is helpless presents itself in Faulkner's novels as the image of the fate or doom that lies upon a family. Certainly, it would be difficult to think of two words used more often in *The Sound and the Fury* and *Absalom* than "fate" and "doom." In the genealogy that Faulkner appended to *The Sound and the Fury*, he begins with the Indian chief Ikkemotube from whom the first Compson got his land—Ikkemotube, whose name was translated into English as "Doom." Of Candace, Faulkner says, "Doomed and knew it, accepted the doom without either seeking or fleeing it. Loved her brother despite him, loved not only him but loved in him that bitter prophet and inflexible corruptless judge of what he considered the family's honor and its doom, as he thought he loved but really hated in her what he considered the frail doomed vessel of its pride and the foul instrument of its disgrace; not only this, she loved him not only in spite of but because of the fact that he himself was incapable of love, accepting the fact that he must value above all not her but the virginity of which she was custodian and on which she placed no value whatever." And of Candace's daughter Quentin: "Fatherless nine months before her birth, nameless at birth and already doomed to be unwed from the instant the dividing egg determined its sex." Her uncle Quentin's whole narrative in *The Sound and the Fury* is simply a prolonged struggle between his sense of fate and his exertions of will, while in *Absalom*, Faulkner makes it clear that Sutpen's hubris called down a destroying fate upon his descendants. Bon, in pursuit of some acknowledgment from his father, is presented as the archetypal fatalist, while Mr. Compson says that Henry knew that he was "doomed and destined to kill" Bon. And when Rosa Coldfield describes Sutpen's first sight of her sister Ellen in church, she says it was "as though there were a fatality and curse on our family and God Himself were seeing to it that it was performed and discharged to the last drop and dreg. Yes, fatality and curse on the South and on our family as though because some ancestor of ours had elected to establish his descent in a land primed for fatality and already cursed with it, even if it had not rather been our family, our father's progenitors, who had incurred the curse long years before and had been coerced by Heaven into establishing itself in the land and the time already cursed."

This feeling that an ancestor's actions can determine the actions of his descendants for generations to come by compelling them periodically to repeat his deeds is the form that the fate or doom of a family takes in Faulkner. Often in his novels the actions of a grandparent preempt the life of a grandchild. One thinks immediately of *Light in August* (1932), where the three principal characters—Hightower, Joanna Burden, and Joe Christmas—have had their destinies determined by the lives of their grandfathers. Hightower originally came to Jefferson because his grandfather was accidentally killed there during a cavalry raid in the Civil War, and he remains in Jefferson even after his disgrace because he is somehow doomed to relive in his imagination every evening at twilight the entrance of his grandfather's cavalry troop into the town. That instant in time, that transitory moment of lost grandeur, has been arrested and preserved by being spatialized in Hightower's imagination, acquiring the status of a painting or of equestrian statuary, and that image has in turn arrested the flow of time in Hightower's life, compelling him to circle back every evening and relive, in the contemplation of that image, his grandfather's death. Joanna Burden has remained by herself in her family home in Jefferson, rather than return to live with her relatives in the North, because her grandfather and brother were shot down on the streets of Jefferson by Colonel John Sartoris, and she will not give the townspeople the satisfaction of thinking that they were finally able to run the Burdens out of town. Joe Christmas's life is, of course, set in its path when his maternal grandfather Doc Hines, who has murdered Joe's father, leaves Joe on the steps of the orphanage and then takes a job at the orphanage to watch the child and make sure that God's curse on Joe, who is the product of miscegenation, is carried out. It is Hines who seals Joe's fate at the end of the novel by inciting the townspeople to lynch his grandson, telling them that Joe is not a Mexican but a black. When Joe is on the run after setting Joanna Burden's house on fire, he approaches Mottstown, where, unknown to him, his grandfather is living; at this point the image of the circle that is a cycle makes its most explicit appearance: ". . . he is entering it again, the street which ran for thirty years. It had been a paved street, where going should be fast. It had made a circle and he is still inside of it. Though during the last seven days he has had no paved street, yet he has travelled further than in all the thirty years before. And yet he is still inside the circle. 'And yet I have been further in these seven days than in all the thirty years,' he thinks. 'But I have never got outside that circle. I have never broken out of the ring of what I have already done and cannot ever undo.' " As Hightower, Joanna Burden, and Joe Christmas resemble one another in the relationship of their lives to the lives of their grandfathers, so their own lives become enmeshed: Joe kills Joanna Burden and is in turn castrated and killed in Hightower's home.

This motif of a grandchild whose destiny is determined by the life of his grandfather is present as well in *The Sound and the Fury*. In one of the conferences at the University of Virginia, Faulkner said that the decay of the Compson family began with Quentin's grandfather General Compson, who had been a failed brigadier general in the Civil War and who put the first mortgage on the Compson property. And in the appendix to *The Sound and the Fury*, Faulkner remarked that from the time of General Compson on, a Compson was doomed to "fail at everything he touched save longevity or suicide." What Faulkner called that "basic failure" that began with General Compson was transmitted to Quentin by his father as a problem *in* time and a problem *of* time. This temporal dilemma makes its appearance at the very start of Quentin's narrative on the day of his death: "When the shadow of the sash appeared on the curtains it was between seven and eight oclock and then I was in time again, hearing the watch. It was Grandfather's and when Father gave it to me he said, Quentin, I give you the mausoleum of all hope and desire; it's rather excruciating-ly apt that you will use it to gain the reducto absurdum of all human experience which can fit your individual needs no better than it fitted his or his father's. I give it to you not that you may remember time, but that you might forget it now and then for a moment and not spend all your breath trying to conquer it. Because no battle is ever won he said. They are not even fought. The field only reveals to man his own folly and despair, and victory is an illusion of philosophers and fools." Before Quentin leaves his room that morning, he twists the hands off his grandfather's watch, the watch that in its passage from generation to generation symbolizes both the transmission of General Compson's failure and defeatism and the burden of remembering a past that paralyzes the present. We might note as an aside that in the decaying, aristocratic families like the Sartorises and Compsons, the given names of the male descendants tend to alternate between two possibilities from generation to generation—between John and Bayard in the Sartoris family and between Quentin and Jason in the Compson family. This alternation is one mark of the inbred character of these families and of the way that the locked-in repetition of traditional patterns has made them unable to cope with changing times. One sign of the mongrel vigor and adaptability of the family that supplants the Compsons and Sartorises is that no member of the Snopes family has a given name that is the same as any other member of that family.

It is tempting to speculate that this motif of a grandfather's life that is repeated in the life of his grandson is a variant of what the psychoanalyst Ernest Jones has called "the phantasy of the reversal of generations." Jones points out that there is a fantasy common among small children that when they grow up and their parents grow old, the children "will become the parents and their parents the children." Jones continues, "The logical consequence of the phantasy, which the imagination at times does not fail to draw, is that the relative positions are so completely reversed that the child becomes the actual parent of his parents. . . . Another way of stating this conclusion is that the child becomes identified with his grandfather, and there are many indications of this unconscious identification in mythology, folk-lore, and custom. . . . The custom of naming children after their grandparents is extremely widespread in both civilised and uncivilised races; among many it is not merely a common habit, but an invariable rule." Indeed, there are primitive peoples who believe "that the grandfather has returned in the person of the child."

Jones suggests that the principal origin of the reversal fantasy is the belief in personal immortality: "Neither the child's mind nor the adult unconscious can apprehend the idea of personal annihilation. . . . This narcissistic conviction of personal immortality extends to persons loved or respected by the ego, so that when such a person disappears it is assumed that it can only be for a time, and that he will surely be seen again, either in this world or the next. To the primitive mind the former place of reappearance is the more natural; hence our children, just like adult savages, imagine that when an old person dies he will shortly reappear as a new-born child."

It is significant that Otto Rank proposes a similar origin for doubling—the narcissistic belief in the immortality of the self. In his essay on the uncanny, Freud summarizes Rank's conclusions: ". . . the 'double' was originally an insurance against the destruction of the ego, an 'energetic denial of the power of death,' as Rank says; and probably the 'immortal' soul was the first 'double' of the body. This invention of doubling as a preservation against extinction has its counterpart in the language of dreams, which is fond of representing castration by a doubling or multiplication of a genital symbol. The same desire led the Ancient Egyptians to develop the art of making images of the dead in lasting materials. Such ideas, however, have sprung from the soil of unbounded self-love, from the primary narcissism which dominates the mind of the child and of primitive man. But when this stage has been surmounted, the 'double' reverses its aspect. From having been an assurance of immortality, it becomes the uncanny harbinger of death." Rank notes that for primitive man the earliest image of the immortal self was his shadow—the shadow which departs with the death of the grandfather but returns with the birth of the grandson. It would seem, then, that in the reversal fantasy we have the archetypal form of the temporal aspect of doubling.

As ambivalence is central to the fully developed figure of the double in that the double in its final form is at once the image of the beloved ego and the image of the feared and hated dissolution of the ego, so Jones points out that ambivalence is also central to the origin of the reversal fantasy—specifically, the child's ambivalence toward his parents. On the one hand, the child's love for his parents takes the form of a parental impulse to care for them as they have cared for him; on the other hand, his hostility toward them expresses itself in a fantasy in which they will be under his power in the same way that he is now under theirs. Jones observes that the most important consequence of the reversal fantasy "is the way in which it determines the later attitude of the individual towards children, especially his or her own," because there "always takes place some transference from a person's parent to the child of the corresponding sex." Thus, a child's personality is "moulded, or distorted, not only by the effort to imitate its parents, but by the effort to imitate its parent's ideals,

which are mostly taken from the grandparent of the corresponding sex."
Jones notes that "the social significance of this should be apparent in
regard to the transmission of tradition," but he adds that one must "take
into account the reaction of the child, which may be either positive or
negative; that is, the child may either accept the transference or rebel
against it, in the latter case developing character traits of exactly the
opposite kind to those it sought to implant." The relevance of the reversal
fantasy to Quentin's situation becomes even more obvious when we
consider the fantasy's relationship to the castration complex. As Jones
expresses it: "A experiences in childhood, and possibly also later, hostile
impulses directed against his father B, and fears that his father will punish
(e.g., castrate) him for them in the appropriate talion manner. When A
grows up, he fears to have a son, C, lest C, the unconscious equivalent of
B, will carry out this punishment on him. There is a double reason, it is
true, for this fear: he fears his son C, not only as a re-incorporation of B,
but also as a separate individual, his son, feeling from his own experience
that sons always tend to hate their fathers. We doubtless have here the
deepest reason for the constant identification of grandson with grandfather; both are equally feared by the father, who has reason to dread their
retaliation for his guilty wishes against them. There are many examples of
this situation in mythology. Thus, Zeus did actually carry out on his father
Cronos the very injury of castration that the latter had effected on his
own father, Uranos; so Uranos is avenged by his re-incarnation, Zeus."

ALBERT J. GUERARD

Faulkner's Misogyny

Faulkner's misogyny presents a special problem: it is unrepressed and even undisguised, is often comically and extravagantly explicit, and offers little resistance to analysis. There is, to be sure, a distinction to be made between misogynous impulse and a healthy satirical intention. Doc Hines, self-appointed instrument of God's abomination of womanflesh, is a great portrait of fanatic puritanism. And Faulkner doubtless did see Caddy and her daughter as victims of "some concept of Compson honor" and of a myth of southern womanhood. He probably thought he admired the forthrightness of Ruby Lamar, offering her body to save Lee Goodwin, and even the mindless naturalism of Lena Grove. Yet there is much evidence that Faulkner shared, imaginatively, no little of the puritanism he satirized; and shared too the Tristan spirituality of Gavin Stevens rejecting both Eula and her daughter, and the monastic integrity of the Tall Convict of *The Wild Palms*, one of his least equivocal heroes. There are other forbidden games to stir Faulkner's imagination, crossrace sexuality most obviously. But miscegenation or sexual abuse (chiefly the abuse of black women by white men) is social history not personal obsession. The more complex question is whether any intercourse with a darker partner is destructive or willfully self-destructive, as it was with Charles Etienne de Saint Velery Bon. Homosexuality, often felt as a menace, is rarely seen in overt form, and the sadistic voyeurism of Popeye is an extreme clinical case. There is also some preoccupation with incest.

It is nevertheless evident that the ultimate and repugnantly forbid-

From *The Triumph of the Novel: Dickens, Dostoevsky, Faulkner.* Copyright © 1976 by Albert J. Guerard. Oxford University Press, 1976.

den game to the Faulknerian imagination was normal intercourse with a woman of marriageable age. We are speaking here, even more than with Dickens and Dostoevsky, of the "writer" not the "citizen," though there are tantalizing areas for speculation about the latter: Faulkner's extreme evasiveness and myth-making (notoriously about his wartime experience), his shyness with women, his aloofness and passivity in his early twenties, his alcoholism. Yet in some respects we know less about Faulkner than about Dickens and Dostoevsky; the very full Blotner biography throws comparatively little light on his psycho-sexual life. Thus it seems more than usually advisable, with an enigmatic near-contemporary, to turn directly to the work.

A first point so obvious that it is rarely made: the misogynist imagination selects, for its female victims, appalling predicaments and punishments, even extreme physical violation and pain: Temple Drake's rape or Charlotte Rittenmeyer's bungled abortion. The mindless niece who persuades the steward to leave the yacht with her, in *Mosquitoes*, for some pages seems likely to be bitten to death. (He in turn, obliged to carry her on his back, evokes the eroticized grass—"monstrous and separate, blade by blade"—and sinister rhythms of the misogynous early Conrad of *The Sisters* and *The Outcast of the Islands*.) We may easily forget, given the Tall Convict's outrage, that his passenger also carries a painful burden. The appalling flood of the Mississippi is suavely counterpointed, in the "Wild Palms" chapters, by knives and iron cold. Faulkner's misogyny, like Conrad's, diminished noticeably with age; this led to the notorious rehabilitations of Eula Varner and Temple Drake, and to the grosser sentimentalities of Gavin Stevens. The sufferings of the later heroines evoke a Dickensian pity: Eula Varner driven to self-sacrifice and suicide, and her daughter Linda gratuitously deafened. The twilight glow of *The Reivers* is less displeasing, and the golden heart of Corinthia Everbe Hogganbeck. For we are now frankly in the age of recollection, and the myth of lost childhood.

Faulkner, like Dostoevsky, had a rather limited feminine typology; but with the great difference that Dostoevsky found, in all of his recurring types, something to love. For Faulkner, young girls before the age of puberty are not sources of anxiety; Caddy "was the beautiful one, she was my heart's darling. That's what I wrote the book about. . . ." Eccentric or benignant old ladies also represented no menace; they were sexually unavailable to the imagination. Various narrators evoke eloquently a brief and precious nymphet phase. Ratliff interprets Gavin Stevens' drugstore dates with the thirteen-, fourteen- and fifteen-year-old Linda Snopes as paternal; he wants to save her soul from "Snopesism." His image of the soul recalls—consciously? facetiously?—Faulkner's image of virginity in his Appendix to *The Sound and the Fury:* so much to be poised precariously on the nose of a seal. Linda's adult appeal, for Gavin, lies in her psychosexual unavailability. To her shocking four-letter word (a blank in the text) he responds, *"because we are the 2 in all the world who can love each other without having to. . . ."* Charles Mallison, shrewder here than Ratliff, notes the repetitive pattern: first the child Melisandre Backus, then Linda. But the children make the mistake of growing older: "they had to be in motion to be alive, and the only moment of motion which caught his attention, his eye, was that one at which they entered puberty, like the swirl of a skirt or flow or turn of limb when entering, passing through a door. . . ." Miss Rosa speaks of herself at fourteen, and the moment only virgins know, "when the entire delicate spirit's bent is one anonymous climaxless epicene and unravished nuptial. . . ." (Epicinity, in *Soldiers' Pay*, evokes "girls in a frieze," "lilies like nuns in a cloister," a "poplar vain as a girl darkly in an arrested passionate ecstasy.") The transitional stage is poetically described by Mr. Compson, as he speaks of Judith between childhood and womanhood, a change from shape "without substance" to womanly flesh, and "that state where, though still visible, young girls appear as though seen through glass and where even the voice cannot reach them. . . ." The glass is related, psychologically, to the urn, itself sometimes decorated by a frieze of arrested motion, so crucial throughout Faulkner's work: an urn that can be alarmingly broken.

There is, however, the moment when sexual availability occurs to the conscious mind. In *Sartoris* Frankie is no more than a tennis partner. But in *Flags in the Dust*, an earlier version of the novel, Horace Benbow's contemplation of her seventeen-year-old virginal grace is interestingly censored, with an actual blank occurring after the word *unchaste*, this followed by a question mark. In both versions Benbow observes Harry Mitchell fondle his daughter Little Belle, while the child watches Horace "with radiant and melting diffidence." Horace's love in *Sanctuary*, of the adolescent Little Belle, now his stepdaughter, is as troubled and poignant as Quentin Compson's for the menaced Caddy, and for him too an odor of honeysuckle is traumatic. He holds Little Belle's photograph, after returning from the unnerving interview at Miss Reba's, and her fatality becomes in his revery that of Temple violated above "the faint, furious uproar of the shucks." She is "bound naked on her back on a flat car moving at speed through a black tunnel. . . ." But the revery begins, sickeningly, with his sense of her sexual attraction for him, a moment reminiscent of Svidrigaïlov's dream of the little girl he had wanted to help greeting him with a prostitute's smile, or Arkady's dream, in A *Raw Youth*, of a shockingly sensual Katerina.

The niece and Jenny, the mindless flappers of *Mosquitoes*, have their small parts in that gently misogynous novel, a minor *Antic Hay*. Jenny comes to Pete in a "flowing enveloping movement"; Mr. Talieferro also feels himself enveloped as she stands beside him, "surrounded, enclosed by the sweet cloudy fire of her thighs, as young girls can." The niece's incestuous interest in her brother is amusingly overt. In an early scene they share a cigarette she has kept in the crown of her hat, now "limp, like a worm"; meanwhile he has been working on a cylinder of wood larger than a silver dollar and about three inches long; it is in two sections that fit together. In the epilogue she comes to his bed, over his protests, to engage in a sisterly version of *fellatio* that leaves him with a moistened ear:

> "Well. Be quick about it." He turned his face away and she leaned down and took his ear between her teeth, biting it just a little, making a meaningless maternal sound against his ear. "That's enough," he said presently, turning his head and his moistened ear. "Get out, now."
> She rose obediently and returned to her room.

With Temple Drake, who is about the same age, we cross the line from mindless *demi-vierge* to accomplished nymphomaniac, though at the Old Frenchman's Place we see her rather as an animal in heat, fearing and wanting to be raped. Mink's future wife, at the lumber camp, was "not a nympholept but the confident lord of a harem." Summoned to her bedroom, Mink found he had entered "the fierce simple cave of a lioness—a tumescence which surrendered nothing and asked no quarter. . . ." The sexual demands of Joanna Burden are, by contrast, neurotic, the perversion cerebral. Her life is rigidly compartmentalized: "The sewer ran only by night." She likes to remind herself aloud that she is having intercourse with a negro; wants to damn "herself forever to the hell of her forefathers, by living not alone in sin but in filth," and invents furious sexual games of concealment and pursuit, fantasies of repeated rape. Joe Christmas's castration need—the striking off of the undergarment buttons as with a knife, the exhibiting himself to the "white bastards"—is in part a response to lifelong identity crisis, but also to Joanna's specific invasions of his identity. To lower the garment is to invite, all unconsciously, an alternative to terrifying normal intercourse: "the cool mouth of darkness, the soft cool tongue" and the speeding car "sucking its dust" and "sucking with it the white woman's fading cry." Conceivably repressed homosexual impulse and the castration need/fear blend in a shared misogynous vision and dread. Perhaps Joe Christmas found, at the hands of Percy Grimm, the freedom he had blunderingly sought all along.

The castrating female with *vagina dentata*, often compared to a cat, is sometimes treated comically, sometimes with unsmiling alarm. Joanna Burden waits for Joe, "panting, her eyes in the dark glowing like the eyes of cats." The powerful woman, ruthless and amoral, and somehow endowed with a sexual knowledge beyond her partner's ("*She already knows*," Ike reflects in *The Bear*, "*more than I with all the man-listening in camps where there was nothing to read ever even heard of*") threatens will, identity, moral purpose. The menace of the child Eula Varner may be engulfment by "mammalian meat," drowning; the castrating female can be more actively dangerous, since she possesses teeth and claws. "Take off your clothes," Ike's wife commands, as forthrightly as Charlotte Rittenmeyer. The hand which draws Ike down is also holding him away, suggesting sexual titillation as well as bargaining refusal. But presently it has the characteristics of a surgical instrument, "as though arm and hand were a piece of wire cable with one looped end, only the hand tightening as he pulled against it." The bed of Mink's insatiable future wife offers, in its imagery, comparable discomforts: "a bed made by hand of six-inch unplaned timbers cross-braced with light steel cables, yet which nevertheless would advance in short steady skidding jerks across the floor like a light and ill-balanced rocking chair." Charlotte Rittenmeyer's eyes, when Harry first meets her, are "yellow, like a cat's." Soon he "seemed to be drowning, volition and will, in the yellow stare. . . ." Later, in Chicago, her terrible honesty emasculates: he blunders and fumbles like a moth, in the "unwinking yellow stare" . . . "a rabbit caught in the glare of a torch; an envelopment almost like a liquid. . . ." She has "the blank feral eyes" of the predatory woman, but the tough blunt vulgarity of the male sexual athlete. In bed she would seem to be the man, "as heedless of the hard and painful elbow which jabbed him as she would have been on her own account if the positions had been reversed, as she was of the painful hand which grasped his hair and shook his head with savage impatience."

The misogynous animal imagery, like the incestuous attraction of Horace and Narcissa, is stronger in *Flags in the Dust* than in *Sartoris*. Belle Mitchell takes Horace to a quiet place while her husband is occupied on the tennis court. "Belle slid her *soft prehensile* hand into his, clutching his hand against her *softly clothed* thigh, and led him into a room beyond *folding doors*." The words I have italicized are omitted or changed in *Sartoris*, where a dusky passage, dangerous enough perhaps, leads not to engulfing doors but to a music room. The most ruthless castrating female of *Flags in the Dust*, Belle's sister Joan, simply disappears from the final version. After seeing her for the first time Horace recalls his first circus, and a tiger "watching him with yellow and lazy contemplation." The tiger was old and toothless, but Joan is not, and Horace finds himself watching her "as a timorous person is drawn with delicious revulsion to a gaze into a window filled with knives." "Carnivorous," Horace reflects, on the occasion of their first conversation, a "lady tiger in a tea gown," possessed of "feline poise." In due time she comes to his house. She has her periods of "aloof and purring repose," though the firelight glows "in little red points in her unwinking eyes," and she is "like a sheathed poniard." The first time she spends the whole night "she revealed another feline trait: that of a prowling curiosity about dark rooms."

There is also the softer menace of the fecund and the bovine. *Light in August*, interpreted schematically, may well seem to offer in Lena Grove a celebration of the natural, against the puritanisms and the self-destructive rigidities, against Byron Bunch's mechanical ordering of his life and Hightower's contemplative death-in-life. But she is, at her best, a serenely comic creation. So too at times is the passenger of the Tall Convict, always associated with the river's monstrous flood, but not comic for him, who wants to turn his back "on all pregnant and female life forever." The misogyny of Gordon in *Mosquitoes*, which induces an early exercise in Joycean stream-of-consciousness, is serious enough. Staring down into the water, he puts aside female temptation ("unmuscled wallowing fecund and foul the tragic body of a woman who conceives without pleasure bears without pain") and expresses a Conradian anxiety over strangling hair. But the great bovine creation—comic, mock-heroic, mythical, ultimately romantic—is of course the child Eula Varner, the object of the schoolmaster Labove's paedophilic obsession. He, the "virile anchorite of old time," finds himself helpless before the eleven-year-old girl who "postulated that ungirdled quality of the very goddesses in his Homer and Thucydides," and who brought a "moist blast of spring's liquorish corruption, a pagan triumphal prostration before the supreme primal uterus." Her passivity is such that even in infancy "she already knew there was nowhere she wanted to go" and "might as well have been a foetus." She emanates, even at eight, "an outrageous and immune perversity like a blooded and contrary filly," and walking to the store gives off, her brother claims, an odor as of a dog in heat. For Labove she may, though terrifying, have the attraction of innocence and sexuality, of being at once child and woman. Yet she seems, with her "kaleidoscopic convolution of mammalian ellipses," more bovine than human. She is "tranquil and chewing," like Ike's beloved cow, and like her invites classical allusions. Eula's mythical properties, turning the schoolroom "into a grove of Venus," prepare the reader for those, some fifty pages later, of the cow (evocative of "Troy's Helen and the nymphs and the snoring mitred bishops, the saviors and the victims and the kings"). And that "triumphal prostration before the supreme primal uterus" prepares us for the moment when Ike, "lying beneath the struggling and bellowing cow, received the violent relaxing of her fear-constricted bowels." The cow is of Olympian seed. Yet the highly poetic treatment may reflect an ambiguous attitude toward the natural functions. For Ike, following the violent relaxing, tries to reassure her that such a violation of "maiden's delicacy is no shame, since such is the very iron imperishable warp of the fabric of love." Orgasm appears to be confused, in Ike's imagination if not the author's, with defecation.

These are some of the dangerous females. The specifically sexual menace appears to have two forms. The first, which dissolves masculine will (Eula's "mind- and will-sapping fluid softness"), is that of engulfment or drowning envelopment. How much such imagery is meaningfully obsessive is hard to say, given Faulkner's extraordinary, often unconscious memory for his own phrases, images, analogies. The older Eula Varner Snopes, offering herself to Gavin Stevens, might leave him "tossed and wrung and wrenched and consumed, the light last final spent husk to float slowing and weightless. . . ." She confronts him "with that blue envelopment like the sea" and looks at him with a "blue serene terrible envelopment" before expressing her extreme feminine amorality: "You just are, and you need, and you must, and so you do." On the following page Stevens can even smell "that terrible, that drowning envelopment." In *Flags in the Dust* Horace is doubly threatened. His spirit drowns in his sister's serenity "like a swimmer on a tideless summer sea"; later he thinks of the older Belle "enveloping him like a rich and fatal drug, like a motionless and cloying sea in which he watched himself drown." Ike McCaslin's one recorded sexual experience, following his surrender to the terrible hand, was a kind of drowning, since "after a no-time he returned and lay spent on the insatiate immemorial beach. . . ." But the drowning sea may also be an engulfing morass. Thus Joe Christmas saw "himself as from a distance, like a man being sucked down into a bottomless morass," submerged "more and more by the imperious and overriding fury of those nights." An amusing variant sees actual quicksand in terms of female sexual organs, rather than the other way around, as old Gowrie helps extract the body of his son, in *Intruder in the Dust*,

> the body coming out now feet first, gallowsed up and out of the inscrutable suck to the heave of the crude tackle then free of the sand with a

faint smacking plop like the sound of lips perhaps in sleep and in the bland surface nothing: a faint wimple wrinkle already fading then gone like the end of a faint secret fading smile. . . .

Small wonder the Tall Convict prefers the "consolingly hard ground that can break your bones" to water, which accepts you "substanceless and enveloping and suffocating, down and down and down."

Some of the Faulknerian envelopments have the familiar ring of the *Auflösung* of romantic literature, and of the impulse (both dreaded and longed for) to lose consciousness in a form of maternal sea. The second sexual menace, most harrowingly experienced by Joe Christmas, involves a horror of menstruation. Christmas, the most clinical "case" in Faulkner's fiction, combines the two fears. His childhood trauma as he ingests the cool invisible worm of toothpaste—hidden among the soft womansmelling garments, as the dietician and the interne make love—is echoed in his first sexual experience, as he takes his turn with the negro girl. "There was something in him trying to get out, like when he used to think of toothpaste." In the dark, "enclosed by the womanshenegro and the haste," leaning, "he seemed to look down into a black well and at the bottom saw two glints like reflections of dead stars." Presently he is sickened to hear that women are "doomed to be at stated and inescapable intervals victims of periodical filth"; his measured response, in attempting to cope with this horror, is to shoot a sheep and immerse his hands in its blood. Quentin Compson recalls his father's comment on women's mysteries:

Delicate equilibrium of periodical filth between two moons balanced. Moons he said full and yellow as harvest moons her hips thighs. Outside outside of them always but. Yellow. Feetsoles with walking like. Then know that some man that all those mysterious and imperious concealed. With all that inside of them shapes an outward suavity waiting for a touch to. Liquid putrefaction like drowned things floating like pale rubber flabbily filled getting the odour of honeysuckle all mixed up.

The horror of lost virginity—of "the swine untethered in pairs rushing coupled into the sea"—is suggested in the instances of blocked phrasing here, as well as by the image of floating contraceptives.

Michael Millgate has commented on the significance of the recurring urn imagery in Faulkner's work, his preoccupation with motion in stasis. But it is surely evident that the urn is also a primary sexual symbol which may or may not be broken: *la cruche cassée* of Greuze as well as Freud. Appalled on his first date with Bobbie Allen, as she informs him it's the wrong time of the month, Joe Christmas leaves her and presently vomits: "In the notseeing and the hardknowing as though in a cave he seemed to see a diminishing row of suavely shaped urns in moonlight, blanched. And not one was perfect. Each one was cracked and from each crack there issued something liquid, deathcolored, and foul." A related horror is suggested by Horace's dream of black matter running from Belle's mouth on galley 22 of the unrevised *Sanctuary*, displaced menstrual flow it may be, though in the final text there is explicit reference to the "black stuff that ran out of Bovary's mouth and down upon her bridal veil." By contrast is the "almost perfect vase of clear amber" created by Horace in *Sartoris:* "larger, more richly and chastely serene, which he kept always on his night table and called by his sister's name in the intervals of apostrophizing both of them impartially in his moments of rhapsody over the realization of the meaning of peace and the unblemished attainment of it, as 'Thou still unravished bride of quietness.' " The word in *Flags in the Dust* is *quietude*. And in *Flags in the Dust* a conversation with Narcissa (removed from *Sartoris* entirely) both makes his incestuous wishes explicit and connects them with virginity. It's "all sort of messy: living and seething corruption glossed over for a while by smoothly colored flesh; all foul, until the clean and naked bone."

The preoccupation with incest is connected both with a veneration of virginity and, less demonstrably, with a dread of normal intercourse. But Horace's love of the chastely serene Narcissa does not preclude physical attraction. About to inform her that he intends to marry Belle, Horace restlessly touches objects on her bedside table, sits on the edge of the bed, lays his hand on her knee, apologizes for leaving her alone at night. "For a while he sat brooding on the wild repose of his hand lying on her covered knee." Presently, after more restless touching of objects, he strokes her knee again. Later, they meet as in a lover's embrace, as he comes in out of the rain, "whipping his sodden hat against his leg. . . ." The presumably unconscious sexual image is worthy of the early Conrad. In *Flags in the Dust* there follows a scene in which Horace conjectures that there are "any number of virgins who love children walking the world today, some of whom look a little like you," whom he might conceivably marry, and this is in turn followed by the compact account of his affair with the feline Joan. But in *Sartoris* we move directly to the car accident and old Bayard's death. The incestuous attraction, reduced with the revision of *Flags in the Dust*, remains very overt in the typescript of the original *Sanctuary*. And Belle has recognized the incestuous drive. "You're in love with your sister. What do the books call it? What sort of complex?"

The most eloquent and most succinct critical statements on Quentin Compson's incest fantasies are, of course, those of Faulkner himself in the Appendix to *The Sound and the Fury:*

> Who loved not his sister's body but some concept of Compson honor
> precariously and (he knew well) only temporarily supported by the
> minute fragile membrane of her maidenhead as a miniature replica of all
> the whole vast globy earth may be poised on the nose of a trained seal.
> Who loved not the idea of the incest which he would not commit, but
> some presbyterian concept of its eternal punishment. . . .

Does the novel itself support so much emphasis on Compson honor? The
most moving recollections would suggest more intimate and more primitive feelings: the knife at her throat which has overtones of dreaded sexual
penetration, during their talk of suicide, with the knife presently dropped;
or the brief memories of physical contact in childhood, in themselves
innocent enough. His deepest concern would seem to be her loss of
virginity *per se* rather than the loss of family honor. A leaf in the water in
which Quentin will drown carries echoes of the maidenhead that obsesses
him; in death there is purity, no touching, no giving or taking in
marriage. We have reached an important moment in Quentin's last day, as
he hides the flat irons under the end of the bridge:

> Where the shadow of the bridge fell I could see down for a long way, but
> not as far as the bottom. When you leave a leaf in water a long time after
> awhile the tissue will be gone and the delicate fibers waving slow as the
> motion of sleep. They don't touch one another, no matter how knotted
> up they once were, no matter how close they lay once to the bones.

The incestuous impulses and relationships in *Absalom, Absalom!*
are complex and intense, but like so much else in the novel are distanced
by the rhetoric of the narrators and by the novel's choreographic formal-
ity. No commentator could hope to improve on Mr. Compson's own
analyses. His reasoning, for Henry, begins with an elaboration on Faulkner's in the Appendix to *The Sound and the Fury*. His "fierce provincial's
pride in his sister's virginity was a false quantity"; it "must depend upon its
loss, absence, to have existed at all." Through the brother-in-law he may,
by identification, enjoy the sister. But also, identifying with the sister, he
may experience a homoerotic connection. That it would be doubly
incestuous is, however, not known to Mr. Compson:

> In fact, perhaps this is the pure and perfect incest: the brother realizing
> that the sister's virginity must be destroyed in order to have existed at
> all, taking that virginity in the person of the brother-in-law, the man
> whom he would be if he could become, metamorphose into, the lover,
> the husband; by whom he would be despoiled, choose for despoiler, if he
> could become, metamorphose into the sister, the mistress, the bride.
> Perhaps that is what went on, not in Henry's mind but in his soul.

Mr. Compson's version of Charles Bon's love is, in turn, a perfect example of René Girard's mediation and triangular desire.

> It was because Bon loved not only Judith after his fashion but he loved Henry too and I believe in a deeper sense than after his fashion. Perhaps in his fatalism he loved Henry the better of the two, seeing perhaps in the sister merely the shadow, the woman vessel with which to consummate the love whose actual object was the youth—this cerebral Don Juan who, reversing the order, had learned to love what he had injured; perhaps it was even more than Judith or Henry either: perhaps the life, the existence, which they represented.

One further misogynous creation, virtually contemporary with *Absalom, Absalom!*, is of genuine and sometimes frightening interest: Laverne of *Pylon*, shared by her husband Shumann and the "parachute guy" Jack, and loved hopelessly by the blundering unnamed reporter (who is at once Christ-figure and a skeletal harbinger of death, an appalled Miss Lonelyhearts and fatally interfering Myshkin). Near the novel's end, and prior to a scene as desolate, direct and stark as any in Hemingway's short stories (as her child is turned over to the dead Shumann's father), three compassionate pages tell of Laverne's victimization, at fourteen and fifteen, by her sister's husband. The adult Laverne is as tough and masculine as Charlotte Rittenmeyer ("pale strong rough ragged hair" . . . "tanned heavy-jawed face"), and her amorality is more forthright. The two men, on the birth of her child of uncertain parentage, and with her approval, at once roll dice to determine which she will marry. The reporter is fascinated by the seemingly disinterested freedom of the threesome, and the fraternity of barnstorming flyers generally. But his voyeurism evokes, at one point, familiar misogynous rhetoric: " 'I could hear all the long soft waiting sound of all womanmeat in bed beyond the curtain.' "

Laverne's response to crisis is fiercely sexual. Angered by Shumann's willingness to risk his life in a dangerous plane (and with both Jack and the mechanic Jiggs in the room) her hard hand strikes his cheek:

> clutching and scrabbling about his jaw and throat and shoulder until he caught it and held it, wrenching and jerking.
> "You bastard rotten, you rotten—" she panted.
> "All right," he said. "Steady, now." She ceased, breathing hard and fast. But he still held the wrist, wary and without gentleness too. "All right, now . . . You want to take your pants off?"
> "They're already off."

From here we move to one of the novel's rare flashbacks, and Laverne's terror on the occasion of her first parachute jump, as she climbs not back into the front seat she had left but into the pilot's, "astride his legs and facing him." The scene, in its comic misogyny and cool treatment of terror, dread both of sexuality and of death, has an audacity belonging more to the 1970's than to the 1930's. The imagery of mutilation is truly Faulknerian, however: a safetywire, a belt that catches him across the legs:

> In the same instant of realising (as with one hand she ripped her skirt hem free of the safetywire with which they had fastened it bloomerfashion between her legs) that she was clawing blindly and furiously not at the belt across his thighs but at the fly of his trousers, he realised that she had on no undergarment, pants.

He soon finds, even as he tries to keep the plane in position, that he is fighting off both Laverne and ("the perennially undefeated, the victorious") his erection. Coming out of a "long swoon" he remembers to roll the plane in the right direction and so rids himself of one burden. The next thing he remembered "was the belt catching him across the legs as, looking out he saw the parachute floating between him and the ground, and looking down he saw the bereaved, the upthrust, the stalk: the annealed rapacious heartshaped crimson bud." She is carried to jail by the outraged village officers on the field, one of whom frenziedly covets her, having seen "the ultimate shape of his jaded desires fall upon him out of the sky, not merely naked but clothed in the very traditional symbology— the ruined dress with which she was trying wildly to cover her loins, and the parachute harness—of female bondage."

Such are some of the terms of Faulkner's misogyny, which would appear to be more intense and more complex than Hemingway's or Conrad's, and more conscious as well. The limitations of this attitude are obvious. Yet it contributed an important share to a small masterpiece, *Sanctuary*.

"SANCTUARY"

Sanctuary is much underrated, partly because of Faulkner's grossly misleading comment that it was a pot-boiler written in a few weeks, but also because it is so unlike the "greatest" Faulkners; seems to lack the manifest seriousness of *Light in August*, *The Sound and the Fury*, *Absalom, Absalom!* and *The Bear*, as well as their difficulty. *Sanctuary* belongs more than most of Faulkner's novels to a recognizable mode of American writing: the tough tight compassionate grotesque picture of suffering, depravity, defeat. There is no redemption in *Sanctuary* other than the redemption of art.

The vision is at best one of stoic defeatism, but concludes in despair and a recognition of the void: Horace returning to the horror of life with Belle; Popeye refusing to appeal his absurd sentence; Temple yawning in the Luxembourg gardens, in the season of rain and death. (The Temple of *Requiem for a Nun* is an altogether different person in an implausible "new life.") The relatively short sentences and objective narration and laconic dialogue may remind us of Hemingway. But the truer affinity is with Flaubert, distancing vulgarity through poetic detail and serenely composed syntax. *Sanctuary* is what Dostoevsky would have called, I think, a *poem*. Meanness and evil and depravity, *seen as such* and with precision, but seen also with compassion, constitute a work of beauty, precisely as does Toulouse-Lautrec's painting of an ugly middle-aged prostitute wearily raising her shift.

Far more than with Dickens and Dostoevsky, the obsession was put to artistic use. Faulkner's misogyny, that is, gave form, solidity, energy to a general vision of contemporary depravity and timeless evil. But *Sanctuary* is a picture, not merely a "vision," of the contemporary depravity, specifically of north Mississippi, more generally of prohibition America. A real lynching occurred at the Oxford courthouse, several years after the publication of *Sanctuary*, and Memphis with its gang conflicts was known as Murder Capital of the U.S.A. The real life contrast for Faulkner was not merely between his somnolent college town and Memphis (where he enjoyed exploring the fringe world of entertainment and corruption) but between the daily tedium of Lafayette/Yoknapatawpha county and its sporadic outbreaks of violence. The "jazz age" students and the resentful townies, Gowan Stevens and his pride in his drinking, the delegation of women protesting Ruby Lamar's stay at the hotel—these are not figures of fantasy, though this might be said of the millionaire lawyer, weighing 280 pounds, who has installed his special bed in Miss Reba's establishment, or the police commissioner discovered there, naked and dancing the Highland Fling. At a fine line between documentary realism and soaring fictional vision stands Senator Clarence Snopes, whose twin brothers Vardaman and Bilbo were named after well-known Mississippi politicians. The soiled hat and greasy velvet collar and "majestic sweep of flesh on either side of a small blunt nose" would have been at home in Dickens's London. He is *non persona grata* at Miss Reba's for feeling the girls' behinds while spending nothing: " 'Look here, mister, folks what uses this waiting-room has got to get on the train now and then.' " The Memphis depravities (except for Temple's) reach us refracted by the grotesque, or by Miss Reba's comic vision, but also by Clarence Snopes's cupidity and cynical humor. Thus the *bas-fonds* misery and exploitation of the negro whorehouse he leads the young innocents to, lest they spend three dollars again:

"Them's niggers," Virgil said.
" 'Course they're niggers," Clarence said. "But see this?" he waved a banknote in his cousin's face. "This stuff is color-blind."

Miss Reba's establishment, except for Temple's room, seems a place of good-humored innocence. Virgil's and Fonzo's classic mistake, and their own innocence sustained for so long, adds to a familiar iconography that tempted even Gide in *Lafcadio's Adventures*. Red's funeral, only a slight parodic extension of gangster ceremonies of the twenties, is also kept at a comic distance. This is but to say that Memphis, the legendary Babylon for north Mississippians, is appropriately stylized. But the "normal" depravities and deprivations of the Old Frenchman's Place, running to ruin and jungle, are intensely real: the slaving Ruby with her sickly child in the box, fiercely cursing; the blind and deaf old man edging his chair into the sun; the mattress of shucks and that other bed of corncobs and cottonseed hulls and the barn loft with its rat. The four men move in somnambulistic, mechanical lust in the room where Temple stands terrified in the corner and the bloody Gowan lies on the mattress. Later the room is in a darkness where Tommy's pale eyes glow faintly, like a cat's, and Popeye's presence is known from the odor of brilliantine. The scenes are taut, spare, intensely real: great dramatic writing.

Interwoven with the general depravity, the picture of the time and place, is Faulkner's deeper vision of evil embodied in the impotent Popeye and the amoral Temple in her nervous animal lust. Theirs is a more than ordinary, "normal" corruption. Popeye reaches us in part through traditional symbolism: evil as blackness, as hollowness, as mechanism. Faulkner like Melville knew the power of blackness, Benito Cereno's sense of "the negro" as a spiritual coloring, though in the 1970's he might have used a different language. Popeye is in fact white, of a "queer, bloodless color"; Temple's early reference to him as that "black man" is a response to the incongruous black suit, which becomes a kind of mask, the accouterment of his gangster role and an assertion of identity. Popeye is simply, as Benbow talks to Narcissa and Miss Jenny, "that little black man." But in a later passage the blackness is generalized: a "black presence lying upon the house like the shadow of something no larger than a match falling monstrous and portentous upon something else otherwise familiar and twenty times its size. . . ."

Popeye is, even more than Conrad's Kurtz or James Wait, a hollow man, bereft of any inner humanity to help him confront the void. He *is* his black suit, his slanting straw hat, his cigarette, his gun; he is his role, perhaps learned from movies as well as life, of a gangster people are afraid of. He is also the mechanical man, composed of inanimate parts, with doll-like hands and eyes "two knobs of soft black rubber," "the face of a wax doll set too near a hot fire," bloodless, and with "the vicious depthless quality of stamped tin." The first compelling image is of inexplicable evil and gratuitous terrorism, as for two hours the squatting Popeye watches Horace across the spring. Through much of the Frenchman's Place section his malice remains shadowy, enigmatic: a pleasureless need to control, humiliate, scorn. The murder of Tommy, coldly casual, disposes of a minor irritant and is punishment for minor disobedience; the murder of Red follows upon a passionless presentation, to Temple, of alternatives. But the evil becomes more meaningful as it is traced to Popeye's impotence. For the relationship of spiritual impotence to individual and collective violence is sociological and psychological reality. Popeye cannot even drink. His only pleasures are smoking and wearing the black suits of his terrorist's role; and the sadistic voyeurism. The voyeurism, the cerebration of sexuality and conversion of thwarted impulse into gesture and sound, is at once an emblem of inhumanity and sad psychological fact. Minutes before the corn cob rape, watching Temple, Popeye "began to thrust his chin out in a series of jerks"; the shooting of Tommy on so little provocation, moments later, may be a first substitute for sexual act. Later, at the brothel, Miss Minnie will see Temple and Red naked as two snakes with Popeye above them making a whinnying sound. But we have already seen, unforgettably, the nervous displacement on his first visit to Temple in the brothel, Popeye crouched "beside the bed, his face wrung above his absent chin, his bluish lips protruding as though he were blowing upon hot soup, making a high whinnying sound like a horse."

The final chapter attempts, with some success, the turnabout of sympathy so effective with Joe Christmas, Thomas Sutpen, Mink Snopes: the revelation of childhood and later deprivation and trauma as cause. There has been some criticism of Popeye's acceptance of the death sentence "for killing a man in one town and at an hour when he was in another town killing somebody else," his refusal to appeal. But these pages are very moving, and Popeye in his cell is one of the loneliest of the many solitaries in American fiction—the "man who made money and had nothing he could do with it, spend it for," and whose last demands are for cigarettes and hair-lotion. The pages have some resemblance to the final ones of *The Stranger*. But unlike Meursault Popeye can take no comfort from the void, and the benign indifference of things; he experiences the void without recognizing that it exists. He merely smokes while the minister prays, where Meursault has his healing burst of rage.

My assumption is sufficiently unusual as to bear repetition: that Faulkner's misogyny, a tendentious attitude consciously indulged in *Sanctuary*, acted as a controlling, selective influence, very much as did the determination to write a spare, objective, nominally impersonal narrative, one relatively free of comment on the thoughts and feelings of the characters. In this his dual strategy had real affinity with Flaubert's in *Madame Bovary* and even more with that of Conrad in *The Secret Agent*, who restricted himself to a bleak vision of London as a slimy aquarium, with its anarchists and policemen essentially kin, and restricted himself too to a coldly ironic, deglamorized style. This is not to say that Faulkner's denigrative view of women was "insincere" in *Sanctuary*, only that it was more than usually unrelieved. The misogyny was not diffuse and compulsive, as often in the early Conrad, but recognized and accepted. Thus the letter to his editor Hal Smith, in which he tells of his "book about a girl who gets raped with a corn cob" and of "how all this evil flowed off her like water off a duck's back." Or, still more succinctly: "Women are completely impervious to evil."

The misogyny can take different forms, as we see if we compare the Narcissa of *Sanctuary* with her portrait in *Sartoris*, where she is, for Horace, the urnlike and unravished bride of quietness. Now, instead, she has the "serene and stupid impregnability of heroic statuary. . . ." She is stupid enough to tolerate Gowan Stevens, but highly efficient in her betrayal of her brother's secret to the District Attorney. She may be a plausible rendering of a southern woman of good family of her time: "I cannot have my brother mixed up with a woman people are talking about. . . ." But convention is carried very far when she says she can't see what difference it makes who committed the murder. "The question is, are you going to stay mixed up with it?" We know that Temple is willing to see an innocent man die. But so too is Narcissa, if only by selective inattention.

The changes in Little Belle, from *Sartoris*, are perhaps the normal ones brought by years. For the child whose "eyes were like stars, more soft and melting than any deer's," has changed for Horace, who now hears "the delicate and urgent mammalian whisper of that curious small flesh which he had not begot and in which appeared to be vatted delicately some seething sympathy with the blossoming grape." He stares "with a kind of quiet horror and despair, at a face suddenly older in sin than he would ever be, a face more blurred than sweet, at eyes more secret than soft." Little Belle, who picks up a man on a train, would seem to owe something both to the daughter Quentin and, as the incestuous fantasy associated with honeysuckle suggests, to Caddy. But no traumatic memory or fantasy of Caddy's brother is as terrible as Horace's, as Little Belle blends into Temple, while the "shucks set up a terrific uproar beneath her thighs." After hearing Temple's story, and as he approaches the house, where he will look at Little Belle's photograph, Horace has a vivid apprehension of the void, Conrad's cooling, dying world: "a world left stark and dying above the tide-edge of the fluid in which it lived and breathed. The moon stood overhead, but without light; the earth lay beneath, without darkness."

The vulgarity of the college girls is unrelieved, as they trade secrets of sexual attraction and prepare for the dance, the air "steamy with recent baths, and perhaps powder in the light like chaff in barn-lofts"; the barn connects them with Temple. The fierce vulgarity of Ruby Lamar is another matter, and the novel's view of her ambivalent. She is loyal, courageous, indestructible, but with some of Charlotte Rittenmeyer's frightening forthrightness. The narrating consciousness would seem to share Horace Benbow's horror over her blunt offer of herself in payment, this in turn not unlike Gavin Stevens's dismay with Eula and later Linda Snopes.

Miss Reba, however, exists in a sphere above and beyond questions of misogyny or moral judgment, and in this is like Sairey Gamp, to whom she may well be indebted. Her memories of life with Mr. Binford, the "two doves" now symbolized by two angry and worm-like dogs, have some of the quality of Sairey's fantasies, though Mr. Binford will, in *The Reivers*, have a material reality. The Miss Reba of *Sanctuary*—ample, commanding, humorous, loquacious—is intimately connected with the dogs, as they moil at her feet, snapping, or are kicked away. They share her asthmatic life, "climbing and sprawling onto the bed and into Miss Reba's lap with wheezy, flatulent sounds, billowing into the rich pneumasis of her breast and tonguing along the metal tankard which she waved in one ringed hand as she talked." She has her fine fictions, as does Sairey, of what is due her profession: "Me trying to run a respectable house, that's been running a shooting-gallery for thirty years, and him trying to turn it into a peep-show." She has her practical realism, assures Temple her maiden blood will be worth a thousand dollars to her, and drinks to the devirgination. The prose, with a macabre precision worthy of Flaubert, comments ironically on the event by describing the drawn shades:

> She lifted the tankard, the flowers on her hat rigidly moribund, nodding in macabre waes hail. "Us poor girls," she said. The drawn shades,

cracked into a myriad pattern like old skin, blew faintly on the bright air, breathing into the room on waning surges the sound of Sabbath traffic, festive, steady, evanescent.

Miss Reba is, like Sairey, an indestructible natural force.

Temple Drake is one of Faulkner's finest brief creations. A casual reader might see her as a run-of-the-mill "flapper" of her time, driven swiftly to nymphomania by the traumatic incident of unnatural rape. (In fact, she is unaware until later of what happened: "You couldn't fool me but once, could you?") Instead she is, as Flaubert saw Emma Bovary, "naturally corrupt," and like Emma comes to take the initiative with her lover and issues her sexual commands. Gowan Stevens, the Frenchman's Place, Memphis simply help her realize her potentialities, which are already indicated by her name on the lavatory wall. She is the good petter, the *demi-vierge* and teaser known for saying, presumably at the moment of truth, "My father's a judge." Two of her protective fantasies before the rape suggest the sexual content of past reveries: she hopes to turn into a boy and to have a chastity belt. The third, to be a veiled bride in a coffin, all in white, may recall Svidrigaïlov's victim as well as Emma's nostalgic reveries of past innocence. But Temple differs radically from Emma, whose provocations were certainly more severe (the two villages and the dull husband), and whose sensuality had its poetry of delicate appearance and romantically dissolving will. Flaubert was, notoriously, ambivalent, and even shared the reveries he scorned. But the portrait of Temple in the taut *Sanctuary* is unequivocal and unredeemed.

The insistent denigrative imagery is remarkably effective. Temple is a mechanical being at the trial, dressed in the role of the gangster's moll. But in other major scenes she is an alert and savage animal, generally a cat: mindlessly springing (into cars and off a train, onto and off the porch, out of the crib and back in), running in animal fear, crouching and writhing, pausing, returning in animal heat. At Miss Reba's she turns restlessly in a littered cage. In the barn loft she is both a girl frightened of rats and herself a cornered rat. But eventually it is the real rat, who has just leaped at her head, that is terrified by the larger animal presence. Its squeaking functions, after a first reading, as brilliant anticipation of Popeye's helpless animal sounds:

> The rat was in that corner now, on the floor. Again their faces were not twelve inches apart, the rat's eyes glowing and fading as though worked by lungs. Then it stood erect, its back to the corner, its fore-paws curled against its chest, and began to squeak at her in tiny plaintive gasps.

The female animal that runs from the house and back wants to be caught. The pattern is set as she gives Tommy one of her slippers to hold ("Durn ef I could git ere two of my fingers into one of them things . . . Kin I look at em?") but jerks her skirt down and springs up when she finds him looking at her lifted thigh. She has been told by Ruby to get away before dark, and is terrified of Popeye, yet is drawn two ways by feline nerves: "Temple met Popeye halfway to the house. Without ceasing to run she appeared to pause. Even her flapping coat did not overtake her, yet for an appreciable instant she faced Popeye with a grimace of taut, toothed coquetry." As real danger looms Temple wedges a chair against the door, but suddenly springs to her feet and takes off her dress, "crouching a little, match-thin in her scant undergarments." The divergent animal impulses to flee and to be caught turn to submission at Miss Reba's. She has played her game with the doctor, holding the covers to her throat. After he has left she springs from the bed and bolts the door. But presently, with fantasies of waiting for a date at home, she gets up and looks at herself in the mirror, at first seeing nothing, then "her breast rising out of a dissolving pall beneath which her toes peeped in pale, fleet intervals as she walked." She unbolts the door through which the two terrified dogs will presently come, to cower under the bed, and later in the evening Popeye.

The dissolving pall might have been imagined by Flaubert; elsewhere too, in this scene, delicate imagery comments in his manner on the sexuality which has become Temple's whole life. We return, several pages after the cracked shade associated with Miss Reba's toast to her maiden blood, to that shade, with everything else now eroticized:

> In the window the cracked shade, yawning now and then with a faint rasp against the frame, let twilight into the room in fainting surges. From beneath the shade the smoke-colored twilight emerged in slow puffs like signal smoke from a blanket, thickening in the room. The china figures which supported the clock gleamed in hushed smooth flexions: knee, elbow, flank, arm and breast in attitudes of voluptuous lassitude. The glass face, become mirror-like, appeared to hold all reluctant light, holding in its tranquil depths a quiet gesture of moribund time, one-armed like a veteran from the wars.

The passage both conveys Temple's consciousness, her drowsing movement toward acceptance (in the next paragraph she will unbolt the door) and, with the last clause, comments ironically on it and on Popeye's impotence as well. Later in the chapter a passage justly admired by Cleanth Brooks, who sees it as relentlessly exposing "the pretentious sleasiness of the room," is also effective for its specifically sexual imagery. A paragraph that begins with imagery of enveloped sexual penetration ends with a slop jar, also enveloped:

> The light hung from the center of the ceiling, beneath a fluted shade of rose-colored paper browned where the bulb bulged it. . . . In the corner, upon a faded scarred strip of oilcloth tacked over the carpet, sat a washstand bearing a flowered bowl and pitcher and a row of towels; in the corner behind it sat a slop jar dressed also in fluted rose-colored paper.

Temple's imaginative anticipation of the rape, as she evokes it for Horace, is a triumph of artistic tact. There is expert modulation from her first simple sentences to efficient narration and imagery of great precision. She conveys her intense ambivalence, dreading and wanting the rape, and suggests persuasively, though indirectly, appalling physical detail. The picture of the completed nymphomania, as we see it at the Grotto and in the room she has commandeered, on the night of Red's death, is conveyed through imagery suggesting a death of her own. Once again there are affinities with Emma Bovary: "shuddering waves of physical desire," the eyeballs drawn "back into her skull in a shuddering swoon":

> Her eyes began to grow darker and darker, lifting into her skull above a half moon of white, without focus, with the blank rigidity of a statue's eyes. She began to say Ah-ah-ah-ah in an expiring voice, her body arching slowly backward as though faced by an exquisite torture. When he touched her she sprang like a bow, hurling herself upon him, her mouth gaped and ugly like that of a dying fish as she writhed her loins against him.

The passage is echoed briefly as she leaves the trial, moving toward the four young men, bodyguards presumably employed by Popeye: "She began to cringe back, her body arching slowly, her arm tautening in the old man's grasp."

The measure of willed evil, as opposed to ordinary depravity and sexual neurosis, is taken twice, as she condemns first Red, then Lee Goodwin to death. She may for a time be under the illusion that Red has some chance for survival, when she telephones to make the assignation, but Popeye sees it as a free choice: " 'I'm giving him his chance,' he said, in his cold soft voice. 'Come on. Make up your mind.' " The risk seems to her worth taking. (*Requiem for a Nun*'s reimagining of this incident radically reduces her guilt.) Her perjury at the trial is unexcited, and like that of a drugged person. The imagery of fish returns: "Above the ranked intent faces white and pallid as the floating bellies of dead fish, she sat in an attitude at once detached and cringing, her gaze fixed on something at the back of the room." Her gazing recurs three times in the short scene. She is perhaps terrified by the bodyguards who, whether hired by Popeye or Eustace Graham, would remind her of the real murderer. But in a larger sense she seems to be gazing past the once familiar world, with its pretenses of order and legality, the world of the baseball game she had wanted to see, into the discovered world of evil; and beyond it into a void.

As Flaubert took commonplace and boring "material" and of it made a thing of beauty, so Faulkner with the sordid and mean; the violent, corrupt, depraved. Corresponding to *Sanctuary*'s ironic, pessimistic, insistently misogynous vision was a willed tautness of narrative method and style. The compression, by no means as natural to Faulkner as to Hemingway or Flaubert, was a source of energizing intensity; the author felt, as the reader feels, the presence of what is left out. The narrative compression is in places extraordinary. Goodwin's trial has only one short chapter and a few paragraphs more; the aftermath of the trial and the lynching even less. (The lynching is merely alluded to in an earlier version.) The poignant evocation of Popeye's background and diseased, neurotic childhood has a few pages only; his trial and the verdict three sentences, less than a hundred words. His jury, like Goodwin's, is out eight minutes. The spare narrative of Popeye awaiting death, quietly and as though indifferently, is as moving as that of Wilbourne in *The Wild Palms*, whose reflections reach us in a rich rhetoric—the one marking his days with cigarette stubs, the other pinching the cyanide tablet in a folded cigarette paper into powder and emptying in on the floor, since between grief and nothing he has elected grief, and fifty years in the penitentiary.

The plot may have been "horrific," in Faulkner's scornful word, but the most violent events are treated very briefly, or merely suggested, or omitted altogether. The death of Tommy comes with a sound "no louder than the striking of a match: a short, minor sound shutting down upon the scene, the instant, with a profound finality, completely isolating it. . . ." And the rape in the next paragraph is distanced for us by Temple's act of self-displacement, which has her tossing and thrashing not in the crib but on the rough, sunny boards outside, beneath the blind and deaf old man. Her harrowing account to Benbow does not reach the rape. She hints at some instrument, in raging at Popeye, but the corn cob is revealed, and then most briefly, only at the trial. The traumatic doctor's examination, at Miss Reba's, occurs between paragraphs; Red's murder between chapters. The movement of the narrative is so swift that little room is left the reader for prurient imaginings.

The compression also obviated the interiority that Faulkner found so tempting, and that does threaten *Sanctuary* when Benbow is on the scene. The account of Temple and Gowan at the Old Frenchman's Place (V–XIV) is a triumph of spare, objective, nominally impersonal narration, as free of characters' thoughts and named feelings as any novel of Hemingway. We have a few laconic mutterings of Tommy, and a few short sentences on the reflections of the disgraced Gowan. Of Temple's interior torment almost nothing is "told." "Now I can stand anything, she thought quietly, with a kind of dull, spent astonishment; I can stand just anything." Four paragraphs later, perhaps deceptively suggesting a rape has already oc-curred, she feels "her insides move in small, tickling clots, like loose shot." Other than that there is only the oblique moment of the rape: "Some-thing is going to happen to me," then the scream "Something is happen-ing to me!" and the fantasy of being outside at the old man's feet. That is all. Elsewhere instead of reflections we see Temple running, springing, crouching; see her moving distractedly in the room; hear her talk; see what she sees.

The narrative is lean, but that is hardly the word for the language. Stylistically there may be some debt to Hemingway as well as to detective fiction, but the greater affinity is with Flaubert. The strategy on the one hand is to juxtapose scenes of natural beauty with the sordid, the mean, the violent, by way of ironic commentary, and to maintain aesthetic distance. The corresponding strategy is to make precison and beauty of language, as it copes with meanness and depravity, function in the same way. Ideally the two strategies go hand in hand. They do in the humble event of Temple relieving herself outdoors. She moves through a lovely Mississippi landscape, but it is not lovely to her, who is almost as alien there as Popeye: the weeds *slash* at her. And the words *scar* and *sunshot*, for all their denotative precision, suggest a world full of menace. The turn of the next to last sentence is Flaubertian, with its denigrative *"kind of despair"*; so too the sentence before that, with its placing of *clung* and its swift dying fall. We are, as often with Emma Bovary, both inside and out; see both Temple and the world she sees, as she stoops and twists "through a fence of sagging rusty wire and ran downhill among trees":

> At the bottom of the hill a narrow scar of sand divided the two slopes of a small valley, winding in a series of dazzling splotches where the sun found it. Temple stood in the sand, listening to the birds among the sunshot leaves, listening, looking about. She followed the dry runlet to where a jutting shoulder formed a nook matted with briers. Among the new green last year's dead leaves from the branches overhead clung, not yet fallen to earth. She stood here for a while, folding and folding the

sheets in her fingers, in a kind of despair. When she rose she saw, upon the glittering mass of leaves along the crest of the ditch, the squatting outline of a man.

Two brief descriptions of Ruby's child combine Flaubert's coldness of clinical detail and composed "written" style with the distancing device of abrupt allusion to something very remote, here Paris street beggars. The two passages come some 20,000 words apart:

> Upon the lumpy wad of bedding it could be distinguished only by a series of pale shadows in soft small curves, and she went and stood over the box and looked down at its putty-colored face and bluish eyelids. A thin whisper of shadow cupped its head and lay moist upon its brow; one arm, upflung, lay curl-palmed beside its cheek.

> It lay in a sort of drugged immobility, like the children which beggars on Paris streets carry, its pinched face slick with faint moisture, its hair a damp whisper of shadow across its gaunt, veined skull, a thin crescent of white showing beneath its lead-colored eyelids.

The last sentence suggests, as Temple remarks after the earlier one, that this child is going to die. Flaubert too, recording the chatter of the shucks inside the mattress where Temple lay, might have seen "her hands crossed on her breast and her legs straight and close and decorous, like an effigy on an ancient tomb."

These remarks are not intended to suggest pastiche, but only to note affinities with the most conscious and controlled of stylists. It is pleasing to see a sentence begin with a Flaubertian notation of the Saturday country-men in town, tranquil as sheep, move to an altogether Flaubertian yoking of cattle and gods, but end with Faulknerian sinuous rhythm and glamor:

> Slow as sheep they moved, tranquil, impassable, filling the passage, contemplating the fretful hurrying of those in urban shirts and collars with the large, mild inscrutability of cattle or of gods, functioning outside of time, having left time lying upon the slow and imponderable land green with corn and cotton in the yellow afternoon.

This is the crowd that, again leaving the land, will be back on Monday to visit the undertaker's parlor where Tommy lies dead.

A novel totally free from "Faulknerese" is inconceivable, and *Sanctuary* has its amusing instances. Temple's limited view of fading light in Memphis gives way, through a clock face, to "a disc suspended in nothingness" and ultimately to no less than "the ordered chaos of the intricate and shadowy world upon whose scarred flanks the old wounds whirl onward at dizzy speed into a darkness lurking with new disasters."

He would be a purist indeed who begrudged such momentary extrava-gances. More regrettable is the highly literary consciousness and decadent rhetoric of Horace Benbow, some of which goes as far back as *Soldiers' Pay:* the view, for instance, of the college girls as "pagan and evanescent and serene, thinly evocative of all lost days and outpaced delights. . . ." Horace's preoccupations are inherited from an earlier version, where he played a more important part. His confrontation with Popeye at the spring is excellent, and his sardonic talk there persuasive. But his drunken monologue in the second chapter reads as though memorized from some-thing he had published in a college literary magazine of the early twenties. "So each spring I could watch the reaffirmation of the old ferment hiding the hammock; the green-snared promise of unease. What blossoms grapes have, this is. It's not much: a wild and waxlike bleeding less of bloom than leaf, hiding and hiding the hammock. . . ." Such writing, and the implausibly remembered dialogue with Little Belle, initiate the misogynous vision. But its prettiness threatens to destroy the reality of the Old Frenchman's Place. The decadent rhetoric has close affinities with Faulk-ner's early poems. Generally speaking, the educated consciousness in Faulkner is at a disadvantage—whether Benbow's, or Gavin Stevens's in other novels—as against the earthy or laconic talk of the blacks and Ratliff, and as against the raw reality of those who physically suffer and die, the criminals and their victims and the very poor.

Horace Benbow is in some ways useful to plot. The confrontation at the spring gives the novel a great start, and there are advantages to seeing the sinister Frenchman's Place environment before Temple and Gowan get there. The novel depends on two coincidences—that Horace should leave the road for a drink at this particular spring, on his walk from Kinston, and that he should meet Clarence Snopes on the train. But these are meaningful enough in a fiction where the ordinary safe world and the hidden criminal society are seen to be so close. Clarence Snopes bril-liantly exemplifies the knowing corrupt politician who moves at ease in both. Horace has his one effective moment of quick intelligence as a lawyer, when he resumes the conversation with Snopes. But Snopes's mind moves quicker still. Horace's education in evil, which has been stressed by some critics, is hardly essential to the novel, though his final surrender is a moving act of despair. He does not, like Temple and her father, go to Europe as he had dreamed of doing; his return to Belle, to the horror, is that of a man whose will has been broken. It is an important moment in the overall misogynous vision. Horace is not necessary, how-ever, as an outside moral intelligence. For that moral intelligence, a very firm one, is supplied by controlling technique and controlled vision, and most obviously by evaluative style.

The essential fact of structure is the willed compression we have noted. The overall movement of the novel is remarkably firm, astonishingly so when we consider how much revision consisted of reshuffling chapters, with much pasting of galleys and rewriting. The introduction of Clarence Snopes, a fine comic rather than sinister portrait, brings new energy when it is needed. But even more important are the justly famous but rarely discussed chapters of Virgil and Fonzo at Miss Reba's (XXI) and of Red's funeral and its aftermath (XXV). Michael Millgate interestingly calls attention to similarities between *Sanctuary* and *Measure for Measure*; we might add that the Virgil/Fonzo episode is altogether Shakespearean, both in its sustained comedy and in the rhetorical effect of its coming at this juncture. In the simplest terms it may be said to bring comic relief and a necessary relief from tension. From the start and through chapter XIV and the report of a death at the Old Frenchman's Place, over thirty thousand words, the taut narrative has commanded exceptional fixity of attention. There are no vacant places or instances of slack, neutral language to invite reader revery. Chapters XV–XVII, largely seen through Horace's eyes, return us to a more ordinary but depressing world. The long chapter XVIII, relieved only by Miss Reba and the snapping dogs, carries the still-bleeding Temple from the Old Frenchman's Place to the bed on which she lies thrashing, with Popeye beside her bed making his high whinnying sound. In Chapters XIX and XX, with Horace again, we contemplate his steadily darkening world, into which the fat obscene reality of Senator Clarence Snopes twice briefly intrudes. Chapter XX ends with Snopes announcing he (who "if it's there" knows "where it is") is going to Memphis.

Instead, with Chapter XXI, it is Virgil Snopes we see arriving in Memphis, with Fonzo: the one pretending to know where things are, the other on his first trip and eager for adventure. The great chapter is so memorable that it is shocking to discover how short it is, some three thousand words: the search for a hotel, and Fonzo's growing awareness of his guide's ignorance, the hesitation before a house with two fluffy white dogs in the yard, the discovery that Miss Reba has daughters, the speculation that she must be a dressmaker (since they have found a woman's undergarment under the washstand), their visit to a brothel which must be kept secret from their "landlady," and the appearance of cousin Clarence, who berates them for their folly in spending three dollars on pleasure, when cheaper negro establishments are available. The chapter, while physically within the novel's world of depravity, has in fact freed us from it into a purely aesthetic world of unalloyed joy, with disbelief suspended. There is no lapse in the bright innocence and gullibility of the two hicks, whose inferences are always wrong. The exchanges are kept very brief, giving the reader no time to protest. No fools outside Shakespeare are more innocent than the two returning from the brothel, worried that Miss Reba will evict them. With Clarence's appearance, and his sardonic comment at the negro whorehouse, we return to a world in which evil and suffering are real. But for these few pages, two-thirds through a dark experience, we have been entirely freed from it, as we are in various Shakespearean interludes.

The relationship of real world and world of aesthetic play is, with Red's funeral party, somewhat more complex. The chapter complements and complicates the novel's darker intensities, rather than freeing us from them entirely. The preceding chapter (XXIV) begins with Temple restless in her cage, demanding more to drink, making what will prove a fatal telephone call. We see her in the car with Popeye, with whom she is now on familiar terms; can call him "daddy" yet pour out her scorn of his impotence, and be silenced by his ringed hand, the ring "like a dentist's instrument." The scene at the Grotto is intensely cinematographic: laconic dialogue, the music and the dancers and the four sinister men; Red standing in the door; the crap-table and Temple's drunken gambling; her demand for a room; the intense dialogue with Red, while her hips grind against him. The brief paragraph of her writhing nymphomania is in a normal novelistic mode. But the rest of the chapter keeps to the cinematographic manner, and creates a world in which gangsters' thugs may force one across a dance floor, and a man condemned to death, perhaps knowing himself doomed, can raise his hand in "a short, cheery salute." By the end of the chapter we are altogether in the world of the movies, a stylized world with its different kind of "reality."

The movement of chapter XXIV, both in timing and in detail, is thus from fairly conventional novelistic realism to the stylization of the gangster film, where death is not quite real. This movement prepares us for chapter XXV's "atmosphere of macabre paradox," and the grotesque and parodic black humor of the funeral party. The initial shock (Red throwing dice, then on the next page in a coffin) is perhaps essential, by way of preparation for the fun, with the mourners as far from the real reality of death as Virgil and Fonzo from the reality of Miss Reba's. Our attention is recurringly fixed on the huge bowl of punch on the table draped in black, which will be a fulcrum for the steadily increasing disorder: "They surged and clamored about the diminishing bowl." But attention is also called to the bouncer, the "bullet-headed man who appeared to be on the point of bursting out of his dinner-jacket through the rear, like a cocoon." For it is he, the professional queller of disorder, who will ultimately bring on the catastrophe, and the corpse tumbling to the floor, the wreath coming too, "attached to him by a hidden end of a wire driven into his cheek." The outbreak of violence matches that of *The Day of the Locust*. But in this moment of chaos Faulkner's imagination anticipates the movement of Flem's spotted horses:

> The bouncer whirled again and met the rush of the four men. They mingled; a second man flew out and skittered along the floor on his back; the bouncer sprang free. Then he whirled and rushed them and in a whirling plunge they bore down upon the bier and crashed into it. The orchestra had ceased and were now climbing onto their chairs, with their instruments. The floral offerings flew; the coffin teetered. "Catch it!" a voice shouted. They sprang forward, but the coffin crashed heavily to the floor, coming open. The corpse tumbled slowly and sedately out and came to rest with its face in the center of a wreath.

As the novel has modulated through the stylization of cinema to this wild anti-realist fun, so now it modulates back toward novelistic realism, and the darkness of Goodwin on trial. It must return from a parodic view of an outside world of anonymous strangers, the gangsters at the funeral party, to the very small world of Horace, Goodwin, Ruby, ultimately Popeye and Temple. The modulation is accomplished brilliantly through a *reprise* of Miss Reba back at home after the party (the two snapping dogs flung back "against the wall in muted thuds"), drinking with Miss Myrtle and Miss Lorraine. At first the talk is playful, and death is still unreal; Red as a corpse "looked sweet." But gradually, as the women go on drinking, and as Miss Reba thinks of herself and Mr. Binford, two doves not two dogs, the talk turns professional, and to Red's folly in taking a chance with Popeye's girl. There is another joking exchange, but with an underlying seriousness: the respectable shooting gallery Miss Reba had run for thirty years, which Popeye tried to turn into a peep-show. The narrative becomes more serious, until Miss Reba at last evokes, for the first time very explicitly, the sexual triad: "Yes, sir, Minnie said the two of them would be nekkid as two snakes, and Popeye hanging over the foot of the bed without even his hat off, making a kind of whinnying sound."

These chapters, and *Sanctuary* generally, reveal much technical expertness and aesthetic tact in which should finally be regarded, like *The Secret Agent*, as a serious and even tragic *entertainment*, one based on a deliberately selective view of reality and an unashamedly misogynous vision. But to say this is not in the least to say that it is not a high work of art. And it is art—as we look back on the kindred challenges of personal obsession: on Dickens's revery in its sentimental extremes, on the great insight but also the disorder of Dostoevsky's—that makes the difference.

DAVID MINTER

The Self's Own Lamp

During the early months of 1928, Faulkner mixed spasmodic efforts to revise *Flags in the Dust* with other activities. He began several new stories and accepted occasional odd jobs, usually as a painter. At one time or another, he painted everything from the domes of large buildings to houses and signs; once or twice he even lacquered brass horns. During these months, he also made a second gift copy of *The Wishing Tree* "as a gesture of pity and compassion for a doomed child." He had told his fairy tale to Margaret Brown many times; she was the youngest child in a family he had known for years. Now she was dying of cancer, and he wanted her parents to be able to read the story to her as often as she wished to hear it. Yet nothing seemed to help Faulkner, neither writing nor odd jobs nor acts of kindness. Failure was not new to him: he had gone along experiencing some of it and anticipating more, trying to prepare defenses that would mute its pain. But the disappointment he felt now was intense, and there was no one with whom he could share it. Although he remained close to his mother, he knew that her tolerance had never extended to complaints, let alone to failure. Relations with his father had eased over the years; by now he felt less shame about being the son of a failure, while his father felt less outrage about being the father of "a bum." But Murry Falkner had never shared his disappointments with others or invited them to share theirs with him.

For different reasons, Faulkner also found it difficult to talk freely with Phil Stone or Estelle Franklin. Pride had always made it hard for him to express his need for tenderness, and now his relations with both Phil and Estelle had become strained. During the writing of *Flags in the Dust*, he had considered breaking with Phil altogether, apparently because he felt that Phil was trying to dictate what he should write. With *Flags* finished, he had enjoyed sharing his high expectations with Phil, and so the tension between them had eased. But he was not ready to share disappointment and failure with Phil, and he had never felt more uncertain about his relations with Estelle. Her divorce would soon be final, and he knew that she was counting on him to marry her. He had continued seeing her so regularly that people in Oxford were gossiping. Yet he felt that he might be in love with someone else. In early 1928 he wrote a letter to his Aunt Bama in which he describes his efforts to revise *Flags* and mentions reviews of *Mosquitoes*. He also refers to a woman he does not name: "We all wish you would [come down]. I have something—someone, I mean—to show you, if you only would. Of course it's a woman. I would like to see you taken with her utter charm, and intrigued by her utter shallowness. Like a lovely vase. . . . She gets the days past for me, though. Thank God I've no money, or I'd marry her. So you see, even Poverty looks after its own." Since Faulkner's lovely vase remainded nameless, it is impossible to know whom he meant. But since Aunt Bama had long since met Estelle, it is clear whom he did not mean. Also unspecified in the letter are the barriers other than poverty that stood between him and his new love. If infatuation with his lovely vase kept him from confiding freely in Estelle, his sense of responsibility to Estelle probably made it difficult for him to confide in another woman. Feeling cut off, finding no one to help dispel his disappointment and doubt, he turned inward. Simply getting through the days became a problem. At odd moments he found himself singing morbid songs, thinking about how he might die, or wondering where he might be buried. "You know, after all," he said to a friend, "they put you in a pine box and in a few days the worms have you. Someone might cry for a day or two and after that they've forgotten all about you."

Soon he was writing stories about some children named Compson. Taking a line from W.C. Handy's "St. Louis Blues," he called one of the stories "That Evening Sun Go Down." Another he called " A Justice." Both were based on memories out of his own childhood, and both concern children who face dark, foreboding experiences without adequate support or adequate sponsors. At the end of "A Justice" he depicts the children moving through a "strange, faintly sinister suspension of twilight." As his imagination played with the Compson children, he began to see them quite clearly, poised at the end of childhood and the beginning of awareness—a moment that possessed particular poignancy for him, as scattered comments suggest, and as both the deep resonance and the making of the Compson stories confirm. "Art reminds us of our youth," Fairchild says in *Mosquitoes*, "of that age when life don't need to have her face lifted every so often for you to consider her beautiful." "It's over very soon," Faulkner later remarked as he observed his daughter moving toward adolescence. "This is the end of it. She'll grow into a woman." At every turn the Compson children see things they cannot understand, feel things they cannot express. In "A Justice," as twilight descends around them and their world begins to fade, loss, consternation, and bafflement become almost all they know.

In early spring, Faulkner began a third story about the Compsons. Calling it "Twilight," he thought to make it an exploration of the moment "That Evening Sun" and "A Justice" had made the Compsons' inclusive moment. By the time he finished it, this third story had become *The Sound and the Fury*, his first great novel. Faulkner was capable, as he once remarked, of saying almost anything in an interview; on some subjects, he enjoyed contradicting himself. In discussing *The Sound and the Fury*, he displayed remarkable consistency for thirty years. His statements vary, of course, in the quality of emotion they express and the quantity of information they convey, but they show that his fourth novel occupied a secure place in his memory, and they suggest that it occupied a special place in his experience. From his statements several facts emerge, all intimating that he wrote *The Sound and the Fury* in the midst of a crisis that was both personal and professional.

The professional dimension to that crisis is clear: Faulkner's high expectations for *Flags in the Dust* prepared for it, Liveright's harsh rejection initiated it, and Faulkner's response intensified it. More and more baffled as well as hurt, Faulkner soon found himself wondering again about his vocation. He probably knew that the threat to sell his typewriter and surrender his vocation was empty, but he apparently believed that he could alter his intentions and expectations—that he could teach himself to live without hope of recognition and reward. For several years he had written in order to publish. After publication of *Soldiers' Pay*, that had meant writing with Horace Liveright in mind. As his work became more satisfying to him personally, it had become less acceptable to his publisher. Refusing to go back to writing books as youthfully glamorous as *Soldiers' Pay* or as trashily smart as *Mosquitoes*, he decided to relinquish a part of his dream. "One day I seemed to shut a door between me and all publishers' addresses and book lists. I said to myself, Now I can write"—by which he meant that he could write for himself alone. Almost immediately, he felt free. Writing "without any accompanying feeling of drive or effort, or any following feeling of exhaustion or relief or distaste," he began with no plan at all. He did not even think of his manuscript as a book. "I was thinking of books, publication, only in . . . reverse, in saying to myself, I won't have to worry about publishers liking or not liking this at all."

But Faulkner was also grappling with personal problems. Protecting his privacy, he remained vague as to what they were. To Maurice Coindreau he spoke of the "severe strain" imposed by "difficulties of an intimate kind" ("des difficultés d'ordre intime"). Though his problems probably had something to do with Estelle and his "lovely vase," and almost certainly had something to do with his loneliness and despair, they remained unspecified. About them, we know only that they ran deep and that they became intimately involved in the writing of *The Sound and the Fury*. About the writing, we know that it brought Faulkner great joy, that it produced great fiction, and that it was carried on with unusual secretiveness. Apparently no one, not even Estelle and Phil, knew anything about *The Sound and the Fury* until it was virtually finished.

Like *Flags in the Dust*, *The Sound and the Fury* is set in Jefferson and recalls family history. The Compson family, like the Sartoris family, mirrors Faulkner's sense of his family's story as a story of declension. But *The Sound and the Fury* is bleaker, more personal, and more compelling. Despite its pathos, *Flags* remained almost exuberant; and despite its use of family legends, it remained open, accessible. Faulkner's changed mood, his new attitude and needs, altered not only his way of working but his way of writing. If writing for himself implied freedom to recover more personal materials, writing without concern for publishers' addresses implied freedom to become more experimental. The novel accordingly represented a move back toward Faulkner's childhood and the family configuration of his earliest years—a move into the past and into the interior. At the same time, through the fictional techniques and strategies that Faulkner used to discover, displace, and transfigure the memories he found waiting for him, his novel represented an astonishing breakthrough. A moving story of four children and their inadequate parents, *The Sound and the Fury* is thematically regressive, stylistically and formally innovative.

Of the several corollaries implicit in its regressive principle, at least two are crucial: first, the presence of the three Compson brothers, who recall Faulkner's own family configuration; and second, memory and repetition as formal principles. Faulkner possessed the three Compson brothers, as he later put it, almost before he put pen to paper. To anchor them in time and place, he took a central event and several images from his memory of the death of the grandmother he and his brothers called

Damuddy, after whose lingering illness and funeral they were sent away from home so that the house could be fumigated. For Faulkner as for Gertrude Stein, memory is always repetition, being and living never repetition. *The Sound and the Fury*, he was fond of remarking, was a single story several times told. But since he used the remembered as he used the actual—less to denominate lived events, relationships, and configurations, with their attendant attributes and emotions, than to objectify them and so be free to analyze and play with them—the remembered was never for him simple repetition. To place the past under the aspect of the present, the present under the aspect of the past, was to start from the regressive and move toward the innovative. Like the novel's regressive principle, its innovative principle possessed several corollaries, including its gradual evocation of Caddy, the sister Faulkner added to memory, and its slow move from private worlds toward a more public world.

The parental generation, which exists in *Flags in the Dust* only for the sake of family continuity, is crucial in *The Sound and the Fury*. Jason is aggressive in expressing the contempt he feels for his mother and especially his father. Attached to them, he nonetheless resents and hates them. Although Benjy feels neither resentment nor hatred, he does feel the vacancies his parents have left in his life. Although Quentin disguises his hostility, it surfaces. Like Benjy's and Quentin's obsessive attachments to Caddy, Jason's hatred of her originates in wounds inflicted by Mr. and Mrs. Compson. In short, each brother's discontent finds its focus in Caddy, as we see in their various evocations of her.

To the end of his life, Faulkner spoke of Caddy with deep devotion. She was, he suggested, both the sister of his imagination and "the daughter of his mind." Born of his own discontent, she was for him "the beautiful one," his "heart's darling." It was Caddy, or more precisely, Faulkner's feelings for Caddy, that turned a story called "Twilight" into a novel called *The Sound and the Fury*: "I loved her so much," he said, that "I couldn't decide to give her life just for the duration of a short story. She deserved more than that. So my novel was created, almost in spite of myself."

In the same discussions in which Faulkner stressed the quality of his love for Caddy, he emphasized the extent to which his novel grew as he worked on it. One source of that growth was technical. The novel, he was fond of remarking, was a story that required four tellings. Having presented Benjy's experience, he found that it was so "incomprehensible, even I could not have told what was going on then, so I had to write another chapter." The second section accordingly became both a clarification and a counterpoint to the first, just as the third became both of these to the second. The story moves from the remote and strange world of Benjy's idiocy and innocence, where sensations and basic responses are all we have; through the intensely subjective as well as private world of Quentin's bizarre idealism, where thought shapes sensation and feeling into a kind of decadent poetic prose full of idiosyncratic allusions and patterns; to the more familiar, even commonsensical meanness of Jason's materialism, where rage and self-pity find expression in colloquialisms and clichés. Because it is more conventional, Jason's section is more accessible, even more public. Yet it too describes a circle of its own. Wanting to move from three peculiar and private worlds toward a more public and social one, Faulkner adopted a more detached voice. The fourth section comes to us as though from "an outsider." The story, as it finally emerged, tells not only of four children and their family, but of a larger world at twilight. "And that's how that book grew. That is, I wrote that same story four times. . . . That was not a deliberate *tour de force* at all, the book just grew that way. . . . I was still trying to tell one story which moved me very much and each time I failed."

Given the novel's technical brilliance, it is easy to forget how simple and moving its basic story is. In it we observe four children come of age amid the decay and dissolution of their family. His sense of it began, Faulkner recalled, with "a brother and a sister splashing one another in the brook" where they have been sent to play during the funeral of a grandmother they call Damuddy. From this scene came one of the central images of the novel—Caddy's muddy drawers. As she clambers up a tree outside the Compson home to observe the funeral inside, we and her brothers see her drawers from below. From this sequence, Faulkner got several things: his sense of the brook as "the dark, harsh flowing of time" that was sweeping Caddy away from her brothers; his sense that the girl who had the courage to climb the tree would also find the courage to face change and loss; and his sense that her brothers, who had waited below, would respond very differently—that Benjy would fail to understand his loss; that Quentin would seek oblivion rather than face his; and that Jason would meet his with terrible rage and ambition. The novel thus focuses not only on the three brothers Faulkner possessed when he began but also on Caddy, the figure he added to memory—which is to say, on the only child whose story he never directly told as well as on those whose stories he directly tells. His decision to approach Caddy only by indirection, through the eyes and needs and demands of her brothers, was in part technical; by the time he came to the fourth telling, he wanted a more public voice. In addition, he thought indirection more "passionate." It was, he said, more moving to present "the shadow of the branch, and let the mind create the tree."

But in fact Caddy grew as she is presented, by indirection—in response to needs and strategies shared by Faulkner and his characters. Having discovered Benjy, in whom he saw "the blind, self-centeredness of innocence, typified by children," Faulkner became "interested in the relationship of the idiot to the world that he was in but would never be able to cope with." What particularly agitated him was whether and where such a one as Benjy could "get the tenderness, the help, to shield him." The answer he hit upon had nothing to do with Mr. and Mrs. Compson, and only a little to do with Dilsey. Mr. Compson is a weak, nihilistic alcholic who toys with the emotions and needs of his children. Even when he feels sympathy and compassion, he fails to show it effectively. Mrs. Compson is a cold, self-involved woman who expends her energies worrying about her ailments, complaining about her life, and clinging to her notions of respectability. "If I could say Mother. Mother," Quentin says to himself. Dilsey, who recalls Mammy Callie, epitomizes the kind of Christian Faulkner most admired. She is saved by a minimum of theology. Though her understanding is small, her wisdom and love are large. Living in the world of the Compsons, she commits herself to the immediate; she "does de bes" she can to fill the vacancies left in the lives of the children around her by their loveless and faithless parents. Since by virtue of her faith she is part of a larger world, she is able "to stand above the fallen ruins of the family." She has seen, she says, the first and the last. But Dilsey's life combines a measure of effective action with a measure of pathetic resignation. Most of Benjy's needs for tenderness and comfort, if not help and protection, he takes to his sister. And it was thus, Faulkner said, that "the character of his sister began to emerge." Like Benjy, Quentin and Jason also turn toward Caddy, seeking to find in her some way of meeting needs frustrated by their parents. Treasuring some concept of family honor his parents seem to him to have forfeited, Quentin seeks to turn his fair and beautiful sister into a fair, unravished, and unravishable maiden. Believing that his parents have sold his birthright when they sold their land, yet still lusting after an inheritance, Jason tries to use Caddy's marriage to secure a substitute fortune.

The parental generation thus plays a crucial, destructive role in *The Sound and the Fury*. Several readers have felt that Faulkner's sympathies as a fictionist lie more with men than with women. But his fathers, at least, rarely fare better than his mothers, the decisive direction of his sympathy being toward children, as we see not only in *The Sound and the Fury* but also in works that followed it. Jewel Bundren must live without a visible father, while Darl discovers that in some fundamental sense he "never had a mother." Thomas and Ellen Sutpen's children live and die without having either an adequate father or an adequate mother. Rosa Coldfield lives a long life only to discover that she had lost childhood before she possessed it. Held fast yet held without gentleness, these characters find repetition easy, independence and innovation almost impossible.

Although he is aggressive in expressing the hostility he feels for his parents, Jason is never able satisfactorily to avenge himself on them. Accordingly, he takes his victims where he finds them, his preference being for those who are most helpless, like Benjy and Luster, or most desperate, like Caddy. Enlarged, the contempt he feels for his family enables him to reject the past and embrace the New South, which he does without recognizing in himself vulgar versions of the materialism and self-pity that we associate with his mother. Left without sufficient tenderness and love, Quentin, Caddy, and Benjy turn toward Dilsey and each other. Without becoming aggressive, Benjy feels the vacancies his parents create in his life, and so tries to hold fast to those moments in which Caddy has met his need for tenderness. In Quentin we observe a very different desire: repulsed by the world around him, he determines to possess moments only in idealized form. Like the hero of Pound's *Cantos*, he lives wondering whether any sight can be worth the beauty of his thought. His dis-ease with the immediate, which becomes a desire to escape time itself, accounts for the strange convolutions of his mind and the strange transformations of his emotions. In the end it leads him to a still harbor where he fastidiously completes the logic of his father's life. Unlike her brothers, Caddy establishes her independence and achieves freedom. But her flight severs ties, making it impossible for her to help Quentin, comfort Benjy, or protect her daughter. Finally, freedom sweeps "her into dishonor and shame." Deserted by her mother, Miss Quentin is left no one with whom to learn love, and so repeats her mother's dishonor and flight without knowing her tenderness. If in the story of Jason we observe the near-triumph of all that is repugnant, in the stories of Caddy and Miss Quentin we observe the degradation of all that is beautiful. No modern story has done more than theirs to explore Yeats's terrible vision of modernity in "The Second Coming," where the "best lack all conviction" while the "worst are full of passionate intensity."

Faulkner thus seems to have discovered Caddy in essentially the way he presents her—through the felt needs of her brothers. Only later did he realize that he had also been trying to meet needs of his own: that in Caddy he had created the sister he had wanted but never had and the daughter he was fated to lose, "though the former might have been apparent," he added, "from the fact that Caddy had three brothers almost before I wrote her name on paper." Taken together, then, the Compson brothers may be seen as manifesting the needs Faulkner expressed through his creation of Caddy. In Benjy's need for tenderness we see signs of the emotional confluence that preceded the writing of *The Sound and the Fury*. The ecstasy and relief Faulkner associated with the writing of the novel as a whole, he associated particularly with "the writing of Benjy's section." In Jason's preoccupation with making a fortune, we see a vulgar version of the hope Faulkner was trying to relinquish. In Quentin's almost Manichaean revulsion toward all things material and physical, we see both a version of the imagination Allen Tate has called "angelic" and a version of the moral sensibility that Faulkner associated with the fastidious aesthete. It is more than accident of imagery that Quentin, another of Faulkner's poets manqués, seeks refuge, first, in the frail "vessel" he calls Caddy, and then, in something very like the "still harbor" in which Faulkner had imagined Hergesheimer submerging himself—"where the age cannot hurt him and where rumor of the world reaches him only as a far faint sound of rain."

In one of his more elaborate as well as more suggestive descriptions of what the creation of Caddy meant to him, Faulkner associated her with one of his favorite images. "I said to myself, Now I can write. Now I can make myself a vase like that which the old Roman kept at his bedside and wore the rim slowly away with kissing it. So I, who had never had a sister and was fated to lose my daughter in infancy, set out to make myself a beautiful and tragic little girl." The image of the urn or vase had turned up in the Hergesheimer review, "Elmer," *Mosquitoes*, and *Flags in the Dust*; it had appeared recently in the letter to Aunt Bama describing his new love; and it would make several later appearances. It was an image, we may fairly assume, that possessed special force for Faulkner, and several connotations, including at least three of crucial significance.

The simplest of these connotations—stressing a desire for escape—Faulkner had earlier associated with Hergesheimer's "still harbor" and later associated with "the classic and serene vase" that shelters Gail Hightower "from the harsh gale of living." In *The Sound and the Fury* Benjy comes to us as a wholly dependent creature seeking shelter. Sentenced to a truncated life of pain—"like something eyeless and voiceless which . . . existed merely because of its ability to suffer"—he is all need and all helplessness. What loss of Caddy means to him is a life of unrelieved and meaningless suffering. For Quentin, on the other hand, loss of Caddy means despair. In him we observe a desire, first for relief and shelter, then for escape. In one of the New Orleans sketches, Faulkner

introduces a girl who presents herself to her lover as "Little Sister Death."
In the allegory he wrote for Helen Baird, a maiden of the same name turns
up in the company of a courtly knight and lover—which is, of course, the
role Quentin seeks to play. At first all Quentin's desire seems to focus on
Caddy as the maiden of his dreams. But as his desire becomes associated
with "night and unrest," Caddy begins to merge with "Little Sister
Death"—that is, with an incestuous love forbidden on threat of death.
Rendered impotent by that threat, Quentin comes to love, not the body
of his sister, nor even some concept of Compson honor, but death itself.
In the end, he ceremoniously gives himself, not to Caddy but to the river.
"The saddest thing about love," says a character in Soldiers' Pay, "is that
not only the love cannot last forever, but even the heartbreak is soon
forgotten." Quentin kills himself in part as punishment for his forbidden
desires; in part because Caddy proves corruptible; in part, perhaps, because he decides "that even she was not quite worth despair." But he also
kills himself because he fears his own inconstancy. What he discovers in
himself is deep psychological impotence that manifests itself in his inability to play either of the heroic roles—seducer or avenger—that he deems
appropriate to his fiction of himself as a gallant, chivalric lover. But
beyond the failure he experiences lies the failure he anticipates, a moment
when Caddy's corruption no longer matters to him. Suicide thus completes his commitment to the only role left him, that of the despairing
lover.

Never before had Faulkner expressed anxiety so deep and diverse.
In Quentin it is not only immediate failure that we observe; it is the
prospect of ultimate failure. Later, Faulkner associated the writing of The
Sound and the Fury with anxiety about a moment "when not only the
ecstasy of writing would be gone, but the unreluctance and the something
worth saying too." In Quentin we see clearly Faulkner's sense that the desire
to escape such anxiety was potentially destructive. If he wrote The Sound
and the Fury in part to find shelter, he also wrote knowing that he would
have to emerge from it. "I had made myself a vase," he said, though "I
suppose I knew all the time that I could not live forever inside of it."
Having finished The Sound and the Fury, he found emergence traumatic.
Still, it is probably fair to say that he knew all along that he would make
that move. Certainly his novel possessed other possibilities for him, just as
the image through which he sought to convey his sense of it possessed
other connotations, including one that is clearly erotic and one that is
clearly aesthetic.

We can begin untangling the erotic by examining the relation between the old Roman who kept the vase at his bedside so that he could

kiss it and the withered cuckold husband who "took the Decameron to bed with him every night." Both of these figures are committed to a kind of substitution, and practice a kind of autoeroticism. The old Roman is superior only if we assume that he is the maker of his vase—in which case he resembles Horace Benbow, maker of his own "almost perfect vase." With Horace and his vase we might seem to have come full circle, back to Faulkner and his "heart's darling." For Horace not only keeps his vase by his bedside; he also calls it by his sister's name. In *The Sound and the Fury* affection of brother and sister replaces affection of parents and children as an archetype of love; and with Caddy and Quentin, the incestuous potential of that love clearly surfaces—as it had in "Elmer," *Mosquitoes*, and *Flags in the Dust*, and as it would in *Absalom, Absalom!*.

The circle, however, is less perfect than it might at first appear, since at least one difference between Horace Benbow and William Faulkner is crucial. Whereas Horace's amber vase is a substitute for a sister he has but is forbidden to possess, Faulkner's is a substitute for the sister he never had. In this regard Horace is closer to Elmer, Faulkner to Gordon in *Mosquitoes*. Elmer is in fact a more timid version of Horace. Working with his paints—"thick bodied and female and at the same time phallic: hermaphroditic"—Elmer creates figures he associates with something "that he dreaded yet longed for." The thing he both seeks and shuns is a "vague shape" he holds in his mind; its origins are his mother and a sister named Jo-Addie. His art, like Horace's, is devoted to imaginative possession of figures he is forbidden and fears sexually to possess. When Horace calls his amber vase by his sister's name, he articulates what Elmer only feels. Like Elmer, however, Horace finds in indirect or imaginative possession a means of avoiding the fate Quentin enacts. Through their art, Elmer and Horace are able to achieve satisfaction that soothes one kind of despair without arousing guilt that might lead to another.

In *Mosquitoes* the origins of Gordon's "feminine ideal" remain obscure, though his art is clearly devoted to creating and possessing it. For Gordon as for Elmer and Horace, the erotic and the aesthetic are inseparable. A man is always writing, Dawson Fairchild remarks, "for some woman"; if she is not "a flesh and blood creature," she is at least "the symbol of a desire," and "she is feminine." Elmer and Horace work in their art toward a figure that is actual; they make art a substitute for love of a real woman. Gordon, on the other hand, makes art a way of approaching an ideal whose identity remains vague. About it we know two things: that it is feminine and that it represents what Henry James called the beautiful circuit and subterfuge of thought and desire. Horace expresses his love for a real woman through his art, whereas Gordon expresses his devotion to his sculpted ideal by temporarily pursuing a woman who happens to resemble it. Horace is a failed and minor artist, Gordon a consecrated one—the difference being that Gordon devotes his life as well as his art to a figure that exists perfectly only in thought and imagination.

On his way to Europe, shortly after finishing *Soldiers' Pay* and before beginning "Elmer" and *Mosquitoes*, Faulkner told William Spratling that he thought love and death the "only two basic compulsions on earth." What engaged his imagination as much as either of these, however, was his sense of the relation of each to the other and of both to art. The amber vase Horace calls Narcissa, he also addresses "Thou still unravished bride of quietude." "There is a story somewhere," Faulkner said,

> about an old Roman who kept at his bedside a Tyrrhenian vase which he loved and the rim of which he wore slowly away with kissing it. I had made myself a vase, but I suppose I knew all the time that I could not live forever inside of it, that perhaps to have it so that I too could lie in bed and look at it would be better; surely so when that day should come when not only the ecstasy of writing would be gone, but the unreluctance and the something worth saying too. It's fine to think that you will leave something behind you when you die, but it's better to have made something you can die with.

In this brief statement the vase becomes both Caddy and *The Sound and the Fury*; both "the beautiful one" for whom he created the novel as a commodious space and the novel in which she found protection and privacy as well as expression. In its basic doubleness the vase is many things: a haven or shelter into which the artist may retreat; a feminine ideal to which he can give his devotion; a work of art that he can leave behind when he is dead; and a burial urn that will contain at least one expression of his self as an artist. If it is a mouth he may freely kiss, it is also a world in which he may find shelter; if it is a womb he may enter, it is also an urn in which his troubled spirit now finds temporary shelter and hopes to find lasting expression.

Of all his novels, it was for *The Sound and the Fury* that Faulkner felt "the most tenderness." Writing it not only renewed his sense of purpose ("something to get up to tomorrow morning") and hope (a task he could "believe is valid"), it also gave him an "emotion definite and physical and yet nebulous to describe." Working on it, he experienced a kind of ecstasy, particularly in the "eager and joyous faith and anticipation of surprise which the yet unmarred sheets beneath my hand held inviolate and unfailing." Since, as Faulkner once noted, *The Sound and the Fury* is a "dark story of madness and hatred," and since writing it cost him dearly, such statements may seem surprising. But he had discovered in *The Sound and the Fury* the kind of work he had anticipated in *Mosquitoes*: one "in which the hackneyed accidents which make up this world—love and life and death and sex and sorrow—brought together by chance in perfect proportions, take on a kind of splendid and timeless beauty." In the years to come he continued to describe his fourth novel as a grand failure. Imperfect success would always be his ideal. To continue his effort to match his "dream of perfection," he needed dissatisfaction as well as hope. If failure might drive him to despair, success might deprive him of purpose: "It takes only one book to do it. It's not the sum of a lot of scribbling, it's one perfect book, you see. It's one single urn or shape that you want."

In a letter to Malcolm Cowley, Faulkner once said that he wanted "to be, as a private individual, abolished and voided from history"; it was his aim to make his books the sole remaining sign of his life. Informing such statements was both a desire for privacy and a tacit conception of his relation to his art. Faulkner assumed that his authentic self was the self variously and nebulously yet definitely bodied forth by his fictions. And it is in this slightly unusual sense that his fiction is deeply autobiographical. "I have never known anyone," a brother wrote, "who identified with his writings more than Bill did. . . . Sometimes it was hard to tell which was which, which one Bill was, himself or the one in the story. And yet you knew somehow that the two of them were the same, they were one and inseparable." Faulkner knew that characters, "those shady but ingenious shapes," were indirect ways of exploring, projecting, and reaffirming both the life he lived and the tacit, secret life underlying it. At least once he was moved to wonder if he "had invented the world" of his fiction "or if it had invented me."

Like imperfect success, however, indirect knowledge and indirect expression imply partial completion and carry several connotations. Both Faulkner's need to approach Caddy only by indirection and his need to describe his novel as a series of imperfect acts only partially completed ally it with the complex. His descriptions of *The Sound and the Fury* are in part a tribute to epistemological problems and in part an acknowledgement that beauty is difficult—that those things most worth seeing, knowing, and saying can never be directly or fully seen, known, and said. But the indirection and incompletion that his descriptions stress are also useful strategies for approaching forbidden scenes, uttering forbidden words, committing dangerous acts. For Elmer Hodge, both his sister Jo-Addie and behind her "the dark woman. The dark mother" are associated with a "vague shape [s]omewhere back in his mind"—the core for him of everything he dreads and desires. Since attainment, the only satisfying act, is not only dangerous but forbidden, and therefore both cannot and must be his aim, Elmer's life and art become crude strategies of approximation. The opposite of crude, the art of *The Sound and the Fury* is nonetheless an art of concealment as well as disclosure—of delay, avoidance, and evasion—particularly where Caddy is concerned. For the work that provides her expression also grants her shelter and even privacy. Beyond Faulkner's sense that indirection was more passionate lay his awareness that it was more permissive. For him both desire and hesitation touched almost everything, making his imagination as illusive as it is allusive, and his art preeminently an art of surmise and conjecture.

In *Flags in the Dust* Faulkner had taken ingenious possession of a heritage that he proceeded both to dismember and to reconstruct. In *The Sound and the Fury* he took possession of the pain and muted love of his childhood—its dislocations and vacancies, its forbidden needs and desires. The loss we observe in *The Sound and the Fury* is associated with parental weakness and inadequacy, with parental frigidity, judgment, and rejection. In the figure of Dilsey Faulkner recreated a haven of love he had learned early to count on; in the figure of Caddy he created one he had learned to long for. If the first of these figures is all maternal, the second is curiously mixed. In the figure of the sister he had never had, we see not only a sister but a mother (the role she most clearly plays for Benjy) and a lover (the possibility most clearly forbidden). Like the emotion Faulkner experienced in writing it, the novel's central figure comes to us as one "definite and physical and yet nebulous." Forced to avoid her even as he approached her, to conceal her even as he disclosed her, Faulkner created in Caddy a heroine who perfectly corresponds to her world: like *The Sound and the Fury*, she was born of regression and evasion, and like it, she transcends them.

By September 1928 Faulkner had finished the manuscript of *The Sound and the Fury* and had begun a typescript. Believing that he "would never be published again," he had no plan for submitting it to a publisher. He wanted something he could bind for himself. Late in September, however, he received in the mail a contract for *Sartoris*. Harcourt, Brace was going to publish at least part of the novel Liveright had rejected. Almost immediately Faulkner decided to pack his manuscript and partial typescript and go to New York. He had a new three hundred dollar advance to live on; he had friends like Lyle Saxon, Bill Spratling, and Ben Wasson to visit; and he could revise and type as well in New York as in Oxford.

For a few days he stayed in Lyle Saxon's apartment; then, wanting a place to work, he found a room of his own. While Ben Wasson cut *Flags in the Dust*, Faulkner revised *The Sound and the Fury*. Although he had always revised with care, he worked now with deep intensity; sometimes his friends did not see him for several days at a time. In part his revisions reflect continuing commitment and affection: "I worked so hard at that book," he later asserted, "that I doubt if there's anything in it that didn't belong there." But they also reflect growing hope that his book might be published. To himself and his friends, he still voiced doubt. He had no intention of building expectations only to see them dashed. It is "the damndest book I ever read," he wrote Aunt Bama. "I dont believe anyone will publish it for 10 years." Yet his revisions reflect a clear effort to enhance the novel's accessibility, to make it less exclusively his own. He increased the number of italicized passages indicating jumps in time; he added passages that clarified episodes; he made links and associations more explicit.

Having finished the revision, Faulkner dated his typescript—"New York, N.Y./October 1928"—and gave it to Ben Wasson. It had been a long, intense, and satisfying labor. "I had just written my guts into *The Sound and the Fury*," he said later. At first he felt exultant. "Read this, Bud," he said to Ben Wasson. "It's a real son-of-a-bitch." But he had learned years before that for him the sense of completion often triggered depression and lifelessness, regret and guilt; that tomorrow he was likely to "wake up feeling rotten." Writing *The Sound and the Fury* had been a deep excursion not only into his imaginative kingdom but into his own interior. Reversing direction proved almost impossible. The end he had labored hard to reach, he had dreaded, as though he dared not "risk cutting off the supply, destroying the source." Perhaps, like Proust and Rilke, he knew that "the gratitude of the completed" implied silence. Perhaps it was not only silence but rejection and punishment that he anticipated. Certainly what he did in the days that followed both imposed silence and inflicted punishment.

Accustomed to the way he worked, his friends scarcely noticed his absence. One night two of them, Jim Devine and Leon Scales, happened by his flat, where they found him alone, unconscious, and lying on the floor, with empty bottles scattered around him. Seeing that he was ill and badly debilitated, they took him with them and nursed him back to health. In later years there were several repetitions of this episode. Sometimes they came with little apparent reason, sometimes in response to painful tasks or unpleasant situations, often after prolonged, intensive writing. In *Mosquitoes*, a character suggests that people not only seek but find moments of "timeless beatitude . . . through an outside agency like alcohol." Although Faulkner's journeys into alcoholic twilight may not always have yielded such visions, they were clearly necessary for him. Sensing in the end of a novel the end of a world, and in the end of a world a final judgment, he often needed and sought an interface.

Able to write again, he stayed briefly with Devine and Scales in the apartment they shared with another friend, then moved in with an artist named Leon Crump. He had had enough of solitude for a time. Both he and Crump worked in the flat, and both worked hard, one painting while the other wrote. Faulkner remained skeptical about the future of *The Sound and the Fury*, but since Horace Liveright had released him from his contract, he was more hopeful. Harcourt, Brace had announced publication of *Sartoris*. In Ben Wasson, he had a loyal friend, in Hal Smith an editor who admired his work.

Wanting to publish and needing to make money, Faulkner began writing stories. He had finished *The Sound and the Fury* before reading any of it to anyone. Now he spent his evenings telling friends versions of the stories he worked on during the day. The war figured in some of them, his trip to Europe in others. In one, called "As I Lay Dying," he reworked material from "Father Abraham." Separately, both the material and the title would become famous; now, together, they found no publisher. Hoping to sell stories before he left New York, Faulkner asked Wasson to introduce him to some editors. Several gave him advice, and at least one, Alfred Dashiell of *Scribner's*, offered encouragement. For a time Faulkner thought he might stay in New York until after the January publication of *Sartoris*. But as Christmas drew near and money ran short, he changed his mind. No one was accepting his stories, and New York was beginning to irritate him. Having jotted down a few addresses, he packed his clothes and manuscripts and caught a train.

Back in Oxford, he continued writing, hoping for some kind of breakthrough. At first his luck held steady; no one wanted anything. Then shortly after publication of *Sartoris*, 31 January 1929, he received a contract for *The Sound and the Fury*. He had been right about Harcourt, Brace. Having kept the manuscript for several weeks, Alfred Harcourt decided to let Hal Smith take it with him when he left to form the firm of Jonathan Cape & Harrison Smith. It was, therefore, with a new publisher, his third, that Faulkner signed a contract for his fourth novel.

The Sound and the Fury was an ambitious undertaking for a new firm: it was a strange book, and it presented special printing problems. But Hal Smith was eager, and he had hired Ben Wasson as an editor. When the proofs arrived in July, Faulkner found changes everywhere. Wasson had removed all the italics and inserted spaces to indicate shifts in time; and he had made a few scattered additions to the text. Although Faulkner knew Wasson meant well, he was angry. Revising carefully, he restored the italics and removed the additions. Writing Wasson, he argued that italics worked as effectively as spacing, and that spacing was unsightly. And he insisted that his text not be tampered with: "Dont make any more additions to the script, bud," he added; "I know you mean well, but so do I. I effaced the 2 or 3 you made." In October the novel was published with italics and without Wasson's additions. Almost immediately it began attracting attention. Even reviewers who found it baffling recognized that it was not simply another novel. But two weeks after its release the economy of the United States collapsed, discouraging sales. In 1931 two small printings followed the first. A total of about three thousand copies would last until 1946.

Between February, when he signed the contract for *The Sound and the Fury*, and July, when he read proof for it, Faulkner made two remarkable moves: he wrote a novel designed to make money, and he married Estelle Franklin. Writing *The Sound and the Fury* had redoubled his old uneasiness about writing for money and recognition. Working without any ulterior motive—not for fame, certainly not for profit—he had "discovered that there is actually something to which the shabby term Art not only can, but must, be applied." Because it was free of ulterior, contaminating motives, *The Sound and the Fury* would always epitomize what he thought art should be. But he had never stopped needing recognition and money, and with publication of *Sartoris* his hope of them had revived: once again he was thinking of himself "as a printed object" and "of books in terms of possible money." Such thoughts might seem base; one part of him, despising them, would always advocate repression. But with *The Sound and the Fury* behind him, he had gone back to writing stories he thought of as public and commercial. Telling them to friends at night, he wrote and hawked them during the day.

His first weeks back in Oxford, he continued writing and pushing stories. At times Alfred Dashiell in particular seemed on the verge of accepting one. But as the mail continued to mix vague encouragement with clear rejections, Faulkner became angry. Internal resistance did nothing so much as redouble the humiliation of failure. It was bad enough to abuse one's talents; it was worse to find no buyers for the products of the abuse. For several years he had worked hard without ever making enough money to live on. Within a few months Estelle's divorce would be final. However uncertain he was about wanting to marry her, he knew that he did not want to do it on borrowed money. Yet he had a publisher for novels that made little or no money and a stack of stories that no one would publish.

As his frustration and anger deepened, Faulkner decided to write a novel that would make money when Hal Smith published it. In late January he began it; in late May he finished it. He called it *Sanctuary*. Disturbed by his motives in writing it, he later disparaged the novel, confusing public response to it. It was, he said, "basely conceived. . . . I thought of the most horrific idea I could think of and wrote it" in order to make money. Suggesting that the work itself must necessarily be contaminated, Faulkner did his novel a disservice. Many readers have followed his lead: assuming that it was basely conceived, they have concluded that it must be base. The disservice aside, however, it is probably fair to say that *Sanctuary* was written less out of injury than anger, and more for money than for itself; and it is certainly fair to say that it is one of Faulkner's bleakest, bitterest, and most brutal novels.

Faulkner began *The Sound and the Fury* knowing little about the direction it would take; he began *Sanctuary* knowing a great deal. Although writing it took several times the "three weeks" he allowed it in retrospect, it was in fact written quickly. In part the speed suggests what the manuscript shows—that Faulkner wrote and revised it with less care than he had lavished on its predecessor. But Faulkner often played with the elements of a story for months, sometimes working them out in detail in his mind before writing a word, and several elements in *Sanctuary* had almost certainly undergone extended gestation. One element was the underworld of rural Mississippi, which revolved around the manufacture and sale of illegal whiskey. Faulkner had been doing business with small, independent "moonshiners" for years, and he admired their courage and resourcefulness, and even shared some of their contempt for "respectable" society. A second element was the gangster milieu of Memphis, where organized gangs battled for control not only of illegal whiskey but of gambling and prostitution. On excursions with Phil Stone, Faulkner had been visiting roadhouses and clubs controlled by Memphis gangs for years. Although he usually watched while Phil gambled, he enjoyed frequenting places like Reno De Vaux's. If most of the customers seemed ordinary, many of the gangsters seemed exotic. From his knowledge of the rural underworld, Faulkner created several crucial figures, including Lee Goodwin and Ruby Lamar, whom he clearly respects. From his knowledge of Memphis he created characters ranging from the comic Miss Reba to the grotesque Popeye. Miss Reba, who would reappear in the last of his novels, *The Reivers*, was based on a well-known Memphis "madam";

Popeye, who had turned up in an early unpublished story, "The Big Shot," was based on a notorious Memphis gangster named Popeye Pumphrey.

Wanting his novel to be popular, Faulkner drew on two kinds of fiction, gangster stories and detective stories, which were read even in Mississippi. He had been reading as well as writing detective fiction for years, and he would continue to experiment with it. Despite the clear and relatively simple models that he had in mind, however, problems pertaining to plot persisted. He needed to find some way of joining the more sensational elements of the underworld to the more familiar social elements of Jefferson; even the several false starts, he continued to revise and shift. He also needed to find some way of controlling his discontent, which included society and men but focused on women. *Sanctuary* displays contempt for the male politicians who control society as well as for the middle-aged matrons who epitomize its hypocrisies. But its action centers on Popeye's brutal victimization of Temple Drake, who is young as well as female; and it reflects deep bitterness toward women. Whether or not this bitterness owes something to the shallow woman Faulkner described to Aunt Bama, or something to old wounds inflicted by Estelle and Helen, or something to the intimate difficulties Faulkner described to Maurice Coindreau, its focus and its depth are clear: as much as any work Faulkner wrote, *Sanctuary* suggests what Albert Guerard has termed a "persistent misogyny." The scenes featuring Temple are so taut, spare, and detached as to seem almost clinical. In the sense that they center on action rather than thought and emotion, they are dramatic. Clearly they were conceived in part as a means of making *Sanctuary* more sensational and more remunerative. But these scences are curious on other grounds, primarily because the depravity in them is overwhelming. During the course of the novel we meet several familiar forms of corruption, from dishonest politicians and cynical socialites to murderers and prostitutes. But both the amoral impotence of Popeye and the corruption of Temple move far beyond usual bounds.

Through most of his life Faulkner felt a "rather strong distrust of women." The move of a young girl through puberty to sexuality seemed to him almost to epitomize the Fall. "It's over very soon," he said later, as his daughter neared that fateful moment. "This is the end of it. She'll grow into a woman." Temple enters *Sanctuary* as a young woman who, having already made this crucial move, is curious to discover its consequences. She loves parties; merely walking, she almost dances. Without fully understanding why, she is playful, flirtatious, provocative. Yet even to readers inclined to censure her curiosity and eagerness, her punishment must seem excessive.

"I am now writing a book," Faulkner told Ben Wasson, "about a girl who gets raped with a corn cob." Having raped Temple, the impotent Popeye takes her to a room at Miss Reba's, where he watches while a surrogate lover named Red so thoroughly corrupts Temple that she becomes both willing and, finally, insatiable. In this curious triangle no character shows any tenderness or affection for another. They are all fascinated by violence and lust. Experiencing this fascination, Temple discovers evil within as well as around her. Because Popeye has introduced her to evil, she is drawn to him as well as repulsed by him. Soon after her rape she passes up a clear opportunity to escape, in part because she is already divided within herself. But her inaction also reflects the influence of her society. Escape, and perhaps survival, interest her less than keeping her refined and respectable friends from knowing what has happened to her because she knows that her society would rather condone evil than acknowledge it. Near the end of the novel, when she returns to the society from which she has been taken, she cynically cooperates in convicting Lee Goodwin of a murder she knows Popeye has committed. She thus comes to us as one who is both instinctually depraved and socially corrupt. Having found lust and violence magical, she becomes totally cynical. Flanked by her powerful father ("My father's a judge; my father's a judge") and four stalwart brothers, she calmly lies.

It may be that Faulkner fails to work out Temple's motivation in committing perjury and convicting an innocent man. But Temple's action presents fewer problems than many readers have suggested. Even before she returns to society, others have begun conspiring to convict Lee Goodwin. The Memphis underworld wants Popeye protected; the district attorney of Jefferson, Eustace Graham, wants a conviction that will enhance his record and help him win election to Congress; Clarence Snopes wants to make a profit and curry influential friends; and Narcissa Benbow Sartoris wants to protect her good name by terminating a sensational trial in which her brother is defending a disreputable man. Although none of these characters commits perjury, none of them shows much interest in truth. Graham is far more interested in his career than in justice; and Narcissa is far less offended by the death of an innocent man than by the scandal of his common-law wife. In Jefferson the law is controlled by men who are interested in power and profit, and the church is controlled by "church ladies" who are interested in convenience and respectability.

Allied against these forces are Lee Goodwin, who knows that Jefferson is indifferent to truth; Ruby Lamar, his wife, who tries to help her husband without incensing the town; and Horace Benbow, Faulkner's improbable knight-errant. Part detective and part trial lawyer, Benbow insists that someone must care enough about truth and justice to pursue them. At times he is resourceful, even energetic and shrewd, and he experiences several fine moments. But in the end, he is overmatched, partly because he is too academic and timid, and partly because the forces allied against him possess great power. "Perhaps it is upon the instant that we realize, admit, that there is a logical pattern to evil, that we die," he thinks at one point. More than defeat, it is the totality of his capitulation that marks him with failure. If Temple's encounter with evil leaves her cynical, Horace's leaves him spent and resigned.

Like "Father Abraham," *Sanctuary* is set in the twentieth century; and like "Father Abraham," it uses the Old Frenchman's Place to evoke the shadowy beginnings of Faulkner's imaginative kingdom. Like *Flags in the Dust*, it suffered a strangely complicated fate between its completion and its publication; and like *Flags*, it underwent substantial revision in the process. While writing it, Faulkner's spirits continued to rise and fall, as they had over the last several years. The more he labored, the more he wanted his new novel to be a work he could regard with pride. But there were times when he felt that whatever he did, he would fail. Shortly before he finished *Sanctuary* he told Phil Stone that he had finally resigned himself: "I think I not only won't ever make any money out of what I write," he said, "I won't ever get any recognition either." Still he could not relinquish hope. In early May, while he was revising and typing his manuscript, he received a new contract and a new advance from Hal Smith. A few weeks later, shortly after mailing his manuscript, he received a largely unexpected response. "Good God," Hal Smith wrote, "I can't publish this. We'd both be in jail." Since Smith's reservations had little to do with the quality of the manuscript, he said nothing to disparage Faulkner's development as a writer. He also refrained from asking that Faulkner return the advance. But he made clear the shock felt by readers at the press, and he said nothing to offer encouragement. Once again Faulkner accepted his failure and hid his disappointment, this time without protest or feigned confidence: he did not even ask his publisher to return his manuscript so that he could try it on someone else. "You're damned," he said to himself, "You'll have to work now and then for the rest of your life."

With his career at yet another turning point, Faulkner began trying to sort out his personal life. The question before him was what to do about Estelle. Her divorce had been granted in April, and he knew that she was waiting. Eleven years before he had felt certain. Now he was less sure, and the signs around him were mixed. Estelle wanted to get married—her younger sister, Dorothy, had called him to say that he should stop stalling. But Estelle's father remained adamant. Faulkner might be interesting, even likeable, but he seemed without prospects at an age when most men had established themselves. Faulkner's own family was scarcely less blunt. His father and brothers said he should get a job and earn some money before thinking about marriage. His mother did not want him marrying anyone, certainly not a divorced woman who was known to drink whiskey. Given more advice than he had sought or wanted, Faulkner decided to ignore it. Some of it seemed to him irrelevant, and some of it presumptuous. He could borrow money to meet immediate expenses; later, if it became necessary, he could get a job. Even with the Depression deepening, he believed that he could earn enough money to support a family.

The larger problem was one of timing. The moment of which he and Estelle had dreamed was gone, and he knew that they could never go back. He may even have known that the residual bitterness within him ran deeper than time's power to heal. Certainly some of it had recently found expression in *Sanctuary*, where Temple's degradation reaches its culmination in scenes that put old preoccupations to new uses. Shortly after she arrives at Miss Reba's, Temple lies in bed remembering the dances she has loved. Later her tireless love of dancing leads directly to uncontrollable desire for fornication. "Call yourself a man, a bold, bad man, and let a girl dance you off your feet," she chides; and then, "Give it to me, daddy." In between these scenes, Popeye watches, "hanging over the foot of the bed," a pale slobbering Mephistopheles, while Red and Temple, "nekkid as two snakes," fornicate. But there was no reason to believe that further delay would soothe problems delay had exacerbated. And despite everything, marriage to Estelle seemed to him inevitable. The first time the Old Colonel had seen Lizzie Vance he had announced his intention to come back and marry her. Several years, one wife, and one child later, he had done just that. The first time Estelle had seen Faulkner, she had made a similar declaration. Now, several years, one husband, and two children later, she was going to do it. There was reversal as well as repetition in the pattern, but both appealed to Faulkner. On 19 June 1929 he and Estelle drove to the courthouse in Oxford and got a marriage license. The next day he went alone to see his mother and Estelle's father. But his mood was no longer interrogative. He and Estelle had listened and waited long enough. With Dorothy as an attendant and a minister's wife as a witness, they were married.

RICHARD H. KING

Working Through:
Faulkner's "Go Down Moses"

Go Down Moses culminates Faulkner's
exploration of historical consciousness which began with *Flags in the Dust*.
With "The Bear" at its center, *Go Down Moses* represents a near perfect
fusion of style, evocation of time and place, and attention to moral
context, framed by the complexities of history and the rhythms of nature.
All of Faulkner's prior fiction points toward this artistic and moral consummation; that which follows betrays a distinct falling off.

Go Down Moses is no recollection in tranquility, no equipoised and
stylized vision; or at least not that alone. Faulkner sounds the agrarian
elegy for a lost world, but never suggests that the Southern tradition is the
cynosure of all virtue; nor does he surrender to the melancholy of his
down-state neighbor, Will Percy, who died in the same year *Go Down
Moses* appeared. *Go Down Moses*, like *The Unvanquished*, begins in a
comic spirit and gradually moves to the tragic. The past discovered by Ike
McCaslin is marked by violation, and the order he inherits is founded
upon the enslavement of blacks and the insatiable exploitation of the land.
If "The Bear" in particular seems to sound the Edenic theme so common
in American writing, it speaks of a paradise already flawed. Unlike
Quentin Compson, Ike McCaslin, the central consciousness of the novel,
is not wrenched apart by the antinomy of past and present. By confronting, and working through, the past of his family and his region, he is able
to transcend it, though not without cost.

There are definite thematic linkages between *The Sound and the*

From A *Southern Renaissance*. Copyright © 1980 by Oxford University Press.

Fury, Absalom, Absalom!, and *Go Down Moses*. In the first version of what was to become "The Bear," Quentin was the narrator, while Ike appeared as an old man. More important, Faulkner, in *Go Down Moses*, again scrutinizes the family romance, the power of the tradition of the fathers, and the tangled relationship of black and white as mirrored in the phenomena of incest and miscegenation within the structured opposition of nature and history (or culture). If the first two novels present the pathology of Quentin's historical consciousness, in "The Bear" we see Ike, having freed himself from the repetitive patterns of the past, able to make a moral choice.

It is crucial to read *Go Down Moses* as a whole. Such a reading forces us to see that it is the history of the McCaslin family not of any one individual which stands for the history of the South. A genealogical reconstruction reveals that the family is composed of black and white members. Blacks are not only metaphorical children, blacks are literal children in the family—and also uncles and aunts, wives and husbands who exhibit all the strengths and weaknesses of their white kinsmen. In uncovering the origins and then narrating the development of the McCaslin family, Ike deromanticizes the Southern family romance.

The larger point is that Faulkner not only reveals the central place of blacks in the "family" but also, contrary to the conventional white Southern wisdom (and here one thinks of Will Percy), celebrates the endurance of the black family as symbolized in the "Fire in the Hearth." For the story of the McCaslin line revolves around the figures of Ike McCaslin *and* Lucas Beauchamp, the last remaining male descendants of the founder, Carothers McCaslin. In the story of Lucas and his family and in the story of the grief-stricken widower in "Pantaloon in Black," Faulkner renders black life with a careful complexity unmatched in his previous work. Gone are the wily but buffoonish retainers of *Flags in the Dust*, the wooden figures of virtue such as Dilsey in *The Sound and the Fury*, or the desperate mulattoes of *Light in August* or *Absalom, Absalom!*

We learn of Lucas's raw courage when he confronts his "brother," Zack Edmonds, over whether Lucas's wife should remain with Zack after the latter's wife has died. In this "risk of life" Lucas wins recognition as an equal, as one "who had never once said 'sir' to his [Zack's] white skin"; and thus he refuses the master-slave relationship (His action does lack any collective, political implication, a problem we will take up later.) Indeed, Lucas rather than Ike inherits—that is, repeats—most of the traits of the family's founding father, Carothers McCaslin: "He's more like old Carothers than all the rest of us put together, including old Carothers. He is both heir and prototype simultaneously of all the geography and climate and biology which sired old Carothers and all the rest of us and our kind . . . nameless now except himself who fathered himself, intact and complete, contemptuous, as old Carothers must have been, of all blood, black white yellow or red, including his own." Thus in the end is the beginning.

But if familial piety is one of the informing values of the novel, it is hard-won and unsentimental. Ultimately, even the traditional form of recognition via the transmission of land from father to son is called into question. The sins of the fathers do weigh heavily on the sons. In "The Bear" we learn that in the 1830s Carothers McCaslin has refused to acknowledge his son by his incestuous union with his slave daughter; and a hundred years later, in "Delta Autumn," Roth Edmonds repeats the failure of his distant relative Carothers when he tries to buy his way out of a marriage to a woman who is distantly related to him and of mixed blood. Incest and miscegenation are the inseparable violations which mark the beginning and the end of the tradition. In "The Bear" their hidden complementarity becomes clear.

As in *Absalom, Absalom!*, Carother's denial of recognition to his black offspring (except for money he leaves in his will) reveals the master-slave relationship which underlies the father-son relationship in the family. The young Ike McCaslin realizes what Quentin had only sensed: the father-son relationship participates in the same dominative mode as the master-slave relationship. The Oedipal relationship remains tainted by enmity because the token of succession—the inheritance of land—is an illegitimate gift. The land does not belong to any one; and the fundamental crime is the will to possession: of land, of slaves, of sons. The family romance masks the history of domination which makes up the history of the family and the region.

For Ike, as for Quentin and Lacy Buchan, the central question is: who is my father and what is my tradition? Ike discovers his grandfather's crimes in the family ledgers, but, fortified by the virtues he has learned from his hunting mentor, Sam Fathers, who is an old man, part Indian and part Negro, Ike transforms the repetitive pattern of the family into an object of recollection and transcends the pattern by relinquishing his inheritance. Quentin can never discover the father or the tradition to order his world. Ike's actual father plays little part in his development, but his cousin, Cass Edmonds, who is "more his brother than his cousin and more his father than either," and his Grandfather Carothers play strong roles. But Ike finds in Sam Fathers a spiritual father worthy to impart to him a set of values, by virtue of which he can reject his family tradition.

The pattern of Sam's life is both repeated and reversed in Ike's life. Sam is denied the land which belonged to his father, an Indian chief, while Ike relinquishes his inheritance voluntarily when he discovers the taint on it. Sam's name means "Had Two Fathers," and this anticipates Ike's appropriation of Sam as a second father, the common experience of the mythological hero and a central theme of the family romance. In this new family romance the "colored" father replaces the white one. Further, Sam is forced to identify with the "out" caste, while Ike identifies with it voluntarily. When Ike travels to Arkansas to give a former slave, Phonsiba, the money left to her by Carothers (her grandfather as well), he asks her how she is. Phonsiba replies, "I am free." This in turn is Ike's response to his cousin Cass when Cass tries to argue Ike out of giving up his inheritance. And at one point in *Go Down Moses* Sam Fathers salutes a majestic buck as "grandfather," while at the end of "The Bear" Ike recognizes his complicity in the evil of the tradition by saluting a snake with the same greeting. This scene in which the son symbolically acknowledges the (grand) father is an assertion of a sort of spiritual mastery, a triumph over the father.

And yet Ike never completely escapes the repetitive pattern of his family. In their desire to be free and equal to whites, Phonsiba and her husband seem to be too much in a hurry to Ike. "Then your people's turn will come because we have forfeited ours. But not now. Not yet. Don't you see?," he says. These are the same words he repeats as an old man to Roth Edmond's mistress. Some day black and white will be able to marry—but not yet. The fact that neither Sam nor Ike leaves a male descendant points to the fragility of the countertradition Ike appropriates. Finally Ike's triumph is not so much an absolute separation from this collective past as it is the awareness, brought home to him by Roth's mistress, of how much he remains trapped in it.

Behind, yet caught in the historical world, stands the presiding presence of the bear, Old Ben. Though most readings of "The Bear" see Ben as the symbol of the wilderness that falls before the onslaughts of human progress, he functions much more ambiguously than that in the story. Early on he is described as moving through the wilderness like a locomotive, which later becomes an emblem of man's invasion and destruction of the wilderness. In this sense Ben represents the same kind of amoral force as old Carothers represents. Also the coincidence of the slaying of Ben and Sam's death indicates a kind of identity between the two: both are self-sufficient, haughty, and heedless of the normal world of men. Ike can only relinquish his heritage once Ben and Sam are dead, which reinforces the connection of Ben, Sam, and old Carothers: Ike's relinquishment slays his grandfather as well. This series of events becomes a metaphor for the murder of the primal father, the incorporation of his strength, and the identification with him. Ike's action both frees and maims him.

Thus in *Go Down Moses* the natural and historical worlds do not stand in contradiction so much as they mirror one another. The former has significance only insofar as man penetrates it. Its natural cycles are mirrored by the yearly ritual of the hunt. The nature of the historical tradition only stands revealed in light of the world of the woods and vice versa. To break the repetitious pattern of the tradition another order of repetition must be set over and against it.

Also, only with "The Bear" can we see the other aspect of Quentin's obsession with incest. Quentin's desire is not only for incest with his sister but for love for and from a father who is worthy to give and receive it. He lacks such a figure and must consequently attempt to become his own father. Ike finds his own father in Sam Fathers, but he is rendered heirless. He repudiates his inheritance in order that his son will not live under its curse, yet this abnegation costs him the love of his wife and hence a son. The remainder of his life is lived out in the increasingly meaningless yearly hunts, and he descends into nostalgic garrulousness.

But such a pessimistic reading neglects the power of Ike's emergence into historical self-consciousness. The occasion for Ike's relinquishment is his investigation of the family ledgers, the best example we have in American literature of the moral task of historical consciousness and the most graphic analogue of the psychoanalytic task of transforming repetitions into recollection. In deciphering the scrawled, nearly illegible entries of his semiliterate father and uncle, Ike, like the patient in analysis, learns to interpret the writing, the traces of past desires. Unlike Sutpen or old Carothers, Ike does not deny his past; and unlike Quentin he avoids the merging with those past desires. Ike literally "remembers" a past which belongs to him and his family. Once acknowledged and worked through ("He knew what he was going to find before he found it"), his past is transcended and becomes "other." He is free of it. According to Freud, we are not only our own individual past, but also the sum of our family's past.

Thus for the first time one of Faulkner's "rememberers" can tell his story to someone else. Ike assumes responsibility for his own story because he assumes responsibility for that which has been done in his family's name. It is this clear recognition of the determining force of the past which paradoxically constitutes the possibility for his saying, "I am free." And this possibility is achieved only by his inscription into another tradition. Only by recognizing another father can he acknowledge, yet be free of, his grandfather.

If it is by virtue of Sam's tutelage that Ike can confront his past, it is Cass Edmonds to whom he must tell his story and give his reasons. Cass's counterarguments are persuasive and rationally unimpeachable. He maintains, and Ike grants, that the Southern tradition is not all bad. Indeed, Ike is able in part to relinquish his inheritance because of what he inherits of old Carothers, "taking with him more of that evil and unregen-erate old man" than he would like. When Cass reminds him of the weaknesses of blacks, Ike responds that those weaknesses derive from their enslavement and what they learned from the white man. Finally, Cass argues that whatever Ike wishes, he cannot be free: "No, not now or ever, we from them nor they from us." This is undeniable, but not to the point. Ike's only response is, "Sam Fathers set me free," by which he means not free from blacks, but free from the history of injustice.

But Ike's ultimate tragedy is that the virtues which enable him to relinquish his heritage are private virtues. His counter-tradition is finally a private and not a collective one. Moreover the space of its realization—the woods—has succumbed to the linear destructiveness of man's fabri-cated world. Indeed, as we have already noted, the principle of destruction was there in the woods all along.

MORALITY AND POLITICS

The significance of Ike's relinquishment has been subject to much critical dispute. Positive readings of the "Ike stories" generally assume two forms. First, Go Down Moses, with particular emphasis on "The Bear," is seen as a modern rendering of archetypal human patterns, most prominent among them being the motif of the "initiation into manhood." Totemic symbols, mythological themes, and anthropological parallels abound; and Ike's story is meant to remind us of our primordial linkage to the natural world. If kept in proper perspective, this type of reading adds richness to the novel. But it tends to undermine the powerful fourth section of "The Bear" by neglecting the specific historical and regional themes in the work.

Another prominent approach to "The Bear" takes it as a story of moral and religious significance in secular garb. R. W. B. Lewis is eloquent in his claim that Ike's relinquishment is an act of religious atonement in the face of the evil of history. According to Lewis, Ike attains a sort of sainthood and thus re-acquaints the secular reader with the Christian notions of suffering, penance, and redemption. This view tempts one to see Ike as a Christ figure and his life as a modern version of the passion. But to see Ike's significance as religious in any but an ironic way is to confuse allusion and analogy with identity, though it must be granted that Faulkner trades a bit too willingly on Biblical rhetoric and parallels. Lewis avoids this sort of religious imperialism and is uneasy about the isolation to which Ike's action leads him.

But there is another line of criticism which fails to be impressed by Ike's religious or moral stature. Richard Adams scores Ike's arguments as illogical and unconvincing, while Herbert Perluck sees Ike's as the "story of a renunciation that fails." In David Stewart's words, Ike's actions provide him with "little more than cheap satisfaction." In this view Ike emerges as a socially irresponsible and a moral trimmer to boot, since he lives off the income from the land he claims to relinquish. Indeed, Stewart includes Faulkner among his accused by claiming that in Go Down Moses Faulkner "induces a condition of paralysis and in this way perpetuates the status quo." Ironically, Faulkner was not adverse to criticizing Ike. Though he did grant that Ike's vision gave him "serenity and wisdom" but "not success," he was also later to say in criticism of Ike that "what we need are people who will say, this is bad and I'm going to do something about it, I'm going to change it." And in the novel itself, Faulkner destroys Ike's wise old man persona.

A conservative critique of Ike (and Faulkner) would echo this impatience with Ike's dithering. It would point to Cass Edmonds's enlightened paternalism as the more realistic and wiser stance for the white Southerner of good will in the late 1880s. But Cass's opposition is too "wise" by a half, too much the wisdom of Job's accusers. Though Cass is apparently a sensitive man and aware of the needs (or at least some of them) of blacks, like Will Percy he insists on their continued subordination. Like Percy, Cass affirms the authority of the tradition not only for its positive qualities but because it is the tradition.

Still neither of these positions seems persuasive. The radical and liberal critiques of Ike ignore the historical possibilities of a young white man in the Mississippi hill country circa 1890. Indeed, until the 1960s, Mississippi was in James Silver's phrase a "closed society." As late as the 1950s Southern moderates such as Mississippi's Hodding Carter, a man of considerable power and influence, continued to express their firm commitment to segregation and white racial purity and superiority, though all the while granting that glaring injustices existed. In short, it is not all clear what sort of political action was possible for Ike in the context of the late 1880s. What was he supposed to do?

But here it must be granted that if Ike's gesture is a morally significant one (and I would insist that it is), it carries no political implication. The world which Faulkner creates and which Ike and Lucas inhabit offers no space of freedom for political or collective action. Indeed there is something to be said for tracing this to Faulkner's own apolitical nature. Despite his courageous pronouncements in support of the 1954 Supreme Court school desegregation decision, he was a States' Right Democrat insofar as he was a political man at all. To insist that he should have made Ike into a political activist is to misconstrue the possibilities of social change in Mississippi in the 1880s (or 1930s) and to misconstrue Faulkner's essential vision of politics and its importance. Still, flawed though it is by the impossibility of political embodiment, Ike's relinquishment is a form of moral triumph, despite what Francis Utley has called his later "backsliding."

But to say that Ike's failure is ultimately a political failure (though not one for which he can precisely be blamed) is another way of saying that Ike's is a tradition of one. He lacks a way of translating this new mythos into a collective historical tradition to replace that of his grandfather, that is, the South's. Nor does it make any sense at all to say, with Olga Vickery, that Ike "evade[s] both the guilt of his grandfather and his own responsibility," for he confronts that guilt and responsibility more forthrightly than any of Faulkner's characters and most of Faulkner's contemporaries. Aside from Lillian Smith and W. J. Cash, it would be difficult to find a Southern writer, sociologist, or historian of Faulkner's era who so clearly identified and critiqued the essential foundations of the Southern tradition. But again it was the tragic fact of Faulkner's (and Ike's) world that historical consciousness and refusal to participate in the skein of injustice did not of itself lead to or suggest a way of translating moral gesture into political action. Though the burden of the fathers had been lifted, the shoulders from which it had been taken remained permanently bent. Only for later generations of readers would Ike's achievement be liberating.

THE COSTS OF CREATION

According to Harold Bloom, all modern creators want priority, to become the first in the series and hence found a new literary or cultural tradition. The way is blocked, however, by a tradition, embodied in literary precursors, whose very existence testifies to the fact that the individual artist is always already too late. The essential vision has been articulated, and nothing new remains to be done. This, according to Harold Bloom, is the anxiety of influence which diffuses the modernist literary enterprise and modernist culture generally.

In his writings on the artist and creativity, Otto Rank anticipated much of Bloom's thesis when he asserted that the "will to immortality" was fundamental to the psychology of creation. "Liberated from God," the artist "himself becomes God." Behind the artificed world lies the historicist anxiety, the will to originality, which is the complementary impulse to the will to immortality. This imaginary world is designed to withstand the ravages of time. The ultimate desire of the artist is to become his own father, to create himself, and thereby deny his father (Time) and all creative priority. Thus behind the artist's desire for immortality stands the fear of death. It is this fear of death, claims Norman O. Brown, which generates time and ultimately culture; but then paradoxically tries to escape them. This is another way of saying the modernist-romantic project is an impossibility. Art is not a way of escaping or stilling the anxiety but of expressing it.

For Faulkner the confrontation with the Southern tradition, a literal historical entity and a fantasy structure, took the form of a confrontation with and critique of various fictional fathers and grandfathers. The various forms of historical consciousness which I have discussed were at the same time an exploration of the burdens of being a writer. This was expressed most centrally in the dialectic between weak sons and strong fathers in Faulkner's work. By *Go Down Moses* the unequal *agon* is inverted and the son triumphs over the father. But not without cost.

Put another way, in Faulkner's work and that of many of his Southern contemporaries, the desire to escape the looming presence of precursors is counterpointed with the desire to find a new father, a new force of tradition that will provide a way of continuing to live and write. This is a standard theme of much of this century's literature and particularly of some of Faulkner's most talented contemporaries and epigones. In Faulkner's work, however, we see the clearest expression of the interaction of these two impulses. For there we see all the essential "moments" in the movement of Southern historical consciousness in the 1930s and 1940s: from the monumentalist attitude of "O, that we could have it back again" to the despairing, anxiety-laden "We can't have it back again" and the even more tortured "Do we want it back again?" Repetition emerges as impossible and recollection alone remains possible. But this victory barely hides the desire to become one's own father. This is granted to Ike McCaslin, but only on the condition that he not become an actual father. In terms of the artist's project it means that the achievement of his vision comes at the cost of isolation and loneliness, for there can never be anyone to follow who will measure up.

Before pursuing this farther, the question of the mother must be raised: where is she? As we have seen in Percy's *Lanterns on the Levee*, she hardly makes an appearance, and Percy's life seems bereft of feminine presences. Tate's *The Fathers* opens with the death of Lacy Buchan's mother, while Lacy's sister is dangerous and destructive. In Lillian Smith's writings her mother remains opaque, and Carson McCullers's fiction lacks the stabilizing or energizing force of (white) female figures. And, indeed, in Faulkner the mother and women in general seem to move more and more to the periphery as we move from *Flags in the Dust* to "The Bear." When a woman makes an appearance she is the promiscuous sister or neurasthenic mother (*The Sound and the Fury*), the ethereal mother and mindless daughter (in *Absalom, Absalom!*), or the grasping temptress-wife in "The Bear." At best, she stands sexless and Cassandra-like on the fringes, passing judgment on the foolishness of men. But she is never at the center.

In the case of Faulkner, at least, we can make some interesting correlations with Freud, our other great critic of the patriarchal tradition. Both were ensconced in and tried to write their ways out of a patriarchal tradition which seemed powerful yet was on the verge of collapse. In both cases, women were conceived of as somehow impenetrable to masculine reason, both less and more than men, more in touch with the primal rhythms of life but also less "civilized" and thus a danger to the fragile cultural order. In both lives there existed a lifelong attachment to the mother, while the literal fathers appeared, against the mother, as weak and ineffectual.

This makes it all the more strange that for Faulkner, as for Freud, the father loomed so large while women were all but ignored in his writings. In placing the Oedipal situation at the center of individual and cultural life and thus making it the focus of his entire system, Freud underplayed the tremendous pre-Oedipal influence of the mother on the child, a neglect that only his followers have rectified.

Not only was Faulkner's mother a powerful force in his life, the desire for his future wife, Estelle Oldham, obsessed him during the 1920s when she was married to another man. Both Faulkner and his biographer are tight-lipped on this matter, but by Faulkner's own testimony he was in the throes of "difficulties of an intimate nature" when he was writing *The Sound and the Fury*; and one can safely guess that they had something to do with sexuality. It is important to remember here that the occasioning image of that novel was "a little girl in muddy drawers" up in a tree, looking in the window of the family house at the death-bed of the grandmother. All the essential elements of this vision—the muddy pants, the tree, the witnessing of a forbidden scene, the connection of death with the bedroom—have to do with sexuality and its fatal lure, with the primal scene and the myth of romantic love. And surely Quentin's agonized but futile efforts to drive away Caddy's suitors reflect Faulkner's memories of his despair over Estelle's suitors and the one who finally married her. Sex, death, and women all seem somehow inextricably linked.

Thus we might speculate that neither Freud nor Faulkner did justice to women and in fact could never quite represent them as "complete" human beings because of the tremendous hold they exerted on each man's life and the powerful resentments each man harbored against their power. Their secret muses could never be acknowledged; the theory and the fiction respectively were "only" delays, ways of avoiding saying what they desired. Creation was a trope itself. This was the anxiety of the mother's influence which underlay the more explicit anxieties that came from the ambitions directed against the fathers. Thus we can read the movement from incest to parricide both ways: the incest desire is the desire to destroy the father; the demystification (symbolic parricide) of the father conceals the incest desire. And this is another way of saying that the creative projects of both Faulkner and Freud, late romantics that they were, were finally unresolvable.

But most interesting, to return to the theme of the creator, is that in the life and work of Faulkner and Freud there was a continual juxtaposition of and vacillation between weak and strong, son and father. Freud, for instance, liked to think of himself as a "conquistador" and identified himself with or greatly admired Hannibal, Cromwell, Napoleon, and Moses. As the founder of a movement he insisted upon loyalty, felt nothing but bitterness and betrayal against those who went astray, and refused to acknowledge them once the break had been made. Yet Freud's theoretical and therapeutic focus was upon the weak and damaged sons and daughters who could not dispel actual or fantasized parental power. In the several fainting spells he experienced when confronted by what he read as signs of disloyalty from his "son," Jung, he displayed a deep fear of being overthrown and hence a vulnerability as a father. Nor is it accidental that the "story" of the murder of the primal father by the sons came in *Totem and Taboo* (1913), not long after his break with Jung. As the primal father of the psychoanalytic movement Freud could scarcely tolerate what he feared: the inevitability of a repetition of the revolutionary impulse at the origins of culture. It is no wonder that he was so taken with the notion that the Jews had slain their deliverer, Moses. To be a father was to be vulnerable and inevitably surpassed.

Though Faulkner was anything but the founder of a movement and remained as far as possible from organizational commitments, there is an analogous ambivalence in his fictional world. He was obviously fascinated with the fathers who were ruthless, cruel, and had founded an order—Sartoris, Sutpen, and Carothers McCaslin. As founders they assumed a certain amoral heroism and were beyond good and evil in any conventional sense. They were demiurges. But then so was the strong artist. Here we should remember that Faulkner labeled the map of Yoknapatawpha County as his: "William Faulkner, Sole Proprietor." This was an appropriately Sutpenian gesture and attached to *Absalom, Absalom!*, though undoubtedly with a hint of irony. At one point in 1939 he blurted out in a letter that "I am the best in America, by god." A certain ruthlessness was revealed in his comment that "If a writer has to rob his mother, he will not hesitate; the 'Ode on a Grecian Urn' is worth any number of little old ladies." (Sutpen apparently felt the same way.) In addition, Faulkner sometimes expressed a feeling of profound detachment from ordinary concerns. For instance, he once said that he would like to be reborn as a buzzard: "nothing hates him or envies him or wants him or needs him." And yet—all of these strong, commanding figures come to grief in acts of hubris which deny the humanity of others and exhibit a heedlessness of the reality: they cannot or do not take time into account. As with Freud this is the anxiety of the strong who know that strength will fade or be subject to challenge.

On the other hand there are the weak figures, the maimed sons rendered ineffectual by powerful fathers and grandfathers. They seem to stand for the other aspect of the artist's persona. In *The Unvanquished* the narrator writes that "those who can, do, those who cannot and suffer enough because they can't, write about it." Later Faulkner was to write to Malcolm Cowley of his passionate desire for anonymity, revulsion against his own existence: "It is my ambition to be, as a private individual, abolished and voided from history, leaving it markless, no refuse save the printed page . . . obituary and epitaph . . . : He made the books and he died." The artist's act of creation was so presumptuous that, whatever hostile end he met, he should expunge himself from memory, leaving only the traces of his existence. Yet these marks of creation, the printed words, were also attempts to stop time which Faulkner saw as the artist's essential task. This was what lay behind his famous statement that he had tried "to get it all in one sentence." If, as Richard Adams asserts (though too abstractly), Faulkner's central theme is the destructive effects of the attempt to stop time, this means that we must see Faulkner's characters who try to overcome time, whether weak or strong, as variations on the portrait of the artist.

This brings us to *Go Down Moses* with its two "sons"—Ike and Lucas. Lucas is a lineal heir of the Sartoris-Sutpen-McCaslin role. Like these precursors he is detached, amoral and indifferent to anything but what he chooses to take as his concern. Like Faulkner himself, Lucas changes his name as though to assert his uniqueness and make himself one of a type. In the latter stories, especially "The Bear," Sam Fathers and even Old Ben embody this same attitude. They are creatures utterly independent and self-sufficient who scorn normal human intercourse. Yet ultimately Faulkner seems less interested in this aspect of the artist than he is in the one represented by Ike, who is clearly a descendant of Quentin and even Gail Hightower and young Bayard Sartoris. Unlike them, however, he can endure the vision he possesses and can act, which is to say he can "say" it and by extension "write" it. With *Go Down Moses* Faulkner finally was able to tell the story he wanted to, or come close to it. For behind it had lain the task of forging "the conscience of his race." And conscience here should be taken to refer both to a new structure of moral perception and to self-consciousness. With this done, Faulkner's great moral and artistic task was essentially complete.

That Ike fails to become the founder himself and to pass on this moral (or aesthetic) vision to anyone else implies, finally, the impossibility of founding any tradition upon art. As with Ike, the artist's epiphanic experience and accompanying vision remain private or at least not compelling for the collectivity. They lack the authorizing power of the great religious visions, toward which Ike—and Faulkner especially later in *A Fable*—strain. Neither Ben (the cultural totem) nor Sam (the mentor) who presides over the moral and artistic "scene of instruction" survives except in the consciousness of one individual. The slaying of the fathers and the undermining of the tradition is finally a negative action. Like Freud's resolutely secular vision or Jung's quasi-religious one, Ike's can provide no basis for a new culture of communal symbolic significance. This is perhaps what Faulkner realized when he denied to Ike any offspring to perpetuate "his" tradition.

Finally, perhaps Faulkner was rendering in fictional form the artistic triumph and impasse, the personal achievement and frustration which he had reached by the early 1940s. Like Ike he was without a son, though he influenced many indirectly through his writing without assuaging his essential loneliness: "a widower now and uncle to half a county and father to no one." Isolated from his community, though he loved it deeply, and caught in a marriage which was anything but sustaining, he had become the old man he already felt himself to be when he wrote how he felt "on the verge of decrepitude" in 1929 at the beginning of his great design. Such were the costs of creation.

ALAN HOLDER

An Odor of Sartoris: William Faulkner's "The Unvanquished"

"An Odor of Verbena," frequently anthologized as a short story complete in itself, also serves as the final chapter of Faulkner's *The Unvanquished*, a novel which appeared in 1938. In that chapter, an extended reference is made to Colonel Sutpen, who figures of course as a central character in *Absalom, Absalom!*, published two years earlier. The allusion to Sutpen only serves to point up the enormous differences between the two novels, in terms of both form and achievement. But while it is a much more conventional piece of storytelling and a much smaller accomplishment than *Absalom, Absalom!*, and while the whole of it has been less highly regarded than its concluding chapter, *The Unvanquished* has an interest of its own, revealing part of Faulkner's overall conception of the Southern past.

The book consists of a series of episodes ranging in time from 1863 to 1874, and related to us by Bayard Sartoris, who figures as a major participant in the work as well as its narrator. Coming from *Absalom, Absalom!* to the adventures Bayard speaks of, one is first struck by the decided absence of the earlier book's elements: the opaque narrative technique, the rhetorical inflation, the tortured questing for the truth of the past. (Such things would probably not have found favor with the readers of *The Saturday Evening Post*, where much of the book first appeared, in the form of stories). It is almost as though writing *The*

From *The Imagined Past.* Copyright © 1980 by Associated University Presses, Inc.

Unvanquished constituted a vacation for Faulkner, a respite from the strenuousness of *Absalom, Absalom!*. Where the story of Colonel Sutpen seemed determined to build up and complicate its subject, to give its materials massiveness, intensity, and large significance, *The Unvanquished*, while drawing its subject matter mostly from the potentially great theme of the Civil War, is to a very large extent content to be relatively low-keyed, relaxed, diminutive.

This is immediately apparent in the treatment of the war action and of the invading Yankees (the story takes place in Mississippi). The Civil War set countrymen killing fellow countrymen, produced an enormous number of casualties, and caused destruction that went, at least in the South, far beyond the confines of limited battlefields. But Faulkner is apparently reluctant to tap these potential sources of drama and intensity. Neither Yankee nor Southerner kill one another before our eyes, though such deaths are alluded to. Much of the war action *per se* is occurring or has occurred offstage, and does not generate a sense of widespread death. It seems to involve, on the part of Colonel Sartoris, much more in the way of stealing Yankee horses than shooting their riders. When the Yankees appear on the home front, the basic locus of the action, they come on mostly as exasperated dupes, frustrated and defeated (in terms of the loss of material goods) by Southern wiles. They do burn down the Sartoris home (as well as others) but that burning is handled in a curiously muted way. For while one chapter concludes with the Yankees being called " 'bastuds' " because they have destroyed the Sartoris house, the destruction takes place almost before we know it, and is not dwelt upon. There is very little bitterness directed against the invaders by either Faulkner or his characters.

Indeed, the Yankee presented most fully is made very attractive. Colonel Dick, knowing that the two boys, Bayard and his Negro companion Ringo, are literally hiding behind Rosa Millard's skirts after having shot at one of his Union soldiers, pretends to believe the lady's assertion that there are no children present. He orders his men not to harass her (the story comes uncomfortably close to being a Confederate version of "Barbara Frietchie"). Later, the Colonel signs an order stating that the silver and mules taken from Rosa should be returned. He is the courteous, considerate gentleman from start to finish, admiring and sympathetic in his response to the Southern civilians. Faulkner's depiction of Colonel Dick would seem to partake of what one historian has found in a number of Civil War novels, the myth "of a war ruled by antebellum courtesies rather than military necessity. . . ." Such a view "avoided violence to the feelings of either North or South. . . ." There is certainly such avoidance here, and it constitutes one of the book's *evasions* of touchy and difficult subject matter. We are given a conflict flattering to both sides, a Civil War which turns out to be a war game more than anything else (the book opens with Bayard playing at war with Ringo, and this turns out to be a comment, intended or not, on much of the book).

There *are* feelings of hatred and revulsion that get into the novel, but these are directed not against the Yankees, but against Southerners preying upon other Southerners. Grumby's Independents are a group of men who begin to loot and terrorize their compatriots as soon as the Northern soldiers are gone. They do not stop at beating women and children, and they end up murdering Rosa Millard. Here are villains of the deepest dye whom everyone can hate with a clear conscience. An easy target for easy feelings is thus provided, making for the complete displacement of the North-South confrontation.

One detects an evasiveness not only in Faulkner's handling of the war, but in his depiction of the relationship between Bayard and Ringo as well—this is part of the larger question of the book's presentation of the Negro. The two characters are twelve-year-old boys when we first meet them. They have long eaten together and slept together, and both call Rosa Millard, mother of Colonel Sartoris and grandmother of Bayard, "Granny." Bayard says of Ringo: "maybe he wasn't a nigger anymore or maybe I wasn't a white boy anymore. . . ." They live a kind of wartime idyll, sharing adventures that are a boy's dream. (The relationship between them links up with the interracial male pairings Leslie Fiedler finds so prominent in American fiction.) In the incident where they shoot at the Yankee soldier they handle the rifle together. During another episode they are riding on one horse, and the symmetry of the action further establishes an "equality" between them: "presently I caught Ringo and held him as he slipped off and then a little later Ringo caught and held me from slipping before I even knew that I had been asleep." Bayard says that the difference in the color of their skins didn't count for them, only the difference in their experiences (at one point Bayard is temporarily "ahead" of Ringo because he has seen a locomotive whereas Ringo has not). If anything, Ringo is regarded by Colonel Sartoris as the smarter of the two boys, and it is he who plays an active role in Rosa's scheme for getting mules from the Yankees under false pretenses. Ringo is a vivid presence in the book, a character of much charm, thoroughly engaging (Faulkner once said he grew up with a boy like Ringo). But apart from that, he has been made by the author into a wholehearted devotee of the old order, perhaps more of a Sartoris than the Sartorises themselves. When the two boys are journeying from home, Ringo trades a prized possession for some of the "Sartoris dirt" that Bayard has taken with him. He is a great admirer of Granny. When he forges copies of the order Colonel Dick had given Rosa, he wants "to sign [General] Grant's name every time, and when Granny said that would not do anymore, Lincoln's. At last Granny found out that Ringo objected to having the Yankees think that Father's folks would have any dealings with anybody under the General-in-Chief." He is plainly unsympathetic to the carpetbaggers who are trying to put Negroes into office. Finally, in "An Odor of Verbena," when Colonel Sartoris is murdered, it is Ringo who comes to inform Bayard and fetch him home, saying " 'we,' " i.e., he and Bayard, could get the Colonel's killer.

But in that chapter, the last in the book, Ringo is ultimately relegated to the background. He and Bayard are both twenty-four now, and Bayard has left home to study law. Just what Ringo is doing is not specified (he is presumably still attached to the Sartoris family in some capacity). Given the prominence of Ringo's role and his relationship to Bayard in the preceding portions of the book, the subordination of these in "An Odor of Verbena" is striking. Such an effect was undoubtedly not intended by Faulkner, and could simply be the result of his bringing together the previously unpublished "Odor" and pieces of the book that had appeared earlier as separate stories. But he has given us *The Unvanquished* as a whole, and looked at as such, the book's shunting aside of the Bayard-Ringo relationship constitutes an evasion of painful subject, namely, the presumable effects that their growing up and out of boyhood, their going the separate ways of white and Negro, have had on their friendship and their views of each other (this would have been particularly complicated by the changed status of the Negroes as a result of the war). Faulkner is certainly entitled to his focus in "An Odor of Verbena," which is the matter of Bayard's entry into moral manhood, but since the story does come as the concluding piece of a larger work, one looks, in vain, for the exploration of a relationship that has figured prominently hitherto. One gets the sense that Faulkner is trying to cover important ground too quickly, too skimpily, that he acknowledges his debt to his character without discharging it, when he has Bayard say that Ringo had changed so much during the time he was engaged in Granny's mule scheme that "I had had to do most of the changing just to catch up with him." What does the change in Ringo consist of, and how do he and Bayard relate to each other now? Only the white character is given a significant development. For if we are to go by what "An Odor of Verbena" does tell us, we see a Bayard who is capable of achieving moral independence, while Ringo seems arrested in a state of Uncle Tom-hood, defined only by his wish to avenge the Colonel's death. The two young men are not adequately placed in relationship to each other in the book's concluding chapter.

The intelligence and resourcefulness that Faulkner ascribes to Ringo in the course of *The Unvanquished* stand out all the more sharply because of the novel's generally condescending treatment of the slaves (the split here in the treatment of the Negro may remind the reader of the clashing elements that went into Mark Twain's portrait of Nigger Jim). For example, the elderly Joby functions exclusively as a comic black, humorously reluctant to do heavy work, and saying "Which?" when one would expect him to say "What?" He is pictured as being in a continual contest with Granny which she always wins. At one point he is portrayed with "his mouth hanging open and his eyes like two eggs" the very model of stage-Negro amazement. His son Loosh is described as having a head resembling "a cannon-ball . . . bedded hurriedly and carelessly in concrete. . . ." (We cannot help laughing at this comparison, albeit guiltily.) Even Ringo does not escape such portraiture, and on one occasion when it is applied to him it robs him of potentially heroic status. He and Bayard have tracked down the infamous Grumby. Bayard is attacked by the outlaw who in turn is attacked by Ringo: ". . . I saw Ringo, in the air, looking exactly like a frog, even to the eyes, with his mouth open too. . . ." Later, he makes an appearance saying " 'I ain't a nigger any more. I done been abolished.' "

Such touches are of a piece with Faulkner's distinctly unreconstructed view of the slaves leaving their masters when they hear of their emancipation. The subject enters in a comical way with Loosh's wife, Louvinia, striking him in the head when he says the Negroes will be freed, and telling him " 'You black fool!' . . . 'Do you think there's enough Yankees in the whole world to whip the white folks?' " Bayard's reaction to Loosh's statement is to tell Granny excitedly that the Yankees are coming " 'to set us free!' " So first, we have Louvinia's amusing distinction between white folks and Yankees, followed by Bayard's inability to distinguish between the status of the white Southerners and the slaves (this last is undoubtedly meant to be amusing also, but is hard to take). After thus availing himself of Bayard's one-time naïveté to try for a comic effect, Faulkner then makes use of the older Bayard's maturity to have him deliver a serious comment on the slaves' attraction to freedom (Bayard is recounting the story's events years after their occurrence, so the narrative is able to move from the child to the man). He speaks of "the impulse to move which had already seethed to a head among [the Negroes], darker than themselves, reasonless, following and seeking a delusion, a dream. . . ."

Faulkner's imagination is engaged by this view (one typical of many Civil War novels), and he provides us with remarkable pictures of the blacks moving in groups along the roads and entering a river in quest of their freedom. We are given a vivid sense of an inexorable, though futile and irrational mass movement, but one wishes Faulkner had allowed his dramatizations to speak for themselves, had been less tendentious and condescending in his treatment of the slaves' drive toward freedom. Drusilla, Bayard's cousin, speaks contemptuously of the slaves tramping the roads all night, " 'waiting for a chance to drown in homemade Jordan. . . .' " Granny lectures a number of slaves on their having left home, telling them to return where they came from. The two ladies appear to be speaking for the author.

Yet there is one notable exception to Faulkner's supercilious conception of the Negroes' hunger for liberty. When Granny asks Loosh if he is leaving the Sartoris home he says that he is: " 'I done been freed; God's own angel proclamated me free and gonter general me to Jordan. I don't belong to John Sartoris now; I belongs to me and God.' " Challenged by Granny on having revealed the whereabouts of the Sartoris silver, Loosh replies: " 'Where John Sartoris? Whyn't he come and ax me that? Let God ax John Sartoris who the man name that give me to him. Let the man that buried me in the black dark ax that of the man what dug me free.' " This is a remarkable moment. A character has broken free of his author's general views and inherited prejudices to present with force and dignity a conception of himself which goes directly counter to the thrust of the story. A piece of Faulkner's imagination seems to have cut loose here and to be operating on its own. The reader finds it hard to believe that the Loosh speaking these lines entered the story possessed of a head like a cannonball embedded in concrete.

Perhaps Faulkner's generally condescending treatment of the slaves leaving their homes to seek freedom comes out of a view of slavery which, at least in The Unvanquished, does not make that condition seem an oppressive one at all. Certainly there is no abuse of Negroes at the hands of the Sartorises anywhere in the book. Also, the wartime conditions depicted seem to have made blacks and whites virtual equals, either in the form of the adventures shared by Bayard and Ringo, or of the common quarters inhabited by members of the two races after the burning of white homes. By such equalization of their condition, Faulkner would seem, as he does in the ultimate subordination of the Bayard-Ringo relationship, to be evading the great, painful fact of the South's old order, the fact of slavery. In the one household beside that of Sartoris where we get a picture of the relations between whites and blacks, there is nothing to suggest the terrible forms slavery could take. The brothers Buck and Buddy McCaslin participate in an elaborate game with their slaves which allows the latter freedom of movement in the evenings. Also, Colonel Sartoris says that the McCaslins are possessed of ideas about social relationships well ahead of their time. In an anticipation of Ike McCaslin in *The Bear*, we are told of the brothers' conception that the people belong to the land and not vice versa. We are told, too, as a presumable extension of this notion, that the brothers have a scheme whereby the slaves will not be given their freedom, but will buy it in work on the plantation. Buck and Buddy have persuaded some poor white farmers to pool their meager land holdings "along with the niggers and the McCaslin plantation, promising them in return nobody knew exactly what, except that their women and children did have shoes, which not all of them had had before, and a lot of them even went to school." Here, too, there is an "equalizing" of whites and blacks, though under conditions of the greatest vagueness, and presided over by members of an upper class exhibiting a spirit of noblesse oblige. The McCaslins' plan seems to represent the book's prescription for the way the slaves should have been freed.

A spirit of noblesse oblige is at work, also, in Granny's disposing of the fruits of her successful swindling. (Repeatedly getting mules free from the Yankees under false pretenses, she sells them back to the Northern soldiers.) She distributes money and mules to her neighbors, but demands that they tell her how they will spend the money, what they will do with the mules, etc. Occasionally, she takes a mule from one person and gives it to another. She is the determined, courageous aristocrat, providing for the less resourceful around her, a Lady Bountiful. When she prays to God, she acknowledges the chicanery of her dealings with the Yankees, but defends it at the same time. Her address to God is a paradoxical thing, a defiant prayer. She is unquestionably admired by Faulkner and part of his portrait of the Old South at its best. (That portrait is highly sketchy, since what the book mainly gives us is the Old South being broken down by the war.)

Granny, or Rosa Millard, was cited by George Marion O'Donnell when he formulated his famous thesis about the Faulkner canon, saying that its unifying principle was "the Southern social-economic-ethical tradition," and that it exhibited "the conflict between traditionalism and the antitraditional modern world in which it is immersed." The Sartorises are people who "act traditionally. . . ." Arrayed against them are "the invading Northern armies" and the landless whites, like Ab Snopes, who aim "to make the traditional actions of the Sartorises impossible." O'Donnell treated *The Unvanquished* first in the development of his thesis, going on to apply his conception of the traditional versus the modern to a number of Faulkner's works, including almost all the major novels. O'Donnell's view proved an influential one, though it has been modified by others since, or called into question as applying to the whole of Faulkner. Putting aside the question of its validity for other of Faulkner's works, we can say that its accuracy with respect to *The Unvanquished* is so dubious that one wonders why it wasn't questioned from the very start. For while Sartorises and Snopes, who are key figures in O'Donnell's formulation, are both present in *The Unvanquished*, O'Donnell's description of the conflict between them, and the respective motivations they embody, does not cover the facts but, rather, misrepresents them.

We might first observe that the invading Northern armies do not represent a principle antagonistic to an "ethical tradition" embodied in the Sartorises. As has been already demonstrated, the chief protrait of a Yankee soldier is highly flattering. Moreover, it is precisely because the Yankees assume that the principle of returning confiscated goods to civilians is at work in the forged military orders Granny presents to them, that she is able to carry out her swindles. They are hardly the enemies of a "traditional" morality here. And just how traditionally ethical is Granny in her dealings with the Yankees? If anything, Sartoris and Snopes *share* a common ability to hoodwink, to outsmart, the invaders. Granny and Abner Snopes make a pair of natural partners until such time as Granny proves the victim of Ab's unscrupulousness with respect to her (only here does O'Donnell's thesis apply). There is in Faulkner considerable admiration for the shrewd dealer, and a delight in his or her manipulations (this is present even in *The Hamlet* where there is much sympathy for the victims of such manipulations). Faulkner's treatment of shrewd operators was probably influenced by tales of outwitting that make up part of the body of "American humor." And while events in *The Unvanquished* ultimately take a terrible turn, the story of Granny's repeated victimization of the Yankees is colored by comedy, as when a Yankee lieutenant asks Granny not to turn a receipt he is giving her into a document that will eventually ruin him. By that point in the story he knows her way with Union Army paper forms.

The talent for outwitting is featured in *the* Sartoris, the Colonel himself. While he is undoubtedly brave, we are made just as conscious of his resourcefulness in *fooling* the enemy. In one episode he gains time for escape by acting like a dimwit. In another, he captures a group of Union soldiers by having Bayard and Ringo make a great deal of noise, giving the false impression to the soldiers that they are surrounded by Confederates. The incident ends with the Yankees sneaking off into the bushes in their underwear. As with the events centering on Granny, the episode is basically comic. Here, too, the focus is hardly on the operation of a traditional morality but on an amoral shrewdness. With the triumphs of both Granny and the Colonel, the reader is not witness to the display of an ethical tradition so much as a capacity to adopt to new circumstances, to improvise, to act in a way that has more to do with spiritedness and imagination than with morality. The results are largely amusing, and rather than adopt O'Donnell's view, it is more to the point to observe that Faulkner's treatment of the Southern past here partakes of the quality of American humor, its amalgam of heroism and comedy.

We should also note that there is a kind of comedy at work in one of the book's chapters other than the sort we have been viewing, and that this too goes counter to O'Donnell's thesis. It is not manifested in terms of Confederate triumphs over the Northerners, but takes the form of satire at the expense of the South. Such humor is not characteristic of the book as a whole, but it does figure as one component in Faulkner's presentation of Southern history. The section called "Skirmish at Sartoris" is largely concerned with the efforts of Bayard's Aunt Louisa to get her daughter Drusilla married to Colonel Sartoris. Drusilla, a cousin of the Colonel's dead wife, had ridden off to war with the Colonel's troop, acting as just one more soldier. Aunt Louisa was scandalized by Drusilla's action, and now insists that she and Colonel Sartoris must get married at once. The women of the town of Jefferson enter into a kind of alliance with Louisa to see that propriety is served. All of these ladies are treated as comic figures, their concern with what they regard as sacred social forms played off against the thoroughly unconventional behavior of Drusilla. Aunt Louisa may be said to embody a "traditional" sensibility, but, whatever O'Donnell might say about the matter, it is not seen by the story as anything to be honored. Aunt Louisa says her husband died in the war *"to protect a heritage of courageous men and spotless women. . . ."* (italics in original). Drusilla has flouted, in her mother's view, "all Southern principles of purity and womanhood that our husbands had died for. . . ." (Aunt Louisa may be regarded as a spiritual ancestress of Mrs. Compson in *The Sound and the Fury*, who is preoccupied with the supposed worth of her family and its good name, which she sees as threatened by the activities of her daughter Candace.) Faulkner plainly cannot take Aunt Louisa or her rhetoric seriously, mocking even her display of mourning (she wears a black crepe bow on her umbrella and carries around with her "a wad of some kind of black knitting"—one thinks of Twain's satire of expressions of ostentatious sorrow in *Huckleberry Finn*). In her comic obsession with getting Drusilla married, she seems to represent for Faulkner a ridiculous elevation of propriety to the supreme value in life, and in her statements about what the Southern dead had sacrificed themselves for, she is seen as advancing an absurd conception of the war. These are components of a Southern sensibility that Faulkner can only laugh at.

Yet even as he shows a readiness to be amused here at the genteel Southern woman's view of the world, Faulkner can be accused of using the humor of "Skirmish at Sartoris" to cloud the issues raised by another element of the South he is presenting to us, the use of violence to maintain the political status quo. Apart from the matter of Drusilla's marriage, the chapter's principal concern is with Colonel Sartoris's response to the machinations of the carpetbaggers. Efforts are being made by Northern whites to get the Negroes of the town to become Republicans and vote a black man into office as town marshal. The Colonel, along with the other white men of the town, is determined that this shall not happen. He ends up shooting the two Northerners who are behind the scheme, saying he allowed them to fire first. He and Drusilla appropriate the ballot box, and in the subsequent "election," all the white men vote against the would-be Negro marshal. "Skirmish at Sartoris" ends with the men cheering Drusilla and the Colonel. The book itself appears to be endorsing the Colonel's action (he claims to be working " 'for peace through law and order' "), evading the question of the means he has employed in pursuing his goal. Faulkner reduces the pressure of such a question by intertwining the story of the ballot box with the comedy of Aunt Louisa confronting a Drusilla who has *forgotten* to get married in the excitement of the action taken against the carpetbaggers. The chapter appears to be presenting an unreconstructed Southern view of the voting episode, with the cheers of the men sounding "high and thin and ragged and fierce, like when the Yankees used to hear it out of the smoke and the galloping. . . ."

However, with the book's final chapter, "An Odor of Verbena," the critique of the Colonel that is conspicuous by its absence from "Skirmish at Sartoris" makes a notable appearance (that critique is not acknowledged at all in the O'Donnell thesis about Sartorises vs. Snopeses). Bayard, now a law student, is called upon by a traditional code to avenge his father's killing (the Colonel has been shot by his one-time business partner, Redmond). He is expected to do so by his fellow townsmen, by Ringo, and most important, by Drusilla, who presents him with a pair of duelling pistols; she is described by him as "the Greek amphora priestess of a succinct and formal violence." However, when he goes to confront Redmond, Bayard does so with no intention of participating in a duel or killing him. This decision marks a significant break with the Sartoris mode. It is obviously approved of by the story and this alone indicates that the way of Colonel Sartoris represents something less than the highest form of conduct for Faulkner. But "An Odor of Verbena" makes unfavorable judgments of the Colonel more directly.

Those judgments must operate against the formidable image of the Colonel that has emerged from the previous chapters. Even as it was being created, that image was partly recognized by Bayard as the subjective product of his younger self, but this distancing acknowledgment still left the Colonel endowed with glamour. The objective facts of the story display his courage and quick-wittedness. He rides a horse named nothing less than Jupiter; it is described at one point as standing in the dawn "as a mesmerized flame. . . ." Effects like this rub off on the man.

But the Colonel's participation in violence is confronted by "An Odor of Verbena" in a way that is new to the book. The chapter tells of how Drusilla, some time before his death, had defended him as having a dream in which " 'all the people, black and white' " would raise themselves by their bootstraps. Bayard, however, had wondered how he hoped to accomplish anything good if he killed people. Bayard reminded Drusilla that the carpetbaggers Sartoris had shot before holding the election were " 'men. Human beings'. " Bayard refers to his father's "violent and ruthless dictatorialness and will to dominate," compares his eyes of those of "carnivorous animals," and sees the hands of the dead Colonel colored by "the invisible stain of what had been (once, surely), needless blood. . . ." The moral question of the Colonel's right to kill, an issue that had been allowed to escape from "Skirmish at Sartoris," is being faced here. Bayard decides that *he* does not wish to continue the pattern of killing in confronting Redmond.

Yet in the last analysis, Faulkner shows a distinct ambivalence towards Colonel Sartoris (a figure based on Faulkner's own great-grandfather). The attraction that the Colonel has for him is by no means purged in "An Odor of Verbena." Faulker cannot bring himself to reject this character clearly and finally. Note, for example, the curious handling of Sartoris's encounters with Redmond. There is one scene which, confusingly, refers to a forthcoming meeting between Redmond and Sartoris but not the one in which the Colonel is killed. During this scene, the Colonel says he is tired of killing and will go to see Redmond unarmed. In the encounter where he *is* killed, he is described as carrying his derringer in its usual concealed place but not using it. Thus, while the Colonel, after his death, is thought of as a man stained with blood, he has displayed, while still alive, a rejection of his usual ways. We have, then, simultaneously, an impulse in the story to judge the Colonel harshly, and a desire to present him

218 • ALAN HOLDER

favorably through his own expression of contrition. Also, while Bayard seems at one point to repudiate the Colonel's "dream" because of his father's readiness to employ violence in seeing it realized, he says, as the book draws to a close, that the dream was "something which he had bequeathed us which we could never forget. . . ."

Finally, there is the symbolic gesture made by Drusilla. It is she who has most passionately expressed the desirability of Bayard's avenging the Colonel's death. When she realizes he is not going to shoot Redmond she becomes hysterical. Yet, ultimately, she pays tribute to Bayard's going unarmed to meet Redmond by placing a sprig of verbena on his pillow. While riding with the Colonel during the war, she used to gather the flower and wear it; it was "the only scent you could smell above the smell of horses and courage and so it was the only one that was worth the wearing." The book concludes with Bayard's discovery of the sprig. In one way Drusilla's gesture can be interpreted as a realization by her that Bayard's course of action is an admirable one, superior to the violence she had originally espoused. But the means by which the gesture is made is linked inextricably to the courage of the Colonel. The odor of verbena takes its meaning from its association with his wartime activities, in which Drusilla shared. The odor evokes the Colonel, and Drusilla's gesture is that of one Sartoris paying tribute to another. So that her act of laying the sprig on Bayard's pillow expresses perfectly Faulkner's mixed feelings toward Sartoris. On the one hand there is the recognition of the courage Bayard has shown in taking a course of action so different from that characteristic of his father. But at the same time the Colonel's courage is evoked, and Bayard in rejecting his father's way, is seen as being worthy of his father. Some critics would argue that there is a progression in the book from the young Bayard's romanticizing of his father to the adult Bayard's recognition of his father's defects. What is being argued here is that alongside its severe judgment of the Colonel, the book manages to retain much of the original glamour it had bestowed on him.

The ending of the book, then, contains a survival of the admiration for the Colonel as a representative of the Old South. In this respect, as well as others, The Unvanquished is very different from Absalom, Absalom!, where Quentin Compson's insistent cry that he does not hate the South strongly suggests just the opposite. The Old South in Absalom, Absalom! seems a much more terrible place than in The Unvanquished, having inhumanity as a part of its structure, as demonstrated in Colonel Sutpen's "design" for founding a dynasty. The recovery of the story of Sutpen oppresses Quentin intensely. In The Unvanquished, the past, even while rejected in one way, is also cherished, and there is a sense of reconciliation and closure at the book's conclusion as opposed to the open-ended pain that Quentin exhibits. The strenuousness and complexity of *Absalom, Absalom!* do not result in release, whereas the relative relaxation and simplicity of *The Unvanquished* produce a Southern past that can be at once rejected and loved, certainly lived with. Everybody would agree that *Absalom, Absalom!* is the greater work and that it acknowledges the cruelty, injustice, and conflicts of the past more fully than *The Unvanquished.* But the latter work is Faulkner's creature as well, and points up what might be called the Confederate component of his sensibility.

When, in a conversation about his great-grandfather and the Civil War, Faulkner was asked the sources of his history, he said:

> I never read any history . . . I talked to people. . . . When I was a boy there were a lot of people around who had lived through it, and I would pick it up—I was just saturated with it, but never read about it.

While we need not accept this statement as the whole truth—there were works on the Civil War in Faulkner's personal library though not a very great number of them—it is undoubtedly the case that Faulkner got much of his sense of the past from oral tradition. Such a source would have tended largely toward a glorification and defense of the past, and certainly influenced *The Unvanquished.* Insofar as it retains the mark of such influence the book is a measure of how far Faulkner had to go from his cultural starting point to be able to write a work like *Absalom, Absalom!* *The Unvanquished* itself is not completely subservient to a narrow, glorified version of the past, being a mixture of the celebratory, the comic, the satiric, and the critical, but it ends up accepting Southern history in a way that *Absalom, Absalom!* cannot.

JAN BAKKER

"As I Lay Dying" Reconsidered

William Faulkner's outrageous story of the Bundren family is undoubtedly one of his most complex and enigmatic novels; complex, because beneath the surface narrative of a grotesque journey we are aware of terrifying depths of human significance; enigmatic, because we never seem to be quite certain in what sense the novel controls our responses. Is the bizarre tale of the Bundrens just macabre comedy or heart-breaking tragedy? Is it a story of heroics or does it mock heroics? Is it an epic with Addie as the dead queen and her sons as the princes carrying out their ritual duties, or does it parody epic? What makes it difficult to find the right answers to these questions is the fact of the irony that informs the novel from start to finish. To appreciate the book's full riches it is therefore necessary to see how exactly the irony works, in its thematics, the characterization, as well as in its vision. Only then will we be in a position to understand that *As I Lay Dying* is at once a comedy and the reverse of comedy, a tragedy and a mockery of tragedy, an epic and the parody of epic, and that instead of detracting from the novel's power these paradoxes tend to intensify it.

With novels like *The Hamlet, The Town,* and *The Mansion, As I Lay Dying* belongs to those works in which Faulkner deals with the Southern poor whites, a group of people long associated in the popular mind with illiteracy, shiftlessness, and brutality. Faulkner did not contribute to this folklore. Although he made use of the comic possibilities of the

From *Costerus,* vol. 26 (*From Cooper to Philip Roth: Essays on American Literature*), edited by Jan Bakker and D. R. M. Wilkinson. Copyright © 1980 by Editions Rodopi (Amsterdam).

type, he generally treats the poor whites in his works with sympathy, seeing in them a dignity and sense of values which, at first sight, seem totally incommensurate with their appalling poverty, illiteracy, and callous and cruel behaviour. A revealing example of this is provided by an episode occurring late in As I Lay Dying. The waggon with its stinking burden approaches Jefferson and is passing three negroes. One of them, shocked at the evil smell, expresses his sense of outrage, and Jewel fiercely curses him, but a white man who is walking in front of the negroes thinks that it is he who is being absued, and immediately takes offence. In the exchange that follows, Darl succeeds in placating the white stranger, while holding Jewel back from starting a fight. What this incident nicely illustrates is a code of honour as elaborate as any upheld by Faulkner's Southern aristocrats. There is a willingness on the part of the Bundrens to apologize for an injustice done, but it must be clearly understood that they are not afraid of facing the consequences if the family honour is at stake.

This sense of family loyalty is even more striking if we remember that Darl is not exactly a believer in idealistic conduct, and that he and Jewel hate each other. The comedy inherent in the situation—the shoddy caravan, enveloped in the appalling stench, the ludicrous cause of the misunderstanding—clearly clashes with the seriousness the Bundrens attach to the issue in question, but the effect on the reader is not an easy laugh but a heightened awareness that life can be laughed at but never laughed away. And this response also applies to the journey the Bundrens undertake to carry the dead body of the mother to a distant graveyard at Jefferson. Although all the other characters in the novel outside the Bundren family circle regard the expedition as foolish and scandalous, there is, with the exception of Darl, no one in the family who opposes the long and dangerous journey. They seem united in their determination to honour the promise exacted by Addie from her husband Anse to bury her bodily remains in Jefferson, beside her father's grave, and even Darl does not shirk the family duty when he sees that his protest is of no avail. Yet, here again, the issues are not as simple as they look, Anse's reply to the question why he is determined to take Addie's body to Jefferson is invariably: "It's Addie I give the promise to. . . . Her mind is set on it"; but there are, as we learn early in the novel, other motivations than mere obedience to the family honour. When Addie dies, Darl imagines Anse saying, "God's will be done. . . . Now I can get them teeth," an observation which proves only too true, as the end of the novel shows. Dewey Dell, the daughter, has also more than one reason: she knows that she is pregnant, and is desperate to get into town, so that she can buy drugs to effect an abortion. And even to the solid Cash the town presents temptations beyond the call of duty. Yet it is Cash, the meticulous craftsman in the family, and Jewel, the fierce, unthinking man of action, whose motivations in undertaking the expedition are most pure, and the fact that they were Addie's favourite sons may be significant in explaining this. Anse himself, in motivating the trip to his neighbours, is hardly credible. Considering his mean selfishness, his blatant hypocrisy, his inertia, one must distrust any form of piety on his part. Beside the set of teeth he longs to have, there is still another secret motive that drives him to town: he wants a new wife to replace Addie. Moreover, Anse can easily impress his neighbours with his concern for Addie, since he knows that he can depend on others to honour his promise. He knows that he can rely on his sons Cash and Jewel, and on other people as well. As he tells Cash: "I reckon there are Christians here." Christians, who will even lend him the spades to dig Addie's grave, so why should he bother to bring them himself?

Anse is the consummate manipulator of men, who knows how to exploit what is good in them, although he is devoid of any himself. Yet, he gets away with it, which shows that it is impossible to dismiss even him as either a caricature or mere type. Despite the impurity of his motivation, Anse remains the driving force behind the expedition, though none of the heroism which the family have to display in bringing it to a successful end falls to him. The responsibility for this is fully shouldered by both Cash and Jewel, whose superhuman efforts to save the coffin from the raging elements fully deserve the qualification heroic. For as Cleanth Brooks has remarked, "heroism is heroism even though it sometimes appears to be merely the hither side of folly." The incredible feats performed by Cash and Jewel in getting the waggon and coffin safely across the flooded river leave no doubt that what we are made to witness here pertains to the epic mode. The description of the crossing itself is brilliantly done. Faulkner's technique enables us to watch it from different points of view, and the composite picture that is thus built up in the reader's mind acquires a larger-than-life vividness and intensity, without its losing touch with reality though. We not only see the events through the eyes of such a level-headed outsider as Tull, whose objective account reveals that the threat the flooded river poses is real enough; we also see them through the keyed-up, though observant imagination of Darl, whose perceptions are always coloured by a touch of the poetic, while the wild agony that the near-loss of the coffin engenders is conveyed through the child Vardaman, who frantically watches it slipping off into the water. No one, then, possesses the whole truth of what really happens, but the sum of their subjective truths lends the reality of the event a scope and depth which it cannot possibly have for those who are directly involved. In this sense art adds a dimension to reality of which the individual in confrontation with his daily existence remains unaware. Cash as well as Jewel are totally ignorant of the fact that what they achieve during the crossing is heroic; to them it is to all appearances the reverse of heroic. The same applies to the comedy that attaches to Cash, sitting on the shore with a broken leg, surrounded by his tools, dived up by a tireless Jewel, who will not think of giving up. It is again a comedy that must escape both Cash and Jewel; to them the whole sequence of catastrophic events is the reverse of comedy. But the heroics and the comedy are there, depending upon the perspective under which the events are viewed, a perspective supplied by art, because Faulkner's technique of multiple presentation of view points prevents it from cancelling those other perspectives which contradict the heroic and the comic. What this achieves for the novel is a density of texture which neither the overtly comic nor the tragic-heroic mode could have given to the writing.

Although both Cash and Jewel seem to emerge from these exploits as mere stock-characters—Cash exemplifying unreflective endurance, Jewel, brainless heroism—the picture is again much more subtle. Jewel is certainly one of the least reflective among the members of the family: of the fifty-nine sections in the novel he is given only one section in which he directly addresses the reader. Yet we get a fairly complete view of Jewel's character; mainly through Darl's eyes, it is true—and Darl is not always to be trusted—but observations of other characters help to rectify this. Faulkner's technique of multiple presentation works admirably here, as, for that matter, it does in his characterization of the other members of the Bundren family. Jewel, then, ignorant, intolerant, and highly strung, is more than a mere automaton. His most precious possession is his horse, for which he has worked so hard that it has nearly ruined his health, and when he allows it to be sold so that the journey to Jefferson can be continued, he makes a sacrifice which reveals unexpected depths of character. But Jewel can only express his feelings through violent and brutal action. His is an unreflective, aggressive masculinity, the stuff epic heroes were made of, and he is destined to perform acts which can either be qualified as heroic (the river-crossing, the barn-burning episode), or as brutal (at the end of the novel when he jumps Darl in order to turn him over to the officers). What makes him recognizable against his Southern background of poor-white stock is the fierce hatred behind all his actions, expressing itself in the ugly violence, engendered not only by the grief about his mother's death, but also in something in his love for Addie which he could never allow himself to become conscious of: the element of incestuous desire.

Like Jewel, Cash is a man of action, and like Jewel he is one of Addie's favourite sons. But there the similarities end. Although Cash, the patient, conscientious craftsman, whose only concern seems to be his tools, begins as a comic figure, and although comedy is always just round the corner when the action involves him, his character shows him for what he certainly is: a quiet, simple and limited man, unimaginative but practical, the solid workman, but as Faulkner makes us look at him from a number of angles, it becomes necessary to modify this verdict considerably. He is unselfish in a quiet, unobtrusive way; the values he believes in may be simple and direct, but he shows dignity and integrity. When a member of the family needs help, he believes that one helps him as a matter of course, without making any fuss about it; one does not set fire to a man's barn, even if one seems to have a valid motive, and one does not help arrest a member of one's own family, as Jewel and Dewey Dell do, even if one agrees that Darl ought to be locked up in an asylum, for his own good, as Cash thinks. His most impressive qualities, however, are his great powers to endure and to suffer without complaining. With his broken leg he rides for six days on a waggon without springs, and does not give so much as a whimper. And when Dr. Peabody expresses his sarcastic indignation about his family's stupidity—they set his leg in a cast by pouring sand and cement around it—he defends this appalling treatment by meekly pointing out that "They just aimed to ease hit some. . . ."

Dr. Peabody's attitude towards Cash is a mixture of amazement, irritation, pity and secret admiration, and one can well understand and share his exasperation, which extends to the other members of the family as well, in particular to the daughter Dewey Dell, the only female character on the seat of the evil-smelling waggon. She, too, looks at first glance like a simple and rather stupid country girl, an easy victim, but like Cash she shows more depth, subtlety, and dignity of character than the circumstances we find her in at the beginning of the novel would lead us to expect. She seems entirely locked up in herself, but there are reasons. Her problem, about which she can only talk with a woman, becomes an obsession after Addie's death, leaving her no time to indulge her grief for her mother. "I wish to have time to let her die," she says, and the Shakespearean echo fittingly intensifies the agony expressed through these words. It's not that she easily accepts the idea of an abortion. As she desperately cries: "I believe in God, God. God, I believe in God," but her pregnancy comes too soon, "it is because in the wild and outraged earth too soon too soon too soon." She could have turned to Dr. Peabody, but her fear and shyness prevent her from doing so. She knows that Darl has discovered that she must be pregnant, but she dislikes him, because she is afraid of his cold, observant intelligence. She is desperately alone and helpless in her confused condition and feels like "a wet seed wild in the hot blind earth." She has to find her own solution for what she calls "the female trouble," and her excursions to the two druggists provide high comedy, without, however, cancelling the poignant pathos of her pitiable situation.

What Dewey Dell exemplifies is the extreme isolation in which all the members of the Bundren family have to come to terms with the death of the mother, the centre which held them together and round which their existence revolved. Their ignorance and inarticulateness prevent them from sharing an experience as profound and uprooting as the death of the mother, and each responds in his own confused and isolating way. Cash, by laying his heart and soul in the making of the coffin, sawing and hammering away under the window of the dying Addie, the rain soaking his clothes; Jewel, through violent, undirected action; Dewey Dell, by frantically concentrating on finding her abortion drugs; Vardaman, the child, by simply refusing to accept his mother's death. He blames Dr. Peabody for it, seeing a causal connection between him and her death, as the physician's arrival coincided with the moment she died. He bores holes in the coffin to allow Addie to breathe, and finally identifies her with the fish he had killed at about the same moment that she had passed away, an analogy which in his prelogical, magical way of thinking begins to constitute a case of transubstantiation, guaranteeing his mother's survival: "And tomorrow it will be cooked and et and she will be him and pa and Cash and Dewey Dell and there won't be anything in the box and so she can breathe." Vardaman's frantic denial of his mother's death, his attempt to liberate her from the coffin, is of course strange, but the boy himself is not an imbecile. It's his way of trying to cope with the terrible shock until he can regain a hold on reality and move towards sanity again. And from his monologues it clearly appears that this process accelerates his attempts at discovering his identity, which, formless as it still is, needs definite shape if he is to make any sense of the disorder he suddenly faces. That in this search for identity he is strictly limited to the narrow circle of a family that has lost its centre of gravity, only adds to the state of utter confusion in which he gropingly tries to find his way, but the family is all he has, and when the end of the novel even this falls apart, his emotional stress finds poignant expression in the compulsive reiteration of his mad brother's name when he cries out: "Darl is my brother. Darl. Darl."

If Addie's death forces the child Vardaman to become trapped in a search for identity that comes too early to be anything but painful and unhingeing, the effect on Darl is even more disastrous: his identity dissolves in madness. The importance of Darl's presence in the novel is unmistakable. In nineteen sections, the greatest number alotted to one single character, we hear his voice, and he is undoubtedly the principal narrator of the book. With Darl's gifts of observation and expression—he is by far the most articulate of the Bundrens—this is not surprising. He represents most strongly Faulkner's own detachment and insight. It is through him that we are most completely informed of the development of the narrative as well as of the hidden motivations that guide the Bundrens' behaviour. Darl sees through his father's hypocrisy, he feels intuitively that Dewey Dell is pregnant, and that Jewel is not Addie's legitimate son. This is not to say that only Darl's view is true—Faulkner's multiple presentation of view points guards us from making this mistake—but the truth he possesses lends a singular depth to the novel. The scene of Addie's death, so convincing in its fine, realistic detail, and the fantastic scene in which Cash works in the rain on the coffin, are imagined by Darl while he is away from home, but there is no reason to suspect that they are not true. They have the truth of the artist's imaginative empathy. But because he is so uncannily perceptive, he sees and knows *too* much, and of all the members of the Bundren family Darl's sense of isolation and alienation is greatest, plummeting to appalling depths when his mother dies. Addie has never accepted, nor loved her second son. Darl knows that he has no mother, and that therefore he cannot love her, but obviously not because he does not want to. Does he hate her? He probably does, but then as a fierce reaction to thwarted love. His setting fire to the barn can be explained by his desire to avenge himself on Addie, but also as an act of piety to end the undignified dragging about of the stinking corpse. That Darl sought his mother's love becomes clear from his relations with Jewel, Addie's favourite son. His fascination with Jewel, however, is not only to be explained by his jealousy of Addie's love for him, but also by his jealousy of Jewel's personality, the man of action, whose firm sense of identity he envies. Jewel knows who he is, Darl says; he, Darl not only doubts his identity, he doubts his very existence: "I don't know what I am, I don't know if I am or not."

Darl is unable to find in life a stable relationship with the world, probably because he has never found it in his relations with his mother. It explains his feeling of not belonging. As Cash perceptively observes: "This world is not his world; this life his life." Darl's tragedy is that he is intensely aware of his predicament, as is shown in his obsession with nothingness and dissolution. After the death of the only person who in some way or other still linked him to the world, even if only in a negative, destructive sense, this obsession grows to such a pitch that the difference between objective and subjective reality ceases to exist for him and he goes mad, laughing with the laughter of the mad, but still in possession of that peculiar lucidity sometimes attached to madness. In the last section that is attributed to Darl, written, significantly enough, not in the first person but in the third to indicate the complete disintegration of Darl's personality, three answers to the question why he laughs are given. They all consist of a crescendo of "yesses," and the bitter irony in these exultant affirmations movingly conveys the tragedy of his mental breakdown, for his laughter becomes the tears which he cannot shed, and who wants to affirm that the only reality women have is in their backs, and that the terrible truth is that Darl is *not* "our brother"?

Not only does Darl have no mother, he does not have a father either. Anse Bundren, as Cleanth Brooks has said, is one of Faulkner's most accomplished villians. He is also one of the most comic, but the outrageous humor with which Faulkner has drawn his character should not make us forget how dangerous he really is. Behind his unbelievable laziness, his crass egoism and despicable stinginess, there hides a predatoriness, which is made even more lethal by his consummate hypocrisy and his relentless knowledge of how far he can go in taking advantage of other people's goodness. Jewel's love of his horse, for which he has worked so back-breakingly hard that it has made his mother cry; Dewey Dell's desperate pleading to let her keep the ten dollars for the abortion drugs, mean nothing to him if they interfere with his own plans. During Addie's illness his stinginess makes him wait till the last moment before calling the doctor, and Cash's sufferings after he has broken his leg leave him completely indifferent. Yet, though he seems contemptible in practically everything he says and does, he is a man who cannot be ignored. He represents, as Cleanth Brooks has again astutely observed, "a force probably necessary to the survival of the human animal though it is terrifying when seen in such simple purity." And the stupendous end of the novel illustrates this with, as Cash describes it, "that kind of daresome and hangdog look all at once like when he has been up to something he knows ma ain't going to like. . . ." His new store-bought teeth are in his mouth, making him look taller and giving him a renewed vitality, and he is accompanied by a "duck-shaped" woman with "hard-looking pop eyes," whom he then introduces to his children: " 'It's Cash and Jewel and Vardaman and Dewey Dell, '[he] says, kind of hangdog and proud too, with his teeth and all, even if he wouldn't look at us. 'Meet Mrs. Bundren,' he says." Anse may have twinges of conscience but they never stop him from satisfying what he considers are his needs. And in this respect he remains very much alive, although to Addie, his first wife, he has been dead for years.

With Addie we come to the central character of the book, as can be inferred from the very title of the story, and the fact that she *is* dead for more than three quarters of the novel no doubt crowns the irony which so all-pervasively informs the writing. In her dual role of wife and mother, Addie, a strong personality, exercises absolute power over her family, even after her death. Of a passionate nature, she is torn by conflicting attitudes to life. On the one hand there is in her a strong inclination to withdraw and to preserve the separateness of her individuality, on the other an equally strong desire to reach out to the world, to reach "the burning heart of life." Before her marriage, when she was a schoolteacher, she used to hate and whip her pupils because they intruded with their noisy and impertinent presence into her separateness, but at the same time the whipping was a desperate attempt on her part to establish some kind of communion, to impress her mark on, and conversely to feel marked by the living. It is also this aching need that makes her marry Anse, a man socially and culturally her inferior—"So I took Anse," she says—believing that it would make her feel part of "the terrible blood, the red bitter blood boiling through the land," and trusting that she could manage to keep whole her integrity as an individual.

Life with Anse, the mean-spirited egoist, the coarse lump of inertia and ignorance, teaches her differently. It violates her separateness "over and over each day," and never as badly as when she is to bear Anse's children. Then she realizes that she is caught in a biological trap, which makes it of no importance whether she feels herself a separate individual or not. She feels "tricked by words older than Anse or love," and Anse might just as well be anybody else, which makes him "dead" to her although he is alive, just as her children might be any children, except Cash because he is her first, and Jewel because through him she has expressed her protest against the words that have proved empty—words like "love," which, when used by Anse, means only more offspring to work his land; or "duty," the duty to have a husband and children, but which, as Addie realizes, can never be the reason of life if, as it seems, it means the starvation of one's identity.

Although Addie hardly strikes us as a woman who believes in the spiritual, there is in her an obstinate yearning for transcendence, for an existence that is not merely vegetative, an existence that not merely happens but is made to happen by the posing of a deed that will lift the individual beyond the anonymity of the passing generations. Whitfield, the minister, seems to present an opportunity to find some higher purpose in life. He becomes her lover, but when he ends the affair, Addie is thrown back on her despairing sense of emptiness within the Bundren family, with Jewel as the visible outcome of her yearning and a renewed disgust at those who merely live through words, although at this stage she also realizes that even empty words are still dangerous because they can be used to manipulate people. Whitfield's monologue, following Addie's shocking, autobiographical account, illustrates that Addie had no reason to think better of the minister than of Anse. While listening to the sermon Whitfield preaches at Addie's funeral, even the prosaic Tull feels the discrepancy between Whitfield the man of words and Whitfield the man of deeds: "His voice is bigger than him. It's like they are not the same. It's like he is one, and his voice is one, swimming on two horses side by side across the ford and coming into the house, the mud-splashed one and the one that never even got wet, triumphant and sad." Whitfield may feel the urge to confess his sin, but he will never really do it, only say that he will do it, and this to him, the man of words, serves as a substitute for the act itself.

Although Addie is domineering and assertive, she remains an intensely feminine woman in that she ultimately only trusts the concrete, and through her physical body tries to gain a hold on reality. But this earth-mother quality is not of the yielding and warmth-generating kind, but is only fierceness and pride, and when she feels that it drags her down in her attempts at transcedence it even becomes destructive. When Cora Tull accuses her of not being a good mother, and reproaches her for her excessive love of Jewel, saying, "There is your sin. And your punishment too. Jewel is your punishment. But where is your salvation?," Addie calmly answers, "He is my cross and he will be my salvation. He will save me from the water and from the fire. Even though I have laid down my life, he will save me." Cora then realizes that Addie does not refer to God but to Jewel, and shocked at what in her eyes is wilful blasphemy and sacrilege, she begs her to repeal her words and to "cast herself upon the mercy of the Lord." But Addie is adamant in her refusal. If the road to spiritual salvation is cut off for her, she will not retreat in resignation, but in defiance, exacting salvation through the very sin she is thought to have committed, a claim made good by Jewel when he saves her coffined body from the flooded river and later from the fire in the barn-burning episode. Addie may not be a good and warm and loving woman, but her unsentimental honesty with herself and her fierce vitality make her a compelling personality of great intensity, who, even after her death, continues to extend her hold on her family, until she is brought to rest next to her father's grave. And it is only through her wish to be buried beside the man who used to tell her that "the reason for living is to get ready to stay dead a long time," and for which she hated him, that we know that she has admitted defeat, which lends her the tragic stature that the macabre comedy of the journey so emphatically denies her.

There is no doubt that the end of As I Lay Dying is grim, leaving no room for any illusions. Addie's death does not change or end anything. It does not effect a catharsis in the family. It does not bring them to greater awareness, either about Addie, about the conflicts that tore her restless life apart, or about themselves. At the end of the novel we are again at the beginning, with a new Mrs. Bundren, guaranteeing the survival of the species, but with Addie's unresolved conflicts transmitted to her children. Addie's sense of isolation and alienation reaches a pitch in Darl, striking him with madness; her outrage at the violation of her individuality whenever she felt life burgeoning in her, is transferred to her daughter Dewey Dell, whose desperate anxiety about feeling trapped and betrayed leaves her no time to mourn her mother's death. Even Cash and Jewel, who one does not expect to change or show greater insight or enrichment from the experience, are worse off at the end. Only Anse, the husband, has profited, and the irony here is in line with the irony of life, which does not concern itself with equity but distributes rewards or punishments regardless of our moral, or lack of moral worth. That this may give us the impression that we live in a mad world rather than in a sane one, is also in keeping with the vision that informs Faulkner's novel. Madness, like death, is never far from our consciousness in As I Lay Dying. The madness of the journey is matched by the madness of the elements that oppose its completion; the madness that drives the Bundrens on, their "furious attitudes," make them unwittingly perform acts of stupendous bravery and endurance but do not cancel the irresponsible folly and the wicked cruelty that accompany these deeds; the mad comedy that attaches to their vicissitudes is overpowering but does not invalidate the tragedy inherent in them. It's all there, in all its heart-breaking confusion, making us pause before the madness of human behaviour, without much greater understanding perhaps, but at least with the kind of acceptance that precludes easy attitudes; neither a sneering dismissal of the human animal, nor a sentimental optimism in the generative forces of the primitive, will reconcile us with the enigmas Faulkner's novel poses. For in the final analysis one does not feel let down by the book. It is the furious energy one feels pulsing in the writing itself that keeps us buoyed, that works as a tonic in revitalizing our sluggishness in the face of the intractable stuff life is made of.

Although the multiplicity of view points, presenting each part of the novel through the consciousness of a particular character, may create the illusion that Faulkner has disappeared as the all-powerful manipulator, it is the style which makes him visible again. Composed of a colloquial diction, freely mingled with high rhetoric, it is this style, often approaching poetry, which is largely responsible for the novel's great power.

What this language incorporates is a vision that underlies not only As I Lay Dying but all of Faulkner's major works, a vision which may be summarized as follows: heroism is to be found in the most unlikely places, endurance in the most unlikely people, and both may be generated by the most unlikely circumstances. While exerting himself in the most unlikely manner for the most unlikely causes, it is impossible for the individual to know the whole truth. All he can hope for is a part of the truth, distorting his perspective and bedevilling his hold on reality. The whole truth may only be known if all the separate truths are brought together, but the ability to do this demands a depth of knowledge, sensibility and wisdom which none of Faulkner's characters will ever obtain. It is here that his characters, even the plainest, attain the tragic stature usually accorded to people of greater awareness and sophistication. That they themselves may be totally unaware of this does not take away from the reality of Faulkner's world. This can be made clear by drawing an analogy suggested by the work of the philosopher Karl R. Popper. In his *Objective Knowledge* Popper distinguishes three worlds—the physical world, the subjective and psychological world, and the world of the products of the human mind (myth, fairy tales, scientific theories, poetry, art, music). Each successive world presents a progressive enrichment of empirical content—an extension of reality, I would say. To explain this Popper introduces the notion of "emergence," that is, new properties and characteristics emerge as the next world extends from the preceding world, a process being complicated by the fact that the worlds continue to interact. In Faulkner's case the same distinctions can be made. We have first the physical world; Yoknapatawpha County, the South; then the subjective and psychological world: the poor whites; and next the world of the products of the mind: the novel *As I Lay Dying*, a world with new properties and characteristics, though originating from the two preceding "simpler" worlds. This is Faulkner's world, in which the South and the poor whites may not be able to recognize themselves, but the reality of which can be looked upon as the progressive enrichment of empirical content underlying their worlds. Faulkner's world as the extension of reality.

JUDITH BRYANT WITTENBERG

William Faulkner:
A Feminist Consideration

During the past four decades, critics attempting to come to terms with the "images of women" as portrayed in the fiction of William Faulkner have more or less arrayed themselves into two groups, those who see Faulkner's females as stereotypical and thus the author himself as either a misogynist or a gyneolatrist (more often the former) and those who regard those same females as complex and variegated and hence see the author as sympathetic to women, even, in a few rare instances, as a proto-feminist. This polarized situation in a field that shows signs, two decades after Faulkner's death, of approaching consensus on other issues has some intriguing aspects that perhaps reveal as much about critical trends and the critics themselves as they do about Faulkner's fictional women.

Maxwell Geismar was the first to raise the specter of misogyny that haunted Faulkner criticism until correctives began to appear in the late 1960s, deeming "the Female" as one of the "twin Furies" that preside over Yoknapatawpha and calling Faulkner's portraits of women a series of "female incubae." Next came Irving Howe, who cited Faulkner's "inclination toward misogyny" and the "ferocity" of his portraiture of "the young American bitch" as indicating "a major failing as a novelist." Leslie Fiedler, the best-known exponent of this critical view, called Faulkner a "serious calumniator of the female," delineated Faulkner's eight-point indictment against women, and divided his nubile female characters into

From American Novelists Revisited: Essays in Feminist Criticism, edited by Fritz Fleischmann. Copyright © 1982 by Fritz Fleischmann. G. K. Hall & Co., Boston.

mindless earth goddesses and bitchy nymphomaniacs. The discussion of Faulkner's misogyny and the pejorative categorization of Faulkner's women informed several subsequent essays, all but one of them written in the 1960s, obviously a not-so-liberal decade in Faulkner criticism. Related to the stereotypers are the archetypers who have seen Faulkner's women as manifestations of the eternal life-giving Earth or as incarnations of the Great Goddess and thus intimated that they regard the author as gyneolatrous rather than misogynistic.

Interestingly, only one of these critics is a woman, and the fact that she is heavily indebted to Geismar and Fiedler for her typology and interpretations raises the issue of such criticism as an exercise at once patriarchal and projective. It has been suggested that Fiedler's categorizing is part of a larger tendency in male critics toward the "biological put-down" of women characters as well as women writers, and the recurrent violation of Faulkner's fictional context by such critics in the pursuit of their misogynistic assessments implies the possibility that such willful misreadings are as often projective as inept, revealing the persistence of such visions in the critics' own psyches. Faulkner himself warned readers on at least two occasions of the dangers of confusing his characters' opinions with his own, yet a number of the misogynist readings do precisely that, accepting the characters who make negative comments as "Faulknerian spokesmen." Another general problem with this critical position is its failure to give equal time to Faulkner's men, or to consider the presence of explanatory or countervailing elements in each work of fiction that serve to qualify many of the superficially negative depictions of women.

A series of critical efforts to countermand the Fiedlerian viewpoint began in the late 1960s, undertaken almost to a person by women, though there are some ironies in that fact, considering that Faulkner's fiction does betray at one level an ambivalent attitude toward females and that he made some overly bitter or implicitly patronizing comments about the sex in essays and interviews, albeit perhaps on occasion with tongue in cheek. Possibly such female revisionists share a faint masochism in the same way the male critics are united by their unexamined patriarchal assumptions. Nevertheless, all of these essays, which range in stance from the cautious to the enthusiastic and in quality from poor to impressive, are significant for their attempts to subvert the reductivist placing of Faulkner's women in narrow categories and to show the author as far more aware of and sympathetic to the complexity of the female psyche than those who deem him a misogynist or gyneolatrist have allowed.

In one of the first of these corrective pieces, Dolores Brien made a number of points which merit consideration by anyone approaching this topic: that Faulkner's work reveals the devastating effect on both men and women of the myth of spotless Southern womanhood, that the women in the novels are usually perceived through the eyes of the male characters, which largely accounts for deficiencies in their individualization, and that one can group Faulkner's male characters according to their attitudes toward women. Two subsequent essays—Elisabeth Muhlenfeld's on *Absalom, Absalom!* and Judith Fetterley's on "A Rose for Emily"—examine thoroughly Faulkner's portrayal in individual works of the way women are constricted or used by males and by the Southern social system. Other essays and a book devoted to Faulkner's women have asserted the infinite variety of his depiction of females and thus should inhibit future critical impulses toward negativism and restrictive categorization.

Although generalizing about Faulkner's female characters is not, as Ilse Lind asserts, "fruitless," it is certainly problematical. Creating any sort of taxonomy, even a complex one, is a transtextual exercise with a number of pitfalls, not least among them the fact that it necessitates a certain distortion of context. Women seemingly alike may play sharply differing roles in their respective narratives, roles qualified by technical elements such as tone and point-of-view, or by Faulkner's having balanced a female "type" with an equivalent male type, or her particular neurosis with a similar one in a male character, thus making it impossible to read any gender-based "message" into the presentation. Moreover, reappearing characters, such as Narcissa Benbow or Eula Varner, may be—or seem to be—quite different in their various fictional manifestations. Another problem is raised by the fact that there is no striking evolutionary pattern in the canon, despite the assertion by Fiedler and Guerard that Faulkner's "rehabilitation" of Temple Drake and Eula Varner in novels of the 1950s reflected a diminishing misogyny; some of Faulkner's feministically most interesting women occur in his fiction of the 1920s and 1930s. Nor is there an artistic correlative, since compelling women characters are found as often in the weak novels as in the great ones.

The extraordinary multivalence of Faulkner's oeuvre as a whole and of each individual work within itself thus makes broad-based assessments hazardous and demands that they be somewhat tentative. One can nevertheless discern some general tendencies in Faulkner's portrayal of women and women-related issues that show him, on the whole, to be neither pro- nor anti-female, but rather an absorbed student of the endlessly variegated human scene.

Faulkner's first two novels, though troubling to the sensitive reader because of their depiction of the first of his series of "mindless cows" and "nubile bitches" and their continual, often pejorative generalizations about women, some by the narrator himself, also evince a number of characteristics that show one cannot simply dismiss them—or any of Faulkner's fictions—as dominated by a negative view of women. *Soldiers' Pay* contains the impressive Margaret Powers, one of Faulkner's most admirable characters—as fine in her way as Dilsey, the Faulknerian female most often invoked as an exemplar of selfless devotion to others, and more thoroughly and complexly depicted and thus more interesting than Dilsey. Margaret selflessly devotes herself to caring for the dying Donald Mahon, even to the point of marrying him, and gladly extends her nurturing to others in need; intelligent and thoughtful, she also serves as a mediator and an instructor, one who manages to change Gilligan's "fixed ideas about women." But Faulkner does not idealize Margaret; he takes us inside her mind to show her struggles with guilt about her dead husband and suggests that she may have serious sexual problems.

In his next novel, *Mosquitoes*, Faulkner portrays two women artists, the poet Eva Wiseman and the painter Dorothy Jameson. Though Faulkner has been criticized for satirizing them, he satirizes everyone in the novel, male or female; moreover, Eva makes a number of valuable contributions to conversations, serving as an intellectual complement to her perceptive brother, Julius. Many of these bright and/or self-sufficient women live in large cities or come from outside the South, implying that, for Faulkner, detachment from the narrow world of a southern small town is necessary for the woman who desires an expanded range of intellectual and vocational options.

Within the restrictive middle-class world of Faulkner's Jefferson, the possibilities for women appear more limited, confined to a choice between spinsterhood or marriage and children, as the comments of Cecily Saunders and Pat Robyn, implicitly members of that middle-class world, and the experiences of the women characters in *Flags in the Dust*, Faulkner's first Yoknapatawpha novel, make clear. The women who evince the serenity of flowers, like Narcissa Benbow (or of cows, like Lena Grove and Eula Varner of later works), are those who accept their narrow options, whereas those who are flirtatious and sexual, like Belle Mitchell and her sister Joan, are at some unspoken level refusing to settle for drab routine and social inhibitions. Faulkner was obviously aware of the effects of a rigidly patriarchal social structure upon its female members. Even though his own status as a product of that structure sometimes led him to imply that it was more admirable to accept than to rebel, his awareness of its oppressiveness was responsible for a number of memorable portraits of women. The papier-mâché virgins and child-women are to be pitied as much as derided, for they have been offered few choices by their society. A number of the women in Faulkner's early fiction call their lovers "papa" and still others remain closely tied to their actual fathers, suggesting that at every level the patriarchy is a powerful force that inhibits their emotional and intellectual development.

Education is not an option for most of the women in Faulkner's fiction. Pat Robyn's dilemma is reminiscent of Maggie Tulliver's: her brother is soon to leave for Yale and she is desperate to go along, though he, like Tom Tulliver, shows little interest in her plight and she herself resignedly concedes, "I guess I'll have to get married and have a bunch of kids." Narcissa Benbow stayed at home while her brother went to Sewanee and then to Oxford, and, although Caddy Compson early showed herself to be the most energetic, curious, and resourceful of the Compson children, it was Quentin who was given the opportunity to go to Harvard. It is hardly surprising that such women frequently become restless and dissatisfied, either finding an outlet in flirtation and promiscuity or internalizing the rigid values that constrict them and turning their hostility on women who seek some form of freedom, even if only a sexual one. Narcissa's cruel treatment of Ruby Lamar in *Sanctuary* is obviously grounded in her inability to come to terms with her own confused longings.

With education rarely available to the women of Faulkner's fictional world, their capacity to be economically self-sufficient is almost nonexistent. Those few who work do so out of economic or emotional exigency, rather than from dedication to an ideal of professional self-fulfillment; because of this and because the range of vocational possibilities is so slight, they usually find little or no satisfaction in their jobs. Very often, because of her economic dependency, a woman's only resource is her body, which she must use as, or exchange for, currency. The women in this category are usually poor whites, such as Ruby Lamar of *Sanctuary*, Everbe Corinthia of *The Reivers*, Mink's wife of *The Hamlet*, Laverne Shumann of *Pylon*, and Dewey Dell Bundren of *As I Lay Dying*, but they may be from the middle class as well—Narcissa Benbow in "There Was a Queen" and Eula Varner Snopes in *The Town* obviously perceive the offer of their bodies as a necessary response to real or figurative blackmail.

A woman's major and virtually only route to social status and/or economic security is marriage, a fact reflected in the desperate maneuvers of Sophonsiba Beauchamp and her brother Hubert in "Was." But here, too, as the hunting and cardplaying metaphors of "Was" suggest, she may be without choice, a mere pawn in a male exchange system similar to that of primitive societies, as Mrs. Maurier of *Mosquitoes*, Ellen Coldfield of *Absalom, Absalom!* and Eula Varner of *The Hamlet* all discover, and even then she may be asked, like Rosa Coldfield, for proof of her ability to perpetuate the male line before receiving her legal "reward." Once married, a woman can demonstrate her energies and talents by able housewifery, like that of Mrs. Varner in *The Hamlet*, or by competent clubwork, like that of Maggie Mallison of *The Town*, though she is equally likely to become a drab "grey wife."

Many of Faulkner's women, however, even the ones ostensibly most confined by the social system, experience a sort of "liberation" in the crucible of war or severe personal crisis which prompts the discovery and display of qualities of strength, resourcefulness, independence, and even tragic grandeur. Two old ladies, Rosa Millard of *The Unvanquished* and Miss Habersham of *Intruder in the Dust*, nurtured under the code of protective gallantry toward "ladies," not only show impressive courage but manage to turn the code upon itself, exploiting it in unexpected ways. Some of the women, like Drusilla Hawk of *The Unvanquished* or Linda Kohl of *The Mansion*, go bravely off to war themselves, proving their worth as fighting participants, though they pay a superficial price—the loss of outward traces of their femininity—and a deeper one—the espousal of a masculine code of violence to the point where they are willing to be implicated in peacetime killings. Other women remain at home during wartime, showing quiet endurance rather than active heroism, learning "masculine" skills and operating family enterprises. Still others are tested by domestic crises and emerge as in some respects admirable, even heroic, figures. In *The Town*, Eula Snopes chooses death rather than elopement with the man she has loved for nearly two decades "in order to leave her child a mere suicide for a mother instead of a whore;" in *Pylon*, after the violent death of her husband, Laverne Shumann gives up her son to his grandparents in order that he have a more stable life; and in *The Wild Palms*, the dying Charlotte Rittenmeyer, recognizing perhaps that she has been wounded as much by her own flawed idealism as by Harry's blundering knife, pleads for his exculpation and succeeds in converting him to her passionate faith in undying love.

If Faulkner was an acute social analyst who understood the plight women (and men) are placed in by the restrictive values of a patriarchal society, he was also, despite his professed ignorance of Freudian psychology, an embryonic psychoanalyst, bringing to and displaying in his fiction a rich awareness of the complex functioning of the human psyche according to many of the principles enunciated by Freud. Of course many feminists have repudiated Freud as a Victorian male chauvinist, but if one accepts Juliet Mitchell's more tempered view of Freud as descriptive rather than prescriptive, then Faulkner's use of psychoanalytical insights, particularly as they affect his portraiture and his male characters' view of women, can be viewed as impressive. At least three psychoanalytical precepts are relevant to a feminist assessment of Faulkner's work: the idea that any individual has the potential to contain traits of both sexes, the belief that a person's character is largely formed by his or her early experiences and family relationships, and the concept of projection, of one's "reality" as created out of one's own desires and fears.

Faulkner's fiction reveals throughout his sensitive perceptions of what one critic calls "the infinite shadings of the masculine and feminine in human beings." From his very first novel, Faulkner shows the way biological gender is modified by emotional ambiguity and portrays a whole array of men with traits traditionally regarded as feminine and women with essentially masculine qualities. Although in some cases these opposite-sex traits undermine the character's attractivness, in still other cases they increase it, so that one cannot make any sort of consistent value judgment about Faulkner's presentation. In *Soldiers' Pay*, for example, though Januarius Jones's effeminate appearance and Cecily Saunders's phallic legs are emblems of their larger distortions, Joe Gilligan's "feminine" intuition and maternalism are positive qualities, as is Margaret Powers's ability to be "one of the boys"—to an extent that almost prompts Joe to call her a "fellow." In virtually every one of Faulkner's subsequent novels, one can find characters who contain traits of the opposite sex, usually one of each gender. In *Mosquitoes*, there is the effete Mr. Talliaferro and the masculine Mrs. Wiseman, the boyish Pat and her brother with a "feminine" jaw. In *Flags in the Dust* and *Sanctuary*, Horace Benbow often seems more helplessly female than the women, especially the predatory Joan and the somewhat mannish Ruby. As a child, Caddy Compson shows a "manly" courage and audacity and wishes to be a king or general, and Quentin's feminine timidity renders him ineffectual, traits similar to those evinced by another young sister and brother, Judith and Henry Sutpen, during the scene in which they watch the naked blacks wrestle. The intuitiveness of Darl Bundren seems as feminine as his mother's harsh philosophizing is "masculine." In *The Wild Palms*, the plump convict appears womanly, and Charlotte looks mannish, her aggressiveness contrasting with Harry's passivity, a trait usually regarded as feminine.

Related to Faulkner's balancing of "masculinized" women with "feminized" men in individual works in his recurrent portrayal of pairs of men and women with similar psychological profiles, so that the reader's tendency to make judgments linked to one sex is controverted. In *Soldiers' Pay*, Margaret Powers and Joe Gilligan are both selfless nurturers, Cecily Saunders and Januarius Jones are both selfish flirts, and the young

Emmy and Donald were both children of nature; in *Mosquitoes*, Mrs. Maurier and Mr. Talliaferro are alike in aging pathetically and spending time as the spiritual parasites of creative people; Horace and Narcissa Benbow of *Flags in the Dust* are similar in their ambivalent fascination-disgust with sexuality; both Mrs. Compson and her son Jason are selfish, immature, and paranoiac. In *Light in August*, Lena Grove and Joe Christmas are both products of an exploited childhood now restlessly on the move and aggressive in different ways; Joe can also be linked with Joanna as outlanders suffering from confused sexual self-images.

Also extensively employed by Faulkner is the psychoanalytical tenet that human beings are shaped in crucial ways by the experiences and relationships of their early years; thus even evil creatures have themselves been victimized at earlier stages and should elicit pity along with condemnation. Though Faulkner doesn't always provide complete data of this sort, he usually offers at least a modicum from which inferences may be drawn. This has feminist implications for all of the women characters usually singled out by critics as proof of Faulkner's "misogyny," most particularly for Temple Drake, who has been called a "Venus flytrap," a "death Goddess," a "violator," and a "trembling, sexless, ferocious bitch." Of course Faulkner himself said that "no person is wholly good or wholly bad," a view that implies that a sympathetically psychoanalytical reading is as appropriate as one that is judgmentally moral, especially in the case of Faulkner's villainous women (and men—but many of these have already been the subjects of sympathetic criticism). Admittedly, Temple Drake is a destructive young woman, responsible directly or indirectly for the deaths of two men and perhaps for the "suicide" of Popeye, but it is important also to see her as a victim not only of rape, but also of her family and of the society of which she is a product. Faulkner tells us little about her family, other than the fact that it consists of a father and four brothers, but we can infer some of the difficulties she has had and continues to have with male figures. Her father is a judge—a towering symbol of the Code—and certainly Temple's confused attitudes toward both her patriarchal family and the patriarchal society are responsible for much of her destructive behavior.

Throughout the novel, Temple is alternately restricted and betrayed by her father and father surrogates. She has obviously received inadequate guidance, for she shows no sense of purpose and has a promiscuous streak that reveals a need to rebel against the forces trying to make her into a "lady." When we first see Temple, she is surrounded by a group of watching, taunting men who represent the voyeuristic, lustful members of the larger male world. When Gowan Stevens drunkenly crashes his car, she receives her first physical wound at the hand of a man, which is followed by a series of others, both physical and spiritual: the invocation of male categories for women, under which Popeye calls her a "whore" and Ruby labels her a "cheap sport," the spying on her by virtually all the members of the Old Frenchman group, Gowan's outright abandonment of her, her rape by Popeye, and her long imprisonment at the brothel in Memphis. This confusing mixture of restriction and betrayal is perhaps a continuation of familial patterns—her father "covers for her" in the newspaper but makes no determined effort to find and rescue her—and it certainly leaves her alternately rebellious and conciliatory toward men. She taunts Gowan and, mentally, her father ("Daddy would just die") but then invokes the parent in the litanous "My father's a judge." Her temporary anorexia, like her wishful visions of boyhood and chastity belts, reveals her basic dis-ease with sexuality, but at every juncture, she shows an acceptance of her plight if not actual complicity in it. In *Requiem for a Nun*, Temple intimates that her "evil" was motivated by rebelliousness toward her father and brothers, and possibly her implication in the deaths of Red and Goodwin, the two "real men" of the novel, was prompted by the same impulses in more exacerbated form. At the end of the novel, she leaves the courtroom physically surrounded by her father and brothers, as she has been emotionally surrounded by men throughout the course of the narrative. Although one cannot condone her actions, one can see them as involving an almost inevitable response to the conflicting messages she has received from a predominantly male world.

This discernment of the origins of emotional and behavioral patterns in early experiences or family dynamics can only increase one's sympathy for other Faulknerian women who seem mindless or destructive, as it does for Faulknerian men like Popeye, Joe Christmas, or Mink Snopes. Cecily Saunders, for example, is certainly erratic and selfish, but she is also to some degree the product of conflicting parental attitudes. The Saunderses alternately press her to marry and treat her like a child; not surprisingly, she vacillates between provocativeness and regressiveness. Narcissa Benbow, early forced by her own mother's death into being a mother to her brother, learned to be possessive about Horace and repressive of her own sexuality, psychological characteristics subsequently responsible for destructive actions and reactions. Caddy Compson, also virtually "motherless," cares for her brothers, becoming promiscuous only when she is taught to regard sex as dirty and thus herself as "bad." Her daughter Quentin has an equally deprived and chaotic childhood with similar results; when Quentin shouts at Jason, "You made me," she speaks, in a way, for all such young women, whose "bitchiness" is a response to circumstances. Mindlessness is another sort of reaction, and the bovine sexuality of Eula Varner in *The Hamlet* can also be seen—though our "seeing" in this case, as in that of Caddy, is filtered through the perceptions of some emotionally involved and thus less than objective male characters—as in some sense induced by her family situation. Eula's father is lazy, lustful, and adulterous, her mother is indifferent, and her brother so hypersensitive to her physicality that he betrays his own attraction to her. Surrounded by lust and unconcern in early pubescence, Eula absorbs her family's dominant traits and becomes what they perceive her to be. Eula is, like most of Faulkner's young "bitches" and "goddesses," invariably influenced, if not fully determined by, the examples of her parents and the messages she receives from them and from her immediate society.

Another psychoanalytical concept that affected Faulkner's portrayal of women is that of projection, the making of reality from desire. Faulkner spoke about this phenomenon in one of its major manifestations when he said, "That is a part of man's or woman's instinctive nature to have an object, an immediate object to project that seeking for love on." Because he was male and most of his narrators, whether omniscient or individualized, are male, the "object" most often "projected" is female, which accounts for a number of qualities in those fictional female "objects" —unreality, mythicity, extremity of desirability or fearsomeness. If Heathcliff represents the male Other to the female imagination of Emily Brontë, all the hyperbolic women in Faulkner's fiction are the Others of the author, the narrators, or the characters. André Bleikasten has written of the way in which Caddy Compson is an empty signifier that speaks the desire of men, a "blank screen" onto which her brothers project their longings and fears, their love and hate. M.D. Faber has asserted that Caddy exists only *in* the men, a "link to the disastrous introjection of the mother." Thus Caddy is not fully recuperable as an autonomous character, for she signifies only in and through her brothers. Virtually the same is true of Addie Bundren, because we see her almost solely through her children, husband, and neighbors, who are in some sense all emotionally and/or judgmentally focused upon her; or the woman in "Old Man," seen only through the tall convict, a product of his anxieties about women; or Eula Varner in *The Hamlet* and *The Town*, a figure raised in the first novel to mythic heights by the titillation of her male observers, or to sphinxlike enigma in the second by the perplexity of another group of males; or, to a lesser degree, Lena Grove and Laverne Shumann, both surrounded, assessed, and pursued by males, largely "made" from masculine responses.

In *Mosquitoes*, Faulkner's characters speak of writing itself as a product of male-originated desire for some elusive ideal woman, and the linkage of "making" women fictionally with "making" them sexually is an intriguing one. Even as Faulkner showed the process of desire-based projection at work inside his fiction, he was aware of its operation from without as enunciative. Though the "shape of love" usually takes a woman's form, it can also be masculine. The elusive empty centers in Faulkner's fiction—the nexuses around which the quest for possession and understanding revolve—are male in at least three instances. Donald Mahon is a silent object of fear or desire to three women and three men; the dead John Sartoris in *Flags in the Dust* becomes a compelling "image" to both Narcissa and Bayard, and Thomas Sutpen of *Absalom, Absalom!* is a figure who exists only in the discourse of the narrators who create him through their efforts to recreate the past; Faulkner shows projection operant in both men and women and makes it a metaphor for creation itself.

Related to the fact that Faulkner's women frequently exist only in the men is their lack of language, Logos, the Word—predominantly a male possession. As Gavin Stevens says in *The Mansion*, Helen left no recorded word, and so, too, are many of Faulkner's nonmythic figures "voiceless." In works narrated omnisciently, most of the women have little to say— Laverne is almost silent, as are the females in *Go Down, Moses*, and male words dominate *Light in August, The Hamlet*, and *Intruder in the Dust*. Moreover, women are frequently perceived to have, or themselves assert, a philosophical opposition to words, and much of the male rhetoric proves to be empty, as in the case of Gavin Stevens and Ike McCaslin, or destructive, as in the case of Mr. Compson of *The Sound and the Fury*. Certainly Faulkner's fiction reveals that women have good reason to be fearful of language, for it is often used to constrict or undermine them: the male obsession with a woman's "good name" hampers her natural impulses, and the assignment of labels such as "lady" or "bitch" or "whore" can have pernicious effects—a few of his women become actual whores only after having been named as such.

Again, however, the generalization must be qualified. Margaret Powers is articulate and thoughtful; she also succeeds in eliciting tales from other females, as at the moment when the previously silent Emmy pours forth the story of her youthful idyll with Donald. The women in *Mosquitoes* speak for themselves, though only Eva Wiseman has much of interest to say. *Flags in the Dust* is a pivotal text in this regard, for Aunt Jenny du Pre is both vocal and interested in words. She tells stories about the family past, recounts bawdy tales in a language of "forceful clarity and a colorful simplicity," generalizes about men, expresses her political views, and responds to the writing of others, especially newspaper accounts of "humanity in its more colorful mutations." Moreover, the quality of her voice is close to that of the narrator's, mingling romanticism and irony as she alternately invokes the heroic past in a voice "proud and still as banners in the dust" and deflates the pretentious behavior of those around her in a voice that is sharp and humorous. She becomes almost a narrator surrogate when the presentation shifts from his to hers with barely a change in tone, as in the graveyard scene, or when she forecasts the major events of the narrative.

A number of women in Faulkner's subsequent novels also have distinctive voices capable of "authoring" the past and affecting others. Rosa Coldfield is Faulkner's most memorable female storyteller, as she creates the first of the visions of Thomas Sutpen, but others, too, discover the satisfactions of narrative—Mrs. Hines of *Light in August* sees Joe Christmas's early history "whole and real" in the moment of recounting it, according to Gavin Stevens, and Drusilla Hawk makes Civil War incidents come alive for her listeners: "We saw it, we were there, as if Drusilla's voice had transported us," says Bayard. Still other women have effective vocal identities, like Linda Snopes Kohl of *The Mansion*, whose "dry harsh quacking voice," the badge of her heroism in the Spanish Civil War, she uses discursively, occasionally becoming as talky as Gavin Stevens. In *Requiem for a Nun*, Temple Drake Stevens's long night of suffering at the hands of her inquisitor, Gavin Stevens, culminates in a fully verbalized reconsideration of her actions in the recent and distant past; in so finding her voice, Temple perhaps also finds the capacity to start, as she says, a "new life," although the bitter irony of her tone suggests that the likelihood of such a possibility is dim. Perhaps the female speaker with the greatest impact is Charlotte Rittenmeyer, whose recurrent statements of passion-ate, if misguided, idealism manage both the outlook and actions of Harry Wilbourne and ultimately effect her own destruction; her voice, with its urgent message, dominates "The Wild Palms" portion of the novel, and she essentially "authors" the central events of the narrative. Thus in his early and late fiction alike, Faulkner presents women who make effective use of language, figures that contrast with and serve to offset the portrayals of those who are voiceless and consequently identified only in and through masculine discourse.

As even this brief survey makes clear, generalizations about Faulk-ner's women and Faulkner's presentation of gender-based issues are prob-lematic, constantly qualified or undermined by the complexity of his vision and the multivalence of his texts. That his women are neither goddesses nor villains seems obvious, just as his men are neither simply heroic nor absolutely evil. The only real "villains" in the Faulknerian world are a restrictive society that is inadequately responsive to the needs and desires of its individual members and a nuclear family that fails its children by offering poor examples or providing inadequate affection—and their victims are both men and women. In *The Mansion*, a novel possibly intended by Faulkner to be his valedictory, two men and a woman comment sadly on the human condition. Miss Reba sympathizes with "every one of us. The poor son of a bitches," as do V. K. Ratliff and Gavin Stevens, echoing her view with their summary comment, "The poor sons of bitches." The male words may be the last words, and their viewpoints the most prevalent in the Faulknerian universe, circumscribing the women and limiting their options, but as the fiction makes clear at every level, men and women alike are poor frail victims of being alive.

PETER BROOKS

Incredulous Narration: "Absalom, Absalom!"

T o a reader concerned with the design
and project of narrative, William Faulkner's *Absalom, Absalom!* is full of
interest. More than Faulkner's other novels, *Absalom, Absalom!* seems to
pose with acute force problems in the epistemology of narrative and the
cognitive uses of plotting in a context of radical doubt about the validity
of plot. Perhaps even more than such cerebral probes into these issues as
Joyce's *Ulysses*, Gide's *Les Faux-Monnayeurs*, Italo Svevo's *La Coscienza di
Zeno*, or Michel Butor's *La Modification*, *Absalom, Absalom!* offers an
exemplary challenge to the critic since it both sums up the nineteenth-
century tradition of the novel—particularly its concern with genealogy,
authority, and patterns of transmission—while subverting it, working this
subversion in a manner that reaffirms a traditional set of problems for the
novel while disallowing its traditional solutions. Here is a novel that in its
appendix provides us with a chronology (as in Freud's final footnote to the
Wolf Man), a genealogy (as in such familial chronicles as Zola's *Les
Rougon-Macquart* and Galsworthy's *The Forsyte Saga*), and a map (fur-
nished implicitly if not literally throughout Balzac, Tolstoy, Hardy, and
other novelists who stake out and order terrain). These are traditional
schemata for the ordering of time and experience from which *Absalom,
Absalom!* markedly departs, yet by which it is also haunted, as by the force
of an absence. *Absalom, Absalom!* may indeed be very much the story of
the haunting force of absences, including formal absences, in the wake of
whose passage the novel constructs itself.

From *Reading for the Plot; Design and Intention in Narrative*. Copyright © 1984 by Peter
Brooks. Alfred A. Knopf, Inc., 1984.

As a first approach to the place of plot in *Absalom, Absalom!*, we can refer again to the concept of narrative as a coded activity, implicit in all narratology and urged most persuasively by Roland Barthes in *S/Z*. That is, a given narrative weaves its individual pattern from pre-existent codes, which derive, most immediately at least, from the "already written." The reading of a narrative then tends to decipher, to organize, to rationalize, to *name* in terms of codes derived from the "already read." We noted that two of Barthes's five codes seem particularly pertinent to the study of plot: the proairetic, or "code of actions," and the hermeneutic, or code of enigmas and answers, ultimately the code or voice of "Truth." The proairetic, it will be recalled, concerns the logic of actions, how the completion of an action can be logically derived from its initiation, and the whole of an action seen as a complete and namable unit, which then enters into combination with other actions, to form sequences. Like its label, this code is essentially Aristotelian, concerned with the wholeness of actions and the logic of their interrelationship. The hermeneutic code rather concerns the questions and answers that structure a story, their suspense, partial unveiling, temporary blockage, eventual resolution, with the resultant creation of a "retarding structure" or "dilatory space" which we work through toward what is felt, in classical narrative, to be meaning revealed. Plot, we suggested, might best be conceived as a combination of the proairetic and the hermeneutic, or better, an overcoding of the proairetic by the hermeneutic. The actions and sequences of action of the narrative are structured into larger wholes by the play of enigma and solution: the hermeneutic acts as a large, shaping force, allowing us to sort out, to group, to see the significance of actions, to rename their sequences in terms of their significance for the narrative as a whole. We read in the suspense created by the hermeneutic code, structuring actions according to its indications, restructuring as we move through partial revelations and misleading clues, moving toward the fullness of meaning provided by the "saturation" of the matrix of the sentence now fully predicated.

A major source of our difficulty in reading *Absalom, Absalom!* may derive from its peculiar use of these two codes, the way they refuse to mesh or synchronize in the traditional mode. As readers, we encounter in the novel certain sequences of action and event that seem to lack any recognizable framework of question and answer, and hence any clear intention of meaning. Worse still, we encounter sequences where the orderly progression of the "proairetisms," the movement of chains of events to their conclusion, is interrupted and interfered with by the formulation of enigmas concerning the actions themselves. It is as if the characters in the novel often turned to the interrogation of a proairetic sequence for its revelatory meaning before we, as readers, have been allowed to see how the sequence runs. The very logic of action is violated by the inquiry into its hermeneutic force, an inquiry that can only derive its sense from an end to the sequence which we have not been privileged to see. Thus it is that we so often find ourselves suddenly faced with hermeneutic shifts of gears, forced to reconsider the very integrity of narrative event in terms of its hermeneutic possibilities and determinations; so that we often find ourselves in the position of Quentin Compson's Canadian roommate at Harvard, Shreve McCannon (relatively, of course, the outsider in the narrative), wanting to shout, as he does, "Wait! For God's sake wait." One quite straightforward instance of the situation I have in mind occurs in the narrative of the killing of Thomas Sutpen by Wash Jones after the birth of the child fathered by Sutpen on Wash's daughter, Milly Jones, where we have this exchange between Shreve and Quentin:

> "Wait," Shreve said. "You mean that he got the son he wanted, after all that trouble, and then turned right around and—"
> "Yes. Sitting in Grandfather's office that afternoon, with his head kind of flung back a little, explaining to Grandfather like he might have been explaining arithmetic to Henry back in the fourth grade: 'You see, all I wanted was just a son. Which seems to me, when I look about at my contemporary scene, no exorbitant gift from nature or circumstance to demand—' "
> "*Will you wait?*" Shreve said. "—that with the son he went to all that trouble to get lying right there behind him in the cabin, he would have to taunt the grandfather into killing first him and then the child too?"
> "—What?" Quentin said. "It wasn't a son. It was a girl."
> "Oh," Shreve said. "—Come on. Let's get out of this damn icebox and go to bed."

We find here a suspension of the revelation that is necessary to make the actions previously recounted (Sutpen's refusal to marry or even to provide for Milly since she has produced a daughter, not a son) into some version of Barthes's fully predicated narrative sentence. This suspension heightens— at the expense of "meaning"—the dramatic rendering of what is the final destruction of Sutpen's life-plot, his "design," itself a major shaping force in the overall hermeneutic code of the narrative.

The reader just as often finds himself witness to a proairetic sequence that appears perfectly logical but lacks the coherence of meaning, as if he had not been given the hermeneutic clues requisite to grasping the intention of event and the motive of its narration. The reader in these cases stands in much the same position as Quentin at the outset of the novel, listening to Rosa Coldfield's narration. I cite a fragment of her narrative from the early pages:

> I saw what had happened to Ellen, my sister. I saw her almost a recluse, watching those two doomed children growing up whom she was helpless to save. I saw the price which she had paid for that house and that pride; I saw the notes of hand on pride and contentment and peace and all to which she had put her signature when she walked into the church that night, begin to fall due in succession. I saw Judith's marriage forbidden without rhyme or reason or shadow of excuse; I saw Ellen die with only me, a child, to turn to and ask to protect her remaining child; I saw Henry repudiate his home and birthright and then return and practically fling the bloody corpse of his sister's sweetheart at the hem of her wedding gown; I saw that man return—the evil's source and head which had outlasted all its victims—who had created two children not only to destroy one another and his own line, but my line as well, yet I agreed to marry him.

This passage in fact gives virtually the whole of the story to be told, from Rosa's point of view, and gives it with the insistent veracity of the eyewitness account: "I saw . . . I saw." What is missing from her account? In some important sense, everything, for it is a largely nonhermeneutic narrative, offering no apparent structure of meaning for this sequence of events, indeed no clue as to how and even why one should look for meaning in it. There is narrative aplenty here, as throughout the novel, but inadequate *grounds* for narrative.

One might generalize from this quotation, to suggest that it characterizes not only a problem *in* the narrative, but the very problem *of* narrative in *Absalom, Absalom!*, where ultimately narrative itself is the problem. Mr. Compson typically generalizes the problem for us, in one of his noble but slightly futile epic evocations:

> It's just incredible. It just does not explain. Or perhaps that's it: they don't explain and we are not supposed to know. We have a few old mouth-to-mouth tales; we exhume from old trunks and boxes and drawers letters without salutation or signature, in which men and women who once lived and breathed are now merely initials or nicknames out of some now incomprehensible affection which sound to us like Sanskrit or Choctaw; we see dimly people, the people in whose living blood and seed we ourselves lay dormant and waiting, in this shadowy attenuation of time possessing now heroic proportions, performing their acts of simple passion and simple violence, impervious to time and inexplicable— Yes, Judith, Bon, Henry, Sutpen: all of them. They are there, yet something is missing; they are like a chemical formula exhumed along

with the letters from that forgotten chest, carefully, the paper old and faded and falling to pieces, the writing faded, almost indecipherable, yet meaningful, familiar in shape and sense, the name and presence of volatile and sentient forces; you bring them together in the proportions called for, but nothing happens; you re-read, tedious and intent, poring, making sure that you have forgotten nothing, made no miscalculation; you bring them together again and again nothing happens; just the words, the symbols, the shapes themselves, shadowy inscrutable and serene, against that turgid background of a horrible and bloody mischancing of human affairs.

This passage alludes to all the enigmatic issues of the narrative: Why did Henry Sutpen kill Charles Bon? What did this killing have to do with Thomas Sutpen, and with the eventual ruin of the house of Sutpen? What does this tale of the ancestors have to do with the present generations? And, especially, how can narrative know what happened and make sense of the motives of events? And if it cannot, what happens to lines of descent, to the transmission of knowledge and wisdom, and to history itself? Is history finally simply a "bloody mischancing of human affairs"? If for Barthes the resolution of all enigmas coincides with the full and final predication of the narrative sentence, Mr. Compson here appears to question the possibility of ever finding a predicate: the subjects—the proper names—are there, but they refuse to accede to meaning.

The quotations from Rosa Coldfield and Mr. Compson both tend to suggest that on the one hand there is a story to be told—perhaps even history itself to be told—and on the other hand there is telling and writing—people writing and reading letters and documents, and especially, talking—but that somehow what should lie in-between, the story-as-told, the narrative as coherently plotted, the hermeneutic sentence, is lacking. Referring once again to Gérard Genette's categories, histoire, récit, and narration—"story," "plot," and "narrating"—it is evident that in Absalom, Absalom! we have on the one hand plenty of narrating, and on the other at least the postulation of a story that may equal history itself. What appears to be missing is the level of plot, the result of Mr. Compson's chemical operation, that comprehensible order of event that was the very substance and raison d'être of the classical narrative.

Another way of stating the problem might be to say that in this novel which pre-eminently concerns fathers, sons, generation, and lines of descent, there seems to be no clear authority, not even a provisional sort, for the telling of the story, and as a result no suggestion of how to achieve mastery of its interpretation. The nineteenth-century novel, we saw, repeatedly concerns issues of authority and transmission, and regularly plays them out in relations of fathers to sons. From Rousseau to Freud, the discourse of the self and its origins—so much a matter of patronymics—ultimately concerns the authority of identity, that knowledge of self which, through all its complex workings-out, aims at the demonstrative statement, "this is what I am." *Absalom, Absalom!* problematizes further this classic issue in that not only does the identity of all the important characters seem to be in question, but the very discourse about identity seems to lack authority. As we have argued in discussion of the narrative situation, stories are told in the name of something or someone; they are told *for* something. The incessant narrating of *Absalom, Absalom!*, however, seems to bring us perilously close to narrative without motive: a collection of "letters without salutation or signature," unable to name their sender or receiver, and unable to define the subject of their narrative discourse. If we ever are to be able to define the status of plot in this novel, we will first have to discover the motives of storytelling. Narrative meaning very much depends on the *uses* of narrative.

These formulations may begin to take on more precise and more useful meaning if I now return to the beginning of the novel, and attempt for the moment to be more explicative. We have at the outset a teller and a listener, or narrator and narratee. Rosa is doing the telling, "in that grim haggard amazed voice until at last listening would renege and hearing-sense self-confound and the long-dead object of her impotent yet indomitable frustration would appear, as though by outraged recapitulation evoked. . . ." This description could stand as emblem for all of Rosa's narrating, and indeed for much of the storytelling in the novel: an evocation through outraged recapitulation, where there is evidently a need not only to remember but also—in Freud's terms—to repeat and to "work through" an as yet unmastered past, from motives that are highly charged emotionally but not specified or yet specifiable. Nor does the listener, Quentin, know why he has been chosen as Rosa's narratee, so that we have from the outset an interrogation of the motive and intention of telling. *"It's because she wants it told,* he thought, *so that people whom she will never see and whose names she will never hear and who will never have heard her name nor seen her face will read it and know at last why God let us lose the war. . . ."* Quentin's explanation here leaps over what we might have expected to be a formulation of the storyteller's intention in terms of the coherent design given to her story by its shaping plot, leaps to the level of history, to the *fabula* as something truly fabulous: the epic of the Civil War, the tragedy of Southern history. The war and the history of the South may in some ultimate sense be both the final principle of explanation for everyone in the novel, and the final problem needing explanation. But to make a direct leap to that level is to elide the intervening level of plot, of coherently motivated and shaped narrative: between story as history on the one hand, and the recapitulative narrating on the other, plot seems to have been lost, to have failed in its role as the cohesive bond of the narrative construction.

It is worth noting that this situation of telling in *Absalom, Absalom!*, which places face to face the one surviving eyewitness to the past (or so we, and Quentin, believe at this point) and the representative of the future, he who is supposed to escape the South, is hermeneutically most significant at the point—the very end of chapter 1—where we are given the fragment of a narrative of what Rosa did *not* see: "But I was not there. I was not there to see the two Sutpen faces this time—once on Judith and once on the negro girl beside her—looking down through the square entrance to the loft." This is far more consequential for a construction of the plot than Rosa's recapitulation of her moral outrage at Sutpen's wrestling bouts with his slaves, which Judith and Clytie are watching from the loft: it is not the seen but the seers, unseen by the eyewitness, which constitute our hermeneutic clue here. For in the doubling of Judith in Clytie, in the Negro version of Sutpen, lies the very trace of difference which is the ironic determinant of Sutpen's plot.

But this is a clue that can only be interpreted later. By the close of the first chapter, I have suggested, there is a split and polarization: narrating on the one hand, an epic historical story on the other, and no narrative plot or design to join them. In this structure of the absent middle, the failed mediation, the problem of the rest of the novel is formulated: How can we construct the plot? Who can say it? To whom? On what authority? The narrative of *Absalom, Absalom!* not only raises these issues, it actively pursues them. The novel becomes a kind of detective story where the object of investigation—the mystery—is the narrative design, or plot, itself.

We might note briefly the forms in which this problem develops over the succeeding chapters. In chapters 2, 3, and 4, Mr. Compson is telling. (One hesitates to label him, or any other of the tellers, a "narrator" in the traditional sense, since narration here as elsewhere in Faulkner seems to call upon both the individual's voice and that transindividual voice that speaks through all of Faulkner's characters. Certainly the narrative is "focalized" by an individual—to use Genette's terminology again—but the question of voice is more difficult to resolve.) Mr. Compson is eminently the figure of transmission, standing between his father, General Compson, the nearest thing to a friend that Sutpen had in Jefferson, and his son Quentin. Mr. Compson fills in some of the background of Sutpen's story, his arrival in Jefferson, his marriage to Ellen Coldfield, the birth of the two children, Judith and Henry, the appearance of Charles Bon. Chapter 3 ends with the evocation of Wash Jones appearing before Rosa's house to tell of Henry's shooting of Bon; then, curiously, chapter 4 ends with the same moment, but with Wash Jones's message fully articulated this time: "Henry has done shot that durn French feller. Kilt him dead as a beef." The two chapter endings force us to ask what has happened in the intervening pages to advance our understanding of this killing, which from Rosa's initial presentation of the elements of the story has stood as a shocking challenge to understanding.

What we have had, essentially, is the elaboration of Mr. Compson's plot, involving Henry and Bon and Judith. It turns on Bon's earlier morganatic marriage to the octoroon woman in New Orleans, making of him an "intending bigamist" in the betrothal to Judith. Mr. Compson is a rich scenarist, imaging the meeting of Henry and Bon at the University of Mississippi, Henry's "seduction" by Bon, the scenes at Sutpen's Hundred during vacations, Henry's trip to New Orleans, and so on. It is a narrative in which we are ever passing from the postulation of how it must have been to the conviction that it really was that way: for instance, Mr. Compson imagines the introduction of Henry to Bon in a series of clauses headed "perhaps," ending: "or perhaps (I like to think this) presented formally to the man reclining in a flowered, almost feminized gown, in a sunny window in his chambers," and then a page later has turned the hypothesis into solid narrative event: "And the very fact that, lounging before them in the outlandish and almost feminine garments of his sybaritic privacy. . . ." And yet, for all his evident will to construct a hermeneutically powerful plot, Mr. Compson encounters moments of radical doubt, most notably in the passage beginning, "It just does not explain," which I quoted earlier. We have a complex, intricate, seemingly highly motivated plot that ultimately appears to get the story of Bon and Henry all wrong. Like Rosa's narrative, however, Mr. Compson's does include some important hermeneutic clues hidden in its mistaken design: the issue of incest, for instance, is suggested in the relation of Henry and Judith—in the vicarious incest Henry would enjoy in Bon's marriage to Judith, whom Mr. Compson does not suspect to be related by blood—and the issue of miscegenation is posed by the very existence of the octoroon woman. These are latent figures of narrative design which will later provide some of the hermeneutic "chemistry" that Mr. Compson's plotting is unable to activate.

With chapter 5, we return to Rosa's telling, and a nearer approach to the moment of murder. "I heard an echo, but not the shot," she says, in a phrase emblematic of her whole relation to narrative event, which is one of secondariness and bafflement. Her narrating takes us precisely to what she did not see and cannot tell: the confrontation of Henry and Judith over Bon's corpse. Imagining the dialogue of brother and sister falls to her listener, Quentin; and we can infer that this need to tell will provide his entry into the narrative structure of the novel more directly than will Rosa's revelation that there is someone other than Clytie currently living at Sutpen's Hundred:

> . . . the two of them, brother and sister . . . speaking to one another in short brief staccato sentences like slaps. . . .
>
> *Now you cant marry him.*
> *Why cant I marry him?*
> *Because he's dead.*
> *Dead?*
> *Yes. I killed him.*
>
> He (Quentin) couldn't pass that. He was not even listening to her; he said, "Ma'am? What's that? What did you say?"
>
> "There's something in that house."
> "In that house? It's Clytie. Dont she—"
> "No. Something living in it. Hidden in it. It has been out there for four years, living hidden in that house."

What is living in the house is, of course, Henry Sutpen, and Quentin's meeting with him, a few hours following this exchange with Rosa, will possibly constitute the most important event of the story that needs telling in *Absalom, Absalom!* and the key motive of its plot, as well as the original impetus to Quentin's narrating. But representation of this event is deferred until the very last pages of the novel. Here, at the close of Rosa's narrative, the narratee—Quentin—apears to fix on one moment of the narrator's account (why is a question we may defer for now) which he cannot "pass." Since, he seems to imply, the narrator has not done justice to this moment, it is up to the narratee to pursue its true narrative implications and consequences. If we may later want to say that Quentin enters the Sutpen *story* through the meeting with Henry at Sutpen's Hundred, he enters the *narrative* on the plane of *narrating*, as the better artist of the narrative plot. Yet, by what right and in what interest does Quentin claim the role of narrator? And if the listener/narratee has moved into the position of narrator, who has come to occupy the position he has vacated?

From chapter 6 through to the end of the novel, the narrating will essentially be Quentin's. His ostensible narratee will be Shreve, yet Shreve will come to participate in the narrating to such an extent that he too must eventually be considered a narrator. The agency of narration will hence be fully dialogic, which both solves and evades the question of the vacancy created by Quentin's movement into the place of the narrator. We need at this point to ask what kind of a narrative principle and authority is provided, can be provided, by these two young men who have usurped narrating, de-authorized the eyewitness account (Rosa's) and the account at one remove (Mr. Compson's) in favor of something at greater distance (both temporally and spatially) but which claims greater hermeneutic force. We need to ask three straightforward, quite naive questions: What do they recount? How do they know it? What is their motive, their investment in what they recount?

Let me start with the second question, that of the epistemology of their narrative. As source of their narrative, there is first of all something in the nature of "documentary evidence." Chapters 6 through 9 in fact are framed by Mr. Compson's letter recounting Rosa's death and burial, and earlier Mr. Compson had shown Quentin the letter Judith had given Quentin's grandmother, the letter written to Judith by Charles Bon in captured Yankee stovepolish in 1865. Then there are the tombstones, as so often in the nineteenth-century novel—in *Great Expectations*, for instance, and in Wilkie Collins's *The Woman in White*—authoritative texts that nonetheless require decipherment. Quentin as his father, out shooting quail at Sutpen's Hundred, come upon five tombstones. These are: (1) Ellen's (ordered from Italy, brought home by Sutpen in 1864); (2) Sutpen's own (of the same provenance); (3) Charles Bon's (bought by Judith when she sold the store); (4) Charles Etienne Saint-Valery Bon's (paid for partly by Judith, partly by General Compson, and erected by the latter); (5) Judith's (provided by Rosa). The aberrant and enigmatic text here—hence the clue—is the fourth tombstone, that of Charles Etienne Saint-Valery Bon (Charles Bon's child by the octoroon woman), who looks white but chooses blackness: who takes a black wife (their child will be the idiot Jim Bond), and in fact his black ancestry in both his mother *and* his father, though we do not yet know this. This Bon, who is hauled into court after a fight and admonished by the justice, Jim Hamblett, for "going with blacks," in fact presents a problem in categorization: Hamblett, following the vocative "you, a white man," turns back on his words to find the sign he has used subverted in its referent: "he looking at the prisoner now but saying 'white' again even while his voice died away as if the order to stop the voice had been shocked into short circuit, '*What are you? Who and where did you come from?*' " In this slippage of signified from under its signifier, we encounter a transgression of categories and accepted patternings which provides an essential trace of hermeneutic design.

More important than the documentary evidence is oral transmission. Quentin's main source of knowledge comes from what Sutpen told his grandfather, General Compson, during the hunt for the French architect, and then on another occasion thirty years later when he came to General Compson's office, a narrative which General Compson passed on to Mr. Compson who passed it on to Quentin. But this narrative lacks meaning until it is retroactively completed by what Quentin himself learns from his visit to Sutpen's Hundred with Rosa in 1909:

> "Your father," Shreve said. "He seems to have got an awful lot of delayed information awful quick, after having waited forty-five years. If he knew all this, what was his reason for telling you that the trouble between Henry and Bon was the octoroon woman?"
> "He didn't know it then. Grandfather didn't tell him all of it either, like Sutpen never told Grandfather quite all of it."
> "Then who did tell him?"
> "I did." Quentin did not move, did not look up while Shreve watched him. "The day after we—after that night when we—"
> "Oh," Shreve said. "After you and the old aunt. I see."

This dialogue marks the supersession of Mr. Compson's, General Compson's, even Sutpen's own narratives in favor of Quentin's, since Quentin has been able to supply essential "delayed information" previously missing, thus creating a narrative that has retroactive explanatory force. The nature of this information is further specified a few pages later:

> "Your old man," Shreve said. "When your grandfather was telling this to him, he didn't know any more what your grandfather was talking about than your grandfather knew what the demon was talking about when the demon told it to him, did he? And when your old man told it to you, you wouldn't have known what anybody was talking about if you hadn't been out there and seen Clytie. Is that right?"
> "Yes," Quentin said.

This information, then, does not come from anything Quentin has read or been told, but simply from seeing Clytie. Here, a decisive clue finally is witnessed and interpreted by an adequate narrator. Clytie, who in Rosa's words *"in the very pigmentation of her flesh represented that debacle which had brought Judith and me to what we were,"* is a Negro Sutpen. Clytie's identity opens the possibility of other part-Negro Sutpen children and alerts the narrators (and readers) to the significant strain of miscegenation; it also sets a model of narrative repetition which will allow Quentin and Shreve to see how Henry and Bon will be acting out Sutpen's script, but in the mode of irony. It is Quentin—the narratee become narrator—who will eventually be able to postulate the essential discovery: that Charles Bon was also Sutpen's child, and that he, too, was part Negro. The source of that postulation, we should emphasize, is the discovery of a certain formal pattern of the crossing of categories: Clytie's Sutpen face with its Negro pigmentation, the very design of debacle. The "truth" of narrative may have come to depend, more than on any fact, on powerful formal pattern-ings, designs, eventually, of the narrative itself; a question to which we shall return.

I have by no means said all that needs to be said about the epistemological issues of Quentin's and Shreve's narrative, but I want for a moment to return to the first of the three questions I identified, the question of what they recount. The story they tell is in the first instance, and essentially, that of Sutpen, which has come to appear the necessary myth of origins of all the problems under consideration, and which in itself very much concerns origins. It has become apparent that nothing can be solved or explained without getting Sutpen's story straight. We could say that it has become apparent that horizontal relationships, those of siblingship and courtship—Judith, Bon, Henry—which were at the center of Mr. Compson's narrative have come to show their hermeneutic inadequacy and their insolubility in isolation. As Quentin reflects, in one of several meditations on the inescapable issue of paternity: *"Yes, we are both Father. Or maybe Father and I are both Shreve, maybe it took Father and me both to make Shreve or Shreve and me both to make Father or maybe Thomas Sutpen to make all of us."* Consideration must now be directed to a vertical problem, an issue in genealogy and the transmission of paternal authority through historical time.

Sutpen's story, filled in mainly in chapter 7, has its thematic summary in the statement, "Sutpen's trouble was innocence." It is the story of a hillbilly boy from the mountains who comes down to the Tidewater with his family and is sent by his father to a plantation house with a message, only to be turned away from the front door and told to come round to the back. In this moment of barred passage, Sutpen discovers the existence of difference: difference as an abstract and formal property which takes precedence over all else—since, for instance, it is more important than the content of the message he was supposed to deliver. Good and evil, morality, social position, worth are not substantial, but belong rather to the order of the signifier. The scenario reads like a version of Rousseau's *Discourse on the Origins of Inequality:* the creation of possession and differentiation where previously there had been none. The difference is symbolized by that between black and white, though this is but the most immediate and visible realization of a larger problem, one indeed so basic that even the boy Sutpen can begin to understand its primordial role in the organization and assignment of meaning. Sutpen's compensatory plot, what he repeatedly calls his "design," will be conceived to assure his place on the proper side of the bar of difference. He goes off to Haiti to make his fortune on a sugar plantation, and there takes a wife who he believes to be part French and part Spanish, but who—after she has borne his son—is revealed to be part Negro, a fact that, as he puts it, makes an "ironic delusion" of his entire design, which depends upon genealogical clarity and purity, on the ability to chart a clear authoritative relationship between origin and endpoint. So Sutpen repudiates his wife and starts over again at Sutpen's Hundred, in a new originating creation: "creating the Sutpen's Hundred, the *Be Sutpen's Hundred* like the olden-time *Be Light.*" But then, his son by the first wife, Charles Bon, appears from the past to threaten "a mockery and a betrayal" of his design: asking through the vessel of Judith that the new pure Sutpen line be intermixed with the dark blood of the past. So it is that Sutpen must turn Charles Bon, his first-born son, from the front door of his own plantation house. In the wake of all disasters, Sutpen goes on trying: after the war, and the disappearance of Henry, he proposes to Rosa that they breed together, then marry if she produces a son. After she has fled back to Jefferson in outrage, he makes a last attempt with Milly Jones—poor white, but white—which results in a daughter, and Sutpen's death at the hand of Wash Jones.

I have dwelt on Sutpen's "design" because it is a key not only to the overriding thematic issues of the novel but, more important, to the symbolic field in which it inscribes its reflection on narrative meaning. Sutpen himself is a master-plotter, endowed with an abstract, formalist sense of what the future shape of his life must be. Yet his repeated attempts to found a genealogy do not work, no doubt because one cannot postulate the authority and outcome of a genealogy from its origin. The authority of genealogy is known only in its outcome, in its *issue*, using that word in all its possible senses. Sutpen attempts to write the history of the House of Sutpen prospectively, whereas history is evidently always retrospective. I have indeed argued that all narrative must, as a system of meaning, conceive itself as essentially retrospective. Only the sons can tell the story of the fathers. Narrative, like genealogy, is a matter of patronymics. And here we may find both a source of Quentin's relative success as narrator of the past and a source of his anguish at being condemned to narrate the past, the world of ghosts which has fallen to his inheritance and which one can attempt to placate only through acts of genealogical narration.

When Quentin and Shreve have given shape to Sutpen's story, they turn to Sutpen's immediate issue, to the sons, Bon and Henry. Bon, too, we learn, has a design. Its parodic form—a parody of all the plots in the novel—is represented by the figure of Bon's mother's lawyer, scheming to blackmail Sutpen through the threat of incest, maintaining his secret notations:

> Today Sutpen finished robbing a drunken Indian of a hundred miles of virgin land, val. $25,000. At 2:31 today came up out of swamp with final plank for house, val. in conj. with land 40,000. 7:52 p.m. today married. Bigamy threat val. minus nil. unless quick buyer. Not probable. Doubtless conjoined with wife same day. Say 1 year and then with maybe the date and the hour too: Son. Intrinsic val. possible though not probable forced sale of house & land plus val. crop minus child's one quarter. Emotional val. plus 100% times nil. plus val. crop. Say 10 years, one or more children. Intrinsic val. forced sale house & improved land plus liquid assets minus children's share. Emotional val. 100% times increase yearly for each child plus intrinsic val. plus liquid assets plus working acquired credit and maybe here with the date too: Daughter and you could maybe even have seen the question mark after it and the other words even: daughter? daughter? daughter? trailing off. . . .

The lawyer's calculations here devastatingly lay bare the plot of the nineteenth-century social and familial novel, with its equations of consanguinity, property, ambition, and eros, that is ever the backdrop for the plottings of *Absalom, Absalom!* Yet Bon appears as the hero of romance, with a simpler and more absolute design. He simply wants a sign—any sign—of recognition from his father. "He would just have to write 'I am your father. Burn this' and I would do it." Bon's insistence on marriage to Judith becomes the choice of scandal in order to force the admission of paternity. What appears to be erotic desire reveals itself to be founded on the absolute demand for recognition by the father.

The working-out of Bon's design leads to the key scene, in 1865, as the Confederate army falls back toward Richmond and final defeat, when Colonel Sutpen summons Henry to his tent and speaks the essential words: "Henry, . . . my son"—the words Bon will never hear—and delivers the final answer to the enigma, completes the hermeneutic sentence that should allow us to explain the mischancings of the affairs of the House of Sutpen: "He must not marry her, Henry. His mother's father told me that her mother had been a Spanish woman. I believed him; it was not until after he was born that I found out that his mother was part negro." And Bon draws the conclusion: "So it's the miscegenation, not the incest, which you cant bear." Thus it is that at this belated point in the novel, knowledge catches up with event, and Henry, along with the reader, learns what those narrators who originally were narratees have learned.

But wait. On what basis and by what authority do Quentin and Shreve narrate this scene, the scene that articulates the revelations necessary to constructing a coherent plot? Whereas for many earlier parts of their narrative we glimpsed sources and documents, here there are none. Indeed, the narrators have clearly passed beyond any possible evidence for their narrative. As Shreve has stated some pages earlier, "Let me play a while now." And before that, "All right. Dont bother to say he stopped talking now; just go on." These and a number of other indications signal clearly that we have passed beyond any narrative reporting, to narrative invention; that narrating, having failed to construct from the evidence a plot that would make sense of the story, turns to inventing it. Even what we normally call "reported speech"—direct quotation—is the product of an act of ventriloquism, in a duet for four voices in which Quentin and Shreve become compounded with Henry and Bon, "compounded each of both yet either neither." To the question, Who is speaking here? the text replies, Everyone and no one:

> . . . it might have been either of them and was in a sense both: both thinking as one, the voice which happened to be speaking the thought only the thinking become audible, vocal; the two of them creating between them, out of the rag-tag and bob-ends of old tales and talking, people who perhaps had never existed at all anywhere, who, shadows, were shadows not of flesh and blood which had lived and died but shadows in turn of what were (to one of them at least, to Shreve) shades too, quiet as the visible murmur of their vaporizing breath.

What can this mean, if not that the narratees/listeners/readers have taken over complete responsibility for the narrative, and that the "voice of the reader" has evicted all other voices from the text, eliminated all the syntactic subordinations of reportage ("He said that she said that . . .") in favor of a direct re-creation, and has set itself up, by a supreme act of usurpation, as the sole authority of narrative? Commenting on a particularly ambiguous case of voicing in Balzac's *Sarrasine*, Barthes reaches the conclusion that ultimately the voice that speaks in the text is that of the reader, in that it is in the reader's interest, in his name, that the story must be told. Here, as narrators, narratees, and characters become compounded and interchangeable—and the narrated and the narrating occupy shifting positions—we have very nearly a literal realization of Barthes's point: the distance between telling and listening, between writing and reading, has collapsed; the reader has been freed to speak in the text, toward the creation of the text.

The passage quoted shows us how narration can become fully dialogic, centerless, a transaction across what may be a referential void—

filled perhaps only with phantasies from the past—yet a transaction that creates, calls into being, a necessary hermeneutic fiction. The narrative transaction thus appears fully consonant with the psychoanalytic transference, a *Zwischenreich* in which narration works through and works out a narrative solution. Furthermore, here the transferential dialogue is carried out by those who were originally narratees and readers, as if the analysts had also become analysands, assuming the burden of all stories, as also the power to reorder them correctly. To the literary analyst, this may imply that the reader, like Quentin and Shreve, will always take over the text, both reading and (re)writing it to his own design, finding in it "what will suffice" to his own hermeneutic need and desire. As Bon's desire once postulated develops by the dynamics of its own internal tension toward the scene in Sutpen's tent in 1865, so the reader's desire inhabits the text and strives toward the fulfillment of interpretation. A further, more radical implication might be that the implied occurrences or events of the story (in the sense of *fabula*) are merely a by-product of the needs of plot, indeed of plotting, of the rhetoric of the *sjužet:* that one need no longer worry about the "double logic" of narrative since event is merely a necessary illusion that enables the interpretive narrative discourse to go further, as in the mind of some Borgesian demiurge. This in turn might imply that the ultimate subject of any narrative is its narrating, that narrative inevitably reveals itself to be a Moebius strip where we unwittingly end up on the plane from which we began. Origin and endpoint—and, perforce, genealogy and history—are merely as-if postulations ultimately subject to the arbitrary whims of the agency of narration, and of its model in readership. Narrative plots may be no more—but of course also no less—than a variety of syntax which allows the verbal game—the dialogue, really—to go on.

To extend these implications further may be simply to encounter the commonplaces of artistic modernism, and these need to be tempered by a sense of the urgency of the narrative act, which may restitute reference and the "double logic" of narrative in other forms. But before turning to that consideration, I want to return to the specific issue of plot, to ask whether the story *Absalom, Absalom!* claims to tell ever gets told: whether the novel ever records the invention of a plot that is hermeneutically satisfying, and where our interpretive desire ought to rest its case. Here we must refer to a scene that ought to be a revelatory moment in both the story and its plot: a scene held in suspense nearly the length of the novel, and one that ought to offer key insight into Quentin's relationship to the narrative since it marks the moment at which the time of the narrators intersects with the time of the narrated—the moment at which it is revealed that one of the protagonists of the past drama lives on into the present of narration, offering the promise that the past can be recuperated within the present. This is of course Quentin's meeting, with Henry Sutpen at Sutpen's Hundred in the fall of 1909, just before his departure for Harvard. What happens in this meeting?

> And you are—?
> Henry Sutpen.
> And you have been here—?
> Four years.
> And you came home—?
> To die. Yes.
> To die?
> Yes. To die.
> And you have been here—?
> Four years.
> And you are—?
> Henry Sutpen.

Does anything happen here? The passage reads as nearly a palindrome, virtually identical backward and forward, an unprogressive, reversible plot. It seems to constitute a kind of hollow structure, a concave mirror or black hole at the center of the narrative. It generates no light, no revelation. If we have been led to feel that we understand the events that precipitated the fall of the House of Sutpen, we may sense that we are still at a loss to understand the larger plot that should link the sons to the fathers, motivate not only the story from the past, but the present's relation to it.

We do know, however, that Quentin's narrating seems to impel him toward recollection and replay of the scene with Henry Sutpen, deferred to climactic position, disappointing in that it offers no revelation, yet evidently constitutive of compulsive narrative desire since the result of this scene for Quentin is "Nevermore of peace": an anxiety never to be mastered, a past come alive that never can be laid to rest. If we can understand in a general way how this "afterlife" of the Sutpen story creates an influx of energy which Quentin's narrative can never quite bind and discharge, can we say specifically why it is Henry Sutpen who emerges as the traumatic figure of Quentin's narrative desire?

We must face the question left hanging earlier: what is the motive of the narrating? One could address this question (and some critics have done so) by way of the intertextual relation between *Absalom, Absalom!* and *The Sound and the Fury*, calling upon Quentin's incestuous desire for his sister Candace to explain his fixation on the story of Henry, Judith, and Bon, equating Judith with Candace and Bon the seducer with Dalton Ames, thus assigning Henry and Quentin to the same tortured place in the triangle of desire. Yet *Absalom, Absalom!* doesn't even mention Quentin's having a sister, and in any case using the intertext to explain, rather than enrich and extend the novel, seems reductive and impoverishing. *Absalom, Absalom!* in fact offers no certain answer to the question of motivation. Yet I think it would also be a mistake simply to note the "arbitrariness" of the narrative and its undecidable relations of event and interpretation: so simplistic and sweeping a deconstructive gesture eludes the challenges the text poses to us. We should rather, I think, consider further how the text may suggest a remotivation of narrative through narration and the need for it.

As its title, and its biblical intertext, so clearly signal, *Absalom, Absalom!* addresses centrally the question of fathers and sons, perhaps the dominant thematic and structural concern and shaping force in the nineteenth-century novel, ultimately perhaps constituting a theme and a structure incorporate with the very nature of the novel as we know it. Circling about the problem of what Shreve calls "that one ambiguous eluded dark fatherhood," *Absalom, Absalom!* raises the related issues of fraternity (Henry and Bon, Quentin and Shreve), paternity (including genealogy), and filiality (if I can know who my father is, will he consent to know me?). Eventually these issues may point to the problematic status of narrative meaning itself: meaning as a coherent patterning of relation and transmission, as the possibility of rule-governed selection and combination, as the sense-creating design of writing. Is coherent understanding, the explanatory narrative plotted from origin to endpoint, possible and transmissible? Do the sons inherit from the fathers, do they stand in structured and significant relation to an inheritance which informs the present? Can the past speak in a syntactically correct and comprehensible sentence?

Two threads of patterning, two elements of design, seem to be woven throughout the book. On the one hand there is incest, which according to Shreve (and Quentin does not contradict him) might be the perfect androgynous coupling, from which one would not have to uncouple: "maybe if there were sin too maybe you would not be permitted to escape, uncouple, return." Incest is that which overassimilates, denies difference, creates too much sameness. If, as Lévi-Strauss has claimed, it is the taboo on incest that creates the differentiated society, the attraction to incest raises the threat of the collapse of difference, loss of tension, and the stasis of desire extinguished in absolute satisfaction. On the other hand there is miscegenation, mixture of blood, the very trace of difference: that which overdifferentiates, creates too much difference, sets up a perpetual slippage of meaning where (as in the case of Charles Etienne Saint-Valery Bon brought before Justice Hamblett) one cannot find any points of fixity in the signifying chain. Incest thus would belong to the pole of metaphor, but as static, inactive metaphor, the same-as-same; whereas miscegenation would be a "wild," uncontrollable metonymy. The story of the House of Sutpen as told by the younger generation seems to be caught between these two figures, never able to interweave them in a coherent design. To give just one brief example, from the scene in Colonel Sutpen's camp in 1865, Quentin and Shreve narrate this exchange between Henry and Bon:

> —*You are my brother.*
> —*No I'm not. I'm the nigger that's going to sleep with your sister.*
> *Unless you stop me, Henry.*

Incest and miscegenation, sameness and difference, here as elsewhere in the narrative—including, notably, the working-out of Sutpen's design— fail to achieve a pattern of significant interweaving, and give instead a situation of paradox and impossibility: for instance, the nigger/brother conundrum that can be solved only by a pistol shot. Shreve at the end offers a parodic summing-up of this problem in design as it concerns the Sutpen "ledger" when he notes that it takes two Negroes to get rid of one Sutpen. "Which is all right, it's fine; it clears the whole ledger, you can tear all the pages out and burn them, except for one thing. . . . You've got one nigger left. One nigger Sutpen left. . . . You still hear him at night sometimes. Don't you?." The one left is, of course, Jim Bond, the idiot, the leftover who can be heard howling at night. The tale he would tell would be full of sound and fury, signifying nothing. He stands as a parodic version of Barthes's contention that the classical narrative offers at its end the implication of a residue of unexhausted meaning, a "pensivity" that remains to work in the reader.

The narrative ledger cannot be cleared by a neat calculation; the tale can never be plotted to the final, thorough, Dickensian accounting; and the *envoi* to the reader—the residual meaning embodied in Jim Bond—seems the very principle of nonsignificance. But of course this is not all that the text has to say about design and the making of patterns. Of the many metaphors of its own status and production presented by the text, all of which would bear consideration, I shall quote only Judith's extraordinary evocation of the loom, which she articulates when she comes to Quentin's grandmother, to ask her to keep the letter she received from Charles Bon during the war, a letter "without date or salutation or signature" which nonetheless constitutes a precious act of communication. It is an extended image, which moves from the letter to the entanglement of marionettes, which then modulates to the loom and the weaving of the rug, then moves on to another kind of text, the legend scratched on the tombstone, then back to the letter and the act of transmission of the letter:

> ". . . and your grandmother saying, 'Me? You want me to keep it?'
>
> " 'Yes,' Judith said. 'Or destroy it. As you like. Read it if you like or dont read it if you like. Because you make so little impression, you see. You get born and you try this and you dont know why only you keep on trying it and you are born at the same time with a lot of other people, all mixed up with them, like trying to, having to, move your arms and legs with strings only the same strings are hitched to all the other arms and legs and the others all trying and they dont know why either except that the strings are all in one another's way like five or six people all trying to make a rug on the same loom only each one wants to weave his own pattern into the rug; and it cant matter, you know that, or the Ones that set up the loom would have arranged things a little better, and yet it must matter because you keep on trying or having to keep on trying and then all of a sudden it's all over and all you have left is a block of stone with scratches on it provided there was someone to remember to have the marble scratched and set up or had time to, and it rains on it and the sun shines on it and after a while they dont even remember the name and what the scratches were trying to tell, and it doesn't matter. And so maybe if you could go to someone, the stranger the better, and give them something—a scrap of paper—something, anything, it not to mean anything in itself and them not even to read it or keep it, not even bother to throw it away or destroy it, at least it would be something just because it would have happened, be remembered even if only from passing from one hand to another, one mind to another, and it would be at least a scratch, something, something that might make a mark on something that *was* once for the reason that it can die someday, while the block of stone can be *is* because it never can become *was* because it cant ever die or perish. . . .' "

If Judith's images suggest an ultimate pessimism about the status of texts—woven or graven or written—her insistence on passing on the fragile letter as an instance of something that possesses ontological gravity because it was written by a living hand, addressed from someone to someone, suggests that the process of sense-making retains a tenuous privilege of which its products are drained. Judith's statement concedes the evanescence or even the impossibility of the "referential" and "meta-linguistic" functions of language (in Roman Jakobson's sense) while arguing the continuing pertinence of and need for the "phatic": the way we use language to test the communicative circuit, to confirm the conductive properties of the medium of words. She makes a claim neither for story nor for plot, but rather for narrating as, in Genette's terms, the narrative act productive of plot and story. This is not simply to state—in a modernist commonplace—that *Absalom, Absalom!* is a "poem about itself," but rather to contend that narrating is an urgent function in itself, that in the absence of pattern and structure, patterning and structuration remain necessary projects, dynamic intentions. Judith's struggle with the tenses of the verb "to be" suggests the whole problem of narrative as recovery of the past and makes us note how in the passing-on of Bon's letter of 1865 (whose very inscription—on the finest watermarked French notepaper taken from a gutted Southern mansion, in stovepolish manufactured by the victorious Union and captured the doomed Confederate raiders in the place of the food or ammunition they had hoped to find—is marked by the cosmic ironic laughter of History) the reader is linked not only to the reading but to the writing of "historical" documents, and how, as a belated reader of the document—following Judith herself, Quentin's grandmother, grandfather, father, and then Quentin himself—he is summoned to take his place in the activity of transmission, to join the ventriloquized medium of history as fiction and fiction as history, perhaps finally to become, in a modification of Proust's phrase, the writer of himself.

The recovery of the past—which I take to be the aim of all narrative—may not succeed in *Absalom, Absalom!*, if by the recovery of the past we mean its integration within the present through a coherent plot fully predicated and understood as past. Yet the attempted recovery of the past makes known the continuing history of past desire as it persists in the present, shaping the project of telling. As the psychoanalyst Stanley Leavy has written, perhaps in too optimistic a tone, "All desire aims at the future, and this especially, because it is a desire for a revelatory knowledge to come, often first and naively experienced as the desire for the recovery of a buried memory, a lost trauma. To speak at all is to express the desire to be recognized and heard, whether the speech is in the form of a demand or not." The seemingly universal compulsion to narrate the past in *Absalom, Absalom!*, and to transmit its words, may speak both of an unmasterable past and of a dynamic narrative present dedicated to an interminable analysis of the past. Faulkner's present is a kind of tortured utopia of unending narrative dialogue informed by desire for a "revelatory knowledge." That knowledge never will come, yet that desire never will cease to activate the telling voices.

Quentin alludes to the tentative and dialogic quality of narrating in a parenthetic reference to General Compson's view of language: "language (that meager and fragile thread, Grandfather said, by which the little surface corners and edges of men's secret and solitary lives may be joined for an instant now and then before sinking back into the darkness where the spirit cried for the first time and was not heard and will cry for the last time and will not be heard then either." This is certainly no triumphant apology for narrative; it makes the patternings of plot tentative indeed, ready to come unwoven as soon as they are stitched together. It is, perhaps, tentatively an apology for narrating, an enterprise apparently nostalgic, oriented toward the recovery of the past, yet really phatic in its vector, asking for hearing. I will here raise the question, to leave it unanswered, whether at the end of the novel Shreve has heard Quentin, whether his last question, "Why do you hate the South?" marks a failure of comprehension of all that has been told, or on the contrary too full an understanding of the desire animating the narrative act. And I will close by returning to the first agent of narration in the novel, Rosa Coldfield, to give her the last word, for it is she who speaks of *"the raging and incredulous recounting (which enables man to bear with living)."*

JUDITH L. SENSIBAR

A New Beginning:
"The Thunder and the Music
of the Prose" (1921 to 1925)

V*ision in Spring* was a pivotal appren-
ticeship work, the one in which we sense the greatest tension as the poet's
faulty vision pits itself against the novelist's increasingly assertive voice.
The meanings of synecdochic scenes in some of Faulkner's finest novels
have their genesis in the "silent music" of all his poetic sequences, but
particularly in this one, his verbal symphony. That his poetry and fiction
are thus connected suggests that the former continually fed and sustained
his imagination. To understand its symbolic meaning and thus how it
encouraged and shaped Faulkner's mature creative vision we turn, finally,
to his life to see what role actual music and poetry played there.

Throughout his life Faulkner closely associated actual music and
poetry with women he loved. But, oddly, Faulkner, like his mother,
Maud, was more than indifferent to music. He often claimed to actively
dislike it. Jill Faulkner Summer says, "He liked to listen to Gershwin and
the Negroes' singing but otherwise I never heard him listen to any music.
He had no ear for it. It was not part of life as far as he was concerned."

In contrast Estelle Faulkner and her daughter loved music. Summer says,

> My mother's family was extremely musical—literally they *all* played
> musical instruments. But my Grandmother [Faulkner's mother] hated

From *The Origins of Faulkner's Art.* Copyright © 1984 by Judith L. Sensibar. University of
Texas Press, 1984.

music. There was never any question of having records to play at her house or at ours. When I was 14 or 15 my brother-in-law [her step-sister's husband] gave me a record player. But I was only allowed to play it when Pappy wasn't there. I was not allowed to play the piano when he was around either. I had to go to my other Grandmother's to have my music lessons and to practice. My mother couldn't play the piano when Pappy was home but when he was away she'd play for hours. She was very good.

Faulkner was no more tolerant of his friends' love for music than he was of his wife's and daughter's. In *A Loving Gentleman*, Meta Wilde writes at some length on this subject. Like his wife and daughter she also loved to listen to and play music. Had she had the talent and money she would, she says, have aspired to be a concert pianist. Instead she worked as Howard Hawks's secretary and "script girl." But she maintained close friendships with many musicians, eventually marrying one. She also played the piano and went to concerts regularly. This is her account of Faulkner's reaction the first time she played for him:

> Glancing his way, I was startled to see that he was squirming in his chair. He had written in *A Green Bough* of "music of lustrous silent gold." Why was he restless? Later, "You didn't like my playing"—the accusation offhand, lightly admonitory.
> "You play very well, m'honey."
> "But it didn't do anything for you."
> "I don't appreciate music as much as I ought to," Bill apologized. "It's one of my flaws I reckon . . . Language is my music," he said. "All I'll ever need."

Wilde concludes, "Faulkner didn't think I played very well." He refused to attend concerts with her and once when he interrupted her as she listened to a love duet from *Tristan und Isolde* the following occurred:

> . . . I waved Bill away as he approached calling my name. For a moment he gazed at me in absolute disbelief, the impact of my impatient gesture drawing the blood to his face, then slammed out of the room.

She apologized profusely, explaining, " 'When I hear music like that, I get lost in it. . . . Nothing else seems to exist for me. . . . Can't you see that music is to me what books are to you?' " His response, " 'I just don't know ma'am.' " She then elaborates:

> But the realization that music possessed me, that I was bonded to it as I could never be to a lover, troubled him. . . . Estelle, who "played piano right well," according to Bill, had never been passionate about music; hers was an accomplishment to be shown off in the front parlor. . . . Bill

began to think of music as a rival and more than once asked how I could be under vassalage to something that he considered "white and opaque and distant." He could no more follow me into my world of symphony, chamber music, recital, and opera than I could enter his innermost domain, where he sat hunched over paper making tiny bird's-feet tracks with his pen.

Since she was not living with Faulkner, Wilde had considerably more leverage with him on this issue, but her leverage seems to have afforded her little insight. Ironically, the metaphor in the lines she quotes from *A Green Bough*, "music of lustrous silent gold," partly explains Faulkner's antipathy. The word "music" was a private, symbolic metaphor whose meaning altered with its context. It stood, apparently, for many things that Faulkner felt were forbidden. But when music was also "silent" it referred to his creative imaginings. Faulkner characterized real music to Wilde as "white and opaque and distant." Music, when it comes from the outside, seems to represent the Pierrot mask's most paralyzing fantasy. Faulkner describes such music with the same adjectives as he uses for the "white woman," the temptress who lures Pierrot and destroys his own "silent music." Wilde further illuminates this issue when she says, "I can be tremendously moved by music. When I'm involved in listening to something fine, tears come. This is just conjecture—it may sound far-fetched—but I wonder if perhaps he didn't feel a little bit left out." Her conjecture, while true, is not the whole story, as her next remark makes clear. She says Faulkner appeared to enjoy her husband's playing: "Wolfgang was different. He was in the presence of an artist." Wolfgang may have been an artist but, more important for Faulkner, he was a man. Thus his "music" did not have the power to threaten Faulkner's imagination. In this sense Wolfgang's music affected Faulkner no more or less than his black servants' singing did.

Since, like his mother, Faulkner disliked or claimed to dislike actual music so much, it seems odd that he chose a wife and a lover who were accomplished musicians. It seems equally odd that he should, in 1921, write a poetic sequence modeled upon Aiken's verbal symphonies and containing poems with musical titles and/or more poems whose subjects are music, musicians, and dancers. (Wilde describes Faulkner as the world's worst dancer. In adolescence he also refused to dance although Estelle loved dancing.) To understand this apparent paradox and its role in shaping Faulkner's art we need to know more about the circumstances under which Faulkner wrote his musical poem sequence.

During the summer of 1921, Faulkner continued, as he had since he returned from the RAF in December 1918, to live at home with his parents. But he gave *Vision in Spring*, a sequence brimming with musical allusions and unfulfilled desires, to a married woman, a musician, and a person for whom his mother had little affection. Jill Faulkner Summers describes these women's relationship:

> Granny was not happy with any of her sons' marriages. There weren't a lot of people she liked besides her grandchildren. She disliked women in general, as a breed I think. She was an extremely down-to-earth, pragmatic little lady and I think she thought my mother was flighty—a sort of butterfly. There was very little interaction between Granny and my mother. Granny always wished that Pappy had not married Mama.

Summers observed that although they shared physical characteristics, her mother and Maud Falkner appeared to have little in common. But together they supplied his antithetical but concomitant desires for what a woman should be:

> My grandmother was very small, less than five feet tall. She was very tough and independent. She had painted above her stove. "DON'T COMPLAIN DON'T EXPLAIN" and she would not answer to anyone for anything she did. She was stubborn with a very quiet wit. Sometimes she would say something and it wasn't until two or three minutes later that you realized how funny it was, or that perhaps you'd been had.
>
> Now one of the qualities about my mother that my father claimed distressed him was her *lack* of independence. In part I think this was because for him, she was the idealized female figure in his poetry, and he saw everything about her through a romantic haze. There were always these two kinds of women in his mind and he needed both. The fact that my mother was physically frail appealed to him. The times he was most caring was when she was not well. He didn't appear to like toughness in her and flatly refused to see the strengths she did have. My mother was very Southern in that she could make any man believe that he was superman. She was also very manipulative for she was, like most Southern women, taught to obey implicitly, "so far as he is wise and she is able."

Faulkner's dual standard for women placed special demands upon his daughter:

> He seemed to feel that frailty was a virtue and liked the idea of little girls in pinafores. I was a terrible Tom-boy and he encouraged it generally—I think because he wished I were a boy. But that wasn't all of it. He wanted women to be self-sufficient and resilient like my Grandmother but he wanted them to *appear* frail and weak. He abhorred women who gave outward and ostentatious signs of proficiency but he also liked the idea of my spending the day on a horse in pants. He just didn't want me

around him otherwise in pants. When I was out riding he liked it because then, for him, I was "Bill" not "Jill."

But there was a dividing point and it took me awhile to understand. It was very easy for him to be many people but it was very difficult for me. Although he encouraged me to be independent he still wanted me to go through the motions of being helpless and female.

To teach her the importance of adhering to his Janus-faced feminine ideal Faulkner did the following:

I can tell you exactly when it was that I at last completely understood where the dividing point lay. It was the early '50's. I was downtown in Oxford in my blue jeans and Malcolm's [her step-brother's] shirt and I saw Pappy coming from the post office. I saw him from far away and I waved. When he came up to me he walked right by me as if I didn't exist. When I got home I was in a lot of trouble. I never went to town in jeans again.

In 1924 Faulkner dedicated his one published sequence, *The Marble Faun*, to his mother (remember the Faun was truly impotent). In 1925 and 1926 he repeated himself as he gave other handmade books—a fable, and his sonnet sequence of love poems, *Helen: A Courtship*—to another unattainable woman, the artist Helen Baird. In the late 1930s he wrote and recited poetry to Meta Wilde. These women resembled each other in several ways: they were independent, they were not available to Faulkner as marriage partners, and their interest was in art forms other than language (Faulkner's mother was also a painter).

Possibly Faulkner chose musical forms and subjects for *Vision in Spring* to please Estelle. It might also be argued that, like other Modernists, he was interested in working within the convention of borrowing musical language and musical analogies for writing poetry. But neither of these explanations addresses the issue of why the language and themes of this sequence permeate so many emblematic scene in Faulkner's novels. Such continuous usage suggests that this sequence served as a touchstone for his imagination, one that continued to inspire him throughout his career.

The subjects of *Vision in Spring*—sex, love, power, impotence, death, and the powers of the imagination—are universal. Faulkner had written of them in earlier sequences but always literarily and obliquely. In *Vision* he comes closer than he ever has to breaking through that "white, opaque, distanced" language: other poets' music. Dimly through this music—to borrow his metaphor—we hear an original author's voice. In *Vision*, particularly in the three poems of its third movement, we begin to hear some life in Faulkner's voices and a hint of genuine emotion. Our reading experience becomes enriched as we see vague outlines of a "story" forming in the intricate formal and thematic connections Faulkner has worked out between the poems in his sequence.

What then is the nature of Faulkner's "poetic" touchstone? Of what is it composed that makes it so rich with invention? The kinds of metaphorical connections Faulkner worked out here between music and vision served as a means for expressing imaginatively a series of conflicts and issues that figured prominently in his real life and in his fantasy life. It seems fair at this point to suggest that these conflicts center on Faulkner's attitudes toward his art and toward women. To say that Faulkner is Pierrot is too simple, but there is enough evidence from Faulkner's art and life to note certain resemblances.

More precisely, Faulkner's conflicts, like those of Pierrot, concern his desire for yet fear of loving a real woman (Estelle and, later, other women who were not his mother). Could he simultaneously love and be loyal to his mother and another woman when his mother had made it quite clear that she disliked and placed no value on either music or other women? (Faulkner maintained his primary allegiance, visiting his mother every day he was in Oxford throughout his married life.) And could he, unlike his fictional would-be artist Elmer, be successful in both art and love? Faulkner's apparent solution in life was to live with other women but to deny that he could take pleasure in or hear their music—real or metaphorical. But even punishing himself and his lovers in this way was not sufficient pay for experiencing the double thrill of artistic creativity and adult sexuality, no matter how surreptitiously. Thus, for much of his adult life he apparently did not sleep with the woman with whom he lived nor did he live with the woman with whom he slept. Faulkner told Wilde he had not had sexual relations with Estelle since Jill's birth in 1933. Whether or not he told the truth is impossible to know. They did have separate bedrooms. Despite this living arrangement, according to Wilde, Faulkner refused either to separate from or divorce his wife. In different ways and degrees Faulkner seems to have withheld sexually and emotionally from both Wilde and his wife.

In 1921, when he wrote *Vision in Spring*, his temporary solution to this conflict was a compromise. In the sequence, real music performed by other artists who also happen to be women—Colombine the actress, the dancers, the musicians—suggests and signifies Pierrot's fear that he will fail as a poet or artist of words. Meanwhile, the sequence itself, love poetry drawing on music for its metaphorical structure and formal organization and addressed to a woman who is not his mother—a woman who loves music—is, in itself, Faulkner's bid for independence from his mother's exclusive love and her values.

Writing "Love Song," a poem whose only music is the "cadence" of Pierrot's feet, allowed Faulkner to make a further bid for independence. There he simultaneously unmasked both Eliot, a recognized poet, and that fearer of women, eternal adolescent, and mother's boy, the would-be poet-actor Pierrot. Parody enabled Faulkner to be more explicit in stating the previously hidden import of his fantasy material. In "The Dancer" and "Marriage" Pierrot confronts a real woman with whom he actually converses. She is no longer the silent dream image of earlier poems like "Portrait." Furthermore, Pierrot begins to express an overt interest in and desire for adult sexual experiences. He no longer dwells exclusively in the isolated world of memory and dreams.

As Pierrot confronts these real women, the symbolic meaning of real music and dance (art forms these women initiate to charm him) is revealed to be death or failure. When he denies women's power over his fantasy life—the dancer is nothing compared to his imaginative impression of her and the piano player cannot banish his sexual fantasy of her—he makes an emotional compromise. This denial permits him to demonstrate his continuing primary love for and attachment to his mother. Faulkner represents her in his poetry as the Marble Faun's and later Pierrot's "moon mother" as well as the Miss Havisham figure in "After Fifty Years" (*The Lilacs*). She always "snares" her young male victim making him impotent, even as he is simultaneously obsessed with and repelled by a desire to experience an adult love relationship.

In Faulkner's novels such male victims persist. Their actual mothers are either malevolent, ineffectual, or dead. Popeye and Joe Christmas are examples. A contemporary critical description of the close relation between Laforgue, the supreme and influential Pierrot poet, and his masks applies, in some ways, to Faulkner's with Popeye and Joe Christmas:

> And yet his poses *pierrotiques* seem to have affected profoundly, and disturbingly, what we can only call his consciousness of self. . . . In one of the most recent studies of the poet, Reboul writes that *"sexuality in Laforgue seems, indeed, to have been abnormal (as one says)—rather weak, irritated by an over-subtle intellect, complicated by a deliberately unchecked imagination, satisfied especially by sight and thought, dulled—notwithstanding its very real presence—by the notion of imperfection and sin."* (emphasis added)

That Faulkner, like Laforgue, may still have not entirely separated his Pierrot pose from his "consciousness of self" is suggested by Meta Wilde's comments and confirmed by one of his few available personal letters, written to his mother from Paris (22 September 1925). It is of interest not only because of what Faulkner writes in it but also because of how he orders his thoughts.

Went to the Moulin Rouge last night. Anyone in America will tell you it is the last word in sin and iniquity. It is a music hall, a vaudeville, where ladies come out clothed principally in lip stick. Lots of bare beef, but that is only secondary. Their songs and dances are set to real music—there was one with not a rag on except a coat of gold paint who danced a ballet of Rimsky-Korsakoff's, a Persian thing; and two others, a man stained brown like a faun and a lady who had on at least 20 beads, I'll bet money, performed a short tone poem of the Scandinavian composer Sibelius. It was beautiful. Every one goes there—often you have to stand up.

They have plays here just for Americans. The suggestive lewd, where it is indicated that the heroine has on nothing except a bath robe, say. Then at the proper time the lights are all turned off and you are led to believe that the worst has happened. Nasty things. But Americans eat it up, stand in line for hours to get tickets. The French of course dont go to them at all. After having observed Americans in Europe I believe more than ever that sex with us has become a national disease. The way we get it into our politics and religion, where it does not belong anymore than digestion belongs there. All our paintings, our novels, or music, is concerned with it, sort of leering and winking and rubbing hands on it. But Latin people keep it where it belongs, in a secondary place. Their painting and music and literature has nothing to do with sex. Far more healthy than our way.

I can tell you about paintings when I get home. I have spent afternoon after afternoon in the Louvre—(that Carnegie was a hot sport) and in the Luxembourg; I have seen Rodin's museum, and 2 private collections of Matisse and Picasso (who are yet alive and painting) as well as numberless young and struggling moderns. And Cezanne! That man dipped his brush in light like Tobe Caruthers would dip his in red lead to paint a lamp-post. . . .

I did this from a mirror my landlady loaned me. Didnt notice until later that I was drawing on a used sheet. This [is] part of 'Elmer.' I have him a half done, and I have put him away temporarily to begin a new one. Elmer is quite a boy. He is tall and almost handsome and he wants to paint pictures. He gets everything a man could want—money, a European title, marries the girl he wants—and she gives away his paint box. So Elmer never gets to paint at all.

My beard is getting along quite well. Vannye laughed at it, because she could see right through it to the little boy I used to be. Both the french language and the French people are incomprehensible to Vannye. She cant even get what she wants to eat. So the other day I took her to lunch and got her a steak, well done, fried potatoes and sliced tomatoes and a cup of coffee. . . .

These righteous remarks to his mother about Paris night life, the art scene, American lewdness, his own writing, his self-portrait, and his Jamesian female relative were written less than a month after he arrived in Paris. They may be, in part, another mask. But if we follow Faulkner's thoughts in this letter as he moves from his observations and judgments about reality to his comments on the novel he is trying to write, the turns his mind takes suggest a very strong moral connection between his life and his art. After commenting on his faunlike self-portrait (am I a man or little boy?) drawn upon a page of his own fiction, Faulkner summarizes his novel (Figure 14). Its hero, a would-be artist (am I a writer or artist?), fails because he succumbs to the prurient leer of gross American female sexuality: "pure beef," "lewd . . . nasty things." Sex for Elmer, as for the Marble Faun or the Americans Faulkner denigrates in his letter, is a "disease." Although Faulkner gives Elmer everything he needs for artistic success, Elmer, whose mother has died, chooses a wife who "gives away his paint box. So Elmer never gets to paint at all."

Faulkner's earlier sequences, *Vision in Spring*, and finally, the unfinished *Elmer* manuscripts themselves make one wonder who really gave away Elmer's paint box (the manuscripts indicate it was Elmer himself), an object whose erotic significance Faulkner describes with loving detail. As the novel begins in what appears to be its earliest version, Elmer lies on the deck of an ocean liner fantasizing:

> . . . to think of nothing consciously: of his comfortable body, of girls without emphasis, of somewhere within him tickling his entrails pleasantly, loneliness.
>
> Then he would rise, and in his cabin draw forth his new unstained box of paints. To finger lasciviously smooth dull silver tubes virgin yet at the same time pregnant, comfortably heavy to the palm—such an immaculate mating of bulk and weight that it were a shame to violate them, innocent clean brushes slender and bristled to all sizes and interesting chubby bottles of oil . . . Elmer hovered over them with a brooding maternity, taking up [the cylinders (deleted)] one at a time those fat portentous tubes in which was yet wombed his heart's desire, the world itself—thick-bodied and female and at the same time phallic: hermaphroditic. He closed his eyes the better to savour its feel. . . .

For Elmer, to paint, to create, is to violate the inviolate, whom he imagines as the supreme maternal image—the "phallic" pregnant virgin. By analogy this fantasy suggests Elmer sees himself as God. Thus his aspirations resemble the Marble Faun's.

Just as he had given up his poetry Faulkner abandoned *Elmer* when it had served his purposes. But he kept Elmer's much-fondled tubes of paint, transforming them in *Light in August* to the tube of toothpaste that both fascinates and repels the child Joe Christmas. Elmer's original paints, "eight colored wax crayons," were given him by his second passionate love, "Jo with whom he slept." This epicene elder sister is androgynously named Jo-Addie (Elmer's nickname is "Ellie"). Elmer's first love is, of course, his mother. He describes his sister and mother as mirror images: Jo has "a bitter beauty," his mother a "stark bitter face." The adjective he chooses also characterizes the quality of his love for them—bitter, because never consummated.

Elmer's mother despises her husband, a useless drunk: "about all Elmer's father had ever given his children was lightish hair, and he hadn't been able to do this for Jo." And Elmer clearly is confused about and questions whether indeed the father is, anatomically, a man, as he calls him "an inverted Io with hookworm."

Consistently in Faulkner's novels, strong, outwardly sexless, man-like women treat all males like fools and children, but few (Addie Bundren excepted) seem to dislike their husbands as much as Elmer's and Faulkner's mothers did. According to Faulkner, the following exchange occurred shortly before his mother died:

> . . . I created a fairy tale for her. I would tell her about Heaven, and what it was going to be like, how nice it was going to be and how she would like it.
> She said, "Will I have to see your father there?"
> "No," I said, "Not if you don't want to."
> "That's good," she said, "I never did like him."

Whether Faulkner actually had this conversation with his mother is irrelevant. What is important is that Faulkner said he did, and therefore it reflects his perception of his parents' relationship. In the story Faulkner tells here, it is he who still, at sixty-three, is his mother's lover, and he who with his art—a "tale"—banishes his father, the husband she claims to hate. As *Vision in Spring* and his other poetry indicate, Faulkner's imaginative powers were not always this potent.

Although Faulkner often referred to himself as a "failed poet" he continued throughout his life to write poetry for the women he loved: Estelle Faulkner, his daughter Jill, Helen Baird, Meta Wilde, and later Joan Williams. Since poetry was the mode in which Faulkner communicated least effectively, it seems paradoxical that he should use it for the language of intimacy. But perhaps that is precisely the point. For Faulkner, love was always "opaque": symbolic of failure or anticipated failure. Thus he reserved his "failed" voice for it. Also he could use poetry—the language he so clearly associated with a dream state—to anesthetize his feelings in a "romantic haze" of false music: other poets' sounds and rhythms. Poetry continued, for Faulkner, to remain the language of his most impossible dreams:

"Perhaps they were right in putting love into books," he thought quietly. "Perhaps it could not live anywhere else."

(Gail Hightower, *Light in August*)

Chronology

1897   Born William Cuthbert Falkner, in New Albany, Mississippi, on September 25; first child of Murry Falkner, then a railroad executive, and Maud Butler.

1914   Leaves school, after long history as a poor student.

1916–17 Lives on fringe of student community at the University of Mississippi.

1918   Tries to enlist in armed forces, but is refused. Works in New Haven, Connecticut for Winchester Gun factory. Changes spelling of name from "Falkner" to "Faulkner." Enlists in Canadian Air Force, but war ends while he is still in training.

1919   Returns to Oxford and enters the University of Mississippi. Writes poems that will be included in *The Marble Faun*.

1920   Leaves the university, but remains in Oxford.

1921   After spending autumn in New York City, he returns to Oxford to work as a postmaster.

1924   Resigns postmastership; *The Marble Faun*.

1925–26 New Orleans period, frequently in circle surrounding Sherwood Anderson. Writes *Soldiers' Pay* and *Mosquitoes*; travels to Europe and resides in Paris; returns to Oxford.

1927   Writes *Flags in the Dust*, which is rejected.

1928   Writes *The Sound and the Fury*.

1929   *Sartoris* (curtailed version of *Flags in the Dust*) published; marriage of Faulkner and Estelle Franklin on June 20; finishes *Sanctuary*; publishes *The Sound and the Fury*; begins *As I Lay Dying*.

1930   Finishes and publishes *As I Lay Dying*; revises *Sanctuary*.

1931   Birth and death in January of daughter, Alabama Faulkner; *Sanctuary* published; begins *Light in August*.

1932   Finishes *Light in August*, which is published after his father's death; begins first Hollywood screenwriting period.

1933   *A Green Bough*; birth of daughter, Jill Faulkner.

1934   *Doctor Martino and Other Stories*.

1935   *Pylon*; begins relationship with Meta Doherty.

1936   *Absalom, Absalom!*

1938   *The Unvanquished.*
1939   *The Wild Palms.*
1940   *The Hamlet.*
1942   *Go Down, Moses.*
1946   *Cowley's Portable Faulkner.*
1948   *Intruder in the Dust.*
1949   *Knight's Gambit.*
1950   *Collected Stories*; Nobel Prize in Literature.
1951   *Requiem for a Nun*; relationship with Joan Williams; electro-shock therapy for depression and alcoholism.
1954   *A Fable*; first assignment for State Department; relationship with Jean Stein.
1955   Goes to Japan for State Department.
1957   *The Town.*
1959   *The Mansion.*
1960   Death of his mother.
1962   *The Reivers*; death in Byhalia, Mississippi on July 6, from coronary occlusion.

Contributors

HAROLD BLOOM, Sterling Professor of the Humanities at Yale University, is the author of *The Anxiety of Influence, Poetry and Repression* and many other volumes of literary criticism. His forthcoming study, *Freud: Transference and Authority*, attempts a full-scale reading of all of Freud's major writings. He is the general editor of *The Chelsea House Library of Literary Criticism*.

CLEANTH BROOKS is Gray Professor Emeritus of Rhetoric at Yale. He is the author of three books on Faulkner, as well as *The Well-Wrought Urn* and *The Hidden God*.

MICHAEL MILLGATE, Professor of English at the University of Toronto, has written *The Achievement of William Faulkner* and *Thomas Hardy*.

RICHARD POIRIER, Professor of English at Rutgers University, is Editor in Chief of *Raritan*. His books include critical studies of Henry James, Robert Frost and Norman Mailer, as well as *A World Elsewhere* and *The Performing Self*.

JAMES GUETTI is Professor of English at Rutgers, and the author of *Word-Music*.

JOSEPH W. REED, JR., Professor of English at Wesleyan University, is the author of *Faulkner's Narrative* and *Three American Originals: John Ford, William Faulkner and Charles Ives*.

IRVING HOWE is Distinguished Professor at the Graduate School of the City University of New York. His best known work is *World of our Fathers*.

HUGH KENNER is Professor of English Emeritus at Johns Hopkins University. He is best known for *The Pound Era*.

JOHN T. IRWIN is Chairman of the Writing Seminars at Johns Hopkins University. His works include *American Hieroglyphics* and *The Heisenberg Variations*, a volume of poems published under the name of John Bricuth.

ALBERT J. GUERARD, Professor of Literature at Stanford University, has written studies of Conrad and Hardy, and is the author of *The Exiles, The Touch of Time: Myth, Memory and Self* and *The Triumph of the Novel: Dickens, Dostoevsky, Faulkner*.

DAVID MINTER is Dean of Emory College and Professor of English at Emory University. His works include *The Interpreted Design* and *William Faulkner*.

RICHARD H. KING is Professor of Philosophy at the University of the District of Columbia, and author of *The Party of Eros* and *A Southern Renaissance*.

ALAN HOLDER, Professor of English at Hunter College, is the author of *The Imagined Past*.

JAN BAKKER, Professor of English at Utah State University, is the author of *Fiction as Survival Strategy* and (with Francelia Butler) *Marxism, Feminism and Free Love: The Story of the Ruskin Commonwealth*.

JUDITH BRYANT WITTENBERG teaches at Simmons College. She is the author of *Faulkner: The Transfiguration of Biography*.

PETER BROOKS is Tripp Professor of the Humanities at Yale. He is the author of *The Novel of Worldliness*, *The Melodramatic Imagination* and *Reading for the Plot*.

JUDITH L. SENSIBAR teaches at the Arizona State University, and has written *The Origins of Faulkner's Art*.

Bibliography

Abadie, Ann J., and Fowler, Doreen, eds. *Faulkner and the Southern Renaissance: Faulkner and Yoknapatawpha*. Jackson: University Press of Mississippi, 1982.

Bassett, John, ed. *William Faulkner: The Critical Heritage*. Boston: Routledge and Kegan Paul, 1975.

Blotner, Joseph Leo. *Faulkner, a Biography*. New York: Random House, 1974.

Brodhead, Richard H., ed. *Faulkner: New Perspectives*. Englewood Cliffs, N.J.: Prentice-Hall, 1983.

Brooks, Cleanth. *The Yoknapatawpha Country*. New Haven: Yale University Press, 1963.

————. *William Faulkner: Toward Yoknapatawpha and Beyond*. New Haven: Yale University Press, 1978.

————. *William Faulkner: First Encounters*. New Haven: Yale University Press, 1983.

Broughton, Panthea Reid. *William Faulkner: The Abstract and the Actual*. Baton Rouge: Louisiana State University Press, 1974.

Dabney, Lewis M. *The Indians of Yoknapatawpha, A Study in Literature and History*. Baton Rouge: Louisiana State University Press, 1974.

Davis, Thadious M. *Faulkner's "Negro": Art and the Southern Context*. Baton Rouge: Louisiana State University Press, 1983.

Gray, Richard. "The Individual Talent: Faulkner." In *The Literature of Memory*. Baltimore: Johns Hopkins University Press, 1977.

Guerard, Albert J. *The Triumph of the Novel: Dickens, Dostoevsky, Faulkner*. New York: Oxford University Press, 1976.

Howe, Irving. *William Faulkner, a Critical Study*. New York: Vintage Books, 1962.

Irwin, John I. *Doubling and Incest / Repetition and Revenge: A Speculative Reading of Faulkner*. Baltimore: Johns Hopkins University Press, 1975.

Jehlen, Myra. *Class and Character in Faulkner's South*. New York: Columbia University Press, 1975.

Kartiganer, Donald M. *The Fragile Thread: The Meaning of Form in Faulkner's Novels*. Amherst: University of Massachusetts Press, 1979.

Kreiswirth, Martin. *William Faulkner, the Making of a Novelist*. Athens: University of Georgia Press, 1983.

Longley, John Lewis. *The Tragic Mask: A Study of Faulkner's Heroes*. Chapel Hill: University of North Carolina Press, 1963.

Malin, Irving. *William Faulkner, An Interpretation*. Stanford: Stanford University Press, 1957.

Matthews, John T. *The Play of Faulkner's Language*. Ithaca: Cornell University Press, 1982.

Millgate, Michael. *The Achievement of William Faulkner*. New York: Random House, 1966.

Minter, David. *William Faulkner, the Writing of a Life*. Baltimore: Johns Hopkins University Press, 1980.

Mortimer, Gail L. *Faulkner's Rhetoric of Loss: A Study in Perception and Meaning*. Austin: University of Texas Press, 1983.

Mottram, Eric. *William Faulkner*. London: Routledge and Kegan Paul, 1971.

O'Connor, William Van. *The Tangled Fire of William Faulkner*. Minneapolis: University of Minnesota Press, 1954.

Oriard, Michael. "The Ludic Vision of William Faulkner." *Modern Fiction Studies* 28 (Summer 1982): 169–87.

Peters, Erskine Alvin. *The Yoknapatawpha World and Black Being*. Ann Arbor: University Microfilms International, 1976.

Schliefer, Ronald. "Faulkner's Storied Novel: 'Go Down Moses' and the Translation of Time." *Modern Fiction Studies* 28 (Spring 1982): 109–27.

Schmitter, Dean Morgan, ed. *William Faulkner: A Collection of Criticism*. New York: McGraw Hill, 1973.

Sensibar, Judith L. *The Origins of Faulkner's Art*. Austin: University of Texas Press, 1984.

Slatoff, Walter J. *Quest for Failure, A Study of William Faulkner*. Westport, Ct.: Greenwood Press, 1972.

Spenko, James Leo. "The Death of Joe Christmas and the Power of Words." *Twentieth Century Literature* 28 (Fall 1982): 252–68.

Sundquist, Eric J. *Faulkner: The House Divided*. Baltimore: Johns Hopkins University Press, 1983.

Wagner, Linda Welshimer, ed. *Four Decades of Faulkner Criticism*. East Lansing: Michigan State University Press, 1973.

Warren, Robert Penn, ed. *Faulkner, A Collection of Critical Essays*. Englewood Cliffs, N.J.: Prentice-Hall, 1966.

Wasson, Ben. *Count No 'count*. Jackson: University Press of Mississippi, 1983.

Williams, David L. *Faulkner's Women: The Myth and the Muse*. Montreal: McGill-Queen's University Press, 1977.

Wyatt, David. *Prodigal Sons, A Study in Authorship and Authority*. Baltimore: Johns Hopkins University Press, 1980.

Acknowledgments

"Discovery of Evil" by Cleanth Brooks from *William Faulkner: The Yoknapatawpha Country* by Cleanth Brooks, copyright © 1963 by Yale University. Reprinted by permission of Yale University Press.

"The Hamlet" by Michael Millgate from *The Achievement of William Faulkner* by Michael Millgate, copyright © 1966 by Michael Millgate. Reprinted by permission of A D Peters & Co Ltd.

"The Bear" by Richard Poirier from *A World Elsewhere: The Place of Style in American Literature* by Richard Poirier, copyright © 1966 by Oxford University Press. Reprinted by permission.

"The Sound and the Fury and *The Bear"* by James Guetti from *The Limits of Metaphor* by James Guetti, copyright © 1967 by Cornell University. Reprinted by permission of the publisher, Cornell University Press.

"Light in August" by Joseph W. Reed, Jr., from *Faulkner's Narrative* by Joseph W. Reed, Jr., copyright © 1973 by Yale University. Reprinted by permission of Yale University Press.

"The Wild Palms" by Irving Howe from *William Faulkner: A Critical Study* by Irving Howe, copyright © 1951, 1952 and 1975 by Irving Howe. Reprinted by permission of the University of Chicago Press.

"The Last Novelist" by Hugh Kenner from *A Homemade World: The American Modernist Writers* by Hugh Kenner, copyright © 1975 by Hugh Kenner. Reprinted by permission of Alfred A. Knopf, Inc.

"Doubling and Incest" by John T. Irwin from *Doubling and Incest / Repetition and Revenge* by John T. Irwin, copyright © 1975 by Johns Hopkins University Press, Baltimore/London. Reprinted by permission.

"Faulkner's Misogyny" by Albert J. Guerard from *The Triumph of the Novel: Dickens, Dostoevsky, Faulkner* by Albert J. Guerard, copyright © 1976 by Albert J. Guerard. Reprinted by permission.

"The Self's Own Lamp" by David Minter from *William Faulkner: His Life and Work* by David Minter, copyright © 1980 by Johns Hopkins University Press, Baltimore/London. Reprinted by permission.

"Working Through: Faulkner's *Go Down Moses*" by Richard H. King from *A Southern Renaissance* by Richard H. King, copyright © 1980 by Oxford University Press. Reprinted by permission.

"An Odor of Sartoris: William Faulkner's *The Unvanquished*" by Alan Holder from *The Imagined Past* by Alan Holder, copyright © 1980 by Associated University Presses, Inc. Reprinted by permission.

"*As I Lay Dying* Reconsidered" by Jan Bakker from *Costerus*, vol. 26 (*From Cooper to Philip Roth: Essays on American Literature*) edited by Jan Bakker and D. R. M. Wilkinson, copyright © 1980 by Editions Rodopi (Amsterdam). Reprinted by permission.

"William Faulkner: A Feminist Consideration" by Judith Bryant Wittenberg from *American Novelists Revisited: Essays in Feminist Criticism* edited by Fritz Fleischmann, copyright © 1982 by Fritz Fleischmann. Reprinted by permission of Twayne Publishers, a division of G. K. Hall & Co., Boston.

"Incredulous Narration: *Absalom, Absalom!*" by Peter Brooks from *Reading for the Plot; Design and Intention in Narrative* by Peter Brooks, copyright © 1984 by Peter Brooks. Reprinted by permission of Alfred A. Knopf, Inc.

"A New Beginning: 'The Thunder and the Music of the Prose'(1921 to 1925)" by Judith L. Sensibar from *The Origins of Faulkner's Art* by Judith L. Sensibar, copyright © 1984 by Judith L. Sensibar. Reprinted by permission of the author and the University of Texas Press.

Index